THE PRICE OF A BARGAIN

THE PRICE OF A BARGAIN

THE QUEST FOR CHEAP AND THE DEATH OF GLOBALIZATION

GORDON LAIRD

For Lisa, Addison and Myles

THE PRICE OF A BARGAIN
Copyright © Gordon Laird, 2009.

All rights reserved.

First published in 2009 by
PALGRAVE MACMILLAN®
in the United States—a division of St. Martin's Press LLC,
175 Fifth Avenue, New York, NY 10010.

Where this book is distributed in the UK, Europe and the rest of the world,
this is by Palgrave Macmillan, a division of Macmillan Publishers Limited,
registered in England, company number 785998, of Houndmills,
Basingstoke, Hampshire RG21 6XS.

Palgrave Macmillan is the global academic imprint of the above companies
and has companies and representatives throughout the world.

Palgrave® and Macmillan® are registered trademarks in the United States,
the United Kingdom, Europe and other countries.

ISBN: 978–0–230–61491–8

Library of Congress Cataloging-in-Publication Data

Laird, Gordon, 1967–
    The price of a bargain : the quest for cheap and the death of
    globalization / Gordon Laird. — 1st ed.
        p. cm.
    Includes bibliographical references and index.
    ISBN 0–230–61491–4
    1. Discount houses (Retail trade)—United States. 2. Deals—United
States. 3. Consumer behavior—United States. I. Title.
HF5429.215.U6L35 2009
339.4′7—dc22   2009035931

A catalogue record of the book is available from the British Library.

Design by Newgen Imaging Systems (P) Ltd., Chennai, India.

First edition: November 2009

10 9 8 7 6 5 4 3 2 1

Printed in the United States of America.

CONTENTS

Wal-Mart shoppers charge security guards at Green Acres Mall, Long Island, November 2008

Credit: Nakea Augustine

INTRODUCTION

BLACK FRIDAY, 2008

They emerged from the darkness and gathered like pilgrims, lining up beneath floodlights in the parking lot. Well before midnight, the first shoppers had already settled into folding chairs and blankets for a long, cold vigil, one that was being staged outside nearly every major discount outlet across America. Facing a deep recession, record numbers of shoppers turned out at ungodly early hours to save a few dollars on Christmas toys for their kids, stock up on necessities, or score a luxury television or stereo before things got worse. In the end, an estimated 172 million people—just over half of North America's total population—would go shopping on the Black Friday weekend in 2008, up from 147 million the previous year. On that morning on November 28, 2008, bargain-hungry crowds were staring down guards and doormen across America. Gunshots were fired at a Toys "R" Us store in Palm Desert, California, and two people were killed. Reports of fighting, damaged property and vandalism filtered through the news. "They're more aggressive," one seasoned Wal-Mart shopper told the *New York Times*. "I've never seen anybody fight like this. This is crazy."

But only one mall would be remembered in the years to come. At 1 A.M. on Black Friday hundreds of shoppers had gathered in front of the Wal-Mart in the Green Acres Mall in Valley Stream, Long Island. Some had come for $9 DVDs and Hannah Montana dolls priced at $5 that Wal-Mart had advertised in local flyers; others wanted the $25 microwaves or 42-inch LCD televisions that had been marked down to $598. Everyone had a game plan for the store's 5 A.M. opening, because when big-box stores open on the Friday morning after the Thanksgiving holiday, shopping becomes a competitive sport. Above the crowd of shoppers, in five-foot high letters, was the Wal-Mart promise: "Satisfaction Guaranteed." In previous years, most retailers only opened for a brief period during the early morning, and offered only limited supplies of aggressively discounted products, so shoppers had come to expect lineups and competition.

This morning was different. Nakea Augustine, a shopper who was there that morning, recounted that when she arrived at Green Acres Mall at 2 A.M., the line was already 2,000 people long. Having studied Wal-Mart's flyer, she was keen on the Hot Wheels Barbie jeep, advertised at more than 50 percent off. As she and a friend stood in line discussing their shopping strategy, they felt a violent surge from behind. "It got scary out of nowhere," said Augustine. "The crowd in the back just pushed." Someone grabbed her pocketbook off her shoulder, ripping her coat open. Other shoppers were punched and pushed to the ground; scuffles broke out.

Desperation and fear bubbled to the surface as the once-orderly lineup turned into a mob. By 4 A.M., it was clear to onlookers that the situation was deteriorating, and police were called. Eyewitnesses recount that police did arrive to monitor the situation, but left before Wal-Mart's doors opened at 5 A.M. ("Can't you see the crowd is out of control?" one eyewitness asked police. "I'm surprised we haven't heard gunshots yet," the officer reportedly replied.)

Above the melee, someone had posted a handwritten sign: "Blitz line starts here." As the rowdy crowd waited for the store's 5 A.M. opening, the fighting and pushing continued. Some shoppers, already injured, left the scene. There were broken arms, bruises, and head injuries. Inside, the eight security guards who had been assigned to the front door began to worry.

From across Long Island, and the New York City boroughs of Queens, and Brooklyn, people converged on the Green Acres Mall with plenty of their own worries. The regional economy had been shedding jobs and struggling with slow growth for the better part of a decade. Consequently, Long Island boasted some of New York State's top foreclosure rates in 2007. Leading up to Black Friday 2008, the downward spiral had intensified: housing values dropped between 10 and 30 percent, putting many homeowners into negative equity status, resulting in foreclosure rates that reached 21 percent by early 2009. Only a few weeks earlier, Long Island had proclaimed itself to be officially in a recession.

If people had any chance of maintaining their standard of living during this holiday season and enjoying the consumer riches they had become accustomed to, they would need bargains—and lots of them. Retailers did not disappoint. With offers of up to 70 percent off—practically giving products away in a calculated effort to bring traffic—Black Friday 2008 marked the very pinnacle of discounting, offering one of the greatest consumer bonanzas of all time.

"Five, four, three, two, one!" At 5 A.M., beneath the blue and white Wal-Mart sign in Green Acres, one of the security guards opened the plate-glass entrance doors a crack. The crowd surged forward with a torrent-like force that knocked one of the doors off its hinges. A security guard tried to use it as a shield against the oncoming crowd but in the melee, the metal part of the door frame crumpled, the glass was smashed, and people and workers began to fall inside the Wal-Mart's entrance passage as more than 2,000 manic shoppers rushed in. There were screams and panic as people poured over several fallen shoppers, security guards, and broken glass.

Security guard Jdimytai Damour, 34, was one of the first to be trampled to the floor. An otherwise unemployed temporary worker, Damour had been recruited for door duty on Black Friday, along with several other workers who were not actually employed by Wal-Mart, but by a service contractor that Wal-Mart had outsourced. He had been working at the Wal-Mart for about a week doing general maintenance and, like most of the others on duty that morning, Damour had no previous training in security or crowd control. Even though Damour was built like a linebacker—six foot five, 270 pounds—when the doors opened, his size and strength were no match for the power of the crowd. He was quickly knocked down as he tried to push people back. Near him was a young woman, Leana Lockley, who had also fallen. "I was screaming that I was pregnant, I am sure he heard that…He was trying to block the people from pushing me down to the ground and trampling me," the nursing student recounted. "Mr. Damour was to the right of me, he was on his knees. I could look at him eye to eye, and he was trying to push them back, and the crowd pushed him down, and he fell on top of me."

Lockley was pulled to safety by her husband. But Damour lay on the floor, gasping for air, according to eyewitness accounts, as people trampled him. Incoming crowds continued to step on and knock against police as they attempted to perform CPR on Damour, who was unresponsive. By the time paramedics were on scene, most of the first wave of shoppers had passed through the entrance and had filled the store. Inside, shoppers guarded the televisions; others swarmed the toy section. Damour died on the concrete floor in between two vending machines, just inside Wal-Mart's entrance only a few feet from where greeters usually stand. While a small crowd had gathered around the horrible scene, many continued to shop, and the store itself only closed well after paramedics gave up their attempt to revive Damour and police had begun to investigate the circumstances of his death. Nassau police later described the scene at the store as "utter chaos" and estimated that Damour had been "literally stepped on by dozens, if not a hundred, people."

A full two hours after the opening rush, and an hour after Damour had been declared dead, Wal-Mart announced that there had been a fatality and that the store was closing. Many shoppers refused to leave. One witness told the New York *Daily News* that shoppers had acted like "savages." "When they were saying they had to leave, that an employee got killed, people were yelling,

'I've been on line since Friday morning!'" said Kimberly Cribbs. "They kept shopping."

Four other shoppers were injured; Wal-Mart would later pay nearly $2 million in damages. Damour's co-workers stood and said a prayer. "They took the doors off the hinges," said fellow Wal-Mart worker Jimmy Overby, in shock. "He was trampled and killed in front of me...I didn't know if I was going to live through it. I literally had to fight people off my back."

* * *

For better and for worse, ours is the age of the bargaineer—the engineer of bargains—whose factory extends from rice paddies to suburban basements everywhere. Each year we are drawn to their doors by the millions. And if it's not Wal-Mart that reels us in, then it is Wal-Mart's big-box brethren, like Costco, Home Depot, Best Buy, IKEA, Kohl's, or smaller outlets like the local dollar store. There are never single, isolated bargains. Most of us stalk value on a serial basis, sometimes in full contravention of common sense. Row upon row, aisle upon aisle, this realm of affordability, selection, and discount is a dominant force in today's world.

It's all here: your next iPod, laptop, snack food, or stuffed animal you take to the hospital when you visit a sick relative. This is you, even before you know it. And all of it is priced to sell. Nearly everything from clothing to electronics has miraculously decreased in price since the early 1990s. And if you're not getting it cheaper, then you've probably gained on quantity or quality, the outcome of a global economy that's been on rollback for the last two decades.

When we buy at our local dollar store or big-box mall, we embrace revolution: the most advanced logistics, marketing and manufacturing network ever invented. At one time, our most expensive commodities—oil, diamonds, metals—were the core business of the planet's largest and most powerful corporations. Today, snack foods, paper goods, and pet supplies are the world's best-selling discount products, and have been the unlikely building blocks of globalization since the 1990s. By 2008, Wal-Mart's $405 billion in annual revenue surpassed the gross domestic product of Saudi Arabia, underlining the degree to which affordable consumerism has come to dominate global trade.

It's all part of a global shopping marathon that helped turn most of the world's developed nations into consumer economies. By the time that Wal-Mart became the world's largest company, in 2002, consumer spending accounted for roughly 70 percent of all employment and economic activity within Organisation for Economic Co-operation and Development (OECD) nations, and it peaked at 78.5 percent for the United States in 2008. It's what economists call the service economy, and it is anchored largely by economic activity in finance, technology, and retail and wholesale trade, as well as all other non-manufacturing business in media, entertainment, airlines, hotels, and restaurants. Rates of personal savings were all but eliminated in the process, with average American households retaining negative after-tax income in annual savings between 2006 and 2009—the lowest in 73 years, equaled only by negative savings rates in 1932 and 1933, during the Great Depression, when nearly one in four adults was unemployed.

Unlike in the Great Depression, today's erosion of household fortunes and the accumulation of massive personal debt is not merely a symptom of economic crisis, but an integral part of growth itself. In an economy dominated by retailing, financial services, and offshore manufacture, the overextension of shopping fuelled broad-based prosperity—not just in America, but around the world. Leveraged on inflated housing prices and generous credit card limits, this unprecedented bonanza of consumer liquidity exploded like a gusher of oil. As shipping traffic and trade deficits boomed, American retail spending increased 43 percent per capita between 1992 and 2005. And Americans weren't the only ones slowly going broke: During the early 2000s, Italy, Britain, Canada, and France actually outpaced the United States in growth of consumer debt with service-dominated economies that long ago eclipsed traditional industry and agriculture. Canada, for example, saw a 50 percent increase in retail sales between 1994 and 2007.

The shift from production to consumption during the late twentieth century represents a transformation in consumerism, trade, and society that had not been seen in several generations. Just as Henry Ford once changed history with the invention of the assembly line in 1913, the quest for cheap goods reworked everything from global commerce to local economies.

The global financial crisis of 2008 was the first large-scale acknowledgment that unsustainable debt lies at the core of Western economies. And with the number of empty malls and bankrupt retailers mounting at the end of the millennium's first decade, it is clear that, even in the age of climate change and energy anxiety, it is consumers themselves who are a diminishing resource.

Unfortunately, the crowds thronging the malls on Black Friday didn't save the economy because shoppers did not return in sufficient numbers: Holiday sales that year were the weakest they had been in more than 40 years. Bankruptcies brought down big-box stalwarts like Linens 'n Things and Circuit City in 2008, and double-digit sales declines and profit losses continued to erode businesses and governments worldwide. By the end of 2008, the wave of retail store closures across the United States reached 6,100, according to the International Council of Shopping Centers (ICSC), with a fifth of all enclosed malls already failing. By early 2009, *Newsweek* reported than an another esti-mated 150,000 retail outlets were expected to close. Only Wal-Mart and sev-eral other discounters and dollar store chains, managed improved growth.

It wasn't just that shoppers had turned ugly. After the wild-eyed hordes in Wal-Mart hauled off their Samsung TVs on the morning of Black Friday and the garbage, glass, and blood were cleaned up, and after all the recrimination and blame for the senseless death of Jdimytai Damour had passed, certain facts remained.

First, the golden age of affordable consumerism was short and poignant in its brilliance. We will very likely never shop this hard again.

And second, our whole system of cheap, from shipping to consumer credit, is leveraged in ways we are only just beginning to understand—and broken in ways that may not be easily fixed.

*   *   *

The glorious thing about the 1990s was that we rarely had to think too hard about where our stuff came from. It just seemed to be there, as stores became bigger, prices decreased, and the depth and selection of goods grew. Banks and credit card companies made it easy to buy and to keep buying. Developing nations like China supplied abundant labor and bought up American debt. Why question a good thing?

In hindsight, it was much like the global financial bubble that burst in 2008, except that instead of collateralized debt obligations and other com-plex financial products, it was globalization itself that had become entangled in growth cycles that turned out to be too good to be true. Instead of faulty investments many times the size of world GDP, our bargain-addicted con-sumer economy is dangerously leveraged on a series of innovations and inven-tions not built to last.

The fundamentals of our global bargain economy—cheap credit, offshore labor, affordable energy and transport—will be less available or disappear entirely during the twenty-first century. This web of interdependence will not un-leverage itself gracefully: there is no going back to normal, no rewind or reboot on global trade. Lack of access to affordable petrochemicals and fossil fuels, for example, could progressively disable whole segments of our economy. Offshore labor, available credit, and affordable transport represent massive productivity and income subsidies that most consumers unwittingly depend upon. Former externalities like climate change and chronic poverty impose additional threats to our supply chains since globalized trade requires stability, not hurricanes and food riots.

The global debt and financial crisis that closed the first decade of the new millennium is just one aspect. It's not just about markets anymore. To grasp what will shape economies, nations, and communities in the years to come, we must look beyond the analysis and assumptions of the financial leaders— the vast majority of whom failed to accurately predict or protect against one of the biggest and most damaging crises of our time. In other words, we have to look at the world not as a growth and wealth machine governed by orderly business cycles, but as something that performs and responds more like a stressed ecosystem, something that requires stewardship and attention.

And at a time when the reality of climate change looms heavily, it is no small irony that so many of our material systems are now full of nonlinear change and modal shifts. Bargaineering multiplied prosperity, but our dependence on deals has also multiplied negative impacts, costs, and risk. What we are discovering is that globalization—productive webs governed by concentrated islands of power—is more vulnerable than many have argued. Traditional, nation-based economic solutions such as tariffs and other protectionist measures are less effective in such an interdependent world. The reality is that in many Western economies, there is surprisingly little productive capacity left to protect. Efforts to localize and live sustainably are obviously critical, yet if the rich tide of globalization fails, as attractive to its many opponents as this may be, there is still surprisingly little ready to fill its place.

It is easy to complain about Wal-Mart, but much more difficult to find anyone who doesn't depend upon or benefit from global trade networks. The world's largest companies depend on cheap. You depend on cheap. Hundreds of millions of people around the world, rich and poor, are part of this web. And, for now, it is still goods trade that drives globalization, worth $13.6 trillion annually, more than four times the global value of services such as finance, software, and travel. And because of this optimized, just-in-time web of production, a growing portion of our world continues to be disproportionately vulnerable to long-term scarcity of petroleum, plastic, labor, and other resources. With millions of people still highly dependent on shipping and shopping across the developed and developing world, it's a risky prospect. The quest for cheap has already consumed much of our easiest and richest gains in energy, transport, and manufacturing. Instead of local, sustainable production, a surprising amount of our ingenuity and capital is still being reinvested into carbon-intensive transport networks, unconventional forms of crude oil, as well as subsidizing market failure—including trillions in bailouts and damage control for failed financial institutions around the world. And from the tar sands of northern Alberta, Canada, to the borderlands of Arizona, in the United States, to the factory zones of mainland China, there is unrest: in lieu of governments and business, citizens and nonprofits are taking bold steps to confront neglected aspects of our social, economic, and environmental troubles.

Consequently, navigating the future isn't as easy as some might think. That we will experience complete economic recovery and a return to growth in the wake of this latest world recession may be wishful thinking since the decades of easy growth are well behind us. Billions spent on stimulus programs since 2008 will not bring back the prosperity of recent decades. Instead, there will, very likely, be fewer Wal-Marts in the face of a long-term contraction, along with the return of a small-portion manufacture and service jobs that had been lost to "offshoring" and outsourcing. Inflation will eventually return and, once again, become chronic: we will pay more for gasoline, shipping, food, and all other products whose cost structure is tied to energy. Conservation and efficiency will begin to drive politics and culture. Commerce will fracture into a series of submarkets dominated by discounting as the ability to freely spend diminishes. Likewise, economies dependant on consumer spending will experience greater volatility, and many nations will turn protectionist as the plentitude created by global trade erodes. Even global security will be affected as trade ties falter, national agendas diverge, and *Pax Americana* fades into history. It could be the death of globalization as we know it, and its passing would deprive us of its many flawed benefits, while bequeathing a global legacy of unresolved problems.

There will be unexpected progress and collapse, new kinds of risk and new kinds of reward. There will be new kinds of change.

When cheap fails us we will have to invent a new status quo, one that more accurately reflects the true cost of things. Our future depends on it. Until recently, the dominant vision of progress was rapid growth, cheap products, and shoppers flush with high credit limits—in other words, the forces that led to the global economic bubble of the 1990s and early 2000s, which many thought would last forever. It was so successful it didn't even seem like gambling. And like a blackjack player on a winning streak, the mistaken assumption was that we could have it all. It was an attitude reinforced by many business and political leaders who promoted self-regulating markets and the kind of high-stakes economism that saw little need for addressing climate change, global underdevelopment, or the impact of unsustainable growth. Even as some of our systems have begun to fail us, many people still gamble on this dream, which now resembles a modern-day cargo cult: plentitude without consequences.

SECTION I

LANDSCAPES OF PLENTY

Discounters converge on Las Vegas, Nevada, the site of North America's largest bargain trade show

Credit: Gordon Laird

CHAPTER 1

THE BARGAINEERS

FEAR AND HOUSEWARES IN LAS VEGAS

Dollar Store Nation

There is a moment, right before dawn, when Las Vegas finally empties out and stands quiet. All the tourists have disappeared, leaving only maintenance workers, security guards, and a few hardcore gamblers hunched over cards amid a sea of empty tables in the casinos. Outside, on Las Vegas Boulevard, a blast of neon light shines down on advertising flyers that are scattered across the sidewalk, offering blackjack games and Barry Manilow tickets to nobody in particular.

Las Vegas has little allure at 5 A.M. Nobody rambles on about the good old days with Dean and Sammy or boasts of winning at the roulette wheel against impossible house odds. There is no excitement, no action. At this hour, Vegas is stripped down and idle—just stucco, glass, and air conditioning, its lights and billboards cycling like a gaudy convenience store vacant between shifts.

It is, however, the beginning of a new day in one of the world's most unlikely economies. In Las Vegas, identical days repeat endlessly, city life is a lucrative grind of shopping, gambling, and serving. It is all based on a deceptively simple business model: a $33.7 billion industry that manufactures virtually nothing.

Las Vegas is one of the purest expressions of the modern service economy. Also called "the knowledge economy" or "New Economy," the modern service economy promised plentitude and productivity, while simultaneously deindustrializing to the point where consumer activity became the dominant source of prosperity. And it was an amazing invention, leveraging everything from massive efficiency gains in shipping, to new pools of cheap offshore labor.

By 7 A.M. the first conventioneers hit the sidewalks and coffee stands, and the taxicab drivers and street cleaners no longer have the city to themselves. Each year, thousands of meetings, events, and industry shows are held in Las Vegas, and everyone from actuarial accountants to adult entertainers now conducts business here. While much of this town is gorging on buffet breakfasts or sleeping off last night's debauchery, professionals and entrepreneurs from around the world convene to meet, deal, and negotiate.

In the shadow of the posh Venetian hotel and casino, attendees for today's big event arrive outside the Sands Expo and Convention Center, carrying boxes, bags, and display cases. Their nametags announce a cross-section of America: Duluth, New Jersey, Pasadena, Dallas. They are the first of nearly 100,000 people who are here to attend one of the world's largest merchandise shows, the ASD/AMD Merchandise Show, a sprawling marketplace of retailers, wholesalers, manufacturers, importers, and amateur hucksters trying to hustle a buck. Their collection of bargain merchandise is so large that it spills over into two other convention halls located nearby.

Laid out on tables and shelves, and almost exclusively manufactured in China and Southeast Asia, are little bits of our everyday lives. There are generic kitchenware items—rubber spatulas, scrubber pads—common to hundreds of thousands of households. I see toys from my kid's playroom: plastic sharks, blocks, stuffed animals. Crowds gather, searching for the world's best bargains. Storeowners from Lima, Peru, browse bed sheets. Iowa wholesalers display replica Tiffany lamps. Chain-store retailers and dollar store managers barter on all things both essential and unlikely—toothbrushes, neon Bob Marley sculptures and Jesus dioramas, samurai swords, witchcraft kits, miniature motorcycles, brand-name toothpaste, Shrek backpacks, and baby shoes.

Nobody knows exactly how many items are on display here, and it would be a superhuman feat to visit all 8,000 booths to find out. But if you have shopped at a discount store, a grocery chain, a dollar store, bought consumer items online or in a flea market, there's a good chance that you've spotted items that first appeared here. Even multinationals like Wal-Mart lurk at the ASD/AMD Merchandise Show in Las Vegas, incognito, looking for new ideas and products to give them a competitive edge over the scores of smaller and mid-size operators that nip at their heels.

Dollar stores, or extreme value retailing, have existed since the 1950s. Yet the strategy of low price point and low profit margin in a no-frills store has only dominated retail since the 1990s, when mass-discount pioneers like Wal-Mart literally destroyed many conventional business practices. As major discounters expanded into new global opportunities, supply chains multiplied, manufacturers spread across greater Asia, and logistics technologies enabled faster, cheaper international trade. Assaulted from unlikely places like Las Vegas and Chinese factory towns like Shenzhen, the very notion of wholesale and retail trade—traditional divisions that once structured business—no longer fully exist.

Commerce in low-cost global merchandise has opened up to anyone with good credit and a business plan. Sam Bundy, president of the trade show's merchandise group, explains how this event is actually an enormous trading floor, a huge international bazaar. "It's not just show—people are here mainly to make deals, find new opportunities, and build existing business relationships," he says as we sit at his command post—a low-walled cubicle next to the constant din of buyers and sellers. "They are trading product, signing contracts, making shipping arrangements as we speak." The products on display here are actually sales samples; a single stuffed animal or small appliance may represent several orders—or hundreds of orders, if it's popular. Twice a year, bartering, buying, and selling at the Vegas show launches hundreds of thousands of products that will, in turn, fill thousands of steel containers to be shipped all over the globe. As offshore goods saturate everyday life, it's the dollar store that increasingly lies at the heart of our economy. According to the trade publication, *Chain Store Guide* (CSG), the number of dollar stores across America nearly quadrupled between 1996 and 2007. "With an increase of over 250 percent over the past ten years, only [Wal-Mart-style] supercenters have exceeded this growth, with a 289 percent increase," says CSG's Arthur Rosenberg. "These numbers ring clear when considering that competing retail [formats] have seen reductions in store counts."

Behind the success of the dollar store is a sea change in global commerce that also fuelled Wal-Mart's rise to power. The lines between buyer and seller, and wholesaler and retailer have blurred. "Many people are learning from what Wal-Mart has done in the past," explains Sam Bundy, president of the trade show's merchandise group. "More and more middlemen are being cut out of supply chains and therefore it's less difficult to source directly than it was five years ago. You don't need the sheer purchasing power of Wal-Mart anymore to find suppliers and go direct."

Many of today's conventioneers are also would-be bargaineers—people who have been downsized or who are currently underemployed and looking for an opportunity. Discount entrepreneurship is the realm of the involuntarily part-time worker. It is a growth sector even in Canada, where part-time work has grown twice as fast as full-time employment since 2001. Amazingly, the number of involuntarily part-time workers in America increased 40 percent in 2008 alone, adding 3.1 million people who were working less because they couldn't find full-time jobs.

"Many people find it an attractive and alluring 'American dream' to run their own business, whether they've been downsized or are looking for alternatives to the typical 9-to-5 job," reports Sam Bundy. "More often than not individuals that have been downsized from large retail operations or wholesale operations are more apt to venture into independent retail." "It's the professional flea marketer, for example, people who make an income and livelihood selling new goods," he says. "Selling a packet of socks for a dollar. They need to find cheap source of product. And you have kiosks, carts in shopping malls, predominantly imports, fashion items, sunglasses, low-end toys. It all opens up new retail opportunities, as there is a very low cost base, a small capital infusion required. Barriers of entry are low, especially compared to a regular storefront."

Others attending the show represent online discount and dollar stores, covering a vast array of websites from eBay spin-offs to mass liquidators like Overstock. com and Woot. Users of eBay, for example, are increasingly selling new products that are sourced directly from the importers and manufacturers represented here in Vegas. "Most eBay super sellers aren't selling and trading collectibles, they're selling consumer goods online, at least $35,000 each month," says Bundy. Fixed-price merchandise, the kind usually sold by online bargaineers, accounted for over one-third of total sales on eBay in 2007. As eBay's traffic plunged late in the first decade of the new millennium, other sites like Amazon, online classifieds, and specialty liquidators came to the fore. (Amazon actually described its 2008–2009 holiday season as "best ever" and, amid a failing retail environment, managed to sell 72 items per second at its peak of sales.)

In other words, bargaineering has become an American pastime. Collectively, small-time bargaineers now have the economic heft of a Fortune 500 company. By the middle of the first decade of 2000, an estimated 200,000 to 250,000 North American dollar stores and microdiscounters posted upwards of $60 billion in annual sales—far less than behemoth Wal-Mart's $374 billion sales for 2007, but roughly equal to those of Costco and Target. When compared to traditional retail, it's a staggering admission: independent and midsized discounters—people and businesses that sell imported party hats, paper plates, and confetti—account for as much annual revenue as many long-standing corporate institutions such as Microsoft, Dow Chemical, BMW, Boeing, and Time Warner. By early 2009, in the midst of global recession, most dollar stores were doing better than ever: Dollar General, the biggest of America's chains, posted nearly 10 percent sales growth at a time when even Target reported a 41 decrease in profits.

"It's an underappreciated part of the economy," says Bundy, noting that the top 1000 independent discounters alone account for $49 billion in American sales, not including small dollar chains, online sellers, and microbusinesses. "Much of the news is focused on the alpha players—the Wal-Marts of the world," he says. "At our show, maybe five percent of businesses service the bigger retail, but the rest of commerce is conducted with independent retail. But there are so many of them, if you were to consolidate all the little guys, they represent a pretty significant impact."

There are no fancy receptions, hospitality suites, or gift bags at this convention. This is global commerce at its grassroots. And no one here expects to discover the next iPod or Blackberry—a singular, killer product that redefines a marketplace. That kind of expectation and hype is for the next electronics conference that rolls through Vegas. What bargaineers care about is price, volume, and speed; everything else is ancillary. The products are often quite generic—it's process that ultimately matters, not content.

Nearby, on the trade floor, someone buys a 40-foot shipping container of sunglasses; someone else sells a shipment of kitchen scrub pads. Bundy gives me a list of some of his longtime contacts, professional bargaineers who are right now bartering, selling, and signing contracts, somewhere out there in an ocean of cheap stuff. Yet he admits that one of the most powerful players isn't even here—the consumer. In the economy of bargains, shoppers play the most ruthless role of all. The growing number of consumers who shop without scruples or loyalty and who expect the best prices are the people whom bargaineers regard with high respect and no small amount of fear. "There is no question that with consumers there are expectations," says Bundy. "And there will be continued pressures driven by the consumer, founded in expectation that we should be able to access these kinds of goods at value prices."

The dark side of the bargain juggernaut is too much success: despite new challenges and fierce competition, consumers still demand perpetual discounts. "That makes for unsustainable growth," warns Bundy. "There will be ups and downs. There will be consolidation."

Despite the near-insatiable consumer demand for bargains, a significant number of bargaineers here will fail, some will go bankrupt, and a few are, right now, probably liquidating everything they have. All it takes is a stalled deal, an extra five-cent loss on a unit, or a lost shipment, and many of the entrepreneurs here could crash. Much like today's consumers, the independent bargaineer is leveraged on credit cards or household equity. There's not a lot of room for failure.

But those who can meet consumer expectation, surpass the competition, and keep product flowing around the world, will win big, Vegas style. Even though it's many months before the global financial crisis hits, everyone here already knows that stakes are high: the memory of failed twentieth-century discounters from Woolworth's to Kmart haunts this global trade floor. And while Woolworth's five-and-dime counters wowed consumers during the late-1800s—and launched retailing into the modern age—today's merciless shopper simply expects Everyday Low Prices as standard. That's what makes bargaineering dangerous. "Before, you got a bargain: 'Wow, what a great find,'" says Bundy. "Now, people just expect to get it."

The Quest for Cheap

It's midday inside the Sands Convention Center. Another plastic spatula, another Barbie doll knockoff. Standing amid the endless rows of kitchenware, toys, small appliances, and novelties, it's hard to believe that this cluttered, generic collection of goods is the vanguard of global trade. Yet this motley bazaar represents the complete and total infiltration of bargain goods into our world. During 2006 alone, over 182,000 new consumer products were introduced, roughly 300 a day, and growing at a rate double that of 2004 and 2005.

Standing behind a cardboard display of batteries, film, and disposable cameras, Carlos Soto runs his own import business out of a small office on the edge of South Central Los Angeles. The Mexican-American Angeleno explains how he imports brand-name products from Korea directly to retailers in Central America, Mexico, and southern California. Filling several 40-foot steel containers each year with Korean Kodak and Duracell products is still cheaper than purchasing identical American-sourced products, even after paying for shipping across the Pacific. "It's an opportunity for small importers like me," he says of the price differentials between national markets. "People don't mind Korean language labels, they want prices."

A soft-spoken family man, Soto is not exactly an obvious choice to be a Wal-Mart giant killer. Yet he sells his products cheaper than almost anyone else in North America, and they wind up in the dollar stores that compete with Wal-Mart supercenters. That's a problem for Wal-Mart, at least as long as Soto can keep filling containers from Korea and negotiating his small business around potential credit crises, lost containers, rising costs, and competitive pressure to lower prices.

Today's new breed of discounters are the daredevils of today's retail economy—risking all to bring you new value—and there are almost as many inventive business schemes at this show as there are products. Entrepreneurs like Soto find opportunity in obscure, unlikely places—and discover ways to deliver affordable batteries and film to strip malls in East Los Angeles, Guatemalan family *tiendas*, and Mexican department stores.

While discounters have been with us since the late 1800s, several late twentieth-century developments helped transform bargain retailers from bottom feeders to global kingpins. First, the invention of advanced logistics and web technologies has enabled whole armies of shipping containers, distributors, and factory workers to be mobilized on the timely delivery of cheap products. Second, the developing world opened for business, led by China, Mexico, and Vietnam, who solicited offshore capital and opened their gates to tariff-free *maquiladora* factories, special economic zones, and other strategies that connected cheap labor to global commerce. Finally, the emergence of postindustrial economies—Western nations with a gross domestic product (GDP) that are dominated by spending—have both accelerated bargains and reinforced dependence on cheap stuff on an unprecedented scale.

In fact, one can track postwar consumerism alongside the gradual rise of discounting. The Las Vegas bargain show began as an Army surplus sell-off in 1961, capitalizing on an excess of Cold War hardware manufactured by America's military-industrial complex; it was a discount business opportunity founded upon government contracts and geopolitical tension. Discounting evolved, and by the 1970s the trade show began primarily featuring general merchandise, following the growing role of dollar store chains and big-box discounters as a dominant force within consumer economies. Bargaineering represents the future, an emerging experiment in globalization and consumerism, but it also represents the past, embodying many of the core ideas of late nineteenth-century business magnate Frank W. Woolworth, who built one of the world's first global retail empires on few scrappy five-and-dime stores in upstate New York.

In 1878, fledgling retailer Woolworth posted a sign in his Watertown store that changed the face business: "Anything on This Counter 5 Cents." Post–Civil War America was fraught with inflation, poverty, and political instability. With so many households displaced or economically troubled and retail of the day bound-up in mandatory counter service and prices inflated by fat merchant mark-ups, the time was ripe for bargains.

After a few initial business failures, Woolworth eventually found huge success with his five-and-dime stores, which featured competitive prices, self-service, and variety. "Patrons of the day could not believe that 'all this' could be had for a few coins a piece," writes historian Karen Plunkett-Powell. "Woolworth was carrying everything from egg whips to tree ornaments to Horatio Alger books. It was the heyday of retail bargains, and Americans were having a field day taking advantage of them."

Customers no longer had to haggle over inflated prices or wait in front of dusty counters. Like Sam Walton, Woolworth learned from his early failures and developed a ruthless, scientific approach to retailing that was only exceeded by Bentonville in the 1990s: strategic location finding, ruthless competition, tight margins and cost controls, emphasis on retail display and signage—and, of course, the aggressively low prices. As Woolworth told one reporter, "Everybody likes to make a good bargain. Let him. Small profits on an article will become big profits if you sell enough articles."

The parallel to Wal-Mart's rise is uncanny: Woolworth brought food into discount stores in 1897, installed cutting-edge technology (cash registers) in 1900. He expanded to 120 stores by 1904, and then went public in 1912 and was worth $65 million, an unprecedented fortune. By 1912 Woolworth's had over 600 stores in the United States and Europe, boasting annual sales that would be equivalent to $1.1 billion today. By early 1900s, serious competition had emerged as other retailers like Kress and Kresge (Kmart) duplicated Woolworth's business model. Retail discounters became standard fixtures in not only all North American towns and cities, but across the United Kingdom, Europe, and Australia; there were 5,000 discount stores in America alone.

Woolworth's success coincided with the twentieth-century shift from agricultural to industrial society. People were moving off farms and into cities, often becoming more active consumers in the process. Five and dime chains became a major force in twentieth-century economies, affecting the same deflationary forces attributed to modern discounters. "According to the U.S. Bureau of Census, in 1935 there were 127,482 chain stores operating in the U.S.," report economists Levy and Young. "It follows, therefore, that a nontrivial proportion of the retail trade was conducted at fixed, nickel and dime, prices for about 40 years or perhaps even more, from the mid 1880s, to the mid 1920s and early 1930s."

By 1961, Woolworth had become the world's first retailer to report $1 billion in annual sales. But the famed skyscraper that Frank Woolworth had built in Manhattan before his death in 1919 had long since ceased to be a center of power. After 117 years, a much-weakened Woolworth's sold off the last of its 400 stores in 1997 and folded its remaining assets into a holding corporation named the Venator Group. What happened? Postwar society became more affluent and suburban and increasingly abandoned the old downtown discounters in favor of enclosed malls. "Woolworth had trouble adapting their cut-rate downtown model to the new suburban shopping centers that sprang up around the country," notes historian Joshua Zeitz. "The company stuck to an updated version of the old five-and-ten even as postwar affluence brought a higher standard of living to many of its customers."

Woolworth's slow decline had everything to do with the birth of new-generation discounters: Wal-Mart, Kmart, and Target all opened within four months of each other in 1962. "By 1970 [these] "big-box" budget retailers, to be joined later by new discount franchises like Toys "R" Us, Circuit City, T. J. Maxx, Office Depot, and Best Buy, outsold traditional department stores as well as five-and-tens," writes Zeitz. "And rang a final death knell for the downtown business districts that Woolworth had long dominated."

The modern age of the bargaineer began with the 1976 opening of Wal-Mart's Price Club in San Diego, California. It wasn't Sam Walton's first store; Chairman Sam had famously failed several times earlier, but it would prove to be a successful experiment in no-frills retailing. Until Sam Walton began building warehouse clubs and supercenters en masse, regular consumers had little access to goods at wholesale prices. Warehouse clubs served up near-wholesale prices by the pallet load, and as the clubs became the fastest growing retail format during the 1980s, a whole new generation of customers began to expect and demand their goods at cost which, in turn, helped accelerate the consumer frenzy that eventually turned Wal-Mart into the world's largest company. "By the late 1980s, the line between the discount industry and other retailers had blurred to the point that the very notion of discounting lost any distinctive meaning," note business sociologists Adele Petrovic and Danica Hamilton, on the end of the first wave of discounting that resulted in consolidation and bankruptcies. While only three of the top ten American discounters of 1980 still survive—Wal-Mart, Target and Kmart—they established market dominance that allowed them to dictate the shape of retail in North America.

As discounting moved into its global phase, making use of cheap transport, labor, and materials in ways never before imagined, international competition became critical. Back in the 1970s, Sweden-based IKEA pioneered an irrepressible template for modern discounting, mixing design, affordability, supply chains, with lots of particle board. Now the world's largest furniture manufacturer, IKEA shares Wal-Mart's secretive approach to global retailing as well as a common talent for giving consumers more for less. In Europe, the success of the hypermarket, a combination supermarket and general merchandise store, launched other global giants: France's Carrefour, the world's second-largest retailer, became the first foreign retailer in Asia in 1989; Britain's Tesco, the world's fourth largest retailer, has managed to so effectively execute its own brand of global discounting that Wal-Mart has copied a number of its core strategies. Together, leading discounters from in Western nations helped break up price monopolies enjoyed by many manufacturers and traditional retailers, often at the cost of domestic manufacturing jobs and local commerce.

As discounters triumph, the department store has turned into an endangered species: store counts for American mass merchandisers—department stores, largely—shrunk by 44 percent between 1996 and 2007. Likewise in Canada, discounters began outselling department stores as early as 1994, adding $2 billion in new sales between 1992 and 1996 while many traditional retailers and grocery stores have suffered a slow decline—including the now-departed Eaton's, once Canada's largest retailer. "Of the forty-two department store chains operating in 1980," note Petrovic and Hamilton, "only 20 remained in business a decade later. Fully 80 percent changed hands during that time."

Carlos Soto owes much to the crushing success of multinational discounters like Wal-Mart who eliminated so many traditional grocery and department stores during the 1990s. When the global standardization of barcodes took place in 2005, for example, the change was largely invisible to shoppers, but an efficiency gain for many major retailers, and a huge boon to independent discounters and retailers, as it allowed for direct and accurate commerce in goods. With access to a universal code for products, "small stores [can] eliminate third, fourth and fifth parties," one independent grocer told Canada's *National Post*. "They won't need brokers; they will be able to deal directly with manufacturers all over the world." Not only were new trade opportunities created, retail began to deconstruct itself. Thanks to Wal-Mart, and to warehouse stores in particular, customers were no longer stuck at the very end of the supply chain with the biggest sticker price.

Wal-Mart's toughest competition in the new millennium comes from small-time discounters like Soto who can now source their own low-price products directly from the same increasingly sophisticated Chinese manufacturers, as well as arrange container shipping around the world with little more difficulty than requisitioning a FedEx delivery. By the mid-2000s, Wal-Mart and other major retailers—Kroger, Save-a-Lot, and Target—added dollar-only sections to existing stores to directly compete with extreme-value pricing, in an effort to win back thrift-obsessed consumers. Wal-Mart's experiments with a dollar-only section underline a harsh reality that Sam Walton himself helped invent: it's all about price. By 2009, in the midst of a consumer spending collapse, major dollar chains such as Dollar General and Family Dollar were actually growing faster than Wal-Mart.

Big or small, today's bargain trader is essentially an arbitrageur—someone who strategically exploits price and cost differentials between markets, leveraging gain on the imbalances. Speed and carefully calculated profit margins are critical. With the kind of strategic precision that would be the envy of Wal-Mart executives, Carlos Soto can purchase foreign brand-name goods, have them delivered halfway around the world, sell them at deep discounts before anyone else can, and still manage to make money. And he does so to the great frustration of his competition. Arbitrage has been more traditionally the dominion of Wall Street—think commodity or bond trades, not dollar stores.

Today's retail-driven economy is leveraged upon a set of systemic imbalances, not the least being the wage/labor differential between China and the West. This is how the biggest trade deficit in human history was launched, one container at a time. "We receive twelve containers every week from Guangzhou, Hong Kong," says Brian Bulley of Encore Sales, a midsize North American distributor of toys, housewares, and novelties. "We deal with quite a number of factories as well as offshore trading companies—one single Guangzhou outfit supplies us with 9000 different items." Like many companies here, Encore supplies design specifications and artwork to factories, some of which might have only eight or twelve workers. It's a system of proxy companies and subcontracts, where buyers effectively lease offshore manufacturing capacity.

There is amazing speed within these production cycles—women's apparel can see as many as 17 different seasons every year—and it is possible for a product to be discontinued even before it reaches the consumer. It's a seemingly infinite network of companies and contracts, one that links hundreds of millions of people around the globe, one shipping container at a time. "You are going to buy our product," says Bulley, "whether you know it or not."

At the ASD/AMD Merchandise Show, a Hasidic trader ambles over to Soto's tables to browse Korean batteries. He has his own booth a few aisles away, proffering toiletries and other drugstore items. "I'm surprised more people don't stop by our booth," he says. "We have a nice booth." Here on the frontlines of the bargain trade, if you don't have either best prices or one-of-a-kind items, business will evaporate, even on the second day of a trade show. He knows that by shaving even a few points off his own profits—which is no small thing in this high-volume, low-margin business—could make for a much busier day tomorrow. The trader praises Soto's business scheme and they trade cards. Nobody bothers to read the fine print on Soto's Korean batteries: Made In China.

Better than Wal-Mart

The bargain has become a cultural icon and an economic monolith, our consumer dreams realized in warehouses. Few have witnessed this transformation as up close as Danny Kole. Back in 1982, the South Los Angeles native and his brother began selling car stereos, tools, and hardware at flea markets.

After scouring California for better merchandise at lower prices, they decided to start importing it themselves and quickly got out of retail and into imports. These days, they operate one of the biggest independent dollar and discount import operations in America and are a major presence at the bi-annual Las Vegas trade event. You probably don't know their business, but you've likely seen products that have streamed through their city of Carson headquarters, not coincidentally located a fifteen-minute drive from North America's busiest container port.

Kole remembers the days when mention of cheap imports conjured scorn and skepticism. Using a telex machine and taking long trips to distant factories on Mainland China, the Koles helped pioneer the kind of direct sourcing and importing that has become the backbone of today's consumer economy. "As dollar stores sprang up around the country, we realized that it was more than a fad," he says. "Without the Asian market, it would have never happened: we used to have 1,000 items in stock, tools and house wares, which increased 20 percent a year. Now we have 4,000 items, [have] diversified to stationary, gifts, toys, photo frames. No single item makes up one percent of our sales."

Kole admits that the staggering growth in his business—his family's jump from flea markets to multimillion-dollar sales—is partially the result of good timing. "We rode the tide of imports," he recalls. "Anything that was a bargain from $1 to 20 cents, we'd try. There was so much out there that the consumer had not seen. And as 99-cent price stores took off, 15 years ago, we went with that. We focused on price point. With so much merchandise available, we found that we could create a huge line of items available for a dollar."

During the 1990s, factories became more sophisticated, barriers to trade were eliminated, shipping costs decreased, and, most importantly, competition among all these elements lowered prices even further. Kole now simply needs to review courier packages full of factory samples that arrive every day. Many are unsolicited submissions from manufacturers who want Kole's business. "We used to travel to Asia and scrounge for as many items as we could find. Now there's not a day that goes by that we don't have several boxes from Chinese suppliers with samples."

For every item you see in a store, bargaineers like Danny Kole reject hundreds more. At best, "we keep 5 to 10 percent of submissions." In other words, Kole might see as many as 240,000 different items in the process of stocking his current stable of 4,000.

This fierce competition to reach Western consumers results in further price drops even before products leave the factory. "New vendors constantly approach us," says Kole. "There is pressure on price. And if suppliers raise prices, we will drop the item." Wal-Mart famously pressures manufacturers to lower prices every year; bargaineers like Kole can simply wait for the next discount to arrive.

The orderly, nation-based commerce of previous generations has been forever changed by this global surge in consumer goods. "The gamut of merchandise available through the sophistication of [offshore] factories has 100 percent changed the landscape of retail," says Kole. "The growth of Wal-Mart and Target has largely been driven by the profitability of imports, not by growth of domestic markets. It's the dollar store-ization of the economy."

New generation importers like Kole will sell wholesale to anyone. With their $100 minimum order—down from $250 a few years earlier—small-time bargaineers don't need to buy whole containers of product. Heck, for $100, local households can shop here wholesale once every few weeks. "Our customers are everyone from a person running an eBay business out of a garage to South Americans buying containers," he says. Many are flocking to the bargain trade simply because people can make quick money. Kole shows a prepackaged display of 1,600 items that can be set down anywhere. "We charge $1,000 for the fully loaded display," he says. "But you're going to turn this into about $2,500."

These are insane bargains. Kole shows me some kitchen knives that would normally retail for $3.99 to $5.99. Kole's price? Fifty-five cents. Pens that sell for $2.99 retail are selling for 39 cents. Indeed, some discounters excel in selling the liquidated stock of big-box retailers—and still manage to gain more revenue per item. Kole displays closeouts it has acquired from major retailers—an increasingly common source of product as retailers cast off seasonal or surplus items in the accelerated push for fresh items and fashions. In his Los Angeles showroom, Kole has a display of kids' college-styled backpacks that were recently bought from Wal-Mart: the Wal-Mart sales tags, still hanging from the backpacks, charge $14.88. "We're selling these for $2.50," he says, with some pride—a discount of nearly 600 percent off the original retail price.

Ultimately, Danny Kole's secret weapon is the universal appeal of discounting. People are simply drawn to deals, says Kole, even if they don't need them. Even before the economic collapse, scores of affluent shoppers could be found snooping about in bargain bins: In 2003, roughly 49 percent of all American households with incomes of more than $70,000 regularly shopped in dollar stores. "We do sell a lot more merchandise to inner city LA than Beverly Hills," Kole admits. "But everyone likes getting a deal. It's the treasure hunt mentality: 'Wow, I bought this for a dollar.'"

Another major trend is the emergence of generic or no-name brands. Also known as private labels, these products are often identical to manufacturer brand-name products, but they are sourced and packaged by retail and whole-sale bargaineers. Wal-Mart's "Great Value" groceries, for example, have made major gains, and the company predicted in 2009 that its 100 different private label brands would gain 40 percent market share by 2012. Meanwhile, tra-ditional retailers and manufacturers continue to invest vast sums on mar-keting and design to cultivate the perception among consumers of brand value—be it perceived status, thrift, style, familiarity, or some other subjective quality. U.S. manufacturers spent $18.45 billion alone on in-store marketing in 2004 for brand-name products. Bargaineers reject the advanced marketing and branding strategies that have been developed over a century of mod-ern commerce by simply offering low prices without fanfare. Brand names are progressively becoming less relevant. In 2009 Procter and Gamble intro-duced Tide Basic, their own knockoff of a premium brand.

Small-time bargaineers here in Las Vegas claim an evolutionary advantage over major retailers, who are locked into massive supply chains and big-box outlets. "Even the Wal-Marts and Targets of the world have become pretty well set," Kole says. "It all looks the same. [We have] the ability to change stores and change the store and change for demographics with neighborhoods. Products aren't fixed to supply or advertising, and can change as needed."

Kole explains that many of his products can quickly be scaled back to ensure the all-important $1 price point that bargaineers strive for. "Facing greater cost, the size or quantity of items is decreased, not price point." Kole gives an example of some generic barbeque brushes that were recently shipped from a factory in China. "We offered them at 3 for $1—an outrageous price," he says. "But when prices went up, we shipped to sell at 2 for $1. The customer won't likely see this as any less of a bargain."

Yet getting less for less is exactly what has been happening in dollar stores and grocery stores in recent years. In an effort to preserve the appearance of low prices, a bar of Dove soap has "shrunk" by half an ounce; a jar of Hellman's mayonnaise is two ounces (56 grams) less then it used to be; and paper towel rolls are shorter, with some brands losing as much as 11 feet per package. (Manufacturers claimed that shortened paper towel rolls were, in fact, "thicker, stronger and last longer.")

Danny Kole's downsized barbeque brushes are a portent of things to come. The "incredible shrinking package" is here to stay, argues Meg Marco of *Consumerist*, because "companies are fearful. There's nothing that sends fear into their hearts as much as price increases, because it makes people think twice—especially in an economic downturn."

For now, nobody seems too bothered at the prospect of getting one less barbeque brush. Want a brand-name backpack from Wal-Mart cheaper than Wal-Mart? Easy, just wait a few weeks and then talk to your local bargaineer or search the Internet. Ours is a future marked by new kinds of risk and reward. And on a planet pulsing with steel containers, the plethora of low-priced product—from backpacks to toothpaste to plastic toys—represents a smart bomb to traditional commerce.

Tomorrowland

In the basement of the Sands convention center, you can browse army surplus and hardware items, just as early bargaineers did during the 1960s, when Sinatra and the Rat Pack were making lounge-lizard history upstairs in the original Sands Hotel. There's a rough edge to these basement bargaineers: biker T-shirts, brass knuckles, SWAT fatigues, bulletproof vests, security cameras, and infra-red goggles—all discounted, of course. Probably the most popular item in the basement is the 150,000-volt stun gun. A gaggle of off-duty security officers are taking turns picking up the pocket-sized weapons, tethered by wire to the display counter, and discharging them with a loud "zap" that echoes throughout the convention hall.

Also on display are full-sized stun batons, purse-sized zappers, as well as concealable stun pens with an 800,000-volt charge, enough juice to knock someone out after just momentary contact. The rent-a-cops wave them around, pretending to chase each other. Unfazed, the vendor behind the counter reads a magazine. Apparently this happens a lot. If people are given the chance to play with electroshock weapons in Las Vegas, even the most mild-mannered conventioneer will pick one up.

That one of the world's largest bargain markets convenes twice annually in Las Vegas is not coincidence, since this city is Tomorrowland for the twenty-first century. Las Vegas has always been an economic frontier zone, where new kinds of commerce have emerged, from money laundering to the modern entertainment corporation. From the beginning, this desert outpost harbored schemers, fringe players, and wise guys. By the turn of the millennium, the Las Vegas "system" had nearly been perfected: millions of people passed through and left behind billions in revenue. Most of them would return home with few winnings, and, if statistics are correct, they returned, under pretenses of doing business or for pleasure. Some, wink, wink, did both.

Shopping and gambling have had a long period of convergence. Well before Wal-Mart became the world's largest company, Las Vegas pushed new frontiers in retail, demonstrating the potential of a nascent service economy. Archetypes for North America's economic future were constructed here, from the enclosed mall of the Circus Circus Hotel big top in the 1960s to today's shopping-integrated entertainment resorts and the network of large satellite casinos that now extends all the way to Macau. Even though many retail developers have largely rejected megamalls and have turned toward deconstructed malls—open-air big-box malls, known as lifestyle centers and power centers—Vegas remains on the cutting edge of retail engineering with its deployment of both spatial and sensory cues to attract, stimulate, and disorient customers, and modern technology that logs detailed customer activity, creates high-resolution data analysis, and allows dynamic adjustments in business strategy in order to extract maximum revenue from every shopper or gambler. In fact, Las Vegas now generates three times more revenue from food, shopping, and accommodation than it receives from its gambling operations, reporting $25 billion in nongaming revenue in 2004 versus $6.8 billion from gaming. Amazingly, even in the world's self-proclaimed gambling and entertainment mecca, the core business is just another day at the mall.

Take away the lights, pirate ships, pyramids, and roller coasters, and many resorts on the Las Vegas Strip would reveal the utilitarian styling of our post-industrial economy—massive parking lots, boxy buildings, and plastic stucco. "Vegas is often described as a city of dreams and fantasy, of tinsel-ish make-believe," writes Marc Cooper in *The Last Honest Place in America*. "But this is getting it backward. Vegas is instead the American market ethic stripped bare, a mini-world totally free of the pretenses and protocols of modern consumer capitalism."

During the early 1970s, America became the first nation "in which the service sector accounts for more than half of total employment and more than half of Gross National Product," wrote Daniel Bell in his prophetic 1973 book, *The Coming of Post-Industrial Society*. "It is the first service economy, the first nation, in which the major portion of the population is engaged in neither agrarian nor industrial pursuits."

As postwar economies matured, industry and manufacturing declined and the service sector grew to nearly 80 percent of America's GDP. Yet as trade-based globalization grew, both production and competition intensified as well. "Like flightless birds on a predator-free island, American companies had no defenses when hungry and hard-eyed competitors finally came hunting from overseas," writes Charles Morris in *The Trillion Dollar Meltdown*. "It was a slaughter. By 1980, for all practical purposes, America no longer manufactured televisions or radios, the Germans and Japanese controlled the machine-tool industry, and American steel and textile industries were a catastrophe. Even IBM's mainframe computers were being challenged powerfully by Amdahl and Fujitsu."

By 2005, retail and wholesale commerce accounted for 35 percent of America's GDP, totaling $4.4 trillion in sales, exceeding industrial, manufacturing, and agricultural production combined. It is as pure a service economy as likely ever invented in human history, with 1.4 million retail outlets employing one in five American workers. Elsewhere, it was much of the same: Retail was the third largest employer in the United Kingdom in 2007 and accounted for one-quarter of all private sector employment in Canada.

Led by the United States and adopted by most Western nations, this change from production to consumption is the hallmark of postindustrial society—an economic landscape characterized by shopping malls, offices, technology, logistics, as well as unprecedented dependence on imports and consumer debt. This transition has created incredible wealth, as well as growing rates of productivity and underemployment.

Wal-Mart emerged as the greatest postindustrial company, one that aggregated power without having to bother with owning factories or natural resources or producing energy. "Thanks to the Arkansas company, retailing trumped the high-tech industry as a contributor to the late 20th century productivity surge," writes James Hoopes. In 2002, business consultants McKinsey found that Wal-Mart created 25 percent of the productivity gains in U.S. economy between 1995 and 1999.

Profound economic imbalances grew over decades in plain view of policy experts and elected officials. It was no accident. Regulatory structures and social supports were dismantled to support deindustrialization and globalization. "Americans were told [that] we would have to submit to the discipline of the free market," recounted the late Ellen Willis in 2006. "[Former president] Carter embraced the neoliberal order with its mantra of austerity; he presided (with the help of the late [Senator] Ted Kennedy) over decontrol of oil prices and deregulation of the airline, trucking, and banking industries. Clinton supported the pro-corporate program of the Democratic Leadership Council and abolished the entitlement to welfare." A similar political-economic transformation occurred in Canada, Britain, New Zealand, among other developed nations, as well as in scores of developing countries around the world.

It's been a core ideology here in Las Vegas, where, practically speaking, self-regulation has been the rule here since the 1960s. Most of the four-mile stretch of the Las Vegas Strip isn't actually inside the city limits of Las Vegas, but exists quietly as an unincorporated part of Clark County, Nevada. Not including state or federal government, one of America's richest commercial areas is presided over by a single elected official. And, as if to clarify its neoliberal stance, in 2006 the city of Las Vegas was the first in America to make it illegal to feed homeless people on public property.

The ideological justification for liberalizing trade and neglecting economic outcomes was simply that prosperity was an end unto itself, the function of free markets. It was, in fact, a hedge—a calculated gamble that there would be enough growth to benefit those who suffered as economic activity was displaced and eliminated. "The ordinary course of change has winners and losers," explained former Federal Reserve Chair Allan Greenspan in September 2008, as the global financial crisis unfolded. "Let's recognize that this is a once-in-a-half-century, probably once-in-a-century type of event."

A thinker who influenced a whole generation of economic leaders, while a professor at the University of Chicago, Milton Friedman championed monetarism and capitalism as the innovation to end innovations, yet this crusade for plenty was, in fact, a policy of "maximum Vegas"—a trade-off of economic growth for new kinds of risk. As economist and *New York Times* columnist Paul Krugman has since argued, the near-religious belief in unfettered markets held by Greenspan and other Chicago School thinkers was just a gambit—and not a very good one either, since it allowed and encouraged growth to be leveraged upon growth and massive amounts of commodified debt to be resold without oversight in a way that would come to resemble a global pyramid scheme. "As long as housing prices kept rising, everything looked fine and the Ponzi scheme kept rolling," wrote Krugman. This, in turn "opened up large-scale funding of subprime lending" through the now-discredited financial innovation of collateralized debt obligation. At the other end of the economy, affordable consumerism continues to fuel another prosperity bubble: unsustainable growth founded on shipping, shopping and spending.

The coy insider adage, which even the squarest tourist at the airport is tempted to echo, "whatever happens in Vegas, stays in Vegas" is no longer true. It probably never was true, for what has been happening in Las Vegas has been on export for the better part of the last 50 years. What happens in Vegas most definitely now happens everywhere.

And in the tradition of Las Vegas' shady past, there were insiders who knew that the great financial gamble was fixed all along, and that their best opportunity was to take a cut, get out, and leave the suckers behind at the table. "Let's hope we are all wealthy and retired by the time this house of cards falters," admitted one Standard & Poor employee as the financial collapse began to build in 2007. This propensity to game the system, even to the point of fraud, wasn't isolated behavior, it was systemic: As New York state attorneys investigated the financial collapse in 2009, it came to light that failed investment house Merrill Lynch "secretly and prematurely awarded approximately 3.6 billion dollars in bonuses" during the fall of 2008, even as its losses mounted towards catastrophic proportions and its new owner, Bank of America, had requested $20 billion in emergency capital from the federal government. While millions of people lost retirement savings, homes, and education funds, "Merrill chose to make millionaires out of a select group of 700 employees," said New York Attorney General Andrew Cuomo.

This is the Las Vegas lesson for our time: One way or another, the house still pretty much always wins. Out on today's casino floor, experienced gamblers still complain about how today's generation of corporate owners—expunged of all known organized crime influences—systematically crashed players' odds on favorite games like blackjack through the calculated introduction of multiple decks, continuous shuffle machines, and advanced surveillance technologies to help identify and eject professional players and lucky rubes who win too much, too often.

At its upper levels, much of the modern service economy—finance, retail, and gambling—is an insider's game. But unlike the financial sector, Wal-Mart and modern Las Vegas leave surprisingly little to chance: engineering out-comes is paramount, simply because ventures like gambling and retail require volume transactions on finely calculated margins. Wal-Mart famously turned American commerce upside down by firmly setting price targets and telling manufacturers to meet the everyday low price and accept future rollbacks; not only did this reverse traditional power relations from manufacturers to retailers, but it began an extraordinary process of transferring the substantial risk of cheap prices, low wages, and exceedingly tight margins—if any profits remained—onto the backs of manufacturers.

Behind this, an even larger process of offloading took place: uncontrolled pollution emissions were unloaded into factory zones and shipping lanes; distant regions were tapped for cheap labor and resources while leaving behind unresolved underdevelopment and political oppression; consumers and companies alike were given access to destabilizing levels of debt, despite obvious risks, because even governments stood to gain from the resultant surge in prosperity. The phenomenal rise of Wal-Mart and other global discounters during the 1990s onward has everything to do with these kinds of external-ized costs, risks, and impacts which were rarely reflected in the business of everyday low prices. Discounters took many risks in retail strategy and global business expansion, but the modern supply chain itself was built upon calcu-lated advantage, technology, and jurisdictional shortfalls. Not having to pay anything extra for carbon emissions, global poverty, or unemployment was what helped make bargaineering the kind of sure bet that a casino executive would love.

In the years before the crash of 2008, Las Vegas attempted to immunize itself against bargains, turning away from families and budget tourists in favor of luxury travelers. The cheap buffets and discount rooms were disappearing. A cold sandwich in the basement of the convention center cost nearly $10; you'd get better value at the MGM Grand down at the fancy end of the Strip, which was perhaps precisely the point.

By 2009, Las Vegas developer Steve Wynn's stock price had crashed 85 percent; Harrah's, MGM, and scores of other hotels and gaming establishments were having serious debt problems. MGM, then controlled by billionaire Kirk Kerkorian, struggled with $13 billion in debt and was selling off properties and other assets in order to stay afloat.

Today, the polyester suits, buffets, and cheap rooms are back again. Cheap prices rule as Las Vegas scrambles to reinvent itself. In a world predisposed towards risk, nobody escapes discounting.

Under the Casino

"Hypocrite!"…"Motherfucker!" In a subterranean maze of meeting rooms beneath Bally's Casino, the American labor movement is falling apart. It's March 2005, and as bargaineers hustle shipping container loads of cheap imports a few blocks north at the Sands convention center, the American Federation of Labor's (AFL-CIO) executive council is fighting it out. The reason? Unions today represent only 15.5 million—12.5 percent—of America's 124 million workers, down from a peak of 33.2 percent of all workers in 1955. And nobody can seem to agree on how to stop what has become, by most accounts, a slow death spiral for organized labor.

The AFL-CIO has been the largest federation of organized labor in America since its inception in 1955, making it the second largest labor body in the world. And in the big casino of global trade, they are the ones who are coming up short. If Fortune 500 retailers and mass bargaineering represent the upswing of postindustrial society, the many woes of organized labor represent its down swing. An estimated 3 million American manufacturing jobs disappeared between 2001 and 2003, striking the very heart of organized labor—nearly 800,000 American manufacturing jobs disappeared in 2008 alone.

"Factory employment is at its lowest level in more than 50 years," reported the National Association of Manufacturers in 2006. "In fact, of the top 28 manufacturing countries in the world (which account for 90 percent of global manufacturing output), just 5 have seen increases in manufacturing employment over the last 5 years: Argentina, Brazil, Spain, Thailand, and Turkey."

The rust-belt decline of manufacturing jobs across the western hemisphere reflects the other side of the bargain boom: Outsourcing, productivity gains through technology, and a whole host of transnational business connections have not created the kind of steady, paid employment that sustained organized labor during the twentieth century. The dual impact of offshore manufacturing and vast increases in productivity through management and technology has helped to shrink union membership worldwide—except China, of course, where a government-backed union is mandatory for most businesses and manufacturers.

And then there is Wal-Mart. The retailer's uncanny ability to bully suppliers into submission—"negotiating" on behalf of consumers—is the same skill-set deployed to drive away unions and play hardball with employees. For decades, Wal-Mart's old-school labor tactics have resulted in unprecedented conflicts, including the world's largest class-action employment discrimination case, *Dukes v. Wal-Mart*; the swift closure of stores that do manage to unionize, such as the 2005 shutting of a newly unionized outlet in Jonquiere, Quebec; as well as publicized individual cases of disabled or low-income workers forced into dismissal, mandatory overtime, or subjected to litigation.

Even in pre-Obama America, a land rife with some of the most lax labor laws in the developed world, Wal-Mart still somehow found a way to embroil itself in massive lawsuits and nasty allegations of misconduct. Between 2000 and 2005, the American National Labor Relations Board's (NLRB) official findings of illegal conduct against major retailers were levied mostly against Wal-Mart: 15 decisions of unfair labor practices out of a total of 19, even though all other major retailers—including Target, Costco, Home Depot, and Albertsons—collectively share more employees than the world's largest company.

While Wal-Mart has liberally stolen from the 1920s antiunion playbook of dirty tricks, the company's labor battles show the underbelly of the service economy. Whatever happens at Wal-Mart does not stay at Wal-Mart: Like Las Vegas, its influence and impact is unprecedented. Launched in 2001, the *Dukes* case encompasses 1.6 million current and former female employees who allege they were wrongfully denied fair pay and promotions on the basis of gender. Their claim was valued at $11 billion as of 2009. And while this charge should not surprise anyone familiar with Sam Walton's good ol' boy management style, Wal-Mart represents a postindustrial vanguard that affects hundreds of millions of other people. In fact, the outcome of a single Wal-Mart lawsuit is monumental: *Dukes v. Wal-Mart* will, as the U.S. Chamber of Commerce argued in a 2007 legal brief, "virtually guarantee that employers will be subjected to large-scale employment discrimination class actions with billions of dollars in potential damages." This prediction would, to some degree, hold true: in December 2008, Wal-Mart paid an estimated $640 million to settle 63 different class-action suits that claimed the company "cheated hourly workers and forced them to work through breaks."

In this context, all the cursing, frustration, and in-fighting here at the Las Vegas labor summit comes as little surprise. Up against Wal-Mart, the union can see the end of an age and the movement into a new one that increasingly excludes them. And as the union leaders duke it out in meeting rooms and staffers scuffle in the halls, media observers and guests can only look at the dour, ashen faces of the leadership as they emerge to make only terse policy statements and wonder what is really being said behind those closed doors.

"These are the darkest days I've seen for American workers across the United States," says federation president John Sweeney, flanked by supporters. "Everything the union has fought for is all under attack." In recent months, Sweeney has blamed Chinese imports, Republican policies, and corporate greed for the decline, noting that nearly 1200 American companies eliminated pension plans in 2003. Burly union kingpins like Leo Gerard (steel workers) and Gerry McEntee (public sector workers), look uncomfortable and play down the rancor. But, tellingly, leaders from three of the four largest unions are nowhere near Sweeney's podium, having mixed it up with the president and his cadre of machinists and steel workers only a few hours before.

Elsewhere, Andy Stern, dissident leader of the powerful Service Employees International Union (SEIU), is circulating an inflammatory resolution. "It is not just hostile employer environment that is undermining our movement's campaign for workers rights," he writes. "It is also the failure of the AFL-CIO." Making the statement even more antagonistic is the fact that Stern was once Sweeney's protégé within SEIU; Stern ran Sweeney's campaign to become federation president in 1995 and soon after replaced him at the helm of what is now North America's largest trade union. Indeed, there are large sums of money involved: Stern advocates a 50 percent cut in union dues to the AFL-CIO, which would result in $35 million more each year for organizing within the SEIU. Conversely, Sweeney proposes a $45 million annual increase in political spending for the AFL-CIO, a continuation of efforts to reform laws that govern capital-labor relations by pumping money into Democratic elections in the hopes that a labor-friendly congress is elected, after years of defeat during successive George W. Bush administrations.

In all of this, there's no small amount of fear. These leaders have to figure out a way to restore membership numbers, win a long list of political battles on worker rights and organizing law, and break the union-free lock of new millennium powerhouses like Wal-Mart. Ultimately, they must be successful or almost everyone at this meeting ultimately loses their jobs. On the surface, the dispute appears ideological: grassroots versus old school, new labor versus big labor. Yet it is far more than that. It is, in fact, a potentially insurmountable conflict that goes to the core of twenty-first century change. The unions are divided by a growing service economy that creates more winners and losers than Vegas could ever dream of.

The hard truth is that there are now more service industry workers in America, some 21 million, than there are union members. The first six years of the twenty-first century were "the first sustained period of economic growth since World War II that fails to offer a prolonged increase in real wages for most workers," most of whom are service based. In the eyes of some service union organizers, this new concentration of service workers represents growth potential, even if it means attempting to unionize retail and technology corporations that consider themselves post-union. Nevertheless, service unions like SEIU and its cousin the United Food and Commercial Workers (UFCW) have had success adding new members to replace losses, and SEIU is actually the fastest-growing union in North America. Yet unions that represent workers in the rust-belt industries—and in some shrinking government sectors—see things differently. In 1969, for example, the machinists' union claimed one million members, but by 2005 had shrunk to 380,000, having lost more than 100,000 members since 2000 alone. The technology, industry streamlining, and offshoring that killed those jobs isn't going away anytime soon and therefore manufacturing sector unions don't see vast potential; they are circling the wagons. Put another way, "Stern insists that given the growing clout of global corporations, unions have no choice but to bulk up and adopt a private-sector growth strategy [of maximizing membership]—a tangibly different take than McEntee's politics-and-public sector approach," observed *Business Week.*

Chatting in-between sessions, observers note that a similar dispute occurred in America during the 1930s, when old-style craft unions faltered in the face of twentieth-century industrialization, with leaders famously coming to blows at a 1935 meeting in Atlantic City. Back then, the fight was about how to respond to industrialization in an age of mass production: the reigning trades and craft unions were losing power as mass industry took over and factories churned out automobiles, appliances, and airplanes. In contrast, today's conflicts are about de-industrialization and the fact that the retail sector represents five percent union membership, yet accounts for one in five of all American workers. This massive shift towards lower-wage, part-time retail-service employment not only vexes unions, but also increasingly touches every aspect of public life. While organized labor has certainly had its low points, labor's slow decline has also meant that issues of broad public benefit, such as health care reform and welfare, received less attention during the years that America was playing casino with itself.

"The stale and paralyzed political dialogue . . . is a direct result of the deterioration of industrial America, followed by the rise of the Wal-Mart economy," noted Matt Bai in a 2006 *New York Times* story on American union woes. "Lacking any real solutions to the growing anxiety of working-class families, the two parties have instead become entrenched in a cynical battle over who or what is at fault. Republicans have made an art form of blaming the declining fortunes of the middle class on taxes and social programs; if government would simply get out of the way, they suggest, businesses would magically provide all the well-paying jobs we need. Democrats, meanwhile, cling to the mythology of the factory age . . . if only Washington would close a few tax loopholes, they seem to be saying, the American worker could again live happily in 1950." Caught between partisan illusions and the relentless influx of offshore goods, organized labor seems almost ready to write its own eulogy.

It hasn't helped unions that Wal-Mart has reformed itself in some areas, albeit not necessarily to union standards. After years of criticism, for example, in 2009 Wal-Mart expanded health coverage, just in time for the recession: only "5.5 percent of its employees now lack health insurance, compared with a nationwide rate of 18 percent" reported the *Washington Post.* These and other troubles are on full display under Bally's. Today's union woes are largely about globalization and de-industrialization—which, in turn, reflects broader conflict and confusion about the growing dominance of postindustrial society, rife with bargains, underemployment, income insecurity, and eroding domestic production. In other words, some of the greatest challenges of our time stem not merely from anxieties about terrorism and geopolitics, but also from the transformation of Western nations into shopping economies.

One starts to wonder if labor's unhappy family might find better odds-to-win upstairs on the blackjack or baccarat tables. Things are that bad. As one senior staffer confides: "We may have a Federation after this week, but I don't know about the week after that."

The Battle of Las Vegas

A few years earlier, Las Vegas had been the site of the first—and possibly last—major battle between organized labor and Wal-Mart. This showdown was a street-level organizing campaign to unionize several Las Vegas Wal-Mart outlets that ran from 2000 to 2004. What actually happened during the failed Vegas campaign does much to explain the bad blood, long silences, and outright fear that grips unionists clustered in the basement of Bally's casino.

With much fanfare, UFCW field organizers rolled into Las Vegas at the behest of the union's head office in Fall 2000. The UFCW was already strong and well-represented in the city's many casinos, restaurants, and grocery stores; it was part of the city's history back when organized crime and the Teamsters help finance some of the strip's first modern resorts. Compared to the rest of America, Las Vegas is highly unionized, a fact that is lost on many tourists, but not on strategists, largely because union membership has grown substantially within the city's many hotel and gambling establishments, which have added over 20,000 members since late 1980s. Many within the UFCW well understood that a David-and-Goliath-style battle between labor and Wal-Mart was overdue—and they needed somewhere that could serve as a fail-safe laboratory for in-store unionizing. It might as well be in Las Vegas, a place that the AFL-CIO president once called "the hottest union city in America."

In fact, a street battle between labor and Wal-Mart could not be avoided. During the 1990s, unions like the UFCW sniped at Wal-Mart regarding child labor abuses and subsidies from local government. But this did little to slow the continued expansion of Wal-Mart and its kin, especially the retailer's Death Star–like strategy of deploying integrated grocery and retail Supercenters across the western hemisphere. ("The Supercenter taught the supermarket industry a lesson in brute capitalism," recounts business journalist Anthony Bianco in *Wal-Mart: The Bully of Bentonville.* "The typical chain supermarket could not slash its prices to match the Supercenter opening across the street and still turn a profit, largely because it was locked into UFCW contracts paying workers 25 percent to 30 percent more than Wal-Mart's nonunion staffers made. The result was that every time a new Supercenter opened up in America, two big supermarkets went out of business, taking some 400 high-paying jobs with them.")

Wal-Mart was doing precisely this in January 2001 when the retailer simultaneously opened four different centers in Las Vegas, over 500,000 square feet of union-free shopping. It was the largest retail opening by a single company in the city's history—no small feat—yet was only part of a national, 46-store deployment across America over three days. It was shock and awe retail strategy, carpet-bombing whole urban zones with bargains in a gambit to secure market share.

"There was a small group of organized Wal-Mart workers under the radar before we arrived," recalls former UFCW organizer Bill Meyer, who coordinated the Las Vegas campaign from 2000 to 2004. "But Wal-Mart sent a slew of folks in there, 'people teams' they were called. It got to the point where workers were scared to death—that they weren't voting on a union but whether to keep the store open. They were scared to death."

Organizers converged on Sam's Club #6382, located due west of the Las Vegas strip. Bill Meyer and others managed to sign a majority of the Las Vegas store workers at Sam's Club #6382 to union cards and the NLRB scheduled an election. The battle escalated: intimidation, firings, and stacking the employee pool with new, union-unfriendly workers became common, some of which would be later documented and found illegal by the National Labor Relations Board (NLRB)—a clear pattern of "of unlawful tactics, forbidden under US as well as international law."

While some Las Vegas workers spoke favorably about Wal-Mart and asserted that no union was necessary, this did little to deter the union's organizing efforts, which became increasingly assertive. "It got to the point where as soon as [union] organizers got out of their cars, the security guards would be in the parking lots telling them to leave," says former cashier Alan Peto, who attempted his own unsuccessful petition against low wages at Wal-Mart, reporting on-the-job harassment, and later filed yet another official labor relations complaint.

In the end, Wal-Mart gained the upper hand. In a last-ditch measure, union organizers filed a complaint to the NLRB in November 2001 and intentionally postponed their election to ensure that Wal-Mart management could not succeed at crushing the vote. As Meyer admits, this strategy probably cost them long-term chance at victory, since it wasn't long before Wal-Mart workers who signed union cards had moved on, were transferred, or were fired. The critical in-store majority was lost. "We had a solid core of people that were going to vote for it," argues Meyer. "But Wal-Mart sent a slew of people in there, destroying the laboratory conditions. We felt confident that if people had been left alone, we would have succeeded."

It was a historic battle that will have implications for decades to come. Yet the odd thing is, none of the union honchos at the AFL-CIO conference wants to talk about the Las Vegas Wal-Mart—especially the UFCW, who appear to be pretending that their campaign never happened. In one public session, a journalist asks leaders about the union Wal-Mart strategy and gets the freeze: "Why would we reveal our strategy?" says one leader, icily. On several occasions, I corner Greg Denier, UFCW communications director, to ask for an interview and some names of UFCW contacts that participated in the Las Vegas campaign. Amazingly, he's got nothing, as if all the labor organizers and millions spent on attempting to unionize Wal-Mart in Las Vegas left no trace whatsoever. It's the same story over at the UFCW 711 local office—"Sorry, no comment." It's as though the whole chapter has been written out of history, like some Soviet-era purge, complete with missing names and faces smudged out of photographs.

It wasn't long ago that union operatives like Greg Denier were attempting to fight Wal-Mart out in the open. "Americans can't live on a Wal-Mart paycheck," Denier told *Mother Jones* magazine in 2003. "Yet it's the dominant employer, and what they pay will be the future of working America."

Despite the official silence, the truth eventually comes out. Las Vegas is a sore point for big labor not because they didn't win—they hadn't officially lost yet, either—but because UFCW themselves pulled the plug on the operation. What really happened, explains Meyer, who only agrees to talk because he is retired from the UFCW, was a leadership change. In July 2004, newly appointed UFCW Organizing Director Bill McDonough terminated the program. "Bill wanted a different course and rode off the path," says Meyer. "There were real battles on philosophy internally. So they set aside the past and moved on." Moreover, an expensive California supermarket strike in 2004 had drained the UFCW's war chest, and "a web-based campaign was cheaper." Even in the labor movement, it seems, there's no escaping downsizing.

The union moved away from organizing Wal-Mart workers to a public relations and internet campaign called "Wake Up Wal-Mart." "I understand why they made their decision," says Meyer. "But I would have done both campaigns." There was, maintains Meyer, visible progress after the unsuccessful 2001 vote drive. Las Vegas union organizers had continued to sign up new Wal-Mart workers, reinforcing union presence and creating confidence. They had launched an independent radio show in Las Vegas to publicize the UFCW and conduct guest interviews with local players—a tactic that was already being employed by labor activists in Hong Kong. But "after we changed philosophies, you didn't see workers as much," says Meyer.

Back at Bally's casino, any mention of Wal-Mart presents an embarrassing contradiction: The UFCW, having eliminated its highly public Las Vegas organizing campaign, was still pushing hard for the same worker-oriented organizing across America—which is also a battle that could raise millions of dollars in new union dues. The campaign in Las Vegas was a wager for everyone, yet when the losses ran high, the union left the game abruptly.

Now all the accusations and cursing make more sense. More importantly, the internal struggle that the UFCW experienced over Wal-Mart is, in essence, the same internal struggle that now threatens to break apart the world's largest labor federation.

For many workers, it's the dark ages of the 1920s all over again, argues Meyer, citing landmark mass layoffs at failed American retailer Circuit City in 2007, when the retailer fired 3,400 senior workers and then offered to hire them back at lower wages. As Daniel Bell predicted more than 30 years ago in *The Coming of Post-Industrial Society,* in the transition from "a goods producing to a service economy, the professional and technical class emerges as the predominant occupational group." And despite the "historical strength of trade unionism, [there are] increasing difficulties within the straights of a service economy and foreign competition." In other words, the so-called knowledge economy that springs from postindustrial society does not favor workers; rather, it often discards or demotes people as the result of what turned out to be unsustainable growth.

None of this is any comfort to the embattled labor unions underneath Bally's casino. After all the acrimony, long silences, and fading hope, everyone leaves Las Vegas unhappy: three of the four of largest unions quit the federation a few months later. In total, seven unions, representing six million workers, abandoned the AFL-CIO. Any hope of a unified labor force that could take on Wal-Mart probably died that day under Bally's casino. What was once Wal-Mart's greatest threat became a series of scattered coalitions and websites.

Wal-Mart eventually did allow some of its stores to unionize—but only in China. Complying with Chinese law, and a four-year ACFTU (All-China Federation of Trade Unions) campaign to shoehorn itself into the 100-plus Wal-Mart outlets operating across mainland China, Wal-Mart adjusted its most fervent antiunion policies for the world's largest marketplace. ("Should associates request formation of a union," read the company's one-line official statement, "Wal-Mart China would respect their wishes.") In a final post-Vegas twist, the enigmatic Stern reportedly played a part in bringing China's Communist Party-controlled union into Wal-Mart's stores.

At the end of it all, Bill Meyer remains philosophic, despite being defeated partially by his own union. "What we learned is that all of this did not go for naught," he says. "We found that many workers actually did want a union. It was the workers themselves. [But] we also learned that our system of labor laws are also deeply flawed," he says, citing delays in the complaints process and employer-friendly labor regulations. "Getting a contract would have almost been impossible, it would have taken years and years. So we were ultimately hampered by labor laws and a company with endless resources." Years later, the NLRB determined that Wal-Mart had acted illegally, and was ordered to pay a few thousand dollars in lost wages and "post notices in its three stores disclosing its federal labor law violations." But it didn't matter anymore. The workers who had originally filed the complaints had long quit their jobs on moved on. "There were a lot of great people who stuck their necks out," admits Meyer, recalling that most everyone who signed union cards either quit, transferred, or were fired. "It was a four-year undertaking and we spent millions of dollars. Many were understandably bitter about it."

But hey, this is Vegas. Losing graciously is part of the drill. Former Wal-Mart workers like Alan Peto have surprisingly little to say about being caught up in a battle of titans. "We went from a high of 30 organizers to only one," Peto says, via email, regarding Wal-Mart's victory and the UFCW's retreat. Peto has moved on and now works in local law enforcement, but he's not forgetting what happened, either. "Basically, everything Wal-Mart said about the UFCW in the anti-union meetings came true," he says, regretfully. "Especially with regards to how the UFCW would ultimately abandon the workers."

In May 2009, the UFCW announced it would once again attempt store-level organizing of Wal-Mart workers on the hopes that newly elected President Obama might facilitate better labor laws. Encompassing 100 stores across America, the union was hopeful about Obama's 2008 election promises on labor reform known as the Employee Free Choice Act which by 2009, had withered under the economic pressure of recession; even the Act's stalwart Democrat supporters had been scared off from supporting anything that resembled growth-stalling legislation. "They know it will fail," said labor historian Nelson Lichtenstein of the UFCW's second quest to unionize Wal-Mart. "It's designed to fail.... [But] demonstrating that failure shows we need something new."

Perpetual Bargain Machine

On the last morning of the Las Vegas bargain show, the trading floor begins to rumble. It's only a few hours before it's time to pack up and clear the building, but there's last-minute action. After four days of bartering and bad coffee, eight thousand vendors start selling off everything—sales samples, display stands, anything not bolted to the floor—to the first person willing to hand over cash. The Sands convention center has just turned into the world's largest dollar store. You want something? Make an offer.

All the strange stuff gets bought up first: electrified mini 4x4 jeeps, faux-antique lighting, imitation motorcycle leathers, giant stuffed animals, and singing Elvis dolls. People are buying more than they can carry, all at super-discount prices.

It is a triumphant moment for those who are at the heart of modern commerce. From the early 1990s to the late 2000s, consumers and bargaineers managed to live the New Economy dream, well outside of the elite circles of Silicon Valley and Wall Street, enjoying uninterrupted growth, cost savings, and possibility, all without having to make a single thing themselves. And while this 20-plus-year span of the bargaineer's ascent to power is hardly a blip in the course of human history, it marks the fullest expression of globalization and its impact on everyday lives.

Even as markets turn sour and consumers stay home, bargains have staying power precisely because cheap stuff delivered a veritable jackpot of value that has become central to our economy. Some analysts estimate that approximately $100 billion in new consumer spending was created through the first wave of the bargain revolution; other estimates claim that imports from China alone have saved U.S. consumers roughly $600 billion. As one 2002 study by the National Bureau of Economic Research claimed: "12 percent of the [American] economy's productivity gains in the second half of the 1990s could be traced to Wal-Mart alone."

Despite the income erosion and corporate command of post-industrialism, bargains are in high demand because they offer an economic boon to regular folks. In glitzy TV ads in 2008 and 2009, Wal-Mart trumpeted savings as a form of income. "Let's say you spent a hundred dollars a week at the grocery store on these kinds of items . . . If you bought these kinds of items at Wal-Mart you could save over $700 per year," says a woman comparing bags of groceries. "What would you do with all that money?" These claims are impressive—shoppers spending $100 per week at a supermarket can save $700 annually on their purchases—yet they come from Wal-Mart's own paid consultants, Global Insight, who in 2006 claimed that whole families of Wal-Mart shoppers saved a total of $2,500 annually.

Wal-Mart has perpetually overstated its benefit to the economy. Globalized bargains are a very small pay raise, contributing only $115 per year to the average American household budget in 2007, according to International Monetary Fund (IMF) statistics on global trade.

Bankruptcy, foreclosure, and employment insecurity across America speak to the fact that the meager gains of affordable consumerism are not shoring up the deeper economic erosion evident in America's heartland. Nevertheless, cheap stuff represents the psychological heart of consumerism: the distant possibility of relative affluence and price accessibility for all classes of people, everywhere. And in our emerging casino economy, where winners and losers abound as wealth and poverty grow in opposite measures, the great majority of consumers continue to cling to bargains in an attempt to beat the odds of an unfair world. Simply put, consumers gorge themselves on imported cheap stuff that inevitably erodes domestic employment, thereby sparking further demand for bargains.

The disintegration of the AFL-CIO represents, among other things, future waves of retail workers and dollar store customers. They are the involuntary bargain shoppers, as are the many former union workers who are already employed as involuntary part-time labor in the service sector. The Vegas bargain show is a prime example of cheap stuff becoming axiomatic, since many bargaineers, especially microbusinesses, eBay sellers and mall cart sellers are, as Sam Bundy noted, also refugees from the world of full-time employment.

Between expected shortages of resources and consumers, Kole sees the potential limits and imperfections of the current system—and knows he'll be one of the businesses caught in the disconnect between expectation and reality. When oil peaked near $150 a barrel in 2008, which increased Kole's costs on everything from plastic to transport, people still demanded bargains. "As times get tougher and tougher, people are even more looking for a deal," says Kole. "Customers are more educated now and if they don't see a good deal, they won't come back." Already, most dollar store chains are stocking more expensive items, partially because income-challenged consumers are doing more one-stop grocery shopping at dollar stores (again, following Wal-Mart's highly successful expansion into groceries), but also because of the gradually declining number of products that can still be sold for a dollar.

"Plastics, anything petroleum-based, have gone up in cost," reports Kole. "Anyone dealing with a plastics factory now receives regular notices announcing regular increases in price. That's the reality of it with plastics: the same person filling up their tanks is doing the same thing buying a laundry basket or a plastic lunch box. They're going to pay more for it next year." Just as five-and-dime stores passed away during a period of industrial expansion during the early twentieth century, so too will dollar stores. This is a little hard to imagine in the midst of the Las Vegas trade floor, where the cheapness seems to run on forever.

Yet Kole imagines a time when bargains will come to resemble natural resources, subject to scarcity and price flux. "Over the long term, bargains will be similar to gas prices, with fluctuations and peak seasons," he says. "So companies will try to adapt, buying when products are less expensive." This is the experiment at the core of a consumer-driven service economy: How far can we bargaineer past known limits? Are there limits? "A postindustrial transformation produces no 'answers'," predicted Bell in 1976. "It only establishes new promises and new powers, new constraints and new questions—with the difference that these are now on a scale that had never been imagined in world history." Consequently, trade in bargains now influences international relations, interest rates, and gross national product on several continents. And what it lacks in imagination, quality, and possibility, it delivered in quantity, low prices, and the ever-present promise of good value.

For now, the Las Vegas bargain show is an oasis. Everyone sets aside business in these last moments and scoops up whatever trinket or household gadget that catches their fancy. Compared to the sterile environments of malls and big-box stores, it's an image of commerce as it appeared well before plastic was ever invented, as thousands of bargaineers barter, haggle, and trade amid half-deconstructed stalls and shipping crates.

For some, today's prize is an executive putting set; for others, it's biker goggles and fake tattoos. I'm laying down a few dollars for some stuffed Hulk and Spiderman dolls for my kids and I negotiate a great price on a toy bin that would never fit on the airplane home. Some folks appear to have a flatbed truck waiting outside on the Strip as they shamelessly haul out everything from fake palm trees, enormous gold-framed Baroque paintings, and life-size statues of American jazz musicians. Poor John Coltrane, strapped to the back of a golf cart. Nearby, a six-foot-tall knockoff of Caravaggio's "Inspiration of Saint Matthew" leans up against a concrete pillar, surrounded by Marilyn Monroe handbags and crates of poker chips.

The random ebb and flow of people and products is more entertaining than Las Vegas itself, much like watching the global economy set to shuffle. And it is the smiles, the genuinely warm glow of the successful shopper that registers as people exit the building, arms filled with loot. This is the kind of magic you don't usually see in Vegas. In this moment, everyone's a winner here, and they know it.

CHAPTER 2

QUANTUM CHEAP

PROGRESS IS PRICE DESTRUCTION

The Fall and Rise of Wal-Mart

Eduardo Castro-Wright has a problem. The CEO of Wal-Mart USA stands before an expectant audience at a posh Arizona golf resort to deliver the convention's keynote address in which he will attempt to explain how Wal-Mart plans to conquer the twenty-first century. Nearly everyone who matters in retail is here: Macy's, Sears, JC Penny, Target, Nordstrom, plus scores of blue-chip manufacturers, consultants, and logistics experts—a veritable brain trust of North America's service economy in a single room. The battles of Las Vegas are behind them; now their main concern is how to maintain revenue and precipitous rates of growth in a world that is filling rapidly with retailers. The problem is that for Wal-Mart, and nearly everyone else, achieving yesterday's success may prove impossible.

Continued growth within saturated and underdeveloped markets is the retail equivalent of what breaking the sound barrier was for postwar America—a quantum threshold that shows what ingenuity and true grit can accomplish. Wal-Mart fancies itself as the one who will unlock this mystery. "Few retailers have changed the marketplace as much as Sam Walton did," says Castro-Wright, reminding everyone of the rags-to-riches story of the world's greatest retailer. "He began in 1962, and it [Wal-Mart] has grown to nearly $300 billion dollars in sales. You do not do that without changing and innovating." The thing is, executives attending this high-level conference aren't buying it. Wal-Mart is in trouble, and everybody knows it.

It's 2007, and Wal-Mart has posted its worst monthly sales results since 1979. The world's largest company actually reached its peak back in 1999, entering the new millennium with a 106 percent increase in stock price and a 9.3 percent same-store growth rate, after incredible gains throughout the 1990s, when it famously opened thousands of new stores around the world and logged record profits. But, to the horror of Bentonville's home office, Wal-Mart's stock value began dropping almost immediately, for a total decline of 38 percent between 2000 and 2007, eliminating an estimated $27 billion in Walton family assets. The company appeared to be in the throes of a middle-life crisis.

Investors had lost faith, smelling failure, despite the company's tremendous profits. In fact, in the 29 years that Wal-Mart reported same-store growth, its profit and store count was still increasing, but actual sales performance declined, from a peak of 13 percent same-store growth in 1987, dropping to an all-time low of 0.8 percent in 2007. Wal-Mart's arch-rival Costco posted as much as 5 percent same-store growth in 2007, more than quadruple the rate of the Arkansas giant, with an estimated one in four American households owning a Costco membership.

Sam Walton was rolling in his grave as Wal-Mart lost ground in the world's most competitive retail market. "Sam was a great innovator," continues Castro-Wright, undaunted. "Sam said, 'everything is changing around you, you can't succeed by if you keep doing what you are doing today. You stay in front of change.'" While Castro-Wright is clearly one of Wal-Mart's brightest and most promising stars, it's clear that he drank the Bentonville Kool-Aid some time ago: With eerie devotion, he invokes Wal-Mart's founder on a first-name basis even though he and other new-generation executives never met the legendary retailer, and, notably, most of Wal-Mart's staggering growth and innovation actually occurred after Chairman Sam had passed on (Walton died in 1992). "We stay on the forefront of everything we do and we remember his teachings: We bring value to customers and communities."

This is, perhaps, how Wal-Mart's top executives rationalize outrageous salaries and bonuses: they don't often take questions and they rarely wander off-message. And today's message is about Wal-Mart's corporate facelift, part of its multi-year plan to get itself back on track—and, most importantly, to regain investor trust. Born in Ecuador, Castro-Wright came from a retailing family. He joined Wal-Mart in 2001, after stints in manufacturing at Honeywell and Nabisco. While at Wal-Mart Mexico (WalMex), he achieved record growth in sales, making it one of the company's most successful international divisions. In 2005, Castro-Wright was appointed CEO of Wal-Mart USA. He is the company's great hope for a turnaround in its critical home market—which, by virtue of Wal-Mart's influence, also means that Castro-Wright literally holds the fate of consumerism in his hands.

So it is that, with great anticipation, today's audience listens for clues in the CEO's speech, that may help them to parse the future. Because Wal-Mart is the still the dominant force in an economy that is dominated by retail and wholesale trade, Castro-Wright could read the phone book and people would still hang on his every word. "We were the first ones to start a distribution network in the 1970s," he continues with casual resolve. "And in the 1980s, we brought in a satellite network. Today, we are continuously driving for innovation."

But the question that everyone with a stake in the world's largest company really wants to know is, where's the growth? It directly concerns the 1.9 million people directly employed by the retailer. After a three-decade period of expansion, Wal-Mart's growth stall causes panic because its core business strategy has always been preemptive growth: breaking into and disrupting markets with low prices before anyone else can get in. Sam Walton's brilliance was in finding untapped potential within the underdeveloped retail markets of rural America; Walton filled in the open spaces on the map, and his successors accelerated this trend globally with logistics technology, offshore production, and aggressive business tactics.

Castro-Wright knows that the stakes are high. Wal-Mart famously cannibalized the top retailers of the twentieth century, just as the dollar stores and fellow big-box discounters now nip at the heels of Bentonville's Goliath. "In less than 40 years, the economic landscape has changed so dramatically that nearly all of the ten largest retailers of the 1970s are no longer the ten largest retailers today," he reminds everyone. "That tells you a lot—retailing is a Darwinian business."

Accordingly, investors had devalued Wal-Mart's share price not because the company lacks profits—its profits actually increased 12 percent in 2007—but because the retailer's past strategy and success appeared to be nearly impossible to duplicate in the future. Retail has become a brutal zero-sum game in the twenty-first century partly because most Western markets are saturated. The most obvious example of this is Wal-Mart's supercentering of America: In its efforts to triple and sometimes quadruple its market share in any given location, Wal-Mart strategically oversaturates its own markets, at least as much as can be supported by its own supply chain network. The result, as was famously demonstrated in Oklahoma City—where, from 1997 onward, the retailer closed an estimated 30 competing supermarkets and reduced food prices by 15 percent with an invasion of 18 different supercenters and markets—is terminal retail saturation. Or, as Sam Walton once bragged, "We became our own competition."

Castro-Wright inherited this end game from Lee Scott, who became Wal-Mart's president in January 2000, just after the company's stock had peaked. Although he presided over the company's massive devaluation, Scott bragged to shareholders in 2005 that, "we estimate there is room for almost 4,000 more supercenters," even though expansion was already flagging at 2,300. By late 2007, Castro-Wright, under investor pressure to curtail operations, downscaled Wal-Mart's expansion plans by 30 percent. At the height of its success, Wal-Mart had successfully managed to open a new store somewhere in America roughly every 26 and half hours.

So, even before the great crash of 2008, Wal-Mart's prospects were looking somewhat dire. "There is turmoil in Bentonville at levels I don't think we've ever seen before," said Mark Hunter, one of America's top retail consultants, when I interviewed him in Tucson in 2007. "For a long time, they have been quietly saying, we're going to become the first trillion-dollar company. They are not going to become a trillion-dollar company. This is a company that is having major problems."

The company had boxed itself in. Wal-Mart can rework its image all it wants, spruce up its stores, and spend millions on public relations, yet it cannot easily escape itself. Its corporate DNA is growth and low prices, built upon mastery of cost, logistics, and scale. Despite this, it wants to pursue customers and markets that purchase more than the cheapest household goods. It wants to be Target, Costco, and Macy's all rolled up into one. The retailer even luxed-out its dowdy stores with brand names and modern color schemes in an effort to appeal to urban shoppers who distained Mr. Sam's hillbilly warehouse aesthetic. Small European-style stores are rumored to be their next big move. "[We're] taking it to the next level," says Castro-Wright. "We don't deal with the blue-grey big box anymore."

"They are trying desperately to move from supply-chain master to merchandising guru," explains Hunter. "They are having problems, a lot of problems.... I think it's one of the bigger reasons for their earnings and store sales problems. They can't quite figure it out—how do we get consumers to buy more than just the basics, underwear and tissues?"

Castro-Wright responded to critics by underscoring the need for Wal-Mart to segment itself, to become more things to more people, expanding into financial services and healthcare, for example, and bringing in groceries and merchandise targeted directly to the Asian and Hispanic markets, who will represent one-third of all customers by midcentury. Wal-Mart has gone environmental, hiring a former Sierra Club president, becoming the world's biggest purchaser of organic dairy and produce, and selling more compact fluorescent lightbulbs than any other retailer—"worth some $3 billion in saved power bills," Castro-Wright reminds his audience, "or one million cars' worth of greenhouse gases."

Wal-Mart also adopted a new marketing strategy and slogan in 2007; it was the company's first slogan change in 19 years: "Save More, Live Better." No longer was Wal-Mart's yellow smiley zooming through stores rolling back prices in the company's television spots; instead, the retailer ran new ads that featured real stories from real shoppers, invoking middle-class dreams and family values instead of everyday low prices.

But Sam Walton never agonized over what a customer feels—he let low prices do the talking. Hunter and others wondered if Wal-Mart was losing its nerve, predicting that this kind of touchy-feely turnaround—save more, live better—was Kremlinesque code for the unmentionable: higher prices, less value. "The move signals a trend they have been establishing in the past several years of increasing their prices on select items," he says. "Wal-Mart is not the low-price leader on every item. They are clearly moving to a strategy of being the low-price leader on key items and taking a higher margins on other items."

This isn't necessarily bad news. A world with fewer of Wal-Mart's aggressive price rollbacks would appeal to many groups, not least to the majority of manufacturers who have frequently been squeezed to the brink of bankruptcy by Bentonville's cheap purchasing department. The unions, workers, activists, and anyone else beaten down by the smiley steamroller would surely claim victory.

Wal-Mart is banking on the fact that it has become a major institution, a third order of public life, powerful enough to defy trends. "89 percent of Americans visited a Wal-Mart store last year," Castro-Wright reminds his Arizona audience. "And our studies showed that many want to feel smart more than trendy; [they want] unbeatable prices for quality product."

But it was not just Wal-Mart that was affected. Well before the 2008 crash, the hypercompetitive markets that sustained the discount boom of the 1990s had begun to stagnate. Consumer bankruptcies, rising business expenses, an ongoing credit crunch, as well as rising gasoline prices, were afflicting many traditional retailers. Macy's, Sears, Nordstrom, and J.C. Penny all experienced depressed same-store sales. Store closures and retail bankruptcies began increasing. Wal-Mart USA alone eliminated 110 store openings in 2005, a 39 percent reduction.

More than anyone, retailers understand what happens in an economy driven nearly 80 percent by consumption when consumers don't show up for shopping duty. "Our customers have been hurting," admitted Office Depot's CEO Steve Odland in October 2008. "The global economy is at stake here."

Some hailed the collapse as an opportunity: This is how we regain balance and common sense after a dizzy boom. This is how we move from debt-fired, high-impact consumerism into something more sustainable.

But Wal-Mart, seeing blood in the water, announced aggressive new discounts. The company's gambit included an ingenious and oddly reassuring early rollout of 2008 holiday-season decorations and 10 percent to 50 percent discounts on toys, including Barbie dolls and Tonka trucks for $10. It was Keynesian retailing; the company "spent" millions in forgone profits on price rollbacks during a recession in order to keep customers. Knowing that more shoppers were living paycheck to paycheck, Wal-Mart put Christmas on the "fast track" because customers would be stretching their budgets over months in order to afford gift-giving season. "It's starting now," said Wal-Mart spokesperson Linda Blakely. "Our price rollbacks make the prices comparable to what they were 20 years ago."

Black Friday 2008 arrived just as U.S. jobless claims jumped to nearly 600,000 in a single month. Wal-Mart had found its mission. As the financial crisis took hold and the world plunged into a broad-reaching and, some feared, potentially bottomless recession, worried retailers lined up their best deals for the final days of a failing holiday season. Taking the lead, Wal-Mart rolled out massive bargains. Most major retailers conceded that there was no choice: Like it or not, they were all competing with Wal-Mart and anyone else who could deliver radical deals. Many discovered that they just couldn't keep up; the venerable retailer Sears posted a 55 percent profit decline.

By February 2009, Wal-Mart had increased same-store sales growth by 50 percent—adding $4.1 billion in additional revenues—compared to same three-month holiday period a year earlier. Back when the economy was booming and shoppers were spending, Wal-Mart couldn't get respect from investors, yet facing the worst economic conditions since the Great Depression, when many retailers were falling fast, it nearly doubled sales growth. (Wal-Mart's same-store sales increased 5.1 percent during February 2009 compared impressive declines of 26 percent for Saks, 30 percent for Abercrombie & Fitch, and 12 percent for the Gap.)

Wal-Mart's epic but often derided quest for cheap suddenly had historic purpose. Wal-Mart's new motto—save money, live better—"has galvanized the entire organization around a common purpose," said Eduardo Castro-Wright, who became vice chairman of Wal-Mart in 2009. The company pledged to feed and clothe its customers more affordably than anyone else on the planet. "Nowhere has price leadership been more important to our customers than in grocery," Mr. Castro-Wright continued, "[and] we continue to increase the price gaps between our competitors and Wal-Mart in food and consumables." At least for that moment, it was clear that discounting, not finance, technology, or any other industry, had become the consumer's last refuge.

Having renewed its success, Wal-Mart proceeded to fire 800 people from its home office in Bentonville. "The business model that Sam Walton created is perfectly positioned for the environment we live in now," said Wal-Mart's new CEO Michael T. Duke. "I do believe this is Wal-Mart's time."

The Tyranny of Price

Sam Walton once claimed that Wal-Mart could "restore manufacturing capacity, improve our national economy, and renew our pride in American craftsmanship." The company's vision today is a little different. Wal-Mart's post-2008 turnaround has much to do with the fact that so many other retailers are failing. Yet, if market failure is a precondition for Wal-Mart's success in the twenty-first century, what does it mean for everyone else?

Wal-Mart created opportunities through "price leadership," adopting policies that multiplied international price reductions in what author Charles Fishman has called the "Wal-Mart effect." "Wal-Mart is the logical end point and the future of the economy in a society whose preeminent value is getting the best deal," economist Robert Reich has written. Yet, in a service economy clogged with retailers, where there are few frontiers left *except* price, we can perceive a fundamental problem with the discount model: in the end, many will not survive a race to the bottom. As Wal-Mart's revitalization demonstrates, new profits or sales will likely be stolen from someone else's bottom line. In this kind of environment, a major retailer who cannot steal growth from competitors cannot survive.

One thing is for sure: the incredible wealth and growth that defined the booming 1990s is history. Evidenced by Wal-Mart's doldrums, there's plentiful concern among Castro-Wright's Arizona audience that the last significant wave of retail growth happened in the 1990s, as new mini-malls and big-box stores cluttered the landscape, leaving a large portion of the greater service economy increasingly vulnerable to increases in energy prices and housing and credit collapses.

Eastern Europe, Asia, and other developing countries are the world's only remaining major growth markets, and they are being pursued by everyone from Wal-Mart to Germany's Metro to Home Depot to France's Carrefour. Yet international expansion has been spotty for many retailers. Wal-Mart's move into Germany was a failure, and its expansion into Japan was a money-losing operation, realities that cloud the retailer's claims that new growth abroad can solve its home market woes. International sales accounted for 22 percent of Wal-Mart's 2006 sales of $345 billion, but most of this came from Canada, Britain, and Mexico, retail markets that are also facing saturation. Developing markets in Central America, Brazil, Argentina, and China hold the most potential for future growth, but there are few guarantees.

Wal-Mart remains addicted to growth. The truth is that consumer-economy stalwarts like Wal-Mart require large economies of scale and competitive expansion to compensate for extremely low profit margins. Deep, perpetual discounting means that Wal-Mart collects as little as half as much profit per revenue as traditional retailers: Wal-Mart earns only 3.24 cents on every dollar it sells. Their success is a testament to their innovation and discipline; no other company in history has managed to make so much money on such low margins. Yet it also means that continued growth is mandatory; Wal-Mart must compensate for rising expenses and consumer demand for deeper discounts with higher sales volumes. So, when investors devalued Wal-Mart at the start of 2000, despite the company's consistently huge profits, it is because they understood the nature of the service economy: if you aren't growing, you're dying.

Wal-Mart's success spawned many imitators. The arrival in North America of the United Kingdom's Tesco, the world's fourth largest retailer, for example, was heralded as a major challenge to Wal-Mart's dominance. Tesco planned to spend $2 billion between 2007 and 2012 to launch Fresh & Easy markets in the United States; by 2008, Tesco was already surpassing most American stores in average sales per square foot and had announced another 150 locations. By tweaking the Wal-Mart model, and opening strategically sized stores with better products and more conveniences—new-school retailers like Tesco and Costco were literally out-Wal-Marting the world's leading retailer, at least before the recession hit.

The future of the modern service economy is evident in the United States, the world's leading consumer market, where new growth is least forthcoming. By 2009, American consumer confidence had reached a 26-year low, and major retail bankruptcies were a near monthly occurrence. "It's no longer reorganization or even liquidation for these companies," bankruptcy lawyer Sally Henry told the *New York Times*, noting the disappearance of retailers like Circuit City, Bombay Company, Linens 'n Things, and Sharper Image. "In many cases, it's evaporation." In the very markets that helped create the world's largest retailers, consumerism was in contraction, not expansion: the International Council of Shopping Centers, a leading retail trade organization, estimated that overall store closings increased 25 percent from 2007 to 2008.

"We have to find a way to help these companies because they're our life-blood," says Marc Hunter. "If we can't find ways, we're going to be in big trouble pretty quickly." John Fleming, the Gallup Poll's chief scientist, concurs. Wal-Mart's fate, to a surprising degree, is our fate, too. "The retail economy *is* the economy, there is no such thing as a [separate] industrial economy and retail economy," he says. "Everything is interconnecting, and one move changes all the dynamics for all the others. And the fact is that we're now connected to markets offshore, so what happens in China tomorrow directly affects us, from currency fluctuations to energy."

The subprime mortgage crisis that began in 2006 is a perfect example of the risks of globalism, says Fleming. Even though some experts had begun predicting the crisis years earlier, the continued ready availability of discount home financing reduced consumer equity, which, in turn, eroded consumer credit and spending. "I think our first big test arrived with trouble in the home finance business," says Fleming. "[It's] a perfect storm where people just can't afford to keep the consumer economy going anywhere because it is fuelled by credit, not real assets." When complex derivatives were sold on that debt, the cumulative effect was crushing: There were eight to ten million American home foreclosures by 2009; by 2010, there will be two million negative-equity homeowners in Britain. "It's innovation coming back and biting you in the ass," says Fleming. "Because all of the financial products that they [the banks]were innovating to get people into homes—and get them into bigger homes than they really could afford—are all the ones that are killing people now because they can't afford the debt payment that they signed up for." By 2009, at least $8 trillion was lost as a result of the resultant credit crisis, which has caused an expected $60 billion reduction in overall consumer spending, a loss that the leading retailers take very personally.

Here in Arizona, the mood surrounding Castro-Wright's keynote presentation is sometimes bittersweet and prescient: not long after assuming top position in the economies of the world, retailers inherited a host of problems that were beyond their ability to control. Fleming and other specialists are here to advise merchants about how to wring new value and customers out of oversaturated markets. And the lessons of a humbled Wal-Mart have not gone unnoticed. "This is the engine of the whole economy," he says. "Look at the auto industry and at housing and at all these sectors of our economy that are so critical to driving the ongoing consumer spending. Those people are feeding money into the Wal-Marts and into all these other companies, our retail space. It is going to be interesting."

Outside the conference hall, golfers tee up in the hot Arizona sun. Because we're near Tucson, gateway city to the largest continual wave of illegal migration in the world, Central American migrants are frequently holed up in the rocky hills above the golf resort, having traveled north through Mexico in search of better wages. From our vantage point, an oasis of air conditioning, concierge service, ice water, and lush, green golf courses that lies in the middle of their escape route, it's possible to see an unwitting convergence of the wildly different elements of today's service economy. Between Castro-Wright's $7.3 million compensation package in 2007 and an average income for an Arizona farm laborer, is a wage differential of about 3,470 percent.

Thousands of migrants pass this way every few weeks, navigating Arizona's deadly Sonoran desert in the dark; thousands more never make it across, intercepted by border patrols, succumbing to heat exhaustion, or killed by thieves that roam the desert before they ever reach the United States. All have bypassed the low-wage *maquiladoras* at the Mexican border, the factories that make affordable textiles and electronics for many of the retailers in Castro-Wright's audience. And those migrants who do survive the trek across the Arizonan desert may wind up standing anonymously outside a Home Depot or a Wal-Mart somewhere else in North America, watching shoppers come and go while waiting for cash labor jobs.

Wal-Mart's newest motto, "Save More, Live Better," explains a lot about why so many different people arrive at big-box malls every day with enough optimism to return again the following week. Shoppers aspire to Save More, while migrants are here to Live Better, and vice-versa. It also underlines the scale of our gambit in the twenty-first century: can we save more and live better?

The Fall of the Mall

It used to be the world's largest shopping mall. Opened in 1981, the West Edmonton Mall, or WEM, in Alberta, Canada, was the ultimate in destination shopping, boasting an indoor roller coaster, an ice rink, a water park, and over 800 stores in a single, enclosed space. Before big-box stores ruled the landscape, the enclosed mall was North America's retail mainstay, featuring large department stores surrounded by smaller outlets, food courts, and specialty shops. During major expansions in the 1980s and 1990s, the WEM aggregated the contents of several big-city regional malls and added a fantasy hotel, a pirate ship, and a mini-golf course.

More than anything, it was a statement of optimism, the expectation that somehow, people would travel hundreds or even thousands of miles to the world's largest mall and the world's largest parking lot set in a suburb of the snowy prairie city of Edmonton. And, despite its cold, remote location, shoppers did converge there, and for 23 years the WEM defended its "world's largest" title against up-and-comers like The Mall of America that opened in Bloomington, Minnesota, in 1992. It was during these last two decades of the twentieth century that jobs disappeared offshore, household debt boomed, and Western economies hedged their futures on consumer-driven growth. The average city mall, even one so preposterously oversized as the WEM, became an agent of a fast-growing service economy. Like Sam Walton's legendary ascent from small-time Arkansas discounter to global retail kingpin, the unlikely success of a massive retail theme park on the northern fringe of urban North America was testament to what seemed to be unlimited growth potential for the shopping economy.

Yet by the mid-2000s, the West Edmonton Mall was already a shadow of its former self, its attractions faded and downsized, its original store count atrophied by 25 percent. The mall's illustrious submarine ride, which moved through a tank replete with live dolphins, had been replaced with bumper boats; vacant spaces left by closed movie theaters were filled in with a skateboard park and paintball gaming area. And there are other newcomers: head shops, dollar stores, and adult erotica outlets. Large parts of the mall still retained its original 1980s motif of chintz glass and mirrors, while other parts had devolved into a sort of "Frankenmall," with cobbled-together plumbing fixes in the bathrooms, broken tiles in its foundations and flooring, and a tired, neglected amusement park.

As supercenters and big-box "power centers" emerged during the 1990s, traditional shopping centers declined, leaving behind a growing number of deserted regional malls. Under the press of Wal-Mart, the hard edge of consumerism emerged, as factors like global competition, distribution networks, and aggressive discounting trumped pirate ships, aquariums, and vacation shopping. Stores became leaner, highly dispersed, and retail itself became riskier and more chaotic.

Shopping and gambling have converged in the twenty-first century, turning places like Las Vegas into shopping destinations and, fundamentally, turning consumerism into an act of embodied risk. Indeed, one of the WEM's busiest areas today is the Palace Casino, a modest two-storey slots and tables establishment with a stucco and neon front that looks out over the mall's vast parking lot. There's a payday loan storefront inside the mall across from the casino and an ATM machine. Inside, the Palace is like any other casino: Stoic players joylessly hand over their hard-earned cash for a chance at a modest windfall. Among shoppers out in the enclosed mall, it's the same thing—a dutiful yet dour observance of shopping, disheartened consumers wandering in a landscape of diminishing rewards.

The WEM's decline was precipitated by the arrival of scores of big-box stores in the surrounding area that were run by chains who regularly close their own stores only to reopen down the street if it means they can capture extra sales or savings in the process. In 2009, for example, Wal-Mart announced that it was closing six Sam's Clubs in Canada, even as it was opening 26 new supercenters there. Wal-Mart is famous for this strategy, to the frustration of many business associations and municipal governments who rightly charge that local economies suffer as a result, especially when millions in development subsidies were granted. Really, what kind of business perpetually and systematically liquidates its own infrastructure?

Some say it all started in Colma, California. Colma is a strange "microcity" on the southern, peninsula edge of San Francisco that boasts more dead residents than living ones: There are 17 cemeteries within Colma's tiny 2.2 square mile footprint. Here, just off Interstate 280, sandwiched between the Woodlawn and Greenlawn cemeteries, is the root of modern retail: the 280 Metro Center—a nondescript open-air mall launched in 1986, which eventually became known as the world's first "power center," or big-box mall.

It's dusk and the sun is setting over nearby San Bruno Mountain. Undeterred by the 1.5 million dead people that surround 280 Metro, shoppers move in and out of cars, carrying bags, children, strollers. A drive-through McDonald's appears to be favored by both local police and teens. Contractors and do-it-yourselfers haul drywall and lumber from the nearby Home Depot. There is steady traffic at the Starbucks inside the Barnes and Noble, which serves as the mall's social center.

In other words, 280 Metro looks much like any other open-air shopping mall in North America: a ring of rectangular buildings around a huge parking lot. There's no commemorative plaque or museum here like the one that hangs outside Sam Walton's first variety store in Bentonville—Walton's Five and Dime—which was long ago converted into a museum/shrine honoring the founder's humble beginnings, complete with his old pickup truck and other sacred memorabilia. The bland, stucco facades of Colma's big-box mall are the true face of bargaineering today.

The power center ushered in the retail surge of the 1990s by featuring "category killer" stores like Office Depot, PetSmart, and Best Buy that ably destroyed local competition by offering superior prices and selection. Home Depot, Bed Bath & Beyond, Nordstrom, and Old Navy collectively anchor 280 Metro Center, and the semicircle of these miniwarehouses dominates all retail within a ten-mile radius. Shopping at the mall is convenient and, since over 70 percent of merchants here are category killers, it meets the high consumer demand for bargains.

Merrit Sher stumbled upon this simple but powerful formula in the mid-1980s. The veteran developer, credited with numerous revitalization projects across the United States, recalls the beginnings of 280 Metro; it was an experiment designed to bring together independent merchants. "We had known Home Depot, Bed Bath, & Beyond, and Trader Joes as independent retailers," he explains, "so we clustered a half-dozen stores and called it a promotional center."

Back in the 1980s, 280 Metro was an anomaly in a retailing world that was defined by large, indoor destination malls that were anchored by department stores like Sears and JC Penny. "It seemed unthinkable to people back then that we could build an uncovered shopping center at an Interstate off-ramp," says Sher. "It began as specialty retail, but it evolved. It was just something ready to happen."

At the time, large, regional malls were always attached to one or two major department or grocery stores, but as bargains began to drive the economy, shoppers increasingly grew frustrated with having to hike extra distances through enclosed malls to get at products. Sher's experiment with clustered retailers began to accelerate as these big box chains became national, then multinational. As Wal-Mart, Costco, and Target defined retail success, power centers became a dominant urban form by the early 1990s. By 1993, for example, 16 new power centers opened in the United States, compared to only four major new malls. By 2007, not a single enclosed mall was being developed, compared to an estimated 60 to 70 that opened each year during the 1980s.

Sher sees the change as evolutionary: what began as an aggregate of specialty stores next to a highway soon became a power center as discounting and category-based stores were added. "Thirty years ago, a store like Woolworth's had all these category-killer stores under one roof: it was called the department store," he says, explaining how retail deconstructed itself during the twentieth century. "Our original power center didn't have discount stores, it was strictly independent and specialty. But after awhile, it became a combination of new things and we define it now as having the discount component."

The big box proved to be an ideal form factor, a meeting ground for consumers and the global supply chain. Consequently, Sher's experiment in retailing spelled the demise of the spacious, covered mall. Despite the high aspirations of traditional enclosed malls, with their fountains, food courts, and arching glass-covered galleries—a utopian vision with roots in the work of the radical French architect Le Corbusier and the Austrian-American architect Victor Gruen—convenience and price-cutting ultimately prevailed, stripping retail down to bare essentials. Ironically, as shopping became more important to the economy, our retail landscapes became more nondescript: retail "boxes" with glass doors, parking lots, and container-loads of product arriving around the back. Whereas Gruen's (and America's) first climate-controlled mall was heralded as a "pleasure-dome-with-parking" by *Time* in 1956, Colma's 280 Metro Center received no such fanfare upon its 1986 launch, although Sher joked at the time that with 280 Metro's adjacent cemeteries, you could "shop till you drop."

Of course, discounting hardly began with Merrit Sher and Sam Walton. Both men merely continued a discount tradition that was established well before the commercial advent of the automobile. "The new discounters took the chain discounting format perfected by Woolworth's and married it to the large floor plans used in regional malls, giving rise to the term 'big box,'" notes retail scholar Michael Tubridy. By 2006, more than half of all purchases were made in retail environments that were under 200,000 square feet—big-box stores, supercenters, neighborhood malls—as opposed to large regional malls and megamalls.

Retail became a new order of public life in the late twentieth century, a vaunted or despised "third space," as the number of shopping centers out-numbered high schools. On average, shopping centers account for 56 per-cent of all sales tax revenues in the United States, worth $124 billion in 2006. At the heart of it all is Sher's power center and its offshoots, such as the more upscale, brand-oriented "lifestyle center," and countless other versions. In Colma, one can witness the apex of retail evolution and not even recognize it because now the format faces its own troubles. The midsize discounters that populate the power centers are the ones at risk in economic hard times, mainly because they don't offer cheap essentials like discounted groceries and staples now common to Wal-Mart and most dollar stores. At 280 Metro, Bed Bath & Beyond suffered double-digit losses and share devaluation as high as 40 percent in 2007. Anchor store Home Depot saw a 24 percent drop in profits in 2006–2007, when $1.4 billion in sales simply "disappeared." By January 2009, it had laid off 7000 workers amid sinking revenues. Nearby, Starbucks had its own well-publicized troubles, pronouncing the late 2000s as the weakest run in the company's four-decade history, during which its stock value depreciated by 50 percent. In 2008, the chain laid off 1,000 employees and closed more than 600 stores.

Like the bargain traders convened in Las Vegas who worry about the pass-ing of the dollar store in the face of chronic inflation, these retailers are wor-ried, but the stakes are even higher here in Colma. Like it or not, the big-box mall has become the Main Street economy in many towns and cities—what happens in Colma definitely matters nearly everywhere else.

You can occasionally detect some crematory smoke from the cemeter-ies wafting above 280 Metro's stores. But the rotten-egg smell isn't the dead people. The center's Home Depot store was built on the site of what had been one of San Francisco's largest solid-waste disposal sites, the Junipero Serra Landfill, which closed in 1983. According to one engineering report, the "store and parking lot [were] constructed over 1,348 piles, each driven approximately 160 ft (49 m) deep into the landfill." An enclosed gas flare vents the methane gas created by 25 years' worth of garbage that is rotting deep beneath the Home Depot to reduce the possibility of an explosion or the formation of a subterranean methane bubble. This means that on any given day, Colma's big-box shoppers are breathing in trace amounts of human ash or gasified garbage—yesteryear's consumers and products—from up and down the San Francisco peninsula.

But graves, garbage, and shopping malls have not been bad for Colma. In 2006, an acre of land there was worth $2 million, and a $20 million casino had been proposed near the Serbian cemetery. Think of Colma as a pioneer city for the twenty-first century: relying on service-sector industries like retail and burial, it has never manufactured anything of note, and its 1,200 living residents enjoy free cable TV that is paid for by the steady streams of tax revenue that the postindustrial business mix generates—as long as people keep shopping and dying, that is. Having a 24-hour Home Depot around the corner, built upon a mountain of garbage, is an added bonus.

"It's great to be alive in Colma!" is the town's unofficial motto.
More like "Coming to a town near you."

Progress is Price Destruction

It's another hot day in Tucson. Outside, golfers continue to tee up on an absurdly green fairway, surrounded by giant saguaro cactus and sun-baked creosote bushes. Heat stroke is a common golf injury here. The yellow desert rolls away into the distance, all the way to the Mexico, where the U.S. military has recently deployed in an attempt to stem the incessant human tide of Mexican immigrants across the border. As golfers work their handicap, and migrants try to outrun Blackhawk helicopters, the world's leading retailers re-convene indoors to agonize about their future.

It's survival of the fittest all the way around, and anyone looking for reassurance will be disappointed. "In a Wal-Mart world, you're either predator or prey," says Michael Bergdahl, point-blank. "It doesn't matter if you are a lion or a gazelle, you and your team had better be up and running every morning."

Bergdahl doesn't work for Wal-Mart anymore, but he served under Sam Walton as "Director of People" during the leader's final years and has since carved out a career as a public intellectual for a company that often refuses to speak for itself. The kill-or-be-killed sentiments are classic Bentonville. For a corporation that has often been associated with Christian fundamentalism and is still pervaded by Sam Walton's Presbyterian notions of "servant leadership," there's a tremendous amount of evolutionary theory bandied about its boardrooms. Wal-Mart's rise is usually attributed to this brute Darwinian streak. Wal-Mart, of course, sat atop the food chain.

But Wal-Mart didn't become the world largest company simply on hustle and competitive drive. If that were the case, shopkeepers and bazaar sellers from Korea to Pakistan would be running the economy. Contrary to popular belief, Sam Walton did not create the new economy. It's the old saw: If Wal-Mart didn't exist, someone else would have invented it.

In fact, history suggests that discounters rise and fall during times of societal transformation. Frank Woolworth, for example, built his F.W. Woolworth empire on North America's first major wave of rural dispossession and urbanization in the great wave of post-war industrialization. The rise of the industry provided Woolworth's not only with hordes of new customers, but technological advancement also made it possible to offer those customers a degree of affordability and selection that ultimately turned Woolworth's Five and Dime stores into a global phenomenon. It was a Wal-Mart prototype in the days before container ships and internet communications. Pioneer mass merchants like Woolworth and Sears grew out of the industrial age and, in turn, their early bargaineering policies helped to accelerate industrialization and consumerism across North America and Europe. "Branded, standardized products came to represent and embody the new networks and systems of factory production and mass distribution," writes historian Susan Strasser. "Formerly *customers*—purchasing the objects of daily life from familiar craftspeople and storekeepers—Americans became *consumers*."

In other words, economic paradigm shifts inspire discounting, and, in turn, bargains expedite change. Progress is price destruction.

Bargains suggest an alternative account of human progress: Great historical watersheds are actually economic shifts, structured around vanquishing costs. Everything from energy supplies to consumerism to colonialism have revolved around price destruction and realizing new value through new processes, such as global sourcing and assemblage. For example, steam-engine efficiencies increased by 50 percent between 1700 and 1930, unleashing tremendous wealth and savings potential. Bread making became much more affordable with the advent of automated mills perfected in the early 1800s; lower bread prices saved consumers money and improved family nutrition. Productivity gains and technological innovations have been slashing prices and displacing workers ever since, making complex technological devices like DVD players and iPods affordable for everyone. Many have bemoaned our big-box world, blaming Sam Walton for starting it. Don't blame Wal-Mart: today's bargain economy stands at the apex of an industrial-economic evolution that began in the nineteenth century with the production of vulcanized rubber, early crude-oil markets, and the combustion engine, and the resulting affordability of goods and services made possible a level of plenitude that had never been seen before. In other words, big-box stores, globalized production, and container ships are not an anomaly. Bargains represent the pinnacle—if not the perfection—of twentieth-century capitalism, in all its creative and destructive capacity.

In North America, for example, business empires have traditionally been founded upon energy, transport, and technology. The five richest barons of industry, measured by wealth as a percentage of the economy, show a clear pattern: John D. Rockefeller, who would eventually control as much as 90 percent of the North America's oil markets, started the Standard Oil Company at the age of 31; Cornelius Vanderbilt commanded steamships and railroads and eliminated competition by fiercely (and sometimes illegally) undercutting prices; John Jacob Astor, pioneer fur trader; Stephen Girard, shipping magnate; and Bill Gates, of course, rounds out the fifth richest-ever with the invention of MS-DOS, helping to launch the global IT boom.

The retailers that rule today's service economy constitute a different order of business: Wal-Mart encompasses energy, transport, *and* technology. From the embodied energy in petrochemical plastics to the logistics technologies and steel containers that deliver that plastic to suburban stores, the modern discounter incorporates the twentieth century's leading industries with surprising effectiveness. As Michael Bergdahl frequently reminds his international clients and audiences, the terms "retail" and "wholesale" are too narrow to describe the modern megaretailer. "Wal-Mart is not a merchandise-driven company," he says. "Wal-Mart is a logistics and retail-driven company that also has retail stores. Everything at Wal-Mart is a commodity."

If Wal-Mart accomplished its rise to power by pushing prices lower than anyone ever before, other barons of industry did the opposite: oil companies conspired to fix prices, OPEC-style, and destroy public transit systems so that people would need cars; Microsoft famously pushed the limits of antitrust law and was fined $899 million euros by the European Commission in 2004; in 2007 there was a lawsuit against five major railroads, including Union Pacific and Santa Fe, alleging that they colluded to fix fuel surcharges.

Wal-Mart's pricing may seem populist, almost egalitarian, but its business practices are ingeniously monolithic. Inside Wal-Mart's circle of influence anything from chasing away union organizers to launching stores in rural China is subject to its monopoly-like grip. Suppliers, manufacturers, and transport companies have been among the notably disciplined. Wal-Mart requires an annual drop in suppliers' prices or quality upgrade, most of which is passed onto consumers. The price squeeze means vendors must be relentless in managing their own costs. They need, in fact, to turn themselves into miniature versions of Wal-Mart if they hope to access the one-fifth of all retail sales that Wal-Mart controls.

The ongoing adoption of radio-frequency identification (RFID) tagging—essentially, a wireless bar code system—is another example of the way Wal-Mart flexes its muscle with its suppliers. RFID tagging will create, executives claim, an estimated $8.35 billion in annual savings for the company. And by using its supplier-integrated supply chain, Wal-Mart's efforts to reduce packaging between 2008 and 2013 will save $3.4 billion. To bring about this kind of systemic change, Wal-Mart "encourages" its suppliers and partners to go along—transform their packaging, add RFID chips, subsidize the retailer's inventory expenses—incurring costs that eat into their own profits.

"Companies like Wal-Mart make money on money because it finds ways of carrying as little inventory as possible," explains Bergdahl. Over a decade ago, Wal-Mart looked at its expenses and decided that it warehoused too many products for too long, tying too much of its money in inventory. It addressed the issue by "inventing" a continuously replenishing supply chain, where manufacturers technically own their own products almost until point of sale. "Wal-Mart doesn't have warehouses anymore. They want as little inventory as possible to ensure 60 day credit terms—it now pays big time to carry only as much inventory as they need in the store." It seems like a minor detail, yet Wal-Mart makes millions by not paying many suppliers for in-store products until a customer actually makes a purchase. In this way, manufacturers and suppliers increasingly assume much of the risk and cost associated with owning unsold products, which are not insignificant.

In fact, the retail aspect of Wal-Mart's operations is almost incidental. The company's profitability lies in its ability to destroy traditional business practices and effect change by its suppliers and shippers. And while corporate giants such as General Motors and Dell outsourced, effectively downsizing themselves to remain competitive, Wal-Mart became bigger. It is a bastion of vertical integration in a world of dissolution. "For Wal-Mart, it is still cheaper to build than to buy, and to employ workers rather than subcontract them," notes Nelson Lichtenstein. "The same technologies and cost imperatives that have led to the decomposition and decentralization of so many other institutions, including government, health care, entertainment, and domestic manufacturing, have enabled Wal-Mart and other retail distribution companies to vastly enhance their own managerial span of control." Or, as Bergdahl likes to note, "even the thermostats in every single one of Wal-Mart stores are controlled from Bentonville: the manager doesn't even control the temperature of his own store."

In some ways, the reasons for Wal-Mart's massive success are still a mystery, even to itself. Although the company revolutionized modern business, it bumbled through the first five years of the new millennium, clearly nostalgic for the 1990s. Yet, when it came out on top in 2009, Wal-Mart's sales were roughly quadruple that of all the top ten American department stores combined: Sears, JC Penny, Nordstrom, and Macy's, among others.

Based on twentieth-century economics, Wal-Mart as the world's largest company and world's largest employer really shouldn't be possible. The theory of the firm suggests that there are practical upper limits to the size of any corporation, mainly due to inefficiencies, costs, and/or managerial failures that inevitably limit growth. The firm simply grows too large to manage, and the humans inside it lack the information and controls to deal with the increased complexity. When General Motors started outsourcing and diversifying, it became smaller, at least in terms of its managerial reach. Wal-Mart has defied these trends, but its success has forced us to question much of what we know about capitalism. Not since the eighteenth- and nineteenth-century era of commercialism, in which monolithic companies like the Dutch East India Company enjoyed state-level powers, has a company as globally influential and powerful as Wal-Mart existed. "Wal-Mart is a living breathing behemoth of a top-down corporation despite the assertion, found in fashionable management theory, that such companies are dead dinosaurs," writes management professor James Hoopes. "Wal-Mart shows that high technology is fostering its own form of the huge, highly centralized corporation run with ruthless, hierarchical efficiency."

Discounting is reinventing capitalism, not through force or a singular commodity or unique invention, but adaptively, with puritanical commitment to price and what Castro-Wright calls "disruptive innovation."

This sea change is still occurring, a paradigm shift that recalls the invention of the automobile. Ford's factory line integrated process and efficiency and helped to underwrite twentieth-century industrial progress. But it wasn't simply that the combustion engine now existed; it was Ford's deployment of process—innovations in manufacture, marketing, and distribution—that created a new system of commerce. It is this continual, behind-the-scenes, re-engineering of process—manufacturing, design, transport, and sales—that today's discounters largely concern themselves with. If crude oil, the assembly line, and the combustion engine were the tools of Ford's success, then offshoring, consumer credit, and logistics are the raw materials of post-industrial powerhouses like Wal-Mart, who have leveraged these resources to attain profits and scale that are rivaled only by energy giants like ExxonMobil.

Like Henry Ford, bargaineers sometimes show a utopian streak. For all their Darwinist bluster, these merchant-pioneers have frequently argued that consumerism can somehow be perfected, not unlike Mao Zedong's exhortations to perfect Chinese Communism. "If we work together, we'll lower the cost of living for everyone," Sam Walton famously claimed. "We'll give the world an opportunity to see what it's like to have a better life."

Unlike Ford and other major twentieth-century manufacturers who created well-paying jobs for generations of Western consumers, Wal-Mart builds stores and sales, both of which have proven to be impermanent. Even Wal-Mart's celebrated reformed health care coverage relies "heavily on the government and other employers to play a role" reported the *Washington Post* in 2009. "Despite revenue that is expected to exceed $400 billion for 2008, the company charges its low-wage workers a substantial portion of their income for medical coverage."

Postindustrial commerce is starting to look a lot like a frontier resource scramble. Are global discounters like Wal-Mart systematically mining our world for opportunity? As a resource, the spending power of Western consumers has largely been tapped, so it is the wave of bankruptcies from 2008 onward that will likely constitute Wal-Mart's next wave of growth: Harvesting displaced customers from the closed stores of competitors is the next frontier. In 2009, Deutsche Bank identified "$9.6 billion of sales up for grabs from stores that are closing and potentially $17.8 billion more from weak stores." It's a commercial pattern that more than resembles a natural resource company, and instead of harvesting minerals or energy, it aggregates many of the same inputs that have been built up over generations of workers and business barons: transport networks, technology, energy, and finance, as well as a global pool of consumers.

Wal-Mart found success through technology, company culture, and managerial strategy. But for the rest of us, the company's innovation also invokes a previous century: dominance, extraction, depletion, and competition for new resources. Check the growing tally of ghost malls and idle big-box stores around the world. Once ExxonMobil is finished with Nigerian oil, for example, the company is unlikely to stick around and support community economic development projects; likewise, Total in Burma and China's state oil companies in Angola and Sudan.

If you don't like Wal-Mart's oddly colonial style of business, tough. If critics want to take the company on, "they need to bring their lunch, because we're not going to lay down," boasted CEO Lee Scott in a 2005 interview, while under fire for exporting jobs and destroying local business. "We've got nothing to apologize for…After all, the economic change [that] Wal-Mart represents creates a handful of losers even as the vast majority of ordinary Americans gain," argued Scott. "But at the end of the day, when someone builds a better mousetrap, it's not the American way to deny average folks the chance to improve their lives. The horse and buggy industry wasn't permitted to crush the car."

New Kinds of Change

The speed with which Wal-Mart's transformation from regional retailer to global kingpin happened is notable: it suggests the kind of major change that many scholars ascribe to the Industrial Revolution, especially the second Industrial Revolution—a period of development during the late 1800s that, among other things, introduced mass-produced consumer goods to the world. And while the technology of today's bargain revolution is not entirely new—container ships, decentralized manufacturing, consumer credit—like the Industrial Revolution, there has arguably been a delay in the impact of many twentieth-century inventions until the end of the century. Atkeson and Kehoe described this as "a productivity paradox, a surprisingly long delay between the increase in the pace of technical change and the increase in the growth rate of measured productivity." Productivity, in this case, is not just machines and factories, but the accelerated output of a global system of production and consumption that defines Western service-sector economies.

In other words, the advent of electricity, the combustion engine, petroleum refining, petrochemicals, telephones, and indoor plumbing did not immediately change the world, just as other more recent innovations, such as the container ship, the computer, the shopping mall, and the credit card—which were all commercially established in the 1940s and 1950s—did not begin to deliver their full impact during the 1990s.

It did not happen overnight, but once it gained momentum, the influence of everyday low prices became profound. The late 1990s spike in America's trade imbalance, consumer debt levels, and Wal-Mart's employee and revenue growth—all of which doubled or tripled between 1995 and 2005—underlines the accelerated growth of retail and wholesale trade in most developed countries. Daniel Bell coined the notion of "post-industrial society" in 1973;

yet it was our late-century discounting boom, technology, and finance bubble that brought it into fruition.

When this sort of accelerated transition occurs, it is often a modality shift that creates imbalances and unpredictable outcomes: precisely the kind of "disruptive change" that today's discount retailer attempts to engineer through outrageously low prices. The nature of this kind of change is not well understood: it is not technology-driven, but technology dependant; it is not cyclical, but it is far from linear; governments and large companies figure in it prominently, but they are nevertheless interdependent with workers and consumers from rural China to northern Canada.

The closest modern analogue to this kind of fluid, systemic change is not economic, but environmental. For example, much of our understanding of climate change, along with its ecological and economic impacts, has mistakenly focused on gradual change, with the ongoing buildup of greenhouse gases in the atmosphere leading to a gradual increase in global temperatures. "This line of thinking, however, fails to consider another potentially disruptive climate scenario," writes Robert Gagosian, president of Woods Hole Oceanographic Institution. "It ignores recent and rapidly advancing evidence that Earth's climate repeatedly has shifted abruptly and dramatically in the past, and is capable of doing so in the future."

NASA's top scientist on climate change, James Hansen, has been studying ocean-atmospheric interactions for decades. "Our climate has the potential for large rapid fluctuations," he writes in a landmark 2007 report. "Indeed, the Earth, and the creatures struggling to exist on the planet, have been repeatedly whipsawed between climate states." Change can build up in the depths and then burst forth, moving rapidly. Polar ice caps, for example, serve as the planet's climate anchors by reflecting solar energy away from deep oceanic currents that, in turn, distribute heat energy across the planet. Melting polar caps have the dual destabilizing effect of not only substantially increasing the solar energy absorbed by oceans, but also freshwater from warming ice and snow also decreases the salinity of vital ocean currents, causing them to stall or fluctuate. "The ocean's slow response delays [climate change] effects," writes Hansen. "But there is the danger of setting in motion a warming of the deep ocean that will lock in disastrous impacts which will unfold for future generations."

Like ecosystems, economies seek out equilibrium. On a planetary basis, we observe this most elemental dynamic within heat energy-transport mechanisms that Hansen and others predict may one day collapse. On a slightly smaller scale, there is also the human attempt to find equilibrium by conjoining Asia's hungry pool of workers with bargain-hungry Western consumers.

And where there is disequilibrium, there is failure: a global economic slow-down marked, alternately, by overproduction and underconsumption in an environment of critical resource scarcity. And, indeed, it will be through the bargain economy—and its dependence on container shipping, fossil fuels, coastal ports, and geopolitical stability—that the heaviest economic impact of climate change is first observed.

Volatility has certainly been a huge part of global food and resource markets during the 2000s. From 2000 to 2006, for example, the United Nations observed a 278 percent increase in mineral commodities; and a 50 percent over-all increase in the real prices of non-fuel commodities. In 2008, in the face of a global incidence of malnutrition and food-based unrest, the United Nations reported that world food prices reached the highest levels in 30 years—increasing 83 percent since 2005. Most notably, the price of Thai medium-quality rice, a global benchmark, more than doubled between 2007 and 2008.

Gone is the time when Western shoppers were not affected by the price of rice, petrochemical feed stocks, or the cost of a steel shipping container. The mass production of cheap stuff shaped globalization as a force of convergence, connection, and interdependence. Yet these connections also amplify market failure. For example, logistics experts at the Port of Los Angeles report that the cost of building a new container ship has increased nearly 50 percent, owing largely to price increases in steel and crude oil—cost increases which, in turn, have been driven by China's double-digit economic growth and Western economies pegged to consumption. Korean shipyards, American SUVs, and Chinese factories compete for the same resources. Eventually it reaches the consumer: American toy manufacturers estimated that between 2006 and 2007 the cost of plastic increased 25 percent due to increased energy prices—even before the price of crude hit $100 a barrel—resulting in 10 percent gains on the retail price of many toys.

The cost of nearly everything from plastic to factory labor has climbed and fallen and climbed again during the first decade of the twenty-first century, accelerated by new demand from developing countries. The price of copper—crucial to electronics, appliances, and home renovations—increased 400 percent between 2004 and 2008. The persistent yet erratic increase of the price of crude oil in recent years has especially led to questioning about the future viability of a bargain-based world, since everything including shipping transport depends on affordable energy and petrochemicals. Chinese logistics costs as a percentage of product price were up to 50 percent higher than in North America or Europe even before the fuel price spike of the late 2000s.

Since most of these commodities are global products, it is globalization that both creates and suffers from this volatility. This is especially so when we suffer through periods of acute scarcity on essentials like oil and rice—especially because they also wear down the resilience of households, countries, and businesses, and compromise their ability to survive difficulty without failure. And patterns of disruptive change, both economic and environmental, pose a threat to the highly refined version of globalization that Wal-Mart and its kin helped invent. And while Wal-Mart is able to prosper in an environment of economic decline, it cannot indefinitely survive a broader disruption of its core resources: affordable energy, logistics, labor and, not the least, consumers. As we've learned since the 1990s, there is very little that is decoupled or independent in our world anymore. Can the supply chain that Wal-Mart pioneered survive the disruptive change that it helped create?

As Thomas Homer-Dixon argues, it's a precursor kind of "synchronous failure" that may already be evident in many of our planet's troubled climatic systems. "In coming years, our societies won't face one or two major challenges at once, as usually happened in the past," he writes. "Instead, they'll face an alarming variety of problems—likely including oil shortages, climate change, economic instability, and mega-terrorism—all at the same time.... [B]loody social revolutions occur only when many pressures simultaneously batter a society that has weak political, economic, and civic institutions."

As global economies and the global climate falls in and out of equilibrium, we experience volatility, strained coping mechanisms, and new patterns of change. "Risks to the growth and stability of the world economy posed by large global imbalances have not receded," warned one UN report in 2007. One could almost tack on Hansen's own climatic warning: "...indications of accelerating change on West Antarctica and Greenland indicate that the [current] period of stability is over."

What climate change also teaches us is that appearances are deceiving—the inertia and size of planetary energy systems create delayed impacts, as well as the possibility for remedial action. Things may look normal, but there is ultimately no way of knowing when a climatic trigger may deploy, causing even greater change. The speed and scope of economic collapse is what surprised many people as the American economy suddenly shed 4.4 million jobs within four months in 2008–2009. Globally, "The current pace of decline is breathtaking," said Robert Barbera, chief economist for Investment Technology Group, in 2009. "We are now falling at a near record rate in the postwar period and there's been no change in the violent downward trajectory."

James Hansen, who spoke out in 2006 about scientific censorship under the Bush administration, argues that we continue to chart new frontiers, likely at our own peril. It is during the current century that we will discover what happens when the Arctic ice cap completely melts for six months of the year. And, not unrelated, can we still fill a Wal-Mart store with bargains when shipping costs have quadrupled and crude oil commands $200 a barrel?

"Civilization developed, and constructed extensive infrastructure, during a period of unusual climate stability, the Holocene, now almost 12,000 years in duration," writes Hansen. "That period is about to end."

The Problem of Value

Even in a world full of change, Wal-Mart still views itself as a catalyst. "How do you bring innovation that is disruptive?" Eduardo Castro-Wright asks the audience near the end of his talk in Tucson. There is a pause. Nobody answers.

As growth frontiers diminish, innovation is in short supply. Here in Tucson, retail true believers like Bergdahl invoke Wal-Mart's talent for survival and adaptation. "Wal-Mart will continuously reinvent itself: it's not going to be the same business we saw last year," says Bergdahl. "Wal-Mart is a very nimble company. You'd think they'd be like an aircraft carrier, and have difficulty turning; but they're more like a PT boat and can change very rapidly. Because change is a way of life at Wal-Mart."

Others, like John Flemming, foresee a much more divisive future, full of winners and losers. "I think we're in for a big come-uppance, which is why it makes it more imperative to focus on ways to drive organic growth with relatively low costs to create change because technology improvements have [already] happened," he says, referring to the past gains of the 1990s retail boom. "We'll see some incremental improvements in the future, but nothing like what we've seen to drive increased productivity." In other words, for discounters, much of the easy growth and profits are finished. "Technology productivity has flattened," says Flemming. "The cost reductions through quality improvements and supply-chain management are going to flat line. Where are we going to get the next frontier of incremental value? It has to be in generating a greater price from products that we offer and increasing the productivity in the people who work for us."

Paradoxically, in the service of bargains, we are having trouble creating value. Even with Wal-Mart's claim to be creating immense value—an estimated 3 percent decline in American consumer prices between 1985 and 2006—our economies are full of bankruptcy, poverty, and worry.

Why? One reason is that while bargains have proven themselves indispensable, they present a fundamental contradiction. Where past business models found ways to create value out of manufacturing, marketing, or technological innovation, the core missive of the modern bargaineer is, in fact, value destruction: undercutting competition, shedding profit, paying suppliers less.

Yet some would say that Wal-Mart has merely been fulfilling its destiny. Discounting's pervasive race to the bottom is merely proof of its influence and success. "A successful discount strategy implies value destruction," argue business professors Anderson and Poulfelt in their 2006 book, *Discount Business Strategy*. Perhaps more importantly, they observe "the potential value destruction stemming from the introduction of a discount strategy is unstoppable once the disruption commences." As examples, they cite successful discounters Skype, IKEA, and Costco, all of whom redefined their respective markets through radically disruptive pricing. "A disruptive strategy, once released into the business world, could have far-reaching consequences [such as] bankruptcy and [industries] falling prey to the disruptive nature of the discount strategy and the value destruction that followed in its wake." In other words, the discounting is proving to be a failure point in what has become a grand, global-scale experiment in production and consumption, connectivity and interdependence. The question of value is critical for the future. "The problem of value must always hold the pivotal position," economist Joseph Schumpeter argued, "as the chief tool of analysis in any pure [economic] theory."

It was back in 1942, during another period of social and economic upheaval, that economist Joseph Schumpeter published his now-famous thesis on creative destruction. Schumpeter viewed capitalism not as a series of rational consumer choices, but as an evolutionary firestorm. This "perennial gale of creative destruction," he wrote, is frequently misunderstood: "the problem that is usually being visualized is how capitalism administers existing structures, whereas the relevant problem is how it creates and destroys them."

Perhaps not coincidentally, Schumpeter paid close attention to retail industries and the greater service sector, which by mid-century had already begun to resemble their modern-day incarnations. With eerie precision, Schumpeter describes Wal-Mart's organizational, logistics and productive assault on traditional commerce. What "keeps the capitalist engine in motion [is] new consumer goods, . . . new methods of production, or transportation, [and] new forms of industrial organization that capitalist enterprise creates," he writes in *Capitalism, Socialism and Democracy*. "In the case of retail trade the competition that matters arises not from additional shops of the same type, but from the department store, the chain store, the mail-order house, and the super market, which are bound to destroy those pyramids sooner or later."

Or as Bergdahl succinctly puts it, "There's no intrinsic value at Wal-Mart to any particular product; the value is about the lowest possible prices." With this simple maxim, the retailer disrupted its market to great advantage, exploited the ensuing destruction of its competition, yet the impact of discounting has continued. Did we assume that large-scale value destruction would affect only Wal-Mart's rivals—or everyone?

Today, the result is not only low prices, but a marketplace that cycles through products at an accelerated rate. One 2007 study examined an average of 650,000 UPC product codes annually for nearly a decade; of these, over 80 percent of the products available in 2003 did not exist in 1994, representing an enormous volume of discrete products that were, in Schumpeterian fashion, created and destroyed as a matter of commerce. Of these 650,000 discrete product codes, which represent roughly 40 percent of America's consumer price index, over 60 percent had been discounted to the seller's minimum reservation price between 1999 and 2003. In other words, the majority of these products were sold at the very lowest price that retailers and manufacturers could tolerate.

This is how local outlet stores and discount fashion boutiques and online liquidators like Woot.com manage to move so much product so cheaply. The global supply chain is perpetually jettisoning surplus goods. Even with this waste and churn, many global supply chains are operating on dangerously low margins, some just one bad deal away from collapse—as evidenced by the epidemic of retail bankruptcies from 2008 onward.

"One of the major trends of retailing is this relentless cycle which turns stuff into commodities," explains Eric Arnold, Distinguished Professor at the Terry J. Lundgren Center for Retailing. "And when things turn into commodities, of course you get into a price race, which is always a price race to the bottom. And so hard discounting as it infiltrates and proliferates and expands, drives more things into a commodity space—that drives down everybody's origins or reduces margins. That is a problem."

Wal-Mart has been rightly commended for some of its efforts to reduce pollution, waste, and greenhouse gas emissions. It has expanded its social and health policies. Yet the company is still dedicated as ever to creating massive change and maximum sales. Its mission remains to sell more cheap stuff than anyone else, even if it does so using less energy per sale. "No other instrument is perceived with such acuity by the customer as the price," David Bosshart writes in *Cheap*. "And no other instrument is more exciting when it is wielded as a weapon." It is much like the volatile capitalism of the financial sector but instead of building bubbles on sketchy assets (as per the 2008 global crisis), the bargaineer sabotages its own market place in the hopes that growth and spending will prevail.

It is discounting's instinct for value destruction that, in the end, makes Wal-Mart its own worst enemy. And if Wal-Mart and other global discounters continue to provide market leadership in the twenty-first century, what does that mean for everyone else?

Retail Economy, Survivor Edition

Who ever thought a $400-a-night golf resort could be so grueling? In this air-conditioned vacuum, time stands still as top executives drone on under artificial lights amid stale coffee. The most barren strip mall begins to hold appeal as the world's leading retailers grind out presentations about their accomplishments and rich futures.

Yet this is the future, or at least one side of it. Some, like retail icon Terry Lundgren of Macy's, obfuscate weak sales by talking about "the relentless pursuit of newness" and boast of spending as much as $1 million per store on fitting rooms. "Great leaders are talent multipliers," says the photogenic Lundgren, smiling for the cameras. Investors were not impressed, as Macy's stock dropped nearly 40 percent between 2007 and 2008. By the time the real trouble hit late in 2008, Macy's offered aggressive copycat discounts, much to the detriment of its profits, which had sunk by 59 percent by early 2009. "Macy's is in huge trouble," predicted J.P. Morgan analyst Charles Grom in 2008. "The only way Macy's will make it is for someone to take it private and spend a few billion dollars re-merchandising the store."

Others, such as Robert Eckert, CEO of Mattel, outline calculated plans for children's "lifestyle products" that sell "consistent emotional connections and turn shoppers into die-hard fans." Not many months later, Mattel would recall more than 20 million lead-tainted toys, many sourced from China, which produces about 65 percent of the company's products—the company closed its last American factory in 2002. "We love Christmas Day at Mattel," jokes the CEO, displaying his new, diversified Barbie collection. Eckert would later claim a 68 percent pay increase, totaling $12.2 million in 2007, despite Mattel's financial losses and damaged reputation. By 2009, Mattel's profits had dropped nearly 50 percent.

One thought occurs. These are people who don't fully grasp what they've tapped into as leading merchandisers and retailers within a faltering service economy. This is the second half of the bargain revolution—a globalized bubble that is contracting—and it's not pretty: value destruction, volatile conditions, and a relentless race to the price bottom. Many others are likewise clueless and unprepared. And yet, for all of the 1990s and much of the 2000s, these business leaders were responsible for a growing segment of the economy, much in the same way that banks were left to grow and self-regulate in their creation of debt derivatives and other highly leveraged products.

One of the few retail honchos talking frankly is Peter Abbot, a Wal-Mart executive who I managed to collar just before Castro-Wright's presentation. He admits that his industry faces major challenges. "You can't please everybody," he says, "but we can make 80 percent of the people happy by [trying] to do what we do right." True to form, Wal-Mart is hoping to engineer its way through the great environmental, social, and economic challenges of the twenty-first century. "We're looking seriously at sustainability—reducing plastic, cardboard packaging—because that's also going to give us the possibility of shipping 20 more cases for the price of one," says Abbot. "We're going to have to understand what makes each store tick, because every time we turn our inventory one full time in a store, we get 7/10ths profit. So we have to keep those turns going, keep that inventory moving."

But Abbot doesn't sugar-coat obvious and immediate facts: slipping consumer fortunes and an over-saturated market. "It's a tough situation [for people] with rent going up, utilities, gas prices," he says. "You've got to bring your 'A' game to work everyday. You can't have any misses."

The dark side of discounting scares even Wal-Mart. When Eduardo Castro-Wright invokes "innovation that is disruptive," he's not wishing for the success of his own firm to be hijacked by dollar stores, unsustainable price competition, and consumer failure. Yet as Schumpeter predicted, the forces unleashed by innovation frequently end in destruction, although what many of his more famous free-market acolytes (such as housing-bubble champion and former U.S. Federal Reserve chair Alan Greenspan) failed to foresee is that not all market-driven destruction is creative or productive.

Bargains are not forever. Over the next several decades, our ability to access cheap consumer credit, cheap shipping, cheap energy, and cheap offshore labor will ultimately decide the fate of globalization. Accelerated by generational issues like climate change, growing competition for natural resources, and chronic underdevelopment, the end of cheap is not merely about price: as a highly distributed and interdependent economic mode, a troubled bargain economy threatens to undo many of the gains of globalization, especially the broad affordability of material goods that most national economies have become dependant upon. It doesn't take much to sabotage this system. By late 2008, for example, the threat of a global cost-price spiral—multifactor inflation that threatens to sabotage supply chains—had become clear: "Since 2002 the [U.S.] dollar has plunged by 30 percent against major world currencies," reported *Business Week*. "Wages in China are rising. [And] the cost of sending a 40-foot container from Shanghai to San Diego has soared by

150 percent, to $5,500, since 2000. If oil hits $200 a barrel, that could reach $10,000."

On one hand, our system of cheap manufacture is a multiplier of value and affordability, one that links critical innovations—rich labor markets, cheap logistics, bountiful energy, and easy consumer debt—into a degree of plenitude and accessibility that is far from perfect yet unprecedented. Moreover, in the developing world, a new middle class has emerged out of the manufacturing zones of Asia and Eastern Europe, and an estimated 500 million people have been lifted out of poverty mostly in China, India, and Southeast Asia partially through the wealth redistribution effected by our singular drive to make more stuff cheaper.

But despite its many gifts, discounting is also a destabilizing force—the greenhouse gas of a consumer-driven economy—that is already threatens to render last decade's gains redundant. Westerners have focused upon security concerns in recent years, and not without justification, yet it is the humble bargain that is associated with some of the greatest long-term social, economic, and environmental issues of our time. Huge trade imbalances, diminishing natural resources, and growing consumer debt threaten a world that has become highly dependent on cheap oil, container shipping, and endless plastic.

We've already seen glimpses of the future. In 2008, for example, Wal-Mart and Costco famously began to ration rice sales to prevent food hording. Home Depot, the world's largest home improvement chain, massively cancelled new store openings in 2008, resulting in the lowest store growth rate in the firm's 30-year history. Collectively, the likes of Starbucks, Foot Locker, and Macy's announced over 1,000 different store closures during the first half of the same year.

In a Schumpeterian twist, the tough times of 2008 onward floated Wal-Mart's fortunes as refugee consumers abandoned their Vegas dreams and went to line up for rationed rice and generic prescription drugs at their local supercenter. Reporting new profits and a rebounding share price, Wal-Mart enjoyed a sales bump as the consumer crisis began to crescendo. As Wall Street crashed in Fall 2008, Wal-Mart's stock prices quickly recovered to 2004 levels, running counter to the precipitous fall of every major stock index.

And not in the least because, according to one survey, an overwhelming majority of consumers—87 percent—still believed that the retailer has world's lowest prices. "Tough times are actually a good time for Wal-Mart," says Thomas M. Schoewe, Wal-Mart's chief financial officer.

The gales of global discounting offer opportunity in hardship. Cheap stuff remains a critical part of our world—and our systems of affordable production and consumption will change, sometimes violently. Like the petroleum that greases our economy, affordable consumerism will ultimately prove to be unsustainable, a twentieth-century boon that, in the face of trade imbalances, consumer failure, and resource scarcity, eventually depletes. This isn't some kind of market-based correction, the kind of sudden crash that affects overvalued stocks and commodities. This could be a corrective on growth itself—the end of cheap production.

"How do I stay in front, and derive value for consumers?" Castro-Wright asks his audience, while searching around for his next flow chart. Again, nobody answers.

SECTION II

OUT OF THE BARGAIN BASEMENT

Wal-Mart CEO Mike Duke rallies shareholders at the company's annual general meeting, June 2008
Credit: REUTERS/Jessica Rinaldi

CHAPTER 3

CHINA CRISIS

THE END OF CHEAP LABOR

Homecoming

North from Hong Kong's central Kowloon station, the train to mainland China snakes through the rolling hills of the New Territories, passing a dense array of factories, farms, and large apartment buildings. The northern edge of Hong Kong is surprisingly lush and green compared to the urban density of its waterfront; small mountain parks, Confucian shrines, and hidden gardens rush past as the express train speeds toward the border. Despite Hong Kong's 1997 reunification with China, the northern border remains a highly controlled zone. The playgrounds, markets, and apartment complexes of the New Territories give way to military bunkers, barbed wire, and army-guard towers as the train nears Shenzhen, a sprawling concrete tower and factory city on Hong Kong's northern border and Guangdong Province's fastest-growing city.

Over 160,000 people cross the Luohu point of entry daily, a tide of businessmen, students, and workers funneling through the armed checkpoint. Shenzhen is the epicenter of bargaineering in today's world, connecting millions of Western consumers with an archipelago of factories in south China that produce the majority of our cheap merchandise. My pants, shirt, backpack, socks, and hat were all made in here in Guangdong Province, so arriving here isn't a journey as much as a homecoming.

The scale of industrial activity in Shenzhen is one of the world's modern wonders. Each day, tons of raw materials arrive by boat, and another 109,000 steel containers of finished product are removed for export. That's about one 20-foot container every second, a veritable river of toys atop cargo ships that sail down the Pearl River towards the open water of the South China Sea.

As of 2001, an estimated 95 percent of Wal-Mart's Chinese purchases were made here in Shenzhen. With the help of Wal-Mart, Home Depot, and other global retailers, China captured over 70 percent of the world's market for toys, furniture, and DVDs and over half of world production of bicycles, cameras, telephones, and shoes. To sustain this output, China has also become the world's largest producer of coal, steel, and cement.

It has everything to do with hundreds of millions of migrant workers stranded on the inside of Shenzhen's foreboding gates. And great numbers of these migrants have left behind family and children to work in special economic zones along the coastline. Most return to their home villages once or twice a year, but religiously send money—which has become the largest source of new income in depressed rural areas. If they are lucky enough to find a good factory, with a fair manager, and avoid being exploited or assaulted along the way, Shenzhen's migrants—along with millions of other dispossessed rural Chinese—can continue to send money home and keep their children, parents, and grandparents out of malnutrition and homelessness by working in distant factory cities, for about $165 a month in wages.

It's a career path that many Western consumers never consider. But, from Mongolia to India, fleeing the countryside with the hopes of finding a factory job and sending money home has defined hundreds of millions of people from the 1980s onward. In China, the total number of farmers turned migrant workers doubled between 1996 and 2008, increasing from 72 million to an estimated 130 to 200 million, based on government estimates. Generations of rural peasants had quietly suffered through Mao's unsuccessful attempts to modernize China—including famine, widespread violence, and isolated bouts of cannibalism—only to become a massive, stranded labor pool.

The train from Hong Kong stops and passengers disembark directly into a drab immigration building. Documents are checked. Everywhere, ads and brochures advertise Shenzhen's enticements: a Hard Rock Cafe, four-star hotels, gourmet restaurants, and several theme parks. After crossing a short bridge that spans the no-man's land between the former British colony and the new China, one descends into the chaos of the train station. Scores of beggars and pimps work the street outside, while kiosks inside the station offer free tours of luxury apartment buildings and upscale housing developments—not unlike the posh, high-security, residential complexes of North America—which were some of mainland China's first gated communities. It is around Shenzhen that many of China's suburbs first took shape. For the first time, wealthy Chinese own property, complete with a two-car garage and a manicured lawn.

By the early 2000s, China had become the Saudi Arabia of cheap. By combining logistics, technology, and hundreds of millions of dispossessed farmers, China created a reported 40 to 50 percent cost advantage on many consumer and industrial products. It was a Schumpeterian price event—nonlinear, disruptive, singular—that offered a quantum leap in profit, growth, and affordability that helped float the postindustrial economies of the developed world. It became a fast-moving feudal state powered by technology and capitalism, with mega-malls for some and mud huts for others. Yet as products flowed and new factories sprung up during the early 2000s, Shenzhen was increasingly marred by battles between militant migrant workers and hired gangs of thugs; worker advocates were brutally attacked; and the streets outside of factory walls sometimes became unsafe. Much to the dismay of government and many factory owners, migrants and workers had been organizing increasingly sophisticated legal challenges, inciting workplace sabotage, and pushing back the restrictions on mobility and residency that made China's labor market critical to globalization. According to China Labor Watch, official labor dispute cases increased nearly fourteenfold between 1995 and 2006, and the estimated number of labor-related riots increased fivefold.

Shenzhen is a window into the uncertain futures of the Western consumer. Facing the fastest-rising prices in more than a generation—food prices jumped by over 23 percent in 2008—China's government raised minimum wages and tightened labor and environmental regulations in order to quell unrest and protest. The impact affected retail prices halfway around the world. After uninterrupted savings since the 1980s, the average price of goods from China began to increase in 2007, peaking in 2008 at an average 9 percent price increase.

Rising costs at home and Western demand for low prices were enough to trigger a wave of factory closures and shutdowns. The Asian Footwear Association estimates that in 2007 alone, nearly 1,000 shoemaking factories out of 8,000 closed or moved out of the region. "There are about 70,000 factories in the Pearl River Delta today. Many of them are talking about reducing their workforce or even shutting down," said Stanley Lau, deputy chairman of the Federation of Hong Kong Industries, to the *New York Times* in 2008. "We expect more than 10 percent of these factories will be closed in a year or two." In early 2009, Lau predicted that another 5 to 10 percent would close due to global recession.

This is highly relevant to Western consumers because contemporary China operates on a growth pact. Either there is 8 percent annual economic growth, or there is trouble. In reality, China's ruling class walks a tightrope in its chosen model of accelerated development, one that includes not only its 1.3 billion citizens but also the developed nations who rely on China for everything from cheap stuff to debt financing. Whereas Wal-Mart is hooked on growth as a matter of profit, China is addicted to growth as a matter of survival. There is a thin margin of error: too little development, and poverty and hunger dangerously afflict 300 million of China's poorest—and the ensuing chaos wreaks havoc with global supply chains. Yet too much development has already created widespread inflation, pollution, and inequity—and fuels the likelihood of collapse.

The global economic crisis that began late in 2008 forced the question of China's precarious balance, since it was unlikely, if not impossible, for the nation to remain unscathed. By the time Prime Minister Wen Jiabao addressed China's National People's Congress in March 2009, the ruling Communist Party of China (CPC) was sparing little expense in its efforts to hold the country together, launching one of the world's largest stimulus plans ($585 billion) and increasing what Wen described as China's "social safety net programs" by nearly 18 percent.

It's hardly the first time China's government has poured resources into saving itself, since it has systematically pumped billions into places that it perceives as vulnerable, from the rebellious central Asian frontier of Xinjiang to the feudal heartland of rural China. Social instability, according to the CPC, has long been the single-greatest threat to modern China. In fact, the last time that China encountered this kind of economic and social strife was probably in the years before the failed democracy uprising of Spring 1989 and the tragic Tiananmen Square massacre that ensued.

We need China. The country's productive role in global commerce has meant that it, like other developing nations, has often internalized and obscured extra costs and impacts—everything from child labor and pollution to national debt. In doing this, China cushioned the global disconnect between high-impact prosperity and lower costs. Offshore labor accounts for only a portion of the overall cost of many of our products, yet not having to pay for things like higher wages, greenhouse gas credits, and worker safety is what helped deliver incredible value to both consumers and corporations since the 1980s. Thanks to China, more than just about any other nation, we do not often pay the true cost of things.

Yet, for these and other reasons, China may need us less in the future. Indeed, China has ample reason to seek out a gradual decoupling with the very nations that helped fund its rise to power, not the least of which the United States. Decades of bargain-fuelled trade and direct foreign investment financed China's transition from a needy developing nation to an emerging global power with growing autonomy. If China can survive itself over the next decade, it may not need low-cost exports as a pillar of its economy. In the meantime, everything from blood oil in Africa to the buying power of Western consumers is now part of its growing sphere of influence.

The great crash of 2008 that wiped out at least $11 trillion in global assets during its first year, mostly sidestepped Chinese households, which carry high savings and don't generally hold stocks and bonds. But millions in the developing world are feeling the effects. What began as a financial crisis turned into a crisis of globalization, one that followed some long-standing fault lines around the world. By the end of 2008, an estimated 63,000 Chinese factories had closed and exports had dropped 25 percent by early 2009. Some economists were betting that China would be lucky to sustain 5 percent growth as the global economic crisis deepened, which would veer into the country's danger zone of destabilized growth. Meanwhile, an estimated 20 million unemployed workers filled the streets of China's factory zones and journeyed back into their home villages and towns—perhaps not unlike the glut of unemployed farmers during Britain's Industrial Revolution. In short, doing business with unstable Western economies has become riskier, and Pacific Rim nations are rightly searching for alternatives. As Chinese prime minister Wen Jiabao worried aloud in March 2009, "We have lent a huge amount of money to the U.S. Of course we are concerned about the safety of our assets," he said. "To be honest, I am definitely a little worried."

The likely "China crisis" of tomorrow isn't so much the collapse of the middle kingdom, but the rise of China as a superpower that no longer chooses to depend on globalization. China's ruling communist party can't abandon its export-dependent model of growth, at least not yet. China needs its U.S. currency assets to stay healthy in the short run and to keep bargain-based globalization alive long enough to stabilize its own domestic troubles. Still, the bargain revolution may one day be remembered as a power transfer from West to East, a new era of geopolitical influence. If China, Taiwan, Korea, and other emerging economies can successfully decouple from the West, unprecedented access to impoverished labor markets will decline as well. Already, China has sought out ways to increase wages and improve labor laws in order to keep value at home instead of subsidizing offshore consumers. This is one way that regional and national forces are undermining globalization in the twenty-first century.

This is also why Western consumers should care more about dirt-poor farmers and migrant laborers in China and beyond: cheap, available labor that long filled our stores with bargains is gradually becoming a threatened resource, for which there is yet no ready alternative.

Into the Bargain Machine

If revolutions during the twentieth century had succeeded in emancipating over one billion rural peasants in Mexico and China, Wal-Mart might be a curious retail phenomenon, not the world's largest company. And yet the greatest productive force of our time was launched by a communist, not Sam Walton: the late Deng Xiaoping—Mao's successor, architect of modern China, and leader of the bloody crackdown against China's democracy movement at Tiananmen Square.

In 1979, when Shenzhen was still knee-high in mud and rice paddies, Deng pronounced Shenzhen as China's first Special Economic Zone, or SEZ, simply, a region whose economic policies are more liberal than those in the rest of the country. At the time, Wal-Mart was a regional merchant spread across 11 states and had just earned its first $1 billion in sales. Deng's then-radical strategy for capitalist development emphasized foreign investment and export. It was a pragmatic plan to kick-start and refinance China's pallid economy by catering to the West's hunger for cheap. Thousands of factories sprouted up across China, creating millions of jobs and an avalanche of products for the world's markets. China doubled its share of the world economy between 1990 and 2000. This unprecedented growth rate was six times that of any other nation. It became, as *Business Week* aptly described it, an "exporting colossus, powering growth of nearly 10 percent a year for the past three decades."

Most of that growth was initially launched from Shenzhen and other industrial centers along the Pearl Delta north of Hong Kong. By 1990, Shenzhen had already captured half of all China's incoming foreign investment, and it continues to capture a sizable portion of the estimated $1 trillion in total foreign investment that has entered China since 1979. According to Hong Kong consultants Enright, Scott and Associates, Shenzhen's economy expanded an astonishing 28 percent annually between 1980 and 2004.

The remittances of migrant factory workers to home villages is an important part of this economy. China's *liudong renkou* (floating population) are not only making bargains for the West, but help keep China afloat as well; the roughly 6 percent increase in rural household income since the early 2000s can be attributed to these cash payments.

"Some will get rich, others will follow," Deng famously predicted in 1985—a prediction that has only become all too true in Shenzhen, where China's richest and poorest citizens jostle for their share of the global bargain trade. Until the 1970s, Shenzhen village was a preindustrial remnant that had remained largely unchanged for nearly two millennia. This coastal village was named Bao'an County in A.D. 331, during the Eastern Jin Dynasty; it was renamed Shenzhen in 1410, during the Ming Dynasty. A few years after the creation of the Shenzhen Special Economic Zone in 1980, the old fishing village was surrounded by 100,000 new residents, and by 2008, an estimated 11 million people had converged on the city. Shenzhen, roughly translated, means "deep drain."

Fittingly, Shenzhen now boasts China's highest per capita ownership of credit cards—several per permanent resident, on average. Hong Kong businessmen have harbored thousands of fatherless children here with Shenzhen girlfriends, many of whom will never travel across Shenzhen's southern gates. Besides having the country's highest concentration of migrant labor, Shenzhen also has more brothels than anywhere else in China. An estimated three-quarters of the city's population of four million do not have a permanent address.

Out on the street, vendors sell a mind-boggling variety of counterfeit consumer goods: huge stuffed Mickey Mouse dolls, Prada and Hugo Boss knock-offs, pirated DVDs, and fake Rolex watches, to name just a few. Hastily erected steel and glass buildings clutter the skyline, and concrete walkways ferry people over dusty, congested avenues. Within minutes, street children swarm visitors. One eight-year-old desperately clings to my leg and refuses to let go. He's either crying or pretending to cry. Locals later explain that Shenzhen gangsters run the kids. Western executives are occasionally kidnapped here, and it's no coincidence that all the major tourist attractions are safely located near the edge of the city. Most of the city's 20,000 foreign expats actually live at scenic Shekou Harbor, about an hour's bus ride from the city's crime-ridden center.

But most people don't come here for the scenery. This is one of the first urban areas in the world created purely for export manufacture, featuring enormous walled factory complexes, streets named for their corporate sponsors, and a constant influx of migrant workers and entrepreneurs. It is a site of enormous hardship, ingenuity, and hope, encompassing tiny workshops and modern megafactories. Here, workers do everything from sort electronic waste that is contaminated with heavy metals for menial pay to operate high-tech assembly machines for wages that rival those of China's middle class. (And everyone suffers China's famous air pollution. An unpublished 2002 study by researchers with the Chinese Medical Association noted that of 11,348 schoolchildren tested in Shenzhen, 65 percent had "unsafe" levels of lead in their blood, according to World Health Organization guidelines—a figure that rises to 80 percent in nearby Guiyu, where families recycle computers, cell phones, and other e-waste.)

Wal-Mart has bravely launched nine supercenters in the Shenzhen area. Decorated according to the company formula—everything red, white, and blue—it sells local specialties, items that you'd find in a typical Chinese grocery store: dried squid snacks, shrimp chips, spicy green peas, and rice cookers. The hope is that the 40,000 employees working in 100-plus stores across China—part of the country's burgeoning consumer class—will train themselves to scavenge for bargains in big-box stores the way North Americans and Europeans do. In 2003, Joe Hatfield, then-president of Wal-Mart China, told the *Los Angles Times* of the great optimism about the Middle Kingdom. "What this place is going to look like 10 to 20 years from now—and what the consumer will be ready to buy—is hard to even think about," Hatfield said. "There are 800 million farmers out there who've probably never even tasted a Coke."

All is not well in the factories that fill our big-box stores: protests, industrial accidents, food riots, and violent attacks against workers and organizers are common occurrences. In a Hong Kong office tower a short train ride from Shenzhen, exiled labor activist Han Dongfang is putting the final touches on his weekly Radio Free Asia program, which broadcasts news and interviews to millions of listeners across China's mainland in Mandarin. Han Dongfang hears it all. "Yesterday, someone called in to report 2,000 people at a protest in front of one factory," he says, estimating that he fields about 80 calls a month. People share information on corruption, human rights abuses, layoffs, and unpaid wages. China's government tries—unsuccessfully—to jam the signal.

"Sometimes people call me from in front of a demonstration of 1,000 people, or when an accident happens, or just to discuss a situation," he says. "And after every incident reported, I do the same thing. I call factories, union leaders, local government officials to prove the story and ask their opinion. Often they say the same general things: 'It's a period of adjustment,' or 'we need to push reform.'" To the chagrin of fellow democracy activists, Han often attempts to mediate disputes with factory managers and party officials in an effort to find solutions without violence, arrests, or job loss.

Based on government sources, "the number of mass protests, demonstrations, sit-ins, and strikes in China soared from around 10,000 in 1993 to 60,000 in 2003, with the total number of participants [totaling] 3.07 million," notes a 2008 report by Han's *China Labor Bulletin* and the Montreal-based advocacy group, Rights and Democracy. (The report, entitled *No Way Out*, compiled five years of research and reported that "there is currently at least one strike involving over 1,000 workers every day in the Pearl River Delta alone.") Or as vice president of Shenzhen's Federation of Trade Unions put it in 2008, strikes had become "as common as arguments between a husband and wife."

Back in May 1989, Han, a former electrician and former People's Liberation Army soldier found himself at Tiananmen Square in Beijing—and founded China's first independent labor union just a few days before the tanks rolled into the square and began shooting. Since then, he had promoted the Chinese vision of democracy—*minzhu* (the people are the master)—that spread across China in the spring of 1989 but was soon driven underground after protests in Beijing and other major Chinese cities were crushed.

Since Tiananmen, explains Han, China has seen successive years of double-digit economic growth, becoming the world's biggest trading nation after Germany, exporting and importing roughly $1.5 trillion worth of goods and services annually. Unlike Germany, which became a leading trading nation through high-value exports—luxury cars, engineering, precision machinery—China's exports run the gamut, from super-cheap to affordable luxury items and high-tech. An estimated 80 million jobs are now directly tied to China's booming export sector, with hundreds of millions more dependent on export revenues.

Yet rural incomes have not kept pace with the rest of China, and the number of Chinese unofficially estimated to be living on less than a dollar a day in 2007 was 300 million. The failure of Mao's revolution kept most of the country frozen for decades, delaying development, education, and income for the majority of Chinese citizens while the rest of the world marched forward. The paradox of uneven development is, of course, that it makes offshore manufacture highly attractive. China's greatest domestic problem is the thing that has made it such an effective instrument of mass production. China can exploit its workers and economy in the short-term, but the poverty, social dispossession, and underdevelopment that created the surplus labor pool is a longterm liability, both for the ruling CPC and the average citizen.

In a global growth economy, these problems are easier to manage. But in a global meltdown, they are direct threats that even China's billions in stimulus funding—nearly $600 billion in 2009 alone—cannot easily mitigate. "Strikes and work stoppages are part of daily life in the Pearl River Delta," says Han. "This is in spite of the fact that, under the current constitution of the People's Republic of China, workers do not have the right to strike." Between limited freedoms and corruption that can reach to the highest levels of business and government, "young workers are without a future," Han says. "Hundreds of thousands of factories are in the same situation: no money, no jobs, no unemployment fund, no retirement fund. Factories are often just a channel for money [management fraud], which is why many fail. Corrupt managers have several houses instead and don't pay their workers."

The biggest threat to China's communist party is not students with democracy banners or Islamic terrorists from central Asia, but millions of scruffy migrant workers who have been cheated out of wages, abused, often injured, and have few prospects. And by early 2009, an estimated 20 million of them were unhappily unemployed. With his unique window on China's hidden struggles, Han's fear is that the Middle Kingdom is not advancing towards stability and market-driven democracy—as many Western politicians once claimed—but towards an uneasy hybrid of diminished freedoms, strife, and unstable development. Han argues no amount of growth or investment alone can fix China, since part of today's emerging crisis began in 1989 when young patriotic Chinese chanted *minzhu* in their unsuccessful call for accountability and good government. "Democracy is more and more out of people's lives," says Han, sadly. "It has become a thinker's activity, not connected with the people."

Instead, mainland China is aflame with a booming middle class, uprisings, depleting food and resources, widespread poverty and crime. And because of this, Han is probably the most popular pirate radio broadcaster in the world. He shakes his head in disbelief. That China has drifted from communism is no secret. But what is it becoming? He doesn't hesitate: "an explosion."

Joint Ventures

Back in the 1960s, Communist cadres ordered Shenzhen farmers and fishermen to sing revolutionary songs on their way to work, in the hope that Hong Kong residents just over the wall would be impressed with their enthusiasm for the revolution. At the time, Hong Kong was Asia's leading global trade and finance hub, a bastion of free-market capitalism, low taxation, and rapid industrialization. Yet after Deng Xiaoping's radical market-based economic reforms began in Shenzhen in 1980, Hong Kong was among the first to outsource. By 1989, most of Hong Kong's manufacturers had been lured across the Shenzhen border. Some of the region's workers, at least the ones who work for Wal-Mart, still sing songs: "My heart is filled with pride...I long to tell you how deep my love for Wal-Mart is..."

The country's ruling class spent the last quarter century building and doing everything it could to be attractive for Wal-Mart and other global retailers. It spent billions on transport networks, its military, and domestic surveillance technologies. China is still unique in the world for its capacity to merge a preindustrial labor pool with twenty-first century technology and infrastructure. "There might be places in other parts of the world where you can buy cheaper, but can you get [the product] on the ship?" Wal-Mart's Shenzhen manager told the *Washington Post* in 2004. "If we have to look at a country that's not politically stable, you might not get your order on time. If you deal in a country where the currency fluctuates, everyday there is a lot of risk. China happens to have the right mix."

In 2002, Wal-Mart opened its global procurement office in Shenzhen, arguably its first major management relocation outside of Bentonville. During the early 2000s, the company's internal sourcing and purchasing agency employed approximately 1,500 people in Shenzhen and two dozen international satellite offices. It was the natural site for Wal-Mart's offshoring efforts: Of the 55 countries from which Wal-Mart imported goods in 2001, China accounted for two-thirds of all purchases. Wal-Mart's Shenzhen procurement headquarters created an estimated $190 billion in sales for the company in 2002, based on $9 billion that Chinese media reported Wal-Mart spent to acquire Chinese products wholesale—suggesting a 21-fold increase from procurement to sales. Wal-Mart doesn't share its data, but the American consulting firm Booz Allen Hamilton estimates that Wal-Mart sourced $2 billion of products from China in 1998, over $18 billion in 2004 and $30 billion in 2008. That's a 15-fold increase within a decade.

Integrating itself with the consumer economics of the West has made Shenzhen an economic trail-blazer for continental Asia. Thousands of other towns and cities across the developing world have studied the Shenzhen model in the hopes that they might transform their own economic backwaters. "Shenzhen will become the most beautiful city in the nation, able to compete with the garden state of Singapore," predicted local Communist party secretary, Zhang Gaoli, in 1999.

Joint ventures began in China as a precondition for foreign investment and manufacture, since Deng and other leaders knew that they needed Western wealth to kick-start China's economy. Known for frequent failures, stranded investment, and scant legal protections, the joint venture has been China's tool for controlling and shaping incoming foreign investment. While China had eliminated mandatory joint venture requirements for corporations by the early 2000s, a grander global joint venture had already been formed. By 2007, Europe and the United States accounted for 41 percent of China's total exports.

In order to maintain their competitive edge, retailers like Wal-Mart integrated even deeper into the economy of the Middle Kingdom, in search of new savings and efficiencies. By the early 2000s, with more than 80 percent of the 6,000 foreign factories that supply Wal-Mart located in China, this exceedingly American corporation had essentially become part Chinese. Between 2001 and 2006, "Wal-Mart was responsible for...11 percent of the growth of the total U.S. trade deficit with China," reports the Economic Policy Institute.

It was an unexpected evolution in Sam Walton's quest, but one that is consistent with his original cost-cutting credo. "For the benefit of the consumer, we should buy merchandise where we get the best value," explained Andrew Tsuei, managing director of Wal-Mart's Shenzhen headquarters. During the period of very low prices during the late 1990s, only 45 cents of the $4.50 retail price of toy sold at Wal-Mart was labor costs. Value was added, as economists often say, along the supply chain, and the consumer ended paying a retail price that is five times the actual labor cost. Following suit, Home Depot and other major retailers, set up their own procurement centers on the mainland.

Like Wal-Mart, China succeeds because it does capitalism better than almost anyone else, often beating former imperialist nations at their own game, dirty tricks and all: currency manipulation, subtle protectionism, economic threats. China's nation-crushing competitive advantage is founded on its capacity for the "disruptive innovation" that Wal-Mart USA's Castro-Wright advocates. Just as Wal-Mart reinvented retailing by bringing together marginal consumer markets and logistics technology, China has reinvented production, combining networked production, transportation, and low-income workers into a global force.

By 2008, China had become a logistics superpower, claiming three out of the five busiest container ports in the world—Hong Kong, Shanghai, and Shenzhen. China adds an estimated 3,000 new kilometers of domestic highway every year. Its national highway network of 30,000 kilometers is second only to America's highway system. Based on China's impressive web of land and sea links, the U.S. Department of Commerce estimates that by 2010, 35 percent of the world's shipping traffic is expected to originate from China.

Manufacturing and information technology is also being used to increase productivity, produce higher-value products, and create new consumer savings. The image of a primitive 1970s-era factory powered by coal furnaces and peasant labor is outdated in major centers like Shenzhen. Higher-value businesses like Dell, Apple, HP, and others have adopted China-based production precisely because of the advanced technology, information management, and automation that is now available. The Chinese factories often also produce discount no-name versions of the brand-name product, much to the enrichment of brand-name companies. As James Fallows reported in 2007, no less than three "competing" brands of low-cost laptop come out of the same Shenzhen factory; an estimated 90 percent of all laptops are now manufactured by one of five Chinese companies—Inventec, Compal, Quanta, Wistron, and Asustek.

Foxconn, the Taiwanese company that is a prime manufacturer for technology titans like Nokia, Dell, and Apple, is the most dominant producer in Shenzhen—most notably, its walled city-factory called Longhua Science & Technology Park, which claims a "population" of 270,000 workers. Foxconn is China's biggest single exporter of goods and a prime example of how special economic zones have diversified into the sort of higher-value products once manufactured much closer to home. Nearly 90 percent of all USB flash drives are manufactured here. What began with Western dollar store wholesalers and discounters scrounging trinkets and housewares in dowdy Chinese factories during the 1980s has resulted in many of our most desirable technologies being bargaineered in much the same way.

Think of Shenzhen every time Apple rolls out another iPod or iPhone—an estimated 10 million iPhones were distributed globally in 2008 alone. There is no other place on the planet that can reliably manufacture and broadcast millions of high-value products and still manage to pass along a healthy profit to Western companies who, at one time, actually made the products themselves. By taking a mere $25 profit per phone, Apple launched the miracle of the $199 iPhone in 2008—an item that originally retailed for as much as $599—and not only helped demolish pricing for many high-end personal devices, but refueled the fading consumer dream. Despite labor shortages and rising costs, Foxconn was producing 800,000 iPhones a week by mid-2008, "above full current capacity."

China's diversification from manufacturing cheap novelties during the 1980s to high-value technologies by the 2000s is one of the most dramatic indications of how China has anchored Western consumerism—with a factory system that could never exist in a Western democracy. China's focused and strategic approach on everything from infrastructure development to macro-economic policy, as well as its ability to manage the consequences of severe underdevelopment, protest, and poverty, wouldn't be possible in a country that had meaningful elections. In fact, the fierce efficiency of mainland China's growth-without-democracy approach is precisely why China maintains an economic lead over other major developing world players like India, even though India's legal system, democratic government, high rates of education, and respect for intellectual property make it an obvious choice for global business.

The reality is that China's one-party state allows for large, radical reconfigurations of work and society that have yet to be reproduced anywhere else.

Foxconn's city-within-a-city factory serves 150,000 lunches daily; its production lines operate around the clock, and the starting wage is 60 cents an hour, Shenzhen's legal minimum. The company expanded to include parts manufacture as well as design and assembly, allowing it to undercut its competitors while increasing profits. Foxconn founder, Terry Gou, is personally worth an estimated $10 billion, and his clients Nintendo (Wii), Apple (iPhone), Motorola (cell phones), Sony (PlayStation) and Dell (computers) represent billions more in domestic sales created through supply chains that no longer represent any clear nationality.

Cheap stuff has created a peace dividend in a globalized world: Nations that share a strong trade in consumer products also share diplomatic stability. More often than not, globalization has taken root developing countries that have suffered through failed revolutions and colonialism: India, China, Vietnam, parts of Southeast Asia, Mexico, Central America, and much of Eastern Europe. As these enclaves opened up for business, global labor supply increased fourfold between 1980 and 2007, according to the International Monetary Fund. In 2008, the World Bank claimed that 500 million people had been lifted out of poverty, mostly in China, India, and Southeast Asia.

On the ground, though, these income gains are not always obvious, and some claimed improvements are outright fabrications. With one of China's worst records for violence and workplace injury in a police state full of industrial accidents, Shenzhen sometimes seems like a scene out of Karl Marx's account of England, despite its growing importance as a high-tech center. Not long before I arrived in Shenzhen on one visit, a fire ravaged a Taiwanese joint-venture electronics factory, where management had blocked fire exits to prevent workers from stealing products, killing 24 women and youth. In keeping with the local business culture, the company's official name is Vast Profit Limited. This is a just a hint of the hardship behind the production of 70 percent of the world's toys. It's no joke that people usually come to Shenzhen for only three reasons: to get rich, to attend to a Shenzhen mistress—or to escape greater hardship back home.

In 2008 a child labor ring was discovered north of Shenzhen. Lured away or captured from the distant, poverty-stricken, rural province of Sichuan, the children, aged 13 to 15, were forced to work up to 300 hours each month for little or no pay. Although 100 children were rescued following this incident, the use of forced labor has increased, despite increased policing and vigilance, another reflection of the desperate economic realities. Faced with a plethora of new costs, many Chinese manufacturers still resort to withholding wages, illegal working conditions, and child labor to meet the low-cost demands of export markets. Later reports from Chinese media suggested that as many as 1000 children were working in factories in Dongguan, directly north of Shenzhen. "[This] case is quite typical," Hu Xingdou, Beijing Institute of Technology, told the *International Herald Tribune*. "China's economy is developing at a fascinating speed, but often at the expense of laws, human rights, and environmental protection." Evidence of slavery also surfaced in 2007, when officials in Shanxi and Henan Provinces rescued hundreds of adults and children who had been captured and forced to work in rural brick kilns.

Pressure to keep costs contained has resulted in persistent labor and human rights abuses, and to periodic waves of faulty products and the use of toxic materials. Facing fierce competition in retail markets, Wal-Mart used its clout to refuse cost increases for labor or materials. This, in turn, puts pressure on Chinese factories, many of which cannot deliver low prices and live up to labor and environmental laws, let alone provide fair wages and safe working conditions. "In the beginning, we made money," one Chinese factory manager told the *Washington Post* in 2004. "But when Wal-Mart started to launch nationwide distribution, they pressured us for a special price at below our cost. Now, we're losing money on every box, while Wal-Mart is making more money."

It's the same value-destruction effect that discounting affected on the retail environments of the West. But its consequences here in the developing world are potentially more serious and threaten to undo some of the income and development gains of past decades. "People have always said foreign investment is the hope of China. This is our bridge to the world," says Han Dongfang. "But what comes across the bridge are 12-hour shifts, seven-day workweeks, and only two trips to the bathroom a day. What comes across are factory fires that kill hundreds of workers who are locked in because their bosses are afraid they will steal the products. The Chinese government has put an invisible net across the bridge that allows money to come in but not the freedoms of a civil society, not the rule of law and not free trade unions."

One result is the illegal strikes and protest and enough random violence to count as a low-level civil war, a fact of life in China's industrial cities that has frequently gone unreported. Readily available explosives from China's countless construction sites, for example, make domestic terrorism a too-common occurrence. On nearly a monthly basis somewhere in China, anonymous disgruntled workers, migrants, and minorities set off bombs and sabotage factories, transport, and government buildings.

It is possible that China may come out ahead of its international joint-venture partners—if it can survive itself, that is. Even after the crash, ongoing trade deficits continue to speak to China's central role within globalization—and of its surprising ability to maintain its current economic model. In particular, China carries special clout as owner of national debt of the developed world, notably its $1.4 trillion surplus of American debt. With its surplus American dollars gained from trade imbalance, the Chinese government has long purchased American debt treasuries with its currency reserves. In other words, the largest trade imbalance in human history—one that inevitably affects all nations—is being underwritten on behalf of the people who tolerate workplace injuries and human rights abuses for the benefit of distant shoppers. "On average, each Chinese peasant owns $1,000 in US Treasury bonds," notes David Dollar, director of the World Bank's Beijing office. "He may not have a tractor and his kids may not have schools, but he has that bond."

Wal-Mart and its kin are just middlemen. The real joint venture is the interdependence that exists between Western consumers, the Chinese government, and migrant labor. We need cheap goods, they need income. It's a relationship that has become more complicated in the twenty-first century. And yet without this compact, there is scant reason to hustle millions of steel containers across the face of the planet.

Mao's Unlucky Heartland

At first glance, rural China is a postcard vision. Oxen, pigs, and ancestral homes dot the countryside blanketed by lush rice paddies that stretch to the horizon. Locals drive ancient tractors and dredge irrigation canals, usually knee-deep in mud. Framed in endless hues of green and brown, Shaoshan village is nearly hidden within the rolling hills of central Hunan Province. It is living history, a place where people tend fields that have been farmed continuously for the last 5,800 years.

What isn't apparent is that pesticides and fertilizer have killed off most marine life in the rivers and lakes. Crops are damaged by acid rain almost as acidic as vinegar, which now falls over parts of central China. Crops that aren't damaged by acid rain may be washed away by annual floods that kill as many as 3,000 people annually, destroying millions of homes and crops, threatening famine. If it's not floods, then it's drought; between here and the Three Gorges Dam, millions lose access to drinking water during semiannual heat waves. Tornadoes and cholera outbreaks also afflict this region during particularly unlucky years.

One emerges from Shaoshan's crumbling train station and the air is humid and heavy; this is a dour, languorous place where the locals still stare wildly at foreigners. It's strangely quiet, deserted-seeming, not the least because so many locals have abandoned the countryside. More than 80 million rural Chinese gave up farming between 1996 and 2006. The estimated 736 million rural Chinese who remain face persistent hardship. Local income remains well below a dollar a day in many areas.

At the center of Shaoshan is a faded tourist attraction. Inside a cluster of Soviet-era hotels, semivacant souvenir stands, and weathered statues is a mud-walled farmhouse with a pigpen, dirt floors, and a kitchen. It was here in Shaoshan that young Mao Zedong once fed chickens and planted rice, and first began to dream of the revolution that would change world history.

Although large by peasant standards—its 13 small rooms and mud court-yard made it a mansion in prewar China—Mao's birthplace isn't much to look at. It is dank and dark inside, and while his old wooden bed still stands inside his room, there are few other signs that a family actually lived here. Mao's modest farmhouse drew as many as 3 million annual visitors at the height of the Cultural Revolution in the late 1960s. Nearby hotels, exhibits, and restaurants are still adorned with socialist banners, grandiose Mao diora-mas and busts of Marx and Lenin. Outdoor loudspeakers blast revolutionary songs from the 1960s most of the day, perhaps to lessen the boredom of the guards and custodians who tend this empty place.

Official signs and plaques, riddled with spelling errors, proclaim mundane aspects of young Mao's life—here, he went swimming; there, he worked in the rice paddy—yet Shaoshan offers little insight into what eventually drove Mao Zedong to the ideological folly that would result in mass persecution and starvation during the cultural revolution. Indeed, Shaoshan represents the persistent poverty of China's heartland. Outside of the affluent cities, infant mortality rates are still high, corrupt officials steal land and money, and an ongoing epidemic of suicides—over half the world's daily total, largely among young rural women—speak to the hardship that has driven millions of rural Chinese to abandon their villages and seek out employment in distant factories.

Many peasants wind up destitute and unemployed in regional cities, such as Changsha, the provincial capital of Hunan, which sits on the Xiang River a short train ride from Shaoshan. It is here that Mao completed part of his education and founded the Hunan branch of the Chinese Communist Party. Even at 6 A.M., all along Wuyi Donglu, Changsha's central avenue, lines of beggars and migrant workers silently wait, many holding up signs offering their skills for pay or begging for money with tales of hardship.

Around the corner on Shaoshan Lu, a new Wal-Mart supercenter waits for customers. It serves the small but growing pool of urban middle class that can be found in most Chinese cities. Including its capital, Changsha, Hunan province holds 68 million people—nearly twice the population of Canada—but only boasts three Wal-Mart outlets. Still, despite being located in one of

China's most depressed provinces, Wal-Mart's Changsha store manages to exceed its $60,000 daily-sales target—paying its workers $84 to $96 a month, well below most of Shenzhen's lowest wages.

Former backwaters like Changsha boomed during the 2000s as they become new bargain zones for export and domestic production, adding chemical factories, heavy machinery, and consumer goods production, and expanding at rates that outpace first-generation SEZs like Shenzhen. Changsha's GDP increased 14 percent annually between 2001 and 2006, compared with China's national average of 9 percent. By 2006, investment was pouring into Changsha at five times the national average, mostly from Hong Kong, Singapore, and Japan, creating a boom economy within the world's leading boom economy.

Why? In 2005, minimum wages in regional capitals like Changsha or Chengdu were roughly half of Shenzhen's minimum wage. Not only did it get more expensive to do business in Shenzhen and other established SEZs, there were chronic shortages of skilled and unskilled workers as materials costs, energy prices, and wages increased. One in six Chinese textile companies was unprofitable in 2007, reports the *Financial Times*, despite an 8 percent increase in export prices. Faced with closure or costly transfer of operations to marginally less expensive countries like Vietnam, many manufacturers moved inland. As the Asia Footwear Association reported in 2007, of the 1,000 shoemaking factories that closed or moved out of the Pearl River Delta region, 50 percent moved inland to places like Hunan.

The list of available products from Hunan's cinder-block factories reads like a manifest list from the Las Vegas bargain show. Your recordable CDs and DVDs may have come from Hunan's Forescape; Hunan Palette Garment offers "deluxe business suits, group uniforms, and shirts"; Shaodong Chenwang hardware specializes in pliers and pincers; nonstick fry pans from Hunan Wujo Light Industry and Chemicals; bamboo flooring from Hunan XiangZhu; and paint rollers and drywall tools from Hunan General Industrial. "Hunan Province has formed a complete industrial system," boasts the regional authority, "with pillar industries like metallurgy, machinery, electronics, food, energy, and building materials."

The Chinese government hopes that rural development will both curb income disparities and promote rapid growth. Launched in 2004, the government strategic plan for this "second-wave" of development—fittingly titled the "Rise of Central China"—seeks to nearly double the shipping, transport, and production capacity of its central provinces by 2012.

Amazingly, a new factory can be built in Hunan's capital region in as little as 45 days. Hunan also plans to make high technology 45 percent of its added value industrial output by 2010—directly competing with the many Shenzhen firms that are looking to relocate inland. Hunan is now one of China's ten most paved regions, boasting 1,800 kilometers of expressway; Changsha's new port on the Xiangjiang River, a tributary of the Yangtze, can transport full containers of product all the way to Shanghai within a few days.

The paradox is that as China's depressed inland regions generate wealth and growth, the world's pool of cheap labor grows smaller. It is true that the spread of factories, technology hubs, and rapid urbanization across the commercial zones of China and Southeast Asia have resulted in gradual decreases in infant mortality, improved healthcare, and a net increase in life expectancy, not to mention color televisions. Yet China's continued growth has everything to do with its longstanding system of rural-urban apartheid that created the world's largest captive labor pool. In China, the labor force was artificially created by a Mao-era policy that established a rigid permit-based separation between city and country residents, known as *hukou* (household registration system). Following the introduction of SEZs and post-Deng market liberalization, migrants began to roam in search of work in cities and factory zones, estranged from the very Chinese countryside that Mao once saw as the core of the revolution. And without official resident status migrants are subject to exploitation and can be denied healthcare, education, and housing. They are, however, welcome in factory enclaves like Shenzhen. It is, as Amnesty International summarized in 2007, "a regulatory and administrative foundation for discrimination against internal migrant workers."

As frontiers like Hunan grow richer and more urbane, a considerable number of people remain on the losing side of China's two-caste system. Wandering Changsha's gritty streets, one sees unemployed soldiers sleeping on traffic dividers between expressways; homeless peasants pushing their belongings past shopping malls; and, as elsewhere in China, the sick, the disfigured, and the disabled—many of whom claim they got that way in workplace accidents— beg for money. Despite official efforts to bring about balance, China's rural-urban disparity is increasing. Over half of China's 1.3 billion residents are still rural—736 million—more than double America's population, knee-high in pig manure and rice paddies.

Hunan Province is a case study in what can happen when economic growth meets generations of poverty, disease, and corruption. Not long before I arrived in Hunan, for example, police clashed with 5,000 farmers in a village outside Changsha, killing at least one person and injuring 100. The farmers had assembled to protest corruption and over-taxation. Several days later, a bomb detonated on a public bus in downtown Changsha, seriously maiming several passengers—an event that police linked to earlier protests. Ten days later, another bomb went off in a village south of Changsha, killing 10 people. Several months later, a man armed with explosives hijacked a city public bus and demanded to be taken to municipal government offices; police sharp-shooters killed him within three hours.

It's not as though country folk are reckless. Indeed, they've been an accept-ing and tolerant bunch for the last 100 years. But the reality is that they have few political options when corrupt state officials steal money, increase prices, or impose unfair taxes. "Legitimate complaints that are repeatedly ignored by the government are the basis of the most incendiary cases [of rural conflict]," explains David Zweig of Hong Kong's University of Science and Technology a few weeks before I travel to Hunan. "They are very, very prepared to use civil disobedience to push their point because they recognize that the legal channels are not going to work."

Another outcome has been a growing environmental movement that is forcing business to pay for pollution through direct action and government regulation. In 2003, Changsha was already China's seventh most polluted city, according to the government's integrated national index. By 2006, an estimated 19 percent of the agricultural land in Hunan and other southern provinces had been damaged by acid rain. Diesel and coal particulates, ran-dom chemical fumes, ozone that grows thick like fog as it bakes in sunlight, and sulphur emissions coming from the factories make Changsha itself a major cause of acid rain. Asthma and respiratory infections are common-place—within a few days arrival, I catch a nasty throat infection that lasts for weeks.

It's a regional smokestack effect. Changsha and eight smaller cities within an hour's drive account for 70 percent of province's economic output and create a similar share of its pollution. No wonder China now leads the world in overall production of airborne particulates. In fact, NASA estimates between 2002 and 2005, the amount of Chinese pollution arriving in North America was "equivalent to about 15 percent of local emissions of the U.S. and Canada."

Consequently, economic and political unrest has given way to some-thing that Mao Zedong would have never imagined: environmental protest. According to China's Ministry of Public Security, pollution is one of the top five threats to China's peace and stability. An estimated 1,000 pollution-triggered "public disturbances" occurred weekly in 2005, *Mother Jones* maga-zine reported in 2008, including riots against proposed chemical plants, lead poisoning, and urban development. And according to China's environment minister "demonstrations or riots of a hundred or more people protesting the contamination of rivers and farms...had increased in recent years by an annual rate of 29 percent."

Even outside of Changsha, the air quality along country roads is bad. Ancient tractors and scooters belch out clouds of black smoke across incredibly beautiful scenes. In the factory lands on the fringe of greater Changsha, mercury and cadmium from smelters and chemical plants pollute the Xiangjiang River, which supplies drinking water for much of central Hunan Province. Until recently, mercury was the main contaminant. The highly concentrated neurotoxin was released in large quantities in the manufacturing of thermometers, barometers, vapor lamps, batteries and in the preparation of chemical pesticides. But cadmium levels peaked to as much as 80 times the national standards after one 2006 industrial accident, endangering the water for 6.5 million people. "About 10 million residents in the [Changsha] cluster have been threatened by industrial discharge which flow into the river," Hunan's head of the provincial environmental department, Jiang Yimin, admitted to the *People's Daily* in 2006. Even "taxi drivers are not willing to drive passengers to the industrial zone in [Changsha's] northern part, where a cluster of more than 200 paper-making, glass-production, melting and even pesticide factories exist."

Headlines continue to leak out. In 2008, sulfuric acid leaked into the water supply from a chemical factory in Chenxi county, poisoning at least 26 villagers. Another 2006 study found that children living in China's industrial areas, on average, show lead blood levels of 11 times the WHO standard. For decades, Hunan was known for revolution, not pollution—Mao's Zigong's utopian China of lush rice paddies, rosy-faced workers, and shiny new tractors.

In 2008, China's government reported that about a quarter of all the water in China's seven main river systems is too toxic for human contact. The result has been a wave of environmental legislation and regulation designed to curb protests, improve public health, and increase energy efficiency. "In recent years, growing pollution concerns have prompted Beijing to pass stricter environmental legislation, including a 2003 law that requires factories gain approval for onetime 'environmental impact assessment' reports," reported journalist Christina Larson in 2008. "China's officials face what may appear to them to be an uneasy choice: allow citizens to use these laws to their fullest extent, or risk a precipitous rise in protests."

In Hunan's most famous village, authorities did what many other governments have done in a crisis—they built a theme park. In 1994, China attempted to reinvent Mao's hometown of Shaoshan by building an $8 million collection of revolutionary vignettes and 3-D dioramas across the road from Mao's original farmhouse. At Mao Zedong Memorial Park, visitors can explore highlights of the brutal Long March to Mao's Yana's cave headquarters, launchpad of the final 1949 campaign on Beijing. As a sign declares outside, visitors are encouraged live China's revolution for themselves "and excitedly read an interesting and vivid no-word history book."

It is retrosocialism at its finest. To many, Shaoshan is still hallowed ground, a pilgrimage site that, at its peak in 1966, received as many as 2.9 million visitors from all over the world annually. By 1980, the inaugural year of the Shenzhen SEZ, visitors had fallen off to 230,000. Lately, numbers have been picking up again as "red tourism" and nostalgia for the stability and isolation of Mao-era China has taken off with growing numbers of disaffected—and increasingly nationalistic—Chinese. The government claimed an estimated 3.2 million visitors in 2008, many of whom attended annual birthday celebrations for the chairman, featuring music and fireworks performances, patriotic tributes and "longevity noodles."

Besides the Mao tourism, the main growth industry within Shaoshan village appears to be prostitution. In the former barber shop of my hotel, a gaggle of young Chinese women lounge and make phone calls, occasionally going upstairs to service single men from the cities who arrive at Shaoshan's largest, slightly decrepit, and very Soviet-style hotel by train and automobile. Some of the girls are clearly underage. They keep ringing up to my room, offering service, which I politely decline at first, then less politely as the evening wears on—*Buyao, Buyao*! (Don't want! Don't want!) One can hear the hotel's ancient phone system ringing throughout the hotel. The hotel management put on dull, unknowing stares when I raise the issue the next day.

Shaoshan's prostitutes likely earn far more than they would make dressed in blue, restocking shelves, and giving the Sam Walton cheer daily at Changsha's Wal-Mart. For what are doubtless legitimate reasons, Shaoshan's working girls have chosen not to venture into the factory lands of Shenzhen.

And by 2009, many workers were returning home in the wave of factory closings that swept across China. China's old system of household registration is gradually being dismantled just as many returning migrants realized that they had nowhere else to go. This sudden exodus, originally estimated to be the better part of 20 million unemployed migrants, has probably not been seen in China since Mao Zedong's Cultural Revolution forced urban youth out of China's cities and farms and prison camps during the late 1960s. But it signals the gradual end of *hukou* policy and the ultra-cheap labor it helped create.

China still faces a foreboding set of social and economic issues, possibly greater than any that Mao Zedong had to face. It is possible that the chairman would have never left Hunan if he were a rural Chinese today. Or, would he have wound up assembling toys for Disney? Would his family have been lucky enough to afford the luxury of secondary schooling that eventually propelled him towards leadership?

After assuming power in 1949, Mao himself seldom visited Shaoshan, favoring luxury resorts like Lushan, an old European-built hideaway in the mountains of Jiangxi. Between 1959 and his death in 1976, he returned home only twice.

How KFC Helped Save the Revolution

It was another busy afternoon in a city that never sleeps. Late in 2007, labor rights activist Huang Qingnan was chatting with his friend Mr. Zhu in front of an apartment block in Shenzhen's Long'gang district. There was a lot to talk about. China's government was getting ready to implement its new Labor Contract Law, which would provide new rights and job security to hundreds of millions of migrant workers. Severance pay, overtime, and employment contracts, which are common in developed countries, were on the table, as the government prepared to make a rare set of concessions designed to help stabilize growing unrest and poverty.

Home to global technology giant and notoriously predatory employer Huawei Technologies, the Long'gang district is a rough-and-tumble factory suburb where an estimated 80 percent of its one million residents are unregistered migrants. As cofounder of Shenzhen's Dagongzhe Center for Migrant Workers, Huang Qingnan was in the neighborhood to inquire about a worker who had been reportedly beaten by a local factory boss over unpaid wages.

Two figures dressed in dark clothing suddenly emerged out of the crowd and approached Huang from behind. Without warning, they drew two 16-inch blades out of newspapers and began hacking at the labor activist's legs and back. He tried to lunge toward one attacker but soon collapsed on the sidewalk, convulsing in a pool of blood. His friend Zhu hurled rocks and chairs at the assailants, who escaped on a motorcycle. Huang's left leg was severed to the bone, and his torso was covered in deep cuts. By the time he reached Long'gang Central Hospital, he had almost died from blood loss. Doctors were able to save the left leg, but necrosis has left him crippled despite multiple operations for skin grafts, nerve, and blood vessel repair. Five men were arrested several months later for the crime.

The attack made headlines across China, but it was no surprise. "Violence has been continuously getting more and more severe [and] the reason I was attacked can only be because they fear the influence of the center," said

Huang as he recovered in hospital. "And they hope that violent means will prevent the center from operating."

Before the attack, Huang Qingnan and his colleagues had been busy at the Dagongzhe Center, a storefront office in a rundown section of Shenzhen that educates workers and provides free legal advice. Piles of books and brochures clutter the desks inside agency; some dusty safety helmets decorate the front window. A poster above the door reads, "Be independent, be self-strong, be united and help each other." As the registered manager of the nonprofit agency, Huang was becoming known as someone who could help workers calculate wages to ensure fair payment, advise them on their legal rights, or help them file private lawsuits, which are the main tool for settling serious grievances with Chinese employers. "Production line workers perhaps do not understand the new law. What we did was just popularize the law," explains Dagongzhe staffer Luo Chunli. "Honestly speaking, companies want to stop us from promoting the law. They are afraid that more workers will fight for their legal rights." Research done in 2007 by China's *Jinan Daily* estimated that 80 percent of all migrant workers "did not know what a labor contract was."

Huang and his fellow advocates had inadvertently tapped into one of the biggest domestic issues in China's twenty-first century: Migrants are the backbone of the economy, making up 70 percent of construction workers, 68 percent of manufacturing employees, and 80 percent of coal miners. (In 2007, Amnesty International reported that approximately 90 percent of workers suffering from workplace-related diseases were migrants; and 80 percent of those who died in mining, construction, and chemical factories were migrants.)

Thanks partially to resource centers like Dagongzhe, migrants have become more militant because many are better educated than first-wave migrants of the 1980s. Many predicted that China's new labor reforms, which came into full effect in mid-2008, would be a disaster for business. In one full-page ad in the *Hong Kong Economic Journal*, a group of local business leaders claimed that the law was making workers "uncooperative" and that activists were exploiting its terms to disrupt production. Another group claimed the new law would be responsible for the closure of 10,000 businesses across Guangdong Province alone. Even before the 2008 reforms, Guangdong had already lost thousands of factories to cost increases, much to the gain of inland provinces like Hunan.

Business had good reason to fear the reforms because an avalanche of legal activism and lawsuits had already begun. As local media reported, the Dagongzhe worker center had "successfully helped workers file a large number of severance pay claims. It now seems that targeted attacks on legal activists like Huang—as distinct from the use of hired thugs to break up wild-cat strikes—may constitute a new stage of retaliation. Local observers speculate on possible collusion between employers and police, government officers or organized crime syndicates in these attacks."

In the end, China's government increased the minimum wage in central Shenzhen by 17.6 percent, despite the fact that China's urban wages had already more than doubled between 1990 and 2004. This is how a dusty little storefront offering legal advice had become dangerous enough to merit an anonymous mob hit. People are fighting over the last dollar as pressures grow. A month earlier, hired thugs had twice smashed windows and desks at the Dagongzhe Center with steel pipes. Without explanation, they tore through the tiny storefront, thankfully sparing the center's sole computer. On the second visit, there was a message: "I'm telling you not to open the center!" shouted one of the gang members. About the same time, Li Jinxin, an assistant with a Shenzhen law firm, was kidnapped and beaten with steel pipes. "[Employers] wish we did not exist." explained Li, who suffered a broken leg and other blunt-force injuries. According to a 2008 United Nations Human Rights Council report, "there were three policemen on patrol outside the offices at the time of the attack who looked on without taking any action against the attackers."

Ultimately, street violence and criminal activity are not the issue. What vexes China isn't insufficient security—after all, it's not hard to find security forces in a police state—but the social and political decay that authorities have attempted to remedy with special economic zones, malls, and lots of jobs.

The main worry for activists like Han Dongfang isn't the dictatorship of the big-box, but the erosion of China's central government and an emerging group of political and economic warlords within the CPC that could be even worse than current plutocrats. Corrupt local officials, well-connected industrialists, and savvy party operatives are well-positioned to exploit any sort of failure in China's monolithic party structure. "The Communist Party is a huge monster, and once it loses control, it will be controlled by local interests." Even China's well-funded army, says the former soldier, cannot be trusted. "What will the army do?" Han asks, worried about the future. "The central Communist Party will lose credibility when enough people can't eat. And who will be the new rulers? The corrupted people. Even worse, they will use democracy to campaign for themselves. After the Communist Party, the country will be ruled by a mafia."

This is a difficult admission for someone who spent several hard years in prison for his role as a democracy advocate and labor organizer in 1989. And, after being tortured, nearly succumbing to drug-resistant TB and losing a lung in prison, Han has lived in partial exile in Hong Kong since 1997, unable to cross over onto the Chinese mainland into Shenzhen and beyond. He notes that poverty, epic corruption and poor working conditions troubled China in the days before students and citizens challenged the government at Tiananmen. During the summer of 1989, some 10 million Chinese were unemployed. "The explosion may eventually come," Han says, looking back on his decade-long crusade for rights and accountability. "People hate their local officials and the local officials hate the central government, which is trying to protect itself. That is why there is so much fighting."

China's Communist Party has been crushing all possible domestic opposition ever since Mao arrived in Beijing. "Because the party knows from its own successful experience 60 years ago that a small but dedicated protest group can take over and control an entire country, it can never let its guard down," writes John Fraser, longtime China watcher. "Not once. Not ever."

Consequently, the calcified, top-down CPC of previous decades does not necessarily have the capacity to manage the complex issues of the twenty-first century. It is very difficult to make reform happen, even initiatives that could help the Communist Party save itself. Within China, activists, intellectuals, and lawyers face severe constraints; fines, prison time, and persecution await anyone who steps outside of an unclear set of official boundaries—someone like Han Dongfang, for example, who formed China's first illegal independent union at Tiananmen Square in 1989.

Yet it was the government that authored the 2008 labor reforms in the first place, and it is the government that also controls the country's only authorized union that represents workers. Even the legal right to strike was floated as a possibility by the Shantou chapter of China's official union in 2008. "This law is beneficial to the job stability for migrant workers," explained Wang Chunguang, of the Chinese Academy of Social Sciences in 2008. "For the entire society's development, this large mobile population should be stabilized, and the premise of that is stable employment."

China's labor reforms had much to do with transferring additional wealth to its vulnerable and explosive migrant population, who comprise an estimated one-third of the population of China's capital city, Beijing, and nearly half of Shenzhen's estimated eight million. Faced with a nascent political movement, China chose to raise wages at the expense of consumers worldwide. Labor reforms and legal accountability are the very things that may well save China from itself—yet at no small cost to corporations and consumers who depend on cheap exports.

Although "some employers continue to turn a blind eye to the new law," Shenzhen Dagongzhe Migrant Worker Center reported in a 2009, it represents a 180-degree turn of events that has affected not only China, but the whole global supply chain. In July 2008, for example, Wal-Mart quietly announced its first-ever collective agreement with a Chinese union in the northeastern town of Shenyang. Not only is the world's largest company the begrudging host to Chinese unions, it also conceded significant wage increases to China's government-controlled union, 8 percent annually until 2009, increases well beyond anything conceded to most workers in North America and Europe.

With over 200 million members, the All-China Federation of Trade Unions (ACFTU) is the world's largest union. It has represented Wal-Mart's 40,000 Chinese retail workers since 2006. "The pressure of workers' actions is changing the legislative landscape in China," confirmed Han Dongfang as he spoke to a US Congressional hearing in 2008. "Laws are being amended to better serve workers' interests."

Major export manufacturers such as Foxconn, which is Shenzhen's largest foreign-owned enterprise, have been similarly targeted. Government-approved unionists approached the electronics giant early in 2007, launching a street-level campaign outside the Longhua Street compounds where many of Foxconn's 200,000 workers live. Chinese unionists canvassed in front of Hui Long Supermarket, imploring Foxconn workers to become union members. "Union cards were issued on the spot," reported *The Beijing News*. "And by midday, the creation of the Foxconn [union] branch was announced."

After KFC, McDonalds, and Pizza Hut were discovered to be paying illegally low wages in 2007, it was the ACFTU that struck an agreement to unionize all outlets across China. And as with Wal-Mart's new wage concessions, the relationship is no longer docile and subservient. ("We are not setting up this union just to have a union," said one KFC worker. "The key issue for us is to form an effective union.")

In KFC's Hubei province outlets, vestiges of independent, local union organizing emerged, precisely the kind of freedom of expression and political activism that has been met with jailings, torture or persecution ever since Mao took power in 1949. "Its significance was extraordinary," reported China Youth Daily in 2008. "Unions at all levels, and the Party and government administration in all localities all unequivocally agree that the interests and dignity of our workers and our national legal system cannot be sacrificed in exchange for foreign investment."

The process that is tipping the balance against "foreign investment" and in favor of Chinese workers actually began at a Wal-Mart outlet in Fujian province in 2006, when China's state union first attempted to unionize the world's most anti-union company. It's a little-known piece of recent history that shows how much things have changed. Much like the failed attempt to organize unions at Wal-Mart, this effort was a covert and grassroots assault on Wal-Mart's monopoly on management. And it was orchestrated with uncharacteristic effectiveness by China's state union. "To force Wal-Mart to establish a trade union, the ACFTU went to the grassroots and covertly organized a small group of workers to apply to set up a union in one of Wal-Mart's stores in Quanzhou City," reports China Labor Translations. "This was the first time that the ACFTU had started the process of union-building from the bottom-up."

The effort was so successful that China's state union decided to unionize all Wal-Mart stores in the same manner, affecting 50,000 Wal-Mart China employees. Faced with defeat, Wal-Mart "chose to formally cooperate with the ACFTU in establishing workplace unions in every Wal-Mart store in China." Consequently, the "Five-Point Memorandum" drafted by Wal-Mart's China head office and union representatives in August 2006 formed the basis for "an open and fair election process" for each and every local-store union committee; it was a grassroots process that ensured national collective agreements and unprecedented wage hikes from 2008 onward. If Wal-Mart China wanted to close stores, lay off workers, or make changes to its operations, it would have to consult the world's largest union, founded in 1925.

Li Qiang regularly travels China to inspect factories and interview workers. As director of New York-based China Labor Watch, he continues to marvel at his country's strange mix of authoritarian rule, free-market capitalism, and re-emergent socialism. It's a new economic model that doesn't follow any previous pattern. Rights and freedoms granted as an economic tool can just as easily be cancelled if foreign investors or global retailers need new incentives. "It's not that workers don't have any rights," he says. "It's that we still ultimately have no way to influence government." China's nongovernmental agencies and civil-society advocates are still either closely watched or outlawed completely. "The law improves labor conditions, but does not provide workers with more power."

And reforms can be used to hide abuses. At one Wal-Mart shoe factory that Li inspected in 2008—Shenzhen's Hantai Shoe Production Ltd.—the union chair is actually a Taiwanese manager who routinely requires workers to work unpaid overtime. "There is no workers' committee, workers' representatives are not elected by workers, and the union has never had to hold any events or protect workers' rights," he says. "The union's establishment is merely a decoration to pass the clients' audits." Most of the 5,000 workers at the suburban factory are required to pay 32 percent of their base monthly wages for food and dormitory lodging; many workers are not permitted food or bathroom usage during shifts; and poor ventilation and blocked emergency exits threaten the health of workers. The company hires security officers to protect workers, yet "securities often attack workers physically at workshop, canteen, and dormitory."

So, even years after Wal-Mart and other multinationals pledged improvements, sweatshop conditions still prevail for migrants who glue and stitch children's footwear for the world's largest company. As Li reports, even though an official Wal-Mart audit of Hantai occurred a few months prior to his inspection, "no conditions were improved," although factory management did post a list of official Wal-Mart regulations.

But this is the strange truth. KFC, Wal-Mart, and McDonald's helped save the revolution by doing precisely what they have often refused to do at home: implement better wages, workplace democracy, and greater accountability. By late 2008, the ACFTU had launched a national campaign that proposed to unionize an estimated 80 percent of the largest foreign companies operating in China, with the goal of having all non-state-owned companies unionized by 2010. Nonconforming companies will be blacklisted by the party and subject to audits, tax investigations, and possible prosecution, making any resistance to unionization within China essentially illegal.

Regardless of whether these reforms and wage increases will survive a global economic collapse doesn't change the fact that China needs to keep more money at home. Having made itself the world Mecca of bargains, it has begun to nationalize its price advantage through labor, environmental, and social reforms, as well as an ever-changing web of tariffs and currency adjustments. The value that was once passed along to consumers is increasingly retained within China's economy, something that is designed to increase the collective wealth of China at the expense of foreign operators and distant consumers.

Why many foreign corporations persist and endure is simply because they badly need China. The average Chinese citizen still only spends half as much as he or she saves, as opposed to many Western consumers who are barely above zero net worth, if at all. That net 50 percent income of savings on 800 million working Chinese is capitalism's holy grail in the twenty-first century. And if accessing that pool of consumer capital means hosting communist unions, swearing an oath to Mao Zedong's memory, or blood sacrifice, there's a pretty good chance that the world's leading service sector corporations would agree.

After fighting vehement battles against worker organizing and activism everywhere else, Wal-Mart was remarkably understated about opening its doors to the world's largest union. "We have a good relationship working with the union," said Jonathan Dong of Wal-Mart China. "The union provides a complement to what we do."

The Beginning of the End of Cheap

In a coastal town near Shanghai, an old friend of mine recalls his days working in a Shenzhen toy factory. It was during the mid-1990s, and he had just graduated university with a degree that wasn't particularly valuable. So he rode a hard-seat train for two days, arrived in Shenzhen, and found work immediately. "It was a job, not very fun," he says. We first met soon after I arrived at his provincial university to study Mandarin language as a foreign exchange student in 1989. Like many Chinese of his generation, he's not jumping up and down ranting about labor abuses or lamenting globalization. It was a job, nothing special, and his recollection sounds a lot like North American kids who worked in a warehouse or washed dishes for summer pay. "Long hours, boring, bad food."

Most Westerners might not last the marathon train ride on a hard Chinese train seat, let alone suffer the working conditions in Shenzhen's factory complexes. His understatement belies the discomfort and long hours that many mainlanders manage without complaint to make a better life for themselves and their families. And thanks to a mildly profitable stay in Shenzhen, he's about to buy his first house, and may one day marry his girlfriend. His career prospects are solid. For him, a sojourn in Shenzhen was a transition—and the world that Wal-Mart and Deng Xiaoping helped build hasn't been without benefit.

But factory labor may have been a permanent prospect if he'd been any more active in the failed democracy movement of May and June 1989, where we became friends as we swarmed the streets along with thousands of other students in one of a hundred mini-uprisings across China inspired by the students at Tiananmen Square. It was the spring of a lifetime as we cut classes, drank tea, and translated slogans. Our university town, while a thousand miles from Tiananmen, still topped 10,000 in the city square before the army massacred thousands in the capital. Then we all scattered. And I returned years later to see what was left behind. "Many of my classmates who were ringleaders still have trouble with the government," he says. "They cannot advance in their jobs and must work for others if they want to succeed. I can talk about this now because we are old and do not have connection with these things anymore." Tiananmen, like Shenzhen, is behind him. He, like others of his generation—the generation that now manages and owns factories as well as works in them—are getting on with their lives.

Years later, we sit together in a chic Taoist teahouse in the same coastal city, catching up on old times, only a train ride away from the incredible glass towers and high-priced designer malls of Shanghai. We're no longer students in a would-be revolution, echoing cries of *minzhu* (democracy) in a crowd of thousands. He has a cell phone, a house, and, I'm guessing, a much larger TV than mine. In this nation of peasants, his arrival into the middle classes from Tiananmen via Shenzhen is China's version of the American Dream.

Just like my old schoolmate, China doesn't really want to build cheap stuff anymore. It wants your job as consumer. In 2007, for the first time, domestic consumption contributed more to China's economic growth than foreign exports (domestic consumption was 37 percent of China's GDP, while foreign demand/net exports were 21.4 percent).

In other words, the very thing that kick-started China's emergence out of the dark days of the 1970s—foreign capital and export manufacture—is slowly being eclipsed by the emergence of other priorities, not the least a Western-style consumer economy. "This is a healthy development trend," argued Shi Jianhuai, of Peking University's School of Economics. "We cannot depend on foreign demand (for economic growth) in such a big economy as China."

This is an important juncture. China's national interests are diverging from those of its major trading partners, not diverging just in terms of export trade, but also energy supplies, currency reserves, and international development. Many Chinese have assumed this from the beginning, knowing that they would not forever manufacture Malibu Barbie or Tickle Me Elmo. Westerners have been slow to recognize this. "The Chinese government is attempting to decrease the gap between rich and poor in China by using rights and legislation as a tool for economic policy," says Li Qiang. "Chinese goods will become more expensive, but the transition from manufacturing to consumerism is an essential path in the view of government."

China's logical trajectory is deglobalization. And in so doing, become the superpower that many predicted it would become. In other words, China cannot reach its goals by continuing to improve the living standards of its trading partners. And as crises emerge in the twenty-first century, the nation's ruling class may be forced to diverge or decouple quicker than Western nations expected.

The end of cheap will not be sudden, but it has already begun. China's move to higher-value products is one aspect since margins on iPhones are better than dollar-store trinkets. China's often-neglected social and environmental problems now create additional drag on Western bargains, as China can no longer fully internalize these costs. (The World Health Organization estimated that excessive air pollution alone eliminated $79 billion of China's GDP in 2000.) Predictably, China has taken a harder line on trade and currency management, which trading partners have long alleged has been undervalued, giving China an unfair trade advantage.

China has been gradually putting the screws to foreign investment and exporters, even as labor costs increased during the start of the century. In 2007, Beijing selectively cut export subsidies, "eliminating rebates...for more than 500 types of high-polluting goods such as fertilizer and leather," reported *Business Week* in 2007, "while further whittling down rates for some 2,800 other low-tech products."

In 2008 China opposed all developed nations in the World Trade Organization on agricultural free trade, effectively undermining seven years of talks. Although it had been eager since the 1990s to join the WTO to gain benefits of greater trade liberalization, China (along with India) would eventually choose instead to protect its farmers against agricultural imports, claiming "a food-security policy of relying on domestic supply" in the face of global rice shortages and depressed rural income. After an estimated 20 million Chinese farmers were evicted between 1992 and 2005 due to land development, China's government claimed it would protect its 750 million rural residents, even at the expense of international trade. Chinese farmers now benefit from additional protections, such as limits on industrial development and the conversion of farmland to factories. In the past, the United States, the EU, Canada, and Japan dominated trade talks. China emerged as an advocate of third-world economies, demanding and largely receiving the dual right for food protectionism as well as continued free trade in goods, much to the dismay of Western nations. "It is a massive blow to confidence in the global economy," claimed Peter Power of the European Commission. "The confidence shot in the arm that we needed badly will not now happen."

Another, potentially huge, consideration is that China, like many other nation investors, was badly burned by its American investments in the early days of the global economic crisis. Will it continue to purchase American debt as an investment? The future of globalization appears to hang on this one question alone.

As James Fallows noted in 2008, much of the $1.4 trillion of China's trade surplus is held as U.S. Treasury notes, which are debt-financing instruments issued by the American government. This, in turn, has allowed Americans to not only finance large government deficits—spending on the Iraq War and bank bailouts—but it has also enabled the continuation of large trade imbalances in general by creating the illusion of stability. "Like so many imbalances in economics, this one can't go on indefinitely, and therefore won't," writes Fallows. "But the way it ends—suddenly versus gradually, for predictable reasons versus during a panic—will make an enormous difference to the U.S. and Chinese economies over the next few years, to say nothing of bystanders in Europe and elsewhere."

This is how the economic DNA of nations has been rewritten. One side of the earth produced a growing range of goods, and the other side consumed them. In the United States, household consumption expenditure nearly doubled between 1990 and 2001, while at the same time, the American trade deficit increased almost fivefold. (In particular, America's trade deficit with China soared to $177.47 billion in 2006 from $102 billion in 2005, and had advanced to $183 billion by 2008.)

It has been assumed that this severe confluence of economies—or "Chimerica" as economist Niall Ferguson describes it—is the trade equivalent of mutually assured destruction. It won't fail because no one can afford failure. Because about 30 percent of America's trade imbalance comes from Chinese imports, the Middle Kingdom knows well that it would be unwise to sabotage the U.S. consumer economy. Moreover, U.S. dollars account for an estimated 70 percent of China's holdings, the largest foreign reserves in the world, and any major move against America could massively devalue China's incredible nest egg. Much depends on how these countries manage their currencies and how much additional debt they create. But tough times have caused strains as well as unprecedented new public and private debt, and as of 2009, America wasn't as great the investment it used to be. The United States "should make the Chinese feel confident that the value of [its American] assets at least will not be eroded in a significant way," said Yu Yongding, former adviser to China's central bank, in 2009, who scolded America for "reckless policies."

In many ways, the trade imbalance is no longer about trade. It is about power and wealth transfer. Networked commerce has resulted in the creation of soft empires, zones of influence and connection that overlap between nations, governments, and companies. For example, the American and Chinese governments and major retailers like Wal-Mart have power and influence well beyond their respective jurisdictions, yet none enjoys full independence. We are still not sure what this means in broad historical terms, but it is significant. "The integration of the four-fifths of the world that is poor with the one-fifth that is wealthy has the potential to be one of the two or three most important economic developments of the past millennium, along with the Renaissance and the Industrial Revolution," argued Harvard economist Lawrence Summers in 2006.

For all its strength as the world's largest country, sitting on top of the world's largest pile of money, China's position as the world's next superpower is surprisingly tentative. In part, China gained strength in the world precisely because it managed to mitigate, defer, and obscure the consequences of unsustainable growth. For over three decades, East and West alike enjoyed a free ride on pollution, social strife, violence, and poverty. But these impacts have most dramatically accrued in China and its government has used up considerable capital, resilience, and goodwill in an impressive attempt to manage the unmanageable.

China is leveraged, but not in the same way as its cash-poor trading partners. In broader terms, it is dangerously top-heavy, since the labor, resource, and environmental capital at the bottom of its economy have eroded. And China has depended on growth—peaking at 11.9 percent in 2007—and the trickle-down effect of new wealth to smooth over the cracks and cleavages that still define its foundations.

In hindsight, China's growth strategy was a gambit on the scale that may not be witnessed for another generation. For years, China was the turn-around story in market-based poverty reduction development. ("Growth of about 9 percent per annum since the late 1970s has helped to lift several hundred million people out of absolute poverty, with the result that China alone accounted for over 75 percent of poverty reduction in the developing world over the last 20 years," claimed the World Bank in a 2005 brief.) But as economies slowed and became more expensive, these market-based gains eroded as well. This was felt not just in China but everywhere, including the estimated 400 million poor in India, and the price-shocked population of Vietnam, who suffered through Asia's worst inflation of 27 percent in 2008.

Now that much of globalization's easy growth is behind us, China's underclass persists, better off than when Mao came to power in 1950, but not improved enough to guarantee stability in the twenty-first century. It turns out that the number of chronically poor may have been vastly underestimated all along—three times that of estimates from the mid-2000s—suggesting that the long-term benefits of globalization and rapid growth are neither as large nor as lasting as expected. "The number of people in China living below the World Bank's dollar-a-day poverty line is 300 million, three times larger than currently estimated," argued leading China commentator Albert Keidel of the Carnegie Endowment for International Peace in 2007. "This more accurate picture of China clarifies why Beijing concentrates so heavily on domestic priorities such as growth, public investment, pollution control and poverty reduction." Keidel recalls that back in the1980s and 1990s, China's dollar-a-day poverty count was likely more than 500 million people. "China has made enormous strides in lifting its population out of poverty," he concludes. "But the task was perhaps more gargantuan than most people thought and progress has been overstated."

China's addiction to economic growth is its defining national liability, in the same way that America and other nations are saddled with debt and financial instability. China's fear of political dissolution through insufficient growth propels the divergence between trading nations, a profound rift at the very heart of globalization. For these and other reasons, the late 1990s probably represented the peak of China's capacity to deliver profit, savings, and incredible volume to Western consumers with minimal risk or negative consequence. These days, nations and investors would be wise to place a risk premium on China. The government's demonstrated resistance to incremental, bottom-up reform is precisely why many observers fear sudden regime change or collapse. Much like the fear of non-linear, rapid change demonstrated in stressed natural systems, China's problematic and highly asymmetrical power structures threatens a similar modal shift studied in climate change science. If it falls, it likely falls big. But instead of melting polar icecaps leading to catastrophic sea rise or rapid temperature gains, China threatens a different sort of change, and not a nice one, either: abrupt, disruptive, and, likely, violent. This of course would cause economic crisis elsewhere, especially considering China's part ownership of the American economy and integration with Europe, Canada, and the rest of Asia. Even China's energy partners in Africa would suffer greatly. In other words, growth without accountability is ultimately problematic, and a random shift within China's simmering internal crisis could sabotage Western economies well before environmental impacts, energy costs, and trade deficits stem the flow of bargains.

Sudden, disruptive change is hardly a rarity in Chinese history. The day before the 1989 massacre at Tiananmen Square that claimed between 800 and 3,000 lives, my Chinese pal decided to show me his family home. As student protests raged on the streets outside and across China, we wandered into a maze of old *hutongs*, mud and brick apartments that surrounded a tiny courtyard. Inside, where his grandmother once lived after previous generations toiled in the countryside, we sat at a tiny square table, drank tea, and he unveiled his prize possession, a 26-inch color television, something that, in 1989, probably cost him dearly. There was no electricity, but we sat there and stared at it anyway.

A day later, China's ruling class turned away from reform, and police and army forces marched to violently quell protests across the country. Former protesters became shoppers and workers. Televisions became larger, cheaper, and more plentiful. Wal-Mart, McDonalds, and Carrefour came calling and students studied business and got jobs and largely forgot dreamy, dangerous notions of a democratic China. After the tanks rolled in Beijing, I remember wandering the streets near Shanghai, buses were overturned, barricades were erected—students had temporarily locked down the city in protest for the killing at Tiananmen. Mostly, the streets were empty, and some of the protesters were already in hiding. It felt as if the whole country had been wiped clean.

The lowly bargain helped build a new empire, yet it is the bargain that heralds the end of an intense but surprisingly short chapter in the history of human development. We rewired global trade and employment, to a significant degree, to leverage a labor resource that is no longer stable. In the process, China and other cheap producers helped insulate many consumers from the consequences of growth and scarcity.

The trouble is, China has now made it clear that it no longer wants that role. It's a risky proposition for everyone involved.

CHAPTER 4

SUPPLY CHAIN NATION

CARGO CULTS OF THE TWENTY-FIRST CENTURY

An Economy on the Docks

From out on the Pacific Ocean, a giant container ship approaches the harbor of North America's busiest port. More like a motorized island than a ship, the Oriental Overseas Container Line (OOCL) *Tianjin* is over 1,000 feet long, 140 feet wide, and more than ten stories high from sea level to bridge tower. Guided by global positioning satellites (GPS), thousands of on-board sensors, and remote video cameras, the ship's pilots carefully steer the vessel into dock at Pier F. Heading north from Hong Kong, up past Japan toward the Aleutian Islands south of Alaska, the *Tianjin* has circled the Pacific Rim and then headed south to here, the combined ports of Los Angeles and Long Beach.

As it settles into dock, the *Tianjin's* massive hull eclipses the horizon. A vessel of this class, one that is too large to fit inside the Panama Canal, sails around the world seven or eight times each year, arriving from Asia full of cargo and returning to the East nearly empty, save for paper and metal recycling. In less than eight hours, the *Tianjin* will unload nearly 8,000 steel containers, each 20- to 40-feet long, that are filled with consumer goods that will, in turn, be loaded onto rail cars and trucks and hauled inland to distribution centers and retail outlets as far as New York, Toronto, and Chicago.

Less than 100 years ago, the port was 800 acres of mudflats at the mouth of the Los Angeles River. But now the area consists of 43 miles of modern harbor, encompassing a total of 15,100 acres of wharves, cargo terminals, cruise-ship docks, roadways, rail yards, and shipping channels that collectively move 11 million containers annually. Past civilizations built pyramids and temples as a testament to their ingenuity and affluence. Today, we move shipping containers on a monumental scale instead.

Beginning in 1980s, our booming trade with Pacific Rim nations turned major port cities like Los Angeles into transport thoroughfares clogged with gigantic container ships, endless trains of intermodal containers, and vast transport-truck fleets that roamed the Interstates the way that bison once roamed the prairie. Amazingly, nearly half of all American container trade manages to travel through Los Angeles, the continent's most congested and traffic-dysfunctional megalopolis. Many people, locals included, would be surprised to learn that goods movement—not tourism or movies—has been one of California's biggest sources of new employment in recent decades, with nearly 900,000 jobs connected to trade activity in 2007.

Consequently, transport just isn't transport in today's world: it is a force multiplier that unlocked new profit, speed, and a cornacopic flood of affordable products that launched globalization into overdrive. In today's global shopping economy, advances like offshore labor, petrochemicals, and credit cards are only enabled and rendered meaningful with modern logistics networks, constellations of technology, and transport hardware that made the earth appear nearly flat with speed, complexity, and affordability. The most successful firms are those that have been able to harness these resources, like Wal-Mart, one of the most resilient corporations of our day.

Yet the transportation solutions of the twentieth century have created new problems. Here in Los Angeles, the persistent soot and haze created by the nonstop transport of goods account for as much as one-third of the city's notorious air pollution. Even during prosperous economic times, Los Angeles's transport-dominated economy was battered by everything from environmental protests to cutthroat global competition for the cheapest shipping rates. When consumer demand began to fall in 2008, containers, cars, and recycling began to pile up in and around the dockyards, and the delicate balance in the Los Angeles's high-volume, low-margin economy began to tilt, in no small way contributing to its struggles with insolvency. Facing over 10 percent unemployment in 2009, California's economy, once seen as a beacon of innovation, was crashing like a played-out resource economy from the previous century, not unlike the frontier oil booms that once defined Los Angeles's waterfront.

Moreover, the shape of global commerce itself is proving to be less than flat. *Wired* magazine famously named the shipping container the "20-ton packet," yet the globalization-as-flat-network metaphor was easier to sustain during the 1990s, when resources and fuel were cheaper than they were in the 2000s. The paradox is that our web of trade and transport is dynamic but often fiercely exclusionary. The pursuit of maximum cheap has meant the creation of larger ports, tighter production clusters, as well as broader trade and currency practices that can discriminate against the cities, countries, and producers that can't compete with the kind of massive economies of scale on display in Los Angeles, Hong Kong, and Rotterdam.

Yet the scene on the docks after the OOCL *Tianjin* docks in the Los Angeles harbor looks pretty routine. Its cargo of two-ton containers is briskly unloaded onto trucks or trains waiting to complete the rest of their journey. Empty ships leave the harbor, and new ones, laden low with new shipments, arrive to unload again. And so it continues, even in the wake of a global economic crisis, partially because there is not yet another plan for the future. You'd never guess that toys covered in lead paint and toothpaste laced with antifreeze chemicals rolled through here not long ago. Or that America's Homeland Security Department can't reliably monitor for dirty nuclear bombs inside containers that could detonate anywhere between here and Duluth.

City of Containers

In the middle of the harbor front, the looming 5,000-foot span of the Gerald Desmond Bridge connects Terminal Island to Long Beach Harbor and one of America's busiest trucking routes, Interstate 710. The bridge has a vertical clearance of 200 feet, but even that is too small for the largest ships. Some ships actually wait for low tide before crossing underneath to gain a few feet of safe clearance. Above, up on the road, container trucks haul past, launching up the incline of the bridge deck and racing down the other side. An estimated 20 percent of America's container traffic passes under this bridge.

But the George Desmond Bridge, the city's "official welcoming monument," is falling apart. It has been crumbling for years, and blocks of concrete occasionally fall off and crash into the ocean below. This huge span isn't adequate: Port advocates say that Los Angeles needs a new bridge system to keep the truck traffic moving, one with four lanes instead of two. At last report, replacing the bridge will cost $800 million. In the meantime, engineers have hung netting beneath the bridge in an effort to catch the larger chunks of concrete. No wonder everyone seems to be in a rush to get away.

Getting out of the port itself is just the beginning. Anyone who drives northbound Interstate 710 out of the harbor knows how congested the traffic is. Drivers can easily get lost in the sea of trailer-bound containers trying to escape the harbor, much like guppies among whales. The rumbling stampede of semis (their drivers exit the port with surprising velocity), which is blamed for everything from the increase in pollution-related deaths to road accidents, is actually part of a highly orchestrated flow of rail and road traffic leaving the harbor 24 hours a day. Miles inland, one is still surrounded by containers. There are the intermodal yards, large staging grounds where the containers will be lifted from the truck beds and loaded onto railway cars to begin the next leg of their journey. Across the Inland Empire, southeast California's second-largest metropolitan region, and beyond, are the warehouses and transshipment docks where containers are unloaded, repacked with goods, and sent directly on to retail stores or even larger regional distribution centers. Inland ports—distant staging grounds connected by rail—have been proposed at Antelope Valley on the edge of the Southwest's Mojave Desert over 70 miles from the harbor. "There is no land to expand the port facilities," argued one government planner in 2007. "You need at least 500 acres for a decent inland port facility, and that kind of land is not available in the urban core."

And when this not-so-graceful ballet of rigs, ships, and trains jams up, the results can be surprisingly devastating. The Ports of Los Angeles and Long Beach have experienced repeated major delays, including a record overflow in 2004 of 100 ships backed up out of the harbor or diverted. The gridlock froze one-third of all American imports at the time, costing as much as $4 billion. One industry trade magazine reported that, "[In 2004,] the Port of Long Beach compared the scene to the World War II invasion of Normandy." In a world of lean inventories, just-in-time production, and high demand, delays cause considerable trouble and expense. A single day's delay at Los Angeles cost the port's clients and trading partners $37 million in carrying costs, $15 million of which was shouldered by China.

Los Angeles has suffered in the past because of congestion. Some ships, following Wal-Mart's lead, now circumnavigate Central America and cross the Panama Canal for Atlantic-side ports along the Gulf of Mexico and the eastern seaboard to gain nominal time savings. In the upside-down world of global transport, many bargains now travel further to arrive sooner.

* * *

Anthony Otto, vice president of OOCL's Long Beach Container Terminal, looks down from an office three stories above the pier and marvels at how much has changed since he first entered the business some 23 years ago. As late as the 1970s, many ships still loaded and unloaded bulk goods and individual boxes, barrels, and pallets. It was the Dark Ages in shipping, before simply putting cargo inside standardized steel boxes created huge savings in costs and shipping speed. "At the time, everyone knew that containerization was growing, but it was not anywhere near the magnitude that it is today," says Otto. "Since then, it has quadrupled in size. Everything got bigger. You've got ships that continue to get bigger and bigger and more 40- and 45-foot long containers," says Otto. "Terminals, big terminals were built quickly; anyone who wanted to sign up for one, anyone who felt they could fill it with international freight, containerized cargo—a terminal was relatively easy to come by."

During a three-decade growth spurt that closed the twentieth century, the Bay of San Pedro on the coast of Southern California, where today's Port of Los Angeles and Port of Long Beach are located, was gradually filled with larger piers, warehouses, cranes, and fuel facilities. Pier F was built in 1965 on the world's largest landfill to date, some 310 acres created out of shallow ocean with 3.35 million tons of rock. On nearby Pier G, Sea-Land Services, Inc. began operating in 1962, introducing an innovative new cargo-handling system using steel boxes. The process became known as containerization— goods, materials, and parts could now be packed into 20- and 40-foot long steel containers.

The precontainer "break-bulk" system of cargo in ship holds dated back to the days of the Phoenicians. Until 1956 when the American entrepreneur Malcolm McLean launched the successful voyage of the Ideal-X container ship from Newark to Houston, it was not unusual for a shipment to incur as much as 50 percent of its costs for a few kilometers of travel portside on either end of its journey: piece-by-piece freight handling was time-consuming and labor intensive. The steel box revolutionized the shipping industry. The process has grown increasingly automated, with cranes, cars, and GPS tracking making it possible to load or unload a single container every one to four minutes. According to the Matson Navigation Company, containerization increased the productivity of the shipping industry, measured on tons of goods moved per working hour, 6,752 percent between 1959 and 1976. It eliminated jobs, accelerated cargo, and average port time shrunk from three weeks to 18 hours.

"Consider the economics," says historian Marc Levinson, author of *The Box*, a popular history of containerization. "Loading loose cargo [was] a back-breaking, laborious business." In 1956, the average medium-sized ship would cost $5.83 a ton, yet on McLean's *Ideal-X*, the world's very first container ship, the cost was already less than $0.16 a ton. "All of a sudden, the cost of shipping products to another destination was no longer prohibitively expensive."

By 1979, the Port of Long Beach had converted most of its facilities to move containers and automobiles, mostly incoming. That same year, Hanjin Container Lines launched regular shipping between Asia and Los Angeles harbor. Within two years, China Ocean Shipping (Group) Company (COSCO), which is wholly owned by the Chinese government, made Long Beach its very first port of call. It went on to become one of the world's largest shipping companies. The local transport industry grew to include air freight, as evidenced by the growth of nearby LAX (Los Angeles Airport), which today is the world's fourth busiest airport, carrying more than 2 million tons of air cargo shipments in 2003. Commerce accelerated as advanced logistics networks evolved in step with containerization to enable all kinds of just-in-time manufacturing and retailing. And, as discounting gradually overtook retailing, Los Angeles harbor grew. Now it is a port where post-Panamax vessels, too large to fit the 110-foot width of the Panama Canal, are commonplace.

But what happens in Los Angeles is just the tip of the iceberg. Global logistics expenditure in 2002 was estimated by Michigan State University to be approximately $6.7 trillion, up from $5 trillion in 1997. This figure suggests that nearly 14 percent of the world economy (by GDP) is given over to fleets of trucks, airplanes, and container ships.

The transport of consumer goods has become a major industry, on a par with one of the world's largest national economies after the European Union and the United States. Greenhouse-gas emissions from international shipping now exceed the total emissions of most nations listed in the Kyoto protocol. Moreover, with the massive clouds of air pollution that float over the Pacific Ocean from Asia's factories and power plants, changing hemispheric weather patterns and raining emissions down on North American shoppers, it is clear that our world has become connected in ways that defy categorization.

Another obvious outcome has been the trade imbalances. Between 1990 and 2001, for example, the American trade deficit increased fivefold. Other Western nations followed suit with smaller but still significant imbalances. And at the same time, Chinese trade increased twice as fast as that of average growth of world trade.

Yet it hardly happened by accident. While the Pacific Rim nations claimed the largest collective GDP output, they also claimed the largest logistics expenditures during much of the 2000s, beating both Europe and North America, and opened up access to cheap and higher-value labor of China. A major factor in creating the new dominance of the East is the fact that China, Vietnam, Korea, and Japan invested in transport. In 2002, for example, these nations spent 40 percent more on logistics compared to North America and Europe, even though the value of overall economic output was no greater than 11 percent difference.

Asian trade now accounts for more than 90 percent of incoming shipments at Los Angeles/Long Beach. And as of 2003, the top 12 importers of containers here were major retailers, and ten of these were discounters: Wal-Mart, Home Depot, Target, Lowe's, Kmart, IKEA, Payless Shoes, Pier 1 Imports,

Big Lots, Toys "R" Us, Limited Brands, and Michaels. In other words, a significant portion of Southern California's economy is now dedicated to unloading ships from China, Vietnam, and Japan that, in turn, fill big-box stores throughout North America.

Container traffic in Los Angles has become a major economic indicator. "Southern California is key for most of the carriers, but also, it is the gateway for 70 percent of the intermodal freight going everywhere else in the country," explains Anthony Otto. "So even though it seems like you have the most dense population, it makes sense from a logistics perspective." Los Angeles delivers an amazing amount of international trade across the continent: Chicago receives 60 percent of its imported goods through Los Angeles, for example, inside steel boxes containing everything from medical supplies to consumer electronics, kitchen utensils, designer clothing, power tools, and automotive parts. On any given day, Anthony Otto or anyone else working on the docks can glance up and know that their next microwave oven or set of golf clubs may be floating by, inside a 100-foot stack of containers.

Somehow, a surprising amount of North American prosperity—and a significant percentage of its incoming bargains—still depends on moving a large number of steel containers through the center of one of the world's most congested cities. Yet, about 40 percent of the containers in movement here are actually empty, and most are returning to the Far East. "The [trade] imbalance is huge," says Otto, eyeing the harbor. "And not a whole lot of finished product is going back that way."

The containers that return with contents, says OOCL service director Paul Connolly, are often filled with low-value goods or recycling. "The majority of the OOCL service [return] cargo is waste paper, scrap metal, a lot of hay, chemicals," he says. "Basically, it's raw materials." Some 11.6 million tons of recovered paper and cardboard were sent from America to China in 2008. Port authorities confirm that the main imports are petroleum, electronics, plastics, furniture, and clothing; the top exports include petroleum products, waste paper, scrap metal, chemicals, and plastic.

It does seem strange that the world's most advanced transport systems is used to deliver recycling to China. This means that 40 percent of the Pacific Rim shipping business often involves cargo that isn't worth the value of the steel box it's shipped in. "Everything [product] that is brought over from Asia is in a [cardboard] box," explains Connolly. "And often those boxes are just thrown away—or they can be taken back, recycled in the paper plants in China and reused to make more boxes to repackage." There is a steady but small flow of trade in certain higher-value goods and parts, such as ball bearings and specialty chemicals, but if any finished product is actually shipped directly back to a Pacific Rim nation, it is likely to be a faulty product being returned to the original factory or supplier.

It is estimated that the global shipping industry spends $11 billion annually managing and moving empty containers around the world. Representing one-twentieth of all global trade, Los Angeles could be spending as much as $550 million annually just to manage its empties. Containers that aren't returned to the Far East, however, pile up like multicolored Lego pieces all over the Los Angeles Basin, turning the City of Angels into a city of containers. And by 2009, with the reduced demand for American exports, the number of empty containers loaded at the Port of Los Angeles actually increased, in contrast to all other container counts at the port complex, which decreased in the wake of the global economic meltdown.

But people still need underwear and toothpaste. At the deep end of Long Beach harbor, a steady parade of rumbling trains and trailer trucks glide a few meters above the ocean on narrow fingers of landfill where saltwater once washed against warships, sloops, and canoes. But it's not like the early 2000s, when everyone remembers that massive container ships like the *Tianjin* were occasionally backed out of Los Angeles's harbor into the open ocean, piled high with flat-screen TVs and gaming consoles.

Recent years are less memorable. The docks are still busy, but with 17 percent fewer shipments in July 2009 than the previous year; overall, global trade had dropped 23 percent. There are also growing piles of near-worthless recycling that China doesn't want anymore, more empty containers than ever, and a glut of Japanese cars that too few people want to purchase. There is no happy medium, it seems.

The Global Pipeline

Modern shipping redefined global trade, in much the same way that railways once revolutionized the landscape of late nineteenth-century North America, and set the pattern for the kind of settlement and sprawl that became the ideal habitat for big-box stores. And despite the trumpeting of the knowledge economy, the vast majority of global trade is still in goods, not services. Materials and goods are worth $13.6 trillion, more than four times the total international trade in services, which includes finance, software, travel, and other New Economy favorites. This differential is profound, given what the OECD describes as the "relatively minor role for services in international trade [versus] the contribution of services in the domestic economies of member countries, where the proportion of total value-added contributed by services is around 70 percent and rising." In plain language: many domestic economies are dominated by consumption and service-related activities, yet the actual business of global trade is still highly material, as it has been since the beginning.

The movement of goods that is on display in Los Angeles's harbor is only part of a vast system of manufacturers, shippers, contractors, merchants, and retailers. Globalization was possible because of the late-twentieth-century emergence of supply-chain management, which realized the full potential of transportation networks by borrowing from advances in military logistics. Complex contractual and logistical arrangements now render an "assembly line" so huge that buyers and manufacturers often never know each other's identities, let alone communicate with each other directly. And the IT and Internet surge of the 1990s created the necessary web-based software and real-time communication links. With thousands of shipping containers crisscrossing the globe, a new science emerged to investigate programs like continuous replenishment (low inventory, manufacture and deliver products rapidly) and disintermediation (eliminating wholesalers and middlemen). Wal-Mart was among the first to take advantage of all logistics advancements, adopting in the 1990s GPS-based tracking, bar-code links, and web-based management systems. It also completed the replacement of paper-based logistics, which began with Japanese just-in-time production for automobiles and now incorporates current space and military technology.

This new phase of global commerce helped giants like Wal-Mart and Carrefour to become bigger than ever, but it also resulted in wholesale outsourcing by many major companies. Dell Computers, for example, built its success on becoming a computer company that doesn't actually make computers, but rather, an aggregate of far-flung production networks.

Companies created alliances with suppliers, sharing information to make ordering, inventory, and accounting more automatic. Wal-Mart was among the first to share sales data with major suppliers. "Every time a box of Tide is rung up at the cash register," according to the company, "Wal-Mart's data warehouse takes note and knows when it is time to alert P&G to replenish a particular store. As a result, Wal-Mart stores rarely run out of stock of popular items."

The nature of goods manufacture itself is highly distributed: More parts, components, and materials are shipped than finished goods. In 2003, 54 percent of global manufacturing imports were actually "intermediate goods"— parts, packaging, materials, all sourced for particular products—en route to assembly, which in turn has increased the number of overall container hauls: An assembled LCD television headed to Best Buy has taken one long trip across the ocean, but its parts have likely traveled even farther. This also means that globalization is doubly dependent on shipping, not only for delivering finished products to stores, but also for ensuring that supply chains are quickly and cheaply replenished with parts and materials.

It is a kind of planetary "Ford-ism," a disjointed but highly coordinated process where manufacturers, traders, and retailers often appear to function as a single, coordinated company. As trade pioneer Victor Fung describes it, the "borderless manufacturing" of the modern supply chain changed production-consumption around the world. The modern supply was invented by people like Fung, whose venerable family company, Li & Fung Limited, the export arm of the Li & Fung Group, was the first Chinese-owned export company. From the success of developing a new kind of firecracker in 1907 to managing the supply chain for fashion, toy, and appliance buyers, everyone from The Gap, Levi Strauss, Marks and Spenser, and Gymboree are creating "a new kind of multinational," as he told the *Harvard Business Review* in 2000.

As befits a global giant, Li & Fung is now incorporated in Bermuda but operates mainly from Hong Hong's Kowloon peninsula. It is one of the world's largest trading companies, with $5.5 billion in sales and 6,000 employees worldwide. And they stay well removed from actual production. "We are a smokeless factory. We do design. We buy and inspect the raw materials," explained Fung. "But we don't manage the workers and we don't own the factories....We work with about 7,500 suppliers in more than 26 countries...more than a million workers engaged on behalf of our customers."

This virtual trading hub—relatively little finished product actually passes through Hong Kong anymore—continues to grow as governments continue to liberalize their economies. In 2004, for example, Li & Fung became the first foreign-owned company to be granted an export company license in China; all previous exporters were state-mandated joint ventures. "Today Asia consists of multiple networks of dispersed manufacturing—high-cost hubs that do sophisticated planning for regional manufacturing," says Fung of the new production networks. "Bangkok works with the Indochinese peninsula, Taiwan with the Philippines, Seoul with Northern China. Dispersed manufacturing is what's behind the boom in Asia's trade and investment in the 1990s—companies moving raw materials and semi finished parts around Asia. But the region is still very dependent on the ultimate sources of demand, which are North America and Europe."

For centuries, merchants were simply brokers and translators, sourcing product for various customers across oceans and continents. As trade accelerated during the late 1980s and 1990s, job descriptions began to expand: traders and merchants extended themselves into manufacturing and logistics and took on design, including the development of prototype products, and management duties, while accelerating shipment times and lowering prices.

In 2007, American business spent an unprecedented $1.4 trillion on logistics, amounting to an estimated 10.1 percent of the nation's GDP. It was the age of FedEx, Amazon, eBay, and booming retail trade. The Americas not only created a hungry consumer base, but pioneered containerization and championed the liberalization of international trade regulations. The United States had played a formative role in shaping and controlling postwar trade agreements like the 1947 GATT, whose primary function was to liberalize global commerce. This resulted in an increase in overall world trade from $365 billion in 1950 to $6.4 trillion in 2000.

Europe dominated the shipping industry during the 1980s, when Maersk Line of Denmark, the world's largest shipping company, seized an opportunity following the 1970s shipping industry collapse—when shipbuilding costs soared 400 percent between 1970 and 1975, largely due to high oil prices—and bought ships and shipping companies at bargain prices. Like retail, the shipping business is highly competitive and its history is littered with failures and bankruptcies. Adding to the volatility created by rapid global growth and pressure for low prices, Maersk discounted its shipping rates and accumulated container ships, while companies from the steamship era slowly died off and America lost its dominance as a merchant marine fleet. In 1999, Maersk purchased container pioneer McLean's Sea-Land Service. By 2005, Maersk had accumulated more than 500 container ships and cornered one-sixth of the global shipping market, becoming the largest container-ship operator in the world.

"In an industry that almost everywhere wrapped itself in nationalist pride, the long-term survivors were profoundly international," writes Levinson in *The Box*. Indeed, Maersk became the Wal-Mart of the logistics world, and the scale and ferocious efficiency with which it operated—pioneering ever-larger container ships and ever-faster port facilities—ultimately helped consolidate the modern supply chain. "Where it sees leverage then expect a list of demands typically involving a reduction in price," wrote the trade magazine *Port Strategy* in a September 2008 editorial. "There is a ruthless determination afoot in Maersk Line to improve business performance with this described as focused on four key elements: filling ships with profitable cargo; product reliability; faster more responsive service; and reduced complexity and cost."

Yet transportation has never been neutral: When the United States completed its network of interstate highways in the 1950s, it was with a mind to national security because ground transportation for mobile missiles in a nuclear world was seen as strategic. Likewise, trade agreements and international systems of currency that were developed during the twentieth century have also tipped the balance of power toward those who already own supply chains and transport networks. As economist Joseph Stiglitz explained in *Making Globalization Work*, an estimated $500 billion flowed from poor countries to rich countries in 2006 simply through the unfair functioning the global reserve system—the system by which countries accumulate foreign currency through trade, mostly in American dollars. The back and forth of trade, represented in resources and container units, creates currency structures and transactions that fund American public debt while eroding the wealth of developing nations. "We can think of this as a round-robin, with money flowing from the developing countries to the United States, and then flowing back again," writes Stiglitz. "There is something peculiar—one might say wrong—with the system, especially since the interest rate they receive ... is so much lower than the interest rate they pay when they borrow the money back again."

Ironically, many poorer countries still hang on to currency as a form of "self-insurance" writes José Antonio Ocampo in a 2007 United Nations study. Currency from a rich country like the United States has been assumed to be assured and stable. But Ocampo warns of the "fallacy of composition," whereby if everyone accumulates the same large currency reserves as insurance, profound instability is created. It is very hard to bail out this system when it collapses, as became evident in 2009 when it became clear that there was too much globally funded debt, distributed unevenly.

The money system behind global trade, it turns out, threatens both rich and poor. It poses a pattern of escalation and risk not unlike the unregulated transactions that precipitated the 2008 financial collapse. "Self-insurance is not only a costly form of insurance for individual countries but [is] also a source of instability to the global economy," concludes Ocampo. There are "many similarities with the instability that a national banking system faced in the past in the absence of a lender of last resort."

On the ground, globalization is governed by supply chains that can, additionally, exclude and disable economies. Regional manufacturing clusters purposefully dominate whole categories of product; there is protectionism; there are pressures for shippers to skip smaller countries and ports in order to save money; global banking and aid agencies require growth-intensive and open trade development.

Globalization in the age of bargains is a series of product pipelines. This reality reflects the natural-resource intensity of major economies, the centralization of economic power as well as the vast network of actual pipelines required to affordably deliver the energy needed to keep ships, factories, and trucks operating. "Container shipping, it is clear, has helped some cities and countries become part of the new supply chains, while leaving others to the side," writes Levinson. "It has assisted the rapid economic growth of Korea while offering precious little to Paraguay."

Poorer countries, whose ports are less busy or less well managed, lose out. Either a country invests billions of dollars or it is passed by, it seems, which does much to explain the vast difference between Asia and other developing nations in overall trade growth. A World Bank report estimated if Peru were as effective at port management as Australia is, its foreign trade would have increased 25 percent.

Globalization is heavily networked but it does not perform like a network; it is selective, and transport can create major obstacles just as easily as it can create the illusion of borderless trade. "The massive ports constructed in China, Malaysia, and Thailand during the 1990s were investments in globalization," says Levinson. "Factories whose goods use those ports will have the lowest rates and the lowest costs in lost time. A country cursed with outmoded or badly run ports is a country that faces great obstacles…The big containerships that link national economies in the global supply chain, carrying nothing but stacks of metal boxes, will pass it by."

The Heart of Los Angeles

Los Angeles didn't want to be passed by. The city bet its future on global transport for the same reason that hordes of people walk into Wal-Mart looking for part-time jobs: it needed cash. As the Cold War drew to a close between 1987 and 1994, its military manufacturing base lost nearly 200,000 jobs, part of a postindustrial unemployment freefall. The new jobs that emerged, such as those within the growing warehousing and transport industry, were temporary and/or paid reduced wages. "LA is the hole in the national bucket," wrote Berkeley's Stephen Cohen at the time. "Twenty-seven percent of [America's] entire 1990-92 job loss took place in Greater Los Angeles."

Things got worse. As unemployment grew, riots exploded in 1992, resulting in 55 deaths and $1 billion in damage. Along with several earthquakes and fires, the Los Angeles riots marked a breaking point, providing a foreboding glimpse of an postapocalyptic city that is often depicted in action movies. It was, as historian Mike Davis notes, "possibly the first multi-ethnic rioting in modern American history [with] economically desperate Latinos in some of the city's poorest neighborhoods, Mexican immigrants from South Central Los Angeles, and Salvadorian immigrants in the Park District in Hollywood

[who] joined in the looting." Facing a grim future, the cities of Los Angeles and Long Beach dredged the harbor and built piers to accommodate ships larger than anyone had ever seen before.

Greater Los Angeles entered a phase of transport megaprojects. "West Coast ports such as Los Angeles and Long Beach made massive investments in container facilities in order to capture larger market shares of the burgeoning trans-Pacific containerized-cargo trade," notes Stephen P. Erie in *Globalizing LA*. Combined, the cities invested $2 billion each on their respective port facilities during the 1990s, in addition to the $2.4 billion Alameda Corridor project—a dedicated freight rail line launched in 2002 that connects the ports of Los Angeles and Long Beach to the national railway system near downtown Los Angeles.

Forget Hollywood and Disneyland. The economic heart of Southern California is container shipping. As port-related employment tripled during the 1990s and early 2000s, logistics trumped tourism, manufacturing, and movie making. Today, the ports are responsible for one in eight of all jobs in the Los Angeles region. In 1994, just as Wal-Mart had set its first $1 billion-a-week sales record, Los Angeles surpassed New York as America's busiest customs district. By 2005, Wal-Mart alone had imported 695,000 container units through the region's ports—much of it consisting of the company's $30 billion in annual Chinese imports (2007)—enough to fill the world's largest container ship, the massive 1,300-foot long *Emma Mærsk*, 63 times. Imports accounted for three-quarters of Los Angeles's trade growth between 1993 and 2000.

Like Asian manufacturing economies and Western retailers, the shipping industry is highly growth dependent. Shipping is where the gigantism of global trade comes into full view—bigger is better, with more and larger container ships and dock facilities and an increased use of automation and technology. The irony is that hardship creates a new growth imperative: The industry requires new efficiencies to regain economies of scale in the face of declining revenues and increased costs.

Los Angeles has found that there are limits, however, not only because this capital-intensive industry hasn't always delivered expected economic benefits, but also because surrounding communities are now protesting against and successfully blocking port expansion. "If the port expands, we're going to reach a point where we are not going to build roads fast enough," says Tom Politeo, a resident of the south Los Angeles harborside community San Pedro.

Politeo's family has lived in San Pedro since the 1940s. He recalls a childhood with clean air, clean water, and towns that were largely free of congestion and disease. He remembers days when his family fished in San Pedro Bay. "There was a time when goods movement did not make up such a large percentage of our economy, and when fishing was the biggest industry."

Between the millions of cars already on the city's roads and highways and the ongoing boom in port traffic, Los Angeles has long been America's capital of traffic congestion. And, although 55 container trains ran daily on the Alameda Corridor in 2007, rigs and trucks still used up an estimated 30 to 40 percent of Los Angeles's freeway capacity that same year. "By the 1990s, the freeways were in existence for 35 years, and at that time we saw significant volumes of trucks," says Politeo as I interview him overlooking the harbor. "Now, everything is jammed up with trucks."

Billions could be spent on upgrading and expanding transport infrastructure and highways. Los Angeles's two main port freeways, the Harbor 110 freeway and I-710, were both built by the government in the 1960s and need serious fixing. As America debated its economic stimulus plan in 2009, sticker prices for trade infrastructure emerged: $6 billion for a truck tollway between Los Angeles and Long Beach and $1 billion to replace the Port of Los Angeles's Schuyler Heim Bridge, the largest vertical-life bridge on the West Coast.

The challenges and failures of privately owned transport networks often end up costing taxpayers money. "We laid the groundwork to move goods very cheaply," says Politeo. "The public picks up the expense, not only the infrastructure, but of pollution as well. So include the social costs of living in a country devoted to transport. There are many costs associated with moving goods and moving people. We don't pay for all this up front. We have a subsidy for mobility."

Some of the greatest costs aren't even counted yet. In Los Angeles, port-related pollution caused an estimated 29 premature deaths, 750 asthma attacks and 6,600 lost work days in 2007. And while the low-grade diesel fuel burned by container ships saves money, the research group Pacific Institute estimated that freight transport would cost California residents $200 billion in health impacts by the early 2020s.

Global connectivity isn't all that it's cracked up to be. After several decades of trade expansion, greater Los Angeles has been reaching its limits. Its highways are nearly full and its air is thick with diesel particulates. In response, the port is attempting to spread itself across the entire geographic area of the Los Angeles Basin and beyond. What began as the shipping and harbor industry is now known generally as the "goods movement industry" since this broad network of transport is no longer bound to the waterfront. It is an industry pushing the geographic and spatial limits of movement.

"Southern California is America's gateway to the global economy and plays a central role in sustaining the nation's prosperity," pledged Los Angeles mayor Antonio Villaraigosa in 2007. "As container traffic continues to grow, we must invest more in our goods movement infrastructure while addressing the environmental and health impacts of ever expanding international trade."

Just as Los Angeles was attempting to address congestion woes, several other issues reached critical mass: air pollution, fuel prices, climate change regulation, and unprecedented global competition for ships and steel. It was a perfect storm of problems. In response, Los Angeles and Long Beach port authorities have proposed spending over $13 billion in expansion projects and upgrades to 2020. New facilities will build vertically, stacking containers like high-rise buildings, creating greater densification and diminishing congestion, in addition to ongoing efforts to optimize Los Angeles's rail corridor and decrease container dwell times on the docks. Portside density would double, (as would estimated capital costs), which could run up to 10,000 container units an acre. The quest for cheap was getting expensive.

Meanwhile, the logistics industry was facing serious difficulty. During a series of commodity and energy price spikes in the first decade of 2000, it became evident that years of easy growth were over, and that supply chains would become increasingly vulnerable. By 2008, the Council of Supply Chain Management Professionals estimated that total logistics costs to American business had increased 52 percent between 2003 and 2008. And even after the recession hit, energy costs remained high. "We will not see a return to prosperity for some time," warned the council's Rosalyn Wilson. "I think logistics costs will claim an even higher percentage of GDP in [the future]." Trucking costs alone increased $36 billion in the United States in 2007, leading to the closure of over 2,000 trucking companies in the same period.

"The cost of shipping a standard 40-foot container from East Asia to the U.S. eastern seaboard...tripled since 2000 and will double again as oil prices head toward $200 per barrel," said economist Jeff Rubin in a 2008 brief for CIBC research. "Unless that container is chock full of diamonds, shipping costs have suddenly inflated the cost of whatever is inside. And those inflated costs get passed on to the Consumer Price Index when you buy that good at your local retailer." Shipping fees slumped after the financial collapse in 2008, but the lesson was clear: The affordability of goods movement is largely governed by the future price of non-renewable energy.

The future threat of increased cost is not limited to international trade. "This is not just about steel, but also maple syrup and avocados and blueberries at the grocery store," said Rubin. "Avocado salad in Minneapolis in January is just not going to work in this new world, because flying it in is going to make it cost as much as a rib eye." Indeed, the Baltic price index, which measures the price of moving major raw materials by sea, changed 50 percent during 2007 and 2008—a volatile trend that hinted that the future of transport was not efficiency, but instability. And this was before the previously externalized costs of air pollution and greenhouse gas emissions had fully entered the shipping-transport equation.

The embodied energy cost of modern transport hits shipping lines hard, the very companies who carry an estimated 90 percent of global goods trade. For much of the 2000s, fuel and steel prices wreaked havoc in the industry while it attempted to fight off demands for lower rates from powerful clients. "A container ship over the last say 5 to 6 years has probably gone up 40 to 50 percent in price," says Paul Connolly. "On the steamship side, steel has been a major factor and the cost of building one of these containerships now has risen exponentially."

Even Maersk lost money on container operations during the early 2000s and was forced to eliminate some of its delivery locations. "Maersk is undertaking the biggest cost-reduction plan in its 103-year history by cutting about 15 percent of the labor force at the container unit," reported Bloomberg in 2008—as many as 10,000 people lost their jobs. Ironically, Maersk's oil and gas division, which operates drill platforms from Qatar to the North Sea, posted a 58 percent increase in profits for the same period, resulting in total profits of $4 billion for the company. Maersk's cost of fuel had nearly doubled between 2007 and 2008 following the price rise of crude oil that eventually peaked at nearly $150 a barrel. "Fuel drives everything," confirms Otto. "Not only the ships but every piece of equipment that we run is on fuel—that consumes a lot of fuel. So everything gets moved around so our fuel costs have gone up tremendously."

That transport is so closely tied to energy prices and consumer demand is a problem for Los Angeles, Rotterdam, Singapore, and other major ports. Many of the cheap efficiencies and quantum savings rendered by modern logistics have already been realized. Geopolitics, congestion, climatic instability, and the growing cost of sustaining far-flung manufacturing empires are constant challenges. Even in tough times, the costs of maintaining idle container ships are considerable.

Los Angeles is a long way from becoming locally self-sufficient. It still needs globalization badly, even if globalization isn't looking so good. As late as 2008, Los Angeles port authorities still optimistically predicted that trade volumes would triple or even quadruple between 2000 and 2020, requiring billions in new port infrastructure. And if global trade crashes, as it did in 2009, then the resulting unemployment, not to mention lost economic growth and investment, would have serious consequences as well. Very likely, global hubs like Los Angeles will suffer both ways, losing business to deglobalization, yet still spending billions on infrastructure updates and environmental reforms.

This is precisely the kind of paradox that dims the once-bright future of globalization. Los Angeles had committed itself to the cost of sustaining a global transport hub, yet even with new trade, environment, and energy costs in the twenty-first century it still shapes itself around goods movement.

The industry is vulnerable in new ways. Port security—searching an annual flow of 3000 incoming container ships for dirty nuclear bombs—is an emerging cost threat. "They are real costs that the shipping industry has to bear at this time," admits Connolly. "The terminals, the steamship lines, the trucking industries—all the various components of the supply chain are subjected. And they are not going to go away; they are real issues that are facing us."

Gridlock

Wilmington, California is the kind of place that you usually never hear about. Part of the 1784 Spanish land grant of Rancho San Pedro, this harborside community was annexed by the City of Los Angeles in 1909 and has dutifully served as the backbone to the city's expansion ever since. It is a working-class community set amid old oil refineries, warehouses, ports, and highways. Besides being the site of the region's first wharf, Wilmington's greatest claim to fame is its modern role as a location for Hollywood movies. Likely you have seen it—if you've seen *Terminator 2*, *Fight Club*, *Crash*, or *Gone in 60 Seconds*, among others.

It was here that one of the town's founders, Los Angeles pioneer Phineas Banning, dredged a 10-foot deep harbor channel through the mudflats in 1871 and moved some 50,000 tons of cargo within a year, giving birth to the modern transport industry. Banning had some notion of the importance of networks: He connected the harbor's muddy berths with a stagecoach line running north to Salt Lake City, Utah, and east to Yuma, Arizona. By 1868, Banning had built one of Los Angeles's first railroads, connecting to San Pedro Bay with the inland settlement of Los Angeles.

The area around Wilmington was gradually developed with oil refineries, a network of freeways, military installations, and America's largest port complex. There are eight major refining facilities within ten miles, many of which date back to the 1930s, when Los Angeles grew up around what is still one of

America's largest-ever oil finds: the 3 billion barrels within the Wilmington field, which lies beneath the harbor, the community, and part of neighboring Long Beach. By the 1940s, Los Angeles and Long Beach had sucked so much oil from under the harbor that the east side of Terminal Island began to sink below sea level until massive amounts of sea water were injected back into the shallow formation. Although much of the original oil supply has been depleted, the refineries remain critical to Los Angeles's economy: Diesel fuel, jet fuel, gasoline, and feedstocks for chemicals and plastics are refined locally from crude oil imported from the Middle East and Latin America— more than 50 percent of its supply—which of course adds to the strategic importance—and congestion—of Los Angeles's port facilities. By 2021, over 90 percent of Southern California's crude oil will be imported through its ports, peaking at an estimated 1.3 million barrels per day by 2040, half of which will be delivered by aptly named "very large crude carriers" (VLCCs) from the Middle East.

Even though much of America's retail inventory travels around or through Wilmington, the community itself has no big-box malls or major retail outlets. There is no Starbucks, Wal-Mart, or Home Depot here, just family-owned corner stores, car washes, and a few fast-food chains, including Los Angeles's first *Der Wienerschnitzel* hot dog restaurant. The reason? Wilmington doesn't have enough people or enough money to attract major retailers. While it is invisible to retail America, Wilmington remains critical to goods movement, since a great many harbor workers live here, plus the community's land base has hosted port expansions and secondary industries since the beginning.

Living in Wilmington is not good for your health. "Almost every family I know has someone suffering from asthma, respiratory health problems, lung disease, or cancer," says Jesse Marquez, founder of Wilmington's Coalition for a Safe Environment. Marquez, a lifelong Wilmington resident, started the group in 2001 to investigate the environmental and public health impact of the ports' expansion projects. "People die prematurely [in Los Angeles] so that Wal-Mart, Nike, Kmart, and others can make billions in profits."

From 2002 on, he says, citing port studies, the harbor has been single-handedly generating more than 20 percent of Southern California's total particulate emissions, considered the most harmful and potentially deadly form of air pollution. And despite new laws and a $2 billion government promise to slash harbor emissions by 50 percent between 2006 and 2012, concerned residents of San Pedro, West Long Beach, and Wilmington are still pushing back hard on development, increasingly galvanized by the deadly air quality and traffic from the harbor's sleepless operation of trucks, ships, and trains.

California's relatively progressive environmental legislation and the fact that neither the ports nor the government can any longer afford to exclude these harborside communities, give locals new clout. "We were totally ignored before," says Marquez, "Now they deal with us."

Some were surprised that a community with a household median income of $35,000 could tackle a multimillion dollar industry. But it's a battle that has been brewing for years. Wilmington and San Pedro to the southwest had previously launched secession movements, environmental coalitions, and countless challenges to what some have described as pollution-based discrimination. Wilmington and west Long Beach are nearly 90 percent Latino, and stand closest to all the refineries, docks, and rail yards.

Southern California has a long and not particularly nice tradition of loading low-income black and Latino communities with pollution from the region's industrial development. This is evidenced by the oil jacks in residential Long Beach neighborhoods, the section of Huntington Park known as "Asthma Town" (for the high number of residents who have asthma as a result of living there), and the high rates of birth defects and cancer discovered in Bell Gardens during the 1980s. In Bell Gardens, high levels of hexavalent chromium were measured from nearby chrome plating facilities, which were also adjacent to Suva Elementary School, a location that became infamous for birth defects and miscarriages.

"Asians, African Americans, and Latinos have the highest population cancer risk estimates, with risks nearly 50% higher [from airborne toxins] than that for Anglos," noted one 2002 study published by investigators from San Francisco State University and University of California. And while land value, or lack thereof, has long been associated with pollution exposure, what has changed in Los Angeles is the kind of pollution: from toxic sites across low-income postal codes to diesel-sourced air pollution affecting poorer neighborhoods near freeways and goods movement sites. Particulate counts near rail yards, trucking corridors, distribution centers, and port terminals are generally 1.5 to 4 times greater than the California average. And while the region has fought smog levels from the 1970s onward with some success, and has reduced overall particulate, it remained America's most polluted city in 2008 on the basis of year-round particulate pollution.

Private transportation has become more efficient and cleaner burning, and many factories have been cleaned up. But portside communities such as Long Beach, San Pedro, and Wilmington still sustain some of the highest levels of particulate matter and ozone in the country.

Decades-old diesel trucks crowd the port area, belching out pollutants and creating some of the worst air quality in the city, leading to the common local observation that "this is where old trucks come to die." Many container ships still burn bunker fuel, the lowest grade diesel fuel available, so coarse and dense that it is mostly solid at room temperature and needs to be heated in order to combust. Coming out of a single smoke stack—such as an enormous prewar coal-fired power plant—this kind of low-grade, inefficient, and highly polluting combustion would never be tolerated in California in the twenty-first century. But because marine vessels are scarcely governed by international regulations on emissions and pollution, and because Los Angeles's truck-dependent port system is populated with independent, low-cost drivers, some of the most primitive, polluting engines outside the developing world have amassed at San Pedro Bay.

Hudson Elementary School, situated on the border between Wilmington and Long Beach next to the Terminal Island Freeway has some of the worst air quality in North America. Parents once counted 590 container trucks passing the school per hour, one of the largest reported truck volumes in the port area. Only a block away is a daycare center that stands within sight of Hudson School and the truck-congested freeway. Within a few miles, radius are major rail yards, railway corridors, and several large oil refineries. When refineries flare off waste gases, the school often locks its students indoors, *if* it is told about it in advance, which doesn't always happen. "Unplanned" flarings around the port area are later reported in the news.

The Hudson School itself looks perfectly normal, a typical, one-story brick building, well-maintained, with the Hudson Hawks team logo painted outside; adjacent to it is a public park with baseball diamonds, trees, and a playground. But a child who dwells here long enough will develop a twofold risk of asthma. "When our team came out here to do air monitoring," says Elina Green, project manager for the nonprofit coalition Long Beach Alliance for Children with Asthma, "in the classroom, particulate counts were 8,000, but out here in the park, it was 40,000. And as different trucks and trains went by, you'd see spikes." In other words, Hudson school kids breathe in air all day that is as polluted as what other Los Angeles school kids might breathe in the middle of traffic en route to school, according to a 2003 study prepared for the California Air Resources.

What local authorities know for sure is that kids are getting sick from the air. Asthma is the leading cause of missed school days in the area, reports Green. It is also the most prevalent admission diagnosis in local pediatric intensive care units. Longer-term effects are highly likely: teens growing up in Southern California's most congested areas show a fivefold risk of reduced lung function. As local emergency room doctor John Miller told PBS in 2006: "You realize from looking at the numbers, looking at the science, that we're living in a diesel death zone."

It's a health crisis, says Green, looking out across the baseball diamonds to the line of trucks driving north on the Terminal Island Freeway. "The thing about particulates is that they are so small that they can bypass front-line body systems, and go deep into parts of the body. And so a lot of the new research is about what sort of impacts these ultrafine particulates have. It's almost a whole new area of study."

The scientific understanding of the air-pollution hazard changed significantly during the period that goods movement became a significant global industry. Beginning in the early 1990s, fine particulate matter—microscopic soot produced by incomplete combustion, particularly of sulphur-rich diesel sources—caught the attention of cancer and air-quality specialists. Other pollutants, such as ozone, irritate the respiratory tract and induce asthma attacks, chest pain, and chronic respiratory irritation; particulates, on the other hand, penetrate deeply into the body, sidestepping many of the body's natural defenses. Particulates that are 2.5 microns or less can find their way throughout the body—entering the brain, inner organs, and deep into the lungs. Particulates are far more dangerous than previously believed because of their deep incursion, but also because they are acidic and can deliver trace amounts of chemicals and heavy metals—benzene compounds, lead, cadmium, and nickel—into the body.

This realization made Los Angeles's ports an environmental hotspot. "Mobile sourced emissions are the primary driver of health risk, accounting for about 70% of the estimated excess cancer incidence, the majority of this from diesel particulate pollution," reported the Pat Brown Institute, a Los Angeles–based think tank, in 2007. "Although much of the Los Angeles region is bathed in a cloud of air pollution, the cancer risk is associated with our transportation network."

Consequently, California's Air Resources Board doubled its estimate of premature, pollution-caused deaths in 2008, based on revisions to risk assessment regarding diesel-related fine particulates smaller than 2.5 micrometers, from 14,000 annually to 24,000 annually, with the most premature deaths occurring close to pollution sources such as freeways, sources of industrial emissions, power plants, and, of course, the port areas. "We're talking about people losing at least ten years of their life," said Linda Smith of the Air Resources Board.

Asthma in children is the front-line effect of chronic air pollution, but there are more disturbing links that may become clearer in coming decades.

For example: a 2003 study with the California Department of Health Services suggested an association between increased childhood leukemia rates and high hazardous air pollution exposure in California, based on data collected between 1988 and 1994. After comparing incidence, location, and relative exposure for a long list of known, probable, and possible carcinogens, researchers "found...a significant trend with increasing exposure level for childhood leukemia in tracts ranked highest for exposure," with highest percentile exposures registering incidence as much as 32 percent above normal. The authors called for further study.

Yet, despite these and other findings, the large rail yard across the highway from Hudson School—Union Pacific's Intermodal Container Transfer Facility (ICTF)—launched a major campaign to expand operations. Already handling 750,000 containers annually, it proposed to increase that number to 1.5 million. And the Burlington Northern Santa Fe Railway proposed building a second facility less than 1,000 feet away from Hudson School, which could, potentially, add as many as 1.5 million containers. While these companies promised cleaner locomotives and electric cranes that would potentially reduce on-site emissions by 74 percent from 2005 levels, there was little provision for dealing with the one-million-plus diesel truck hauls required to fill their railway cars with steel containers.

"Proximity to the school is the big issue. We're already talking about a heavily impacted area. At what point do we say enough is enough?" says Green, recalling how over 700 community members had attended a recent consultation meeting on the proposed ICTF facility, and many have attempted to block the ICTF and other expansion projects.

Green believes that land at the ports would be better used by removing truck traffic in favor of more dedicated rail lines, yet this kind of upgrade, which is common in Europe, is considered impossible to do here. "They have land, but it's about political will. They want that land for other uses, such as new shipping berths. We've been opposing that. New intermodal facilities [near Hudson School] could be unnecessary. We could modernize and clean up around here." By 2008, there were already 16 major expansion projects planned for the ports. Yet many of these were being blocked or stalled by community opposition.

Gridlock in Los Angeles involves far more than ships, containers, and traffic. The entire urban basin is at odds with itself: Having lost several generations of manufacturing jobs, the region needs all the transport-related jobs it can scrounge. Inner-city communities are fighting hard in the face of increased port traffic and the dire consequences of diesel pollution; and profit margins are drying up for shipping companies and trucking contractors, leading to new pressure for cost-cutting and expansion. At the same time, population density will increase across Los Angeles Basin, with major growth near the ports in West Long Beach.

In the conventional wisdom of the transport industry, expansion has been synonymous with efficiency. Yet, when Los Angeles attempted to solve congestion in this way, they largely failed. "In the 1980s, they claimed that new rail yards would take trucks off the freeways," says Green. "But that never happened. They look short term, on a project by project basis, and their net goal is to allow capacity or increase capacity.... If it were up to them, I think they would love to be able to pay to move the community."

Tom Politeo suggests that Los Angeles's dependence on trucks—and publicly subsidized highways and facilities—was an ideological choice that reflects the brute side of Los Angeles's legacy of frontier commerce. "What we have is an economy not based on free trade but [on] privilege," he says. "And that is part of the reason we are so dependent on trucks, for example. We've painted ourselves into a corner as the system that is connected to truck access, not rail access. Trucking was deregulated in the 1970s, for much reduced cost and much reduced responsibility." Port-related sprawl happened because it was cheap; truck-based connections to rail yards persist because they utilize public road connections to private rail facilities.

In 2008, California introduced comprehensive land-use laws in an effort to reduce sprawl, a major cause of transport-based air pollution, yet the crux of the ports' problems remained: the crumbing bridges, highways, and stacked-up containers everywhere. Green says expanding infrastructure in high congestion areas can result in greater congestion. "The common argument is that to improve emissions, you make freight move faster. So you expand the freeway to improve emissions. We know that if trucks drive between 40 and 70 miles an hour, we can reduce pollution. But we also know that if they expand a freeway, then growth is expected to triple. In ten years, we could find ourselves back where we are right now."

Full-Cost Progress

Responding to years of protest and impasse, Los Angeles's $2 billion green plan, launched in 2006, was the most ambitious of its kind in North America. But the greening of Los Angeles's sometimes ancient fleet of deregulated and independently owned haul trucks is no small undertaking. Nor are efforts to persuade marine operators, whose ships do not fall under the jurisdiction of local or state agencies, to burn cleaner fuel while near the coast. Elsewhere, goods-transport pollution remains a serious problem. Voluntary guidelines in

New York have not been successful. "Unfortunately, little of the enthusiasm for environmental protection engendered by [NYC's] Green Port Program has produced concrete air pollution reductions," says researcher James Cannon. And Houston's port remains fraught with pollution.

In Southern California, few question the reality of traffic congestion, air pollution, and the public health crisis. But deciding who pays to fix the problems remains difficult. Who can reform globalization in south Los Angeles? It turns out that the higher cost of cleaner fuel and lower emissions is, like $150-a-barrel oil, a mortal threat to both the industries and the politicians who built their livelihoods on cheap.

Several months after diesel fuel was named top port pollutant in 2008, for example, California air regulators approved new guidelines to reduce ocean-going ship emissions. A program promoting low-sulfur fuels was launched in 2009; stringent international rules on shipping fuels are to take full effect in 2015. Some shipping companies volunteered immediate fuel upgrades, while the Pacific Merchant Shipping Association complained about jurisdiction. Indeed, shippers had already blocked a 2006 state regulation to impel cleaner fuel usage.

Typical bunker fuel contains up to 45,000 parts per million (ppm) of sulfur; by comparison California diesel trucks can burn diesel that contains no more than 15 ppm sulfur. The cost is not insignificant: Ships entering California waters will spend an extra $30,000 per trip simply to burn cleaner fuel within 24 nautical miles of the coast.

In 2008, the ports launched its clean-truck replacement effort, and offered subsidies to replace an aging fleet of about 16,800 run-down rigs: Truckers can purchase a new $100,000 diesel rig with latest in emissions technology for a mere $30,000. Yet the American Trucking Association filed a federal suit to block the effort, claiming that it was the result of "intrusive regulatory systems."

Like a bad traffic day on I-710, the gridlock seems endless. In July 2008, California State Senator Alan Lowenthal succeeded in passing a bill to impose a fee on cargo containers that would levy millions to help clean up the ports and reduce community impacts. For a fee of $30 per twenty-foot container unit (TEU), the added expense would be about half a cent per laptop, or five cents per big-screen television. California's Chamber of Commerce derided the legislation, which it claimed "Increases the cost of shipping goods and makes California less competitive by imposing an illegal per-container tax." And when a coalition of environmental groups sued the county government over laxity in dealing the air pollution in 2008, Jack Kyser, chief economist with the Los Angeles County Economic Development Corporation, threatened that lawsuits and reforms "could choke off a lot of international trade" and result in cost increases for all imported goods. "Sometimes, people don't understand the ultimate consequences of what they do," said Kyser. "Start stocking up on your tennis shoes and other necessities."

By mid-2009, the U.S. Environmental Protection Agency had announced plans with Canadian regulators to designate the entire North American coastal region as an "emission control area." Extending nearly 400 kilometers from the coastline, the zone would require shippers to burn cleaner fuel in order to reduce sulfur emissions by 96 percent by 2015. The new standard will prevent an estimated 8,300 deaths annually, a small but significant portion of the 60,000 deaths worldwide attributed to shipping emissions. The total cost of the new North American fuel standard will be $3.2 billion, or $18 per container.

It is a war over pennies, yet the total amounts are huge. A 2007 study by the Pacific Institute estimated that the total cost of adopting cleaner technology in the ports will be $6-$10 billion by 2020, while California's Clean Air Resources Board reports this would save $3 to $8 billion in total health impacts. As California debated a 2008 container-tax bill, the California State Board of Equalization estimated that each new percentage increase in overall sales tax could eliminate as many as 58,000 jobs.

In a cost-critical environment, there are fewer win-win solutions, and the political landscape really does begin to look like a parking lot. Los Angeles mayor Antonio Villaraigosa pledged to transform his city into "the greenest big city in America," yet he has reportedly refused to limit port growth. "When we met him last year," Jesse Marquez recounts, "he could not accept one thing: no port growth. Port growth was where his head was at."

Few political leaders can deny the economic importance of port activity. By 2007, dockside labor payrolls had increased to $1 billion, up from $400 million a decade earlier, echoing the estimate that roughly one in eight of all Los Angeles jobs is port related. There is a broad consensus across government that port growth is the key to replenishing the gradual loss of high-quality manufacturing jobs that have been disappearing since early 1990s.

Marquez wants his community to be known for more than dirty ports and that crazy helicopter chase scene from 1991's *Terminator 2*. Filmed on the Terminal Island Freeway. Arnold Schwarzenegger, the Terminator-turned-California governor, roared past local oil refineries, pursued by an unstoppable assassin from the future. The Hudson School was somewhere outside the frame as Schwarzenegger blasted his way toward port facilities at Terminal Island, which also happens to be one of the locations in 1977 cult classic *Pumping Iron*, which began his film career.

As governor, Schwarzenegger had already vetoed several earlier attempts to impose an environmental container fee on port traffic which would pose a significant cost and job loss threat for a regional industry that needs to move 11 million containers annually to stay solvent. There are few easy choices when it comes to California's ports, and harbor-front gridlock has traveled up the food chain. Marquez, however, makes no apologies for helping to block port development. The founder of Los Angeles's Coalition For A Safe Environment and co-chair of the Los Angeles chapter of the Sierra Club's Harbor Vision Taskforce reports that community opposition helped stop seven different proposed terminal projects since the early 2000s. "They had nearly zero port growth in 2007 and 2008. Some of that is the economy, but some of that is the growth factor. That's good news. Before, development was based on their needs and didn't take the community into account."

Others argue that zero growth would be good for the ports. "Globalization is peaking as a result of oil production peaking, and that we are about to enter an era of increasing local production to meet local needs," notes Tom Politeo. "Flat trade growth may actually mean that many half-measures to improve the environment will show some absolute benefit, since they won't have to peddle faster than the growth, something they've never been able to do."

Things have changed. The first new ship terminal to be added to the Port of Los Angeles in years is the TraPac container facility, which would be erected on one of the few patches of unused waterfront land in the region. When plans to build it were announced in 2003, there was strong opposition from community and environmental groups. With the help of Natural Resource Defense Council, Marquez and others gained a $57 million community-based trust fund for cleaner technologies, renewable power, air cleaners for medically vulnerable residents, as well as fund impact and advocacy studies. "We went way beyond anything we accomplished in the past," he says. "Every single mitigation measure we have identified over the last seven years, we finally achieved. This is about full-cost accounting."

Finally, Wilmington has clout. In 2010, Wilmington will see construction begin on a $57 million parkland buffer along Avalon Boulevard next to the harbor, which will include 6,000 new trees, a $212 million waterfront project, as well as a green technology center. "Wilmington will not be forgotten," said Mayor Villaraigosa in 2009. "We've got a lot of work left to do."

Marquez has just returned from Germany, where he toured the ports of Rotterdam and Hamburg, marveling at the electric trains and windmills, the automated cranes, and dedicated on-dock rail. Not a diesel rig in sight. The self-described "Wilmington homeboy" says that he has seen the future, and it looks a lot different than the industrial waterfront that lies at the end of many local streets. Clean, efficient cargo-transportation technologies, such as magnetic transport and electric trains, he says, would make an enormous difference, yet North Americans have trouble investing in long-term gain.

"Before, investments were based on corporate need, and they didn't take into effect the environment, they didn't take into effect any of the public health concerns or other socio-economic impacts. But now they are having to assess that and include that. All of a sudden the true value, the real cost-benefit of what they are doing comes to light. Before, they were in denial." But, says Marquez, it's still a lot better than China. "This is America. They can't just push projects through and then put us in jail."

*　*　*

It's not a victory for discounting, however, because these incremental increases in the cost of transport are inevitably passed along to consumers. And, as shippers and other port industries begin to suffer losses and insolvency in the wake of the global economic crisis, there may be fewer resources for addressing the issue of greenhouse gas emissions and less compliance with existing regulations. People like Otto and Connolly at OOCL are now responsible for responding to vast external changes that are affecting their business, even as they must deal with growing volatility in prices, global trade, labor, and environmental issues.

"On a per unit basis, it is actually on a per unit basis about a break-even," says Otto. "You are able to squeeze that much more through [but] you consider what your lease agreement is with the port. While the labor and certain costs associated with the operation go up, incrementally, I still think you are much better off the denser you go." Industry doesn't have much of a choice but to create vertically-stacked container cities like those already operating in China and Europe; yet this kind of vertical expansion is far more capital-intensive than the horizontal port expansions of the past. Many shippers and logistics companies will fail, given that years of potential losses lay ahead.

It is the Schumpeterian curse: innovation expedites an economic model toward its limits. Solutions like containerization and massive ships provided new productivity, affordability, and speed to consumers and global business; yet as the cost structure of transport and manufacture changes during the twenty-first century, they require increasing amounts of capital, natural resources, management, as well as public sacrifices and environmental impacts to sustain. Inputs increase (energy, capital investment, technology expenditure), yet returns are static or decreasing. In the terms of modern economic theory, one emerging view is that the "scale-effects property" of mature systems is broken: increased investment in technology and research for example, does not yield increased results. "Evidence shows that resources devoted to R&D have been increasing exponentially, but the growth rates remain roughly constant over time," note economists Dinopoulos and Şener in a 2007 paper on Schumpeterian growth theory.

The drive to recapture yesterday's prosperity and affordability is still strong. This is why ports like Los Angeles, along with manufacturers, retailers, and consumers, are still spending extra billions for incremental gains. In other words, containerization helped liberate trade during the twentieth century, but as we move deeper into the new millennium, we are clearly stuck inside the box. Indeed, by 2009, Los Angeles's port authority was offering a 10 percent discount on container traffic as an incentive to keep business moving.

If only to prove the point, major clients like Wal-Mart keep asking for discounts, according to other harbor professionals, even though it is clear that the shipping industry is managing a long-term crisis. "They will sit down there and say 'look, this is what we are going to pay. Take it or leave it. And if you do not do it, you are going to lose these 29,000 containers a month," explains Manny Aschemeyer of California's Marine Exchange.

When the going gets tough, everyone wants a deal. "Oh yeah, everybody wants their stuff," says Otto. "And quicker and cheaper."

The Hill and the Harbor

There's a spot in Long Beach where hulking steel pump jacks still dot the hillside. This is Signal Hill, a minicity enclave less than 2.5 square miles, that is peppered with the wells that tap into the Long Beach oil field, the site of the first of the major oil discoveries of the 1920s. The Signal Hill discovery launched America's first great oil boom, which soon made Southern California the world's biggest oil producer, responsible for roughly one quarter of world oil supply by 1923. At that time, Signal Hill was the biggest oil field of all. Yet, with nearly 300 wells squeezed within its tiny municipal footprint, the city within a city resembled a cluttered forest of drilling derricks.

These days, the oil doesn't run quite as thick, so the shrinking collection of oil jacks that robotically lurch up and down, plunging the earth's crust for hydrocarbon, has been surrounded by malls, hospitals, and houses. There are still whole city blocks of reddish earth dotted by occasional oil jacks, dilapidated machinery, and pipeline connections where nothing grows. Long Beach's Memorial Medical Center, where childhood asthma cases are reported at double the rate of the rest of California, is down the hill on the edge of this former cluster of derricks.

A few blocks away from the medical center is a lone pump jack, still work-ing an old oil deposit. It is encircled by a newly built wooden fence, and around it, like a large black moat, is a parking lot. Built around this two-story jack is a 24-acre big-box mall anchored by Home Depot, built in 2005. It nestles up to the San Diego Freeway to the north. Unlike the Colma Home Depot that was built on a mountain of garbage, this mall sits atop an old oil field, a so-called brownfield site—made famous by Upton Sinclair's novel *Oil!* and, more recently, by Paul Thomas Anderson's 2007 Oscar-nominated film, *There Will Be Blood*—which, since the 1920s has, along with other Signal Hill rigs, pulled nearly one billion barrels of oil out of the ground, including 614 million barrels extracted by 1938. This was the birthplace of industrial California, and of the oil riches that helped to build Hollywood, new highways, huge real estate developments, and glamorous family dynas-ties. "Southern California was the Kuwait of the Jazz Age," journalist Eric Schlosser told the *New York Times* in 2008. "An enormous amount of money was quickly made there and spent in all kinds of extravagant ways. . . . This was a whole new society in the making, and it was being fueled by oil money the likes of which no other city had ever seen before."

Looking south from the Home Depot parking lot, you can see the city of Long Beach unfold toward the harbor; massive gantry cranes unload con-tainer ships, some of which are 25 stories high, grazing at the water's edge. Directly across the street from Home Depot, just the other side of East Spring Street, are at least 20 square blocks of dusty moonscape in the middle of the city, the remains of Signal Hill's oil boom. The EPA estimates that 60 per-cent of the land within Signal Hill's tiny municipal enclave has contamina-tion issues, both real and perceived. At the centre of it all is an EPA-certified brownfield, fifty-six acres of rusting tanks, pump jacks, metal scrap, and large expanses of dark soil and gravel dotted by shrubs and ratty-looking palm trees. Here, seepage from over 80 years of petroleum development, laced with aro-matic hydrocarbons, heavy metals, and methane gas, runs as deep as 10 to 15 feet underground. A broken network of old oil pipelines, some buried just beneath the surface, some exposed above, traverses the site. It's been slated for multiple developments—most recently as a sports park—but nothing has happened, possibly because of the potentially large cost of removing contam-inated topsoil.

Signal Hill won't stay idle for long. Over time, inner-city land has grown potentially more valuable than some of the remaining oil wells and is now gradually being decommissioned and sold off as real estate—including "50 acres of former petroleum sites [turned] into a 150 unit single-family resi-dential project with a retail value of over $100,000,000" reports owner-operator

Signal Hill Petroleum. Indeed, some homes nearby with ocean views now fetch nearly $1.5 million. The Home Depot at the top of the hill will soon have a Starbucks, giving shoppers their own ocean view while they drink $5 lattes and shop the iTunes store via wireless internet.

It's hard to imagine the dangerous and blatantly corrupt place that Sinclair wrote about. But it's the story of Los Angeles and many postindustrial centres. Signal Hill's transition from oilfield to big-box mall are two sides of an economy built upon extraction. The large pump jack that stands in front of Home Depot is sucking increasingly valuable crude out of the ground, and passing it along to local refineries for upgrading. Modern retail operations follow a similar trajectory: supply chains extract cheap resources and labor, pipeline it through international ports and other logistics channels, and create profit margins on large sales volumes. The modern supply chain was meant to achieve efficiency and competition, speed and precision. The supply chain goes deeper than that, since much of our bargaineered world is actually embodied hydrocarbon: crude oil, petrochemicals, plastics, steel.

The actual energy cost of shipping transport is just one part of the cycle. A large container ship can burn through 46,200 liters of fuel every 100 kilometers, and emits the equivalent air pollution of 12,000 automobiles. If it is steaming toward Los Angeles, its cargo contains tons of plastic, much of which actually contain more raw energy value than crude oil. Add to this the trucking and rail transport on both ends of the journey, plus the final drive home from the big-box store with the customer.

There is progress. Governments outside Los Angeles are pushing for reduced emissions and more stringent fuel requirements—most notably a European initiative to limit all marine fuels to 1.5 percent sulfur, less than one-third of the UN's 2005 standard—and shipbuilders are creating larger, more energy efficient vessels. Wal-Mart has made much of its own cost-saving efforts: cutting total packaging by 5 percent by 2013 will, it claims, save 1,358 barrels of oil, 5,190 trees, and 727 shipping containers annually. Moreover, the company has pledged to improve the energy efficiency of its suppliers as well, leveraging its command-control mastery of the supply chain to institute emissions savings.

Shippers themselves have been divided on fuel solutions: in 2007, a group of independent shippers and tankers called for a moratorium on bunker fuel, with a move to fuels that contain less than one percent sulfur. The International Bunker Industry Association countered, arguing that if ships did in fact burn higher-quality fuel—as opposed to the cheap sludge from refinery waste streams—"refineries would need to process roughly 12 million additional barrels of crude oil daily, more than the entire output of ɔaudi Arabia." Moreover, the United Nations Conference on Trade and Development reported in 2008 that operational productivity in world shipping (measured in ton-miles) actually decreased slightly between 2004 and 2006, after a near-continuous 50 percent increase since 1984. Great gains were made over decades with increases in port productivity, yet the more recent decrease "reflects the faster rate of fleet expansion."

In other words, the quantum savings rendered by modern container shipping were created through what could be our last societal binge of affordable crude oil. Unlike other transportation challenges, there are few transitional technologies for the modern bulk, tanker, and container ship: there is no Prius, no hybrid solution, for the shipping world. While some experiment with sail technologies to capture wind, and hull coatings to reduce barnacle accumulation and friction, the vast majority of our trade—again, an estimated 90 percent of global goods trade—sails under combustion just as it did a generation or more earlier. Unlike Wal-Mart, Office Depot, or other big-box chains who have added solar panels to stores and gained upwards of 25 percent immediate energy savings, there is no similar solution for what is still the most vital transport link in the global supply chain. Some argue that global population increases alone will cancel out transport efficiency gains.

"A conceit of the New Economy is that it promises freedom from the smokestacks and sweatshops of the past two centuries," writes journalist Wade Graham. "In some swaths of formerly industrial North America, factories have been replaced by Wal-Marts and FedEx vans. But this is only a local illusion, a magic trick of trade and geography, obscuring the underlying fact that the New Economy not only rests on the grimy, polluting old one but propagates, multiplies, and feeds it, spreading it around the world.... We click off our wishes on Web sites, setting in motion diesel engines by the tens of thousands: trucks, loaders, cranes, and locomotives, armadas of little smokestacks toiling to deliver us the goods."

It's a dual threat: cost and emissions. And hazards abound for an energy-intensive world that sustains itself on global trade. What we do know is that logistics networks are proving exceedingly effective at telegraphing and amplifying problems just as they multipled savings. When our systems are stressed and pressed toward their limits, not only do savings diminish and costs increase, but the broad interconnectedness of these systems itself becomes a liability, and problems crop up simultaneously: air pollution, congestion, climate change, affordability, and public health. Even terrorism is a factor here, since a single hit to the ports could quickly disable one of the world's largest regional economies.

The fate of Los Angeles is a global story. And while oil deposits financ_ the development of Los Angeles Basin—and many large public works project_ that ensured the city's future growth into one of world's great global cities—it tied its fate to shipping and shopping. It now manages the ups and downs of globalization, pollution impacts, economic health, and countless other varied and competing interests. Goods movement has been a windfall, like the oil rush and Cold War military manufacturing that preceded it, yet economic cycles aren't what they used to be; they are now fraught with new variables, challenges, and constraints. In many ways we played globalization like an oil or gold boom, extracting as much as possible as quickly as possible, and staging areas like Southern California and South China were transformed in the process.

In a Terminator-style twist, California has returned to the past to help save the future. Late in 2008, it was revealed that the old Wilmington oil field beneath the harbor could still hold $1 billion in revenue by 2018. It's an unexpected cash windfall for cities like Los Angeles and Long Beach, who have begun to strain under growth and cost pressures at their respective ports, as well as California state and Occidental Petroleum, who would deploy new injection technology to squeeze hidden hydrocarbons out of the recesses of the muddy harbor. The Wilmington field has 4,000 different wells; new technology could squeeze a 63 percent increase in oil output out of the last remaining producers, plus add several new wells.

Long Beach mayor Bob Foster touted the plan to protract the life of an aging oil field as a "win-win for everyone." The ports themselves could gain $150 million alone, and some valued relief from their current entrapment within billions of new environment-related expenses, increased operating costs, and continued threat of decreased growth in container traffic. Oil money could offer some latitude to address the environment-community gridlock that threatens the ports. Yet new exploration and new drilling opens up the specter of longstanding contamination and health impacts, not just the barrens of Signal Hill, but also of more recent fiascos, such as the 1969 oil spill from a platform in Santa Monica Bay which leaked 200,000 gallons of crude into an 800 mile oil slick that covered local beaches. On the other hand, with predictions of a growing flotilla of large oil tankers arriving in San Pedro Bay, adding more congestion, pollution, and risk of spill, homegrown crude does have some advantages.

In September 2008, U.S. Congressional Democrats reversed a decades-old policy against offshore drilling, potentially opening up vast stretches of ocean from Florida to California. (Not unrelated, oil companies contributed $90 million to California political campaigns in 2006.) On shore, depleted fields across the Los Angeles Basin are being drilled again, from Beverley Hills to the harbor and beyond. In 2008, several new wells were sunk into the depths of Signal Hill. One exploration company estimated that Signal Hill itself has two billion more barrels of recoverable oil hidden deep beneath the shallow formations previously claimed by drillers in the 1920s.

With the new scramble to secure oil, Los Angeles is rediscovering its identity of the 1920s. Then, as now, Los Angeles's "homegrown wealth and commerce were insufficient to support the region's lavish superstructures of consumption," writes historian Mike Davis. "As Upton Sinclair noted, Los Angeles was fundamentally 'parasitic' on prosperity produced in other regions—a kind of 'cloud society,' levitated by the influx of wealthy migrants."

Unlike Sinclair's 1920s microcosm of frontier industry, today's players in Wilmington and Long Beach are also the world's largest corporations, representing the vanguard of the global economy: Wal-Mart, Chevron, ConocoPhillips. Los Angeles launched the modern oil industry, pioneered automobile culture and urban sprawl, and helped deliver the world into container ship consumerism. And on many fronts, it is attempting to reinvent past growth patterns—drilling deeper, shipping faster—as future challenges bear down, based on an irrepressible optimism about the limits of our material world.

Sinclair made Signal Hill famous, yet his tales of desperation, corruption, and conflict seem nearly quaint in hindsight. Sadly, in our time, squandered fortunes, depleted economies, and polluted zones are no longer limited to a dusty little 2.5 square mile patch of land.

CHAPTER 5

ALL IS PLASTIC

THE SMALL WORLD OF HYDROCARBONS

The Wal-Mart of Oil

Flying a few hundred feet above the forest, the helicopter swings into a turn. Below are countless trees—pine, spruce, and larch. There are small green lakes amid the trees, and swaths of open muskeg that look like verdant meadow from above. This is the boreal forest, or Taiga, a dense and huge swath of biome that circles the Subarctic from Alaska to Northern Europe to eastern Siberia. It is the Amazon forest of the north, the biggest terrestrial ecosystem in the world.

The muskeg is what makes the boreal unique: a biomass-rich sponge of sphagnum moss, water, dead plants, and small shrubs and trees, it can reach as deep as 100 feet underground. Eventually, the trees and muskeg give way to cut lines, which turn into sandy berms dotted with black puddles. This is the outer edge of a huge tailings pond, part of a series of oily lakes and contaminated sand flats created by the mass production of synthetic crude.

It's all part of an estimated $218 billion in oil mining projects proposed for northern Canada, covering an area the size of Florida or Great Britain. Bitumen crude is heavy oil laced with soil and water that is found in Alberta's Athabasca region and beyond. Other forms of "unconventional" crude can be found around the world, from the light-heavy oil of Venezuela to the bitumen-like gravel of American oil shale.

Unconventional crude has become a strategic energy source in the twenty-first century, ever since high oil prices and shrinking global reserves of conventional crude made it economically attractive to energy multinationals. The International Energy Agency (IEA) reported in 2007 that the global oil industry will likely invest $5.4 trillion between 2006 and 2030 just to maintain production capacity. "Twenty-two trillion dollars of investment in energy supply infrastructure is needed to meet projected global demand [because] the world's primary energy needs are projected to grow by 55 percent between 2005 and 2030," notes the IEA. About half of the increase in global demand goes to power generation and one fifth to meeting transport needs—mostly in the form of petroleum based fuels." Even in the midst of the 2008 global economic crisis, the IEA still predicted a 45 percent increase in overall demand by 2030.

In North America alone, there are an estimated 1.1 trillion barrels of recoverable unconventional crude. Canada's tar sands represent the largest portion of this virtual reserve, marshalling new investment and production capacity that already provides one-fifth of all American oil imports. Yet there are an estimated total of 100 billion barrels of heavy oil in California, Alaska, and Utah, as well as Alabama, Kentucky, Missouri, and Texas. The tar sands of northern Alberta are only the largest of many global unconventional energy plays that will run for at least the next 50 to 100 years. Heavy oil, shale or bitumen deposits of commercial magnitude are already in production in Russia, Venezuela, Iran, and China.

The helicopter banks again and reveals the grand Syncrude tailings pond in the distance. At about 540,000 cubic meters in volume, this pond and its huge earthen berm, so big that it is rated as the world's second largest dam after China's Three Gorges. Other tailings ponds—large lakes really—litter the landscape below. The massive tailings ponds tell their own story: Each day, Canada exports one million barrels of oil to the United States and dumps 90 percent of the three million barrels of water used daily in its production into the tailings ponds. It's as much water as might be used by a city of 2 million people, and it's toxic enough to kill any fish within a few days.

The ground changes from dirty gold sand to deep black as we pass over the edge of the outflow and into the pits. Here in the black expanse of the strip mine, which is dug into the boreal forest 50 or even 75 meters deep, the huge trucks rumble from even larger electricity-powered excavators that unload house-sized chunks of oily earth into the truck's payloads. Many are the mighty Caterpillar 797B, the largest operating trucks in the world, roughly 48 feet long and three stories high and worth about $5 million each, and they are designed specially for bitumen mining. There are about 185 Caterpillar 797Bs working the pits, plus countless smaller trucks and support vehicles that move among them, at some peril. Only the month before, a contractor from a Caterpillar dealership was crushed by one of them; a few months earlier, a 797B ran over a Suncor Energy employee who was driving a small pick-up truck. Despite safety precautions and an elaborate system of traffic management, driving the world's largest trucks much like maneuvering a small apartment building set on giant pontoon tires, while hauling 400 tons of muskeg at 30 miles an hour.

Extracting oily dirt and turning it into gasoline or diesel is no small undertaking. Based on technologies developed during the 1940s and 1950s, tar-sands mining is an extremely physical, resource-intensive process that has turned into a full-fledged oil rush. Where just two companies toiled along the banks of the Athabasca River during the 1970s, methodically digging out huge open-pit mines to expose the bitumen underneath the muskeg, there are now 87 major excavation projects underway, representing nearly all of the world's major oil companies.

This is the future of oil: a high-impact war on scarcity waged by giant machines and giant corporations. In the aggregate, it is the largest industrial project on the planet. With an estimated 173 billion barrels of recoverable crude, it is advertised by government reports as the second-largest proven reserves after Saudi Arabia. Only about 3 percent of the available bitumen has already been recovered. Once the tar sands reach full production later this century, it is expected that Canada will become the second-biggest oil producer in the world.

From the air, the mining process resembles a gigantic rally race, as trucks accelerate away from excavators in sequence, rumble around twists and turns within the mine toward the hopper bins at to the center of the facility to unload. The dumped loads are crushed by enormous rotating steel teeth at the bottom of the hoppers and sent by conveyor belt to the long cone-shaped extractor cells that will begin to wash the bitumen out of the soil. Meanwhile, the trucks turn around and race back to the excavator, governed by a central dispatch that plots and monitors their progress with GPS.

Viewing this spectacle of the world's largest trucks on a race to fill the tanks of North American SUVs may be entertaining from above, but the traffic is purposeful and precise. Each excavator is designed to fill the truck's payload in four timed scoops. The 797Bs burn 105 liters of fuel each hour (less than 1 mile per gallon) and must be operated near-continuously for maximum operating returns. In each of the large excavator shovelers is a microwave oven and a restroom, which allows workers to stay inside their machines and not require cafeteria visits or bathroom breaks—a Wal-Mart-style productivity gain that will bring in $700 million in additional revenue during the lifetime of Suncor's mine operations.

This is probably what an oil boom would look like if Bentonville ran things: advanced logistics, communications technology, and disciplined management, all to deliver an affordable product across great distances. Unlike conventional energy developments where billions are spent just to locate hydrocarbon deposits, exploration costs here are minimum, since everyone already knows where the resource is located, more or less. In other words, tar sands are really about manufacturing process and logistics.

Wal-Mart, as the market-shaper of the 21st century economy, has been described as a global logistics and management company that also happens to run retail stores. Here in the tar sands, an operation like Suncor is the Wal-Mart of the energy world: it requires scale, abundant inputs, merciless engineering, profit-oriented efficiency, as well as plentiful public subsidies such as tax allowances, royalty holidays, lax regulation, as well as no-limits emissions and expansion. The modern tar sands operator is a fully integrated manufacturing operation and third order of government that also happens to sell energy.

The helicopter finally reaches the edge of the Athabasca River, having traversed miles of black pits and racing trucks. Across the river lies Suncor's city of steel: a Disneyworld-sized extraction and refining site that is the pride of the industry. For decades, few investors bothered with the tar sands, simply because it was too costly. Today's collection of megaprojects is a cutting-edge experiment in creating new energy, yet there is no guarantee that unconventional crude will keep energy affordable. During late 1970s, the per-barrel operating cost in the tar sands was roughly the same as the price of conventional crude; profits were often consumed by the cost of making the oil. Thanks to technology and engineering advances, Suncor's per-barrel costs dropped as low as $8.30 during the late 1990s and early 2000s—a significant advance in cost reduction on par with Wal-Mart's supply chain miracle of the 1990s. And like Wal-Mart, Suncor and other companies improved its cost advantage based on operational scale—getting bigger, always—and from regulatory laxity that minimized or deferred its environmental and climactic responsibilities, allowing it to pursue lower-cost, self-regulation and voluntary measures.

"We're the single largest player in the world's biggest oil basin," Suncor CEO Rick George told *Forbes* magazine in 2003. "And we're next to the world's biggest market." At the time, George disclosed that his ultimate goal, besides adding another 140,000 barrels a day, would be to decrease per-barrel costs to $6, making Suncor North America's cheapest and likely most profitable producer of oil. But in 2008, Suncor's costs boomed to $30 dollars per barrel, one company rep told me, because of increased costs of labor, steel, and energy. By the time that energy prices peaked in 2008, operators like Suncor had incurred a 55 percent operating cost increase since 2005. By late 2008, companies with projects still in development stated that they would need to price their oil at a minimum of $100 per barrel in order to break even. And when oil prices crashed as the financial crisis hit, the industry announced waves of project cancellations and delays, shelving $39 billion worth of projects by February 2009.

This is mainly because the tar sands manufacture high-quality energy by using other forms of high-quality energy and resources. For every barrel of synthetic crude, it takes two tons of soil, as much as four barrels of water, and, on average, between four and six times more energy than conventional oil extraction. "The entire process is fueled by natural gas, and the energy consumed is awesome," writes journalist Andrew Nikiforuk in *The Tar Sands*. "Every 24 hours the industry burns enough natural gas to heat four million American homes in order to produce one million barrels of oil." Natural gas consumption is expected to triple between 2005 and 2015, according to Canada's National Energy Board.

Behind the scenes, there have been significant improvements. Early on, for example, it required almost as much energy to produce a barrel of oil than was embodied by the oil itself. By 2008, the average natural gas requirement was about one-sixth energy the value of a finished barrel. But the process still generates up to three times the greenhouse-gas emissions of conventional oil production. By late 2008, tar sands production was still predicted to nearly double by 2015, and its greenhouse emissions are likewise predicted to increase from approximately 40 million tons of carbon to 67 million tons during the same period. For most of the 2000s, uncontrolled greenhouse-gas emissions were one of the great competitive advantages of the tar sands, since provincial goals for carbon reduction have been largely intensity-based (percentage reduction per barrel) and none have actually been subjected to absolute limits nor subject to required cap and trade reductions; essentially, as of 2009, a green washed emissions regime helped keep manufactured crude as cheap as possible.

If all the estimated 1.1 trillion barrels of unconventional oil in North America is eventually exploited, the climactic impact could be catastrophic. A 2008 report by WWF and the Co-operative Financial Services estimated that this maximum-extraction scenario could result in atmospheric carbon dioxide increases of between 49 and 65 parts per million, pushing past existing climate stabilization targets and potentially forcing a two-degree increase in the global mean temperature—a new peak that could lead to far greater climactic volatility, disease, and famine. "The human race is going to extreme lengths to 'recarbonize' its activities, at a time when rapid decarbonization is needed," charged the WWF.

The helicopter returns with its cargo of passengers, all stunned at the scale of devastation levied against the boreal forest; toxic sand flats, acidic lakes full of hydrocarbon effluent, and open-pit mines that go on for miles. Yet the billions of dollars behind the tar sands is the true wonder, since this is part of a larger story about the persistence of hydrocarbons, our deep dependence on combustion, and the impetus to make unconventional fuels more affordable while undermining long-term energy security.

The revolution of cheap that made Wal-Mart king—and made life more affordable for millions of cash-strapped people—was actually part of the world's last great resource boom. When oil nearly hit $150 in 2008, the modern supply chain began to falter under higher prices, proving more vulnerable than many imagined. All the transport, plastic, and urban sprawl associated with discounting are actually a story about energy. And while our first hundred years was about the discovery of energy supply, our next hundred years will be defined by energy scarcity and a global scramble to control some of the dirtiest hydrocarbon deposits.

Modern consumerism has never been without reliable supplies of affordable energy. And the tar sands of northern Alberta, and its expensive oil manufacturing operations, is a well-financed gamble in favor of chronically expensive crude oil. Does the quest for cheap end here?

Race for Crude

Journalists who arrive in Fort McMurray to visit the tar sands report the obligatory scenes from a town that is bursting at the seams: the Tim Horton's coffee drive-through that is backed-up even at 4 A.M.; the scores of workers who live in campgrounds, converted garages, or who sleep in trucks; the incredulous locals, amazed that the town population could explode from 25,000 twenty years ago to an expected 250,000 in the next twenty years. Between construction projects for bitumen mining and extraction facilities, and the ramped-up pace of existing operations, the tar sands are a seemingly endless fountain of high-paying jobs. This is a place where a high school dropout can make $100,000 in the first year; drug abusers get rehired at the next company down the road; and people come from thousands of miles away to work for a year or two, and then stay for ten.

New jobs and new fortunes are being created out of a global anxiety over the end of affordable energy. The social impact of a $218 billion oil rush is considerable. "Look at the parking lots around here," says union organizer Leroy Nippard. "They're full: multiple families living in a two-bedroom apartment. You need $200,000 salary to get by." The rush of capital into the tar sands has resulted in a rush of people—thousands of workers who live in work camps near the project sites and around Fort McMurray; 40,000 arrived between

2003 and 2008. With all the new crime, drugs, and lack of available health-care, it's a challenging place even if you have a job. But it's likely the only place on the continent where people can sell a mobile home for $500,000, or where companies have been so desperate for skilled workers that they some-times offer complimentary flights, rent support, and generous cash incentives to get them to sign on. It's also the only place on the continent, where union membership has increased substantially—Nippard's union of operating engi-neers has nearly doubled its membership in the last two years—and only half of tar sands construction sites are unionized. "Basically, we're just getting in there and taking it out as fast as possible," says Nippard.

Yet the convergence by world's largest companies here is still surprising, considering the relatively small amounts of oil involved. By the 2020s, for example, the Athabasca mines will deliver over 3 million barrels a day into a world that, as of 2005, was already consuming 83 million barrels a day. Indeed, the unconventional crude of Canada's tar sands is a mere drop in the bucket of the world's daily consumption of oil.

Those extra few millions are critical, not only because global demand continues to grow, but also because bitumen deposits represent a signifi-cant portion of new oil reserves that are not controlled by OPEC, China, or Russia. Moreover, our pool of conventional energy resources is shrinking as state-owned oil companies—represented by OPEC, China, Russia, Mexico, and South America—have come to control the vast majority of proven oil reserves. In 1978, major oil corporations controlled approximately 70 percent of all oil and gas reserves; by the late 2000s, they controlled 20 percent. Put another way, of the world's largest oil and gas producers by company in 2005, the top five were all state-owned oil companies: Saudi Arabia, Russia, Iran, Mexico and China.

This makes large new sources of unconventional energy like the tar sands far more strategic and valuable than previously thought. "The international oil companies cannot dictate the tempo any more," said analyst Fadel Gheit of Oppenheimer & Co. in 2008. "They can try projects that didn't work two years ago, but it's not a question of money. They don't have access to resources."

Combined with demand from emerging markets like China and finan-cial speculation, which can drive prices 20 to 30 percent higher, it's hard to imagine oil remaining affordable forever. Indeed, the billions invested in the tar sands are proof that the world's largest nonstate companies believe in the inevitable rise of crude—and long-term problems with available sup-ply. "Normally, high prices would mean higher supply," said former Iraqi oil ministry undersecretary Fadhil Chalabi in 2008. "What is happening is something different. The international companies are denied access to areas of abundant oil within OPEC, and it's getting costlier in other areas."

At the 2008 World Petroleum Congress, it was announced that the reach of state-owned companies has increased. About 90 percent of world reserves are located in countries that limit foreign investment in energy. The ability of the remaining 10 percent of oil reserves to support North America, much of Europe, and the developing world is in doubt, says the International Energy Agency based on a forecast of non-OPEC supply that one analyst described as "paltry." Looking ahead, the IEA predicted some demand caused by high prices, yet production and available oil supply will decrease at an even faster rate. "We are clearly in the third oil shock," said executive director Nobuo Tanaka. Even as oil prices crashed during the global financial crisis, the IEA continued to predict the return of $100 per barrel oil, doubling to $200 by 2030. ("It is becoming increasingly apparent that the era of cheap oil is over," noted the IEA's World Energy Outlook in November 2008.)

It is for this reason that the International Energy Agency noted that Canada will lead all non-OPEC nations in new production, adding an expected 1.2 million barrels daily by 2013, followed by Brazil, which in 2008 boasted the world's largest single, new oil discovery in nearly a decade in an ultradeep—4.5 miles—offshore basin off the country's Atlantic coast. Previously strong exporters like Mexico and Iran are beginning to weaken, possibly becoming chronically dependent importers of oil like the United States, a one-time world leader in crude exports (back when Los Angeles was known for its oil wells, not movies and container ships).

With the rise of unconventional crude, it would be wrong to suggest that the oil age is ending. In fact, there is much evidence to suggest that we are only just now entering the last oil age—a potentially very expensive and high-impact one. This scenario is potentially more destructive than the notion of peak oil—the near-term decline of hydrocarbon that is widely and often fervently predicted—because it represents a revival of marginal forms of nonrenewable energy that threatens our long-term environmental and economic security. Collectively we could spend the next hundred years paying even more for fossil fuels, investing valuable resources into developing them and significantly increasing greenhouse gas emissions in the process, while displacing efforts to create renewables and conserve carbon.

Peak oil, at least, held out the promise of scarcity-induced change. As we reach finite limitations of growth-dependent globalization, our hydrocarbon chain has begun to cannibalize itself. According to 2008 projections, for example, much of the natural gas from the yet-to-be-constructed Arctic pipelines from Alaska and Canada's Mackenzie Delta could easily be consumed by the energy needs of tar sands producers. In other words, clean-burning natural gas, which has only recently become one of our most strategic energy sources, is being turned into an energy source to make synthetic crude for a continent whose auto fleet is nearly as fuel inefficient as it was in the 1970s.

Countries and corporations are competing not just for new energy supplies, but whole energy supply chains: pipelines, petrochemicals, refining, and low-cost regulatory zones with lax emissions controls in places like Africa, South America, Central Asia and Canada. And not coincidentally, it is debtor nations—both developing countries and overspent Western powers—who are losing out in this contest. Excluding Canada, "oil from the Organization for Economic Cooperation and Development (OECD) nations, Russia, non-OPEC producing states, Mexico, and the United States, the total is a mere 232 billion barrels—or just over 17 percent of the world's reserves," noted Herbert London, president of Hudson Institute, in 2003. And as America's Energy Information Agency noted in its 2008 forecast, it is the non-OECD nations, rich with population and resources, that will nearly double the average economic growth of the high-income economies of the West between 2005 and 2030. The crusade for the world's last affordable hydrocarbons has already begun and this contest has everything to do with the quest of emerging powers like China to secure new energy sources.

At different points during the twentieth century, America led the world in oil exports, manufacturing, and, more recently, in spending and imports. In terms of global dominance, it's a pattern of decline. Collectively, Western nations still hold much clout—diplomatic, military, engineering, consumer culture, etc.—but this is not the same as controlling or better conserving what Thomas Homer Dixon has described as "society's critical master resource."

Energy is essential for maintaining stability and prosperity. "When it's scarce and costly, everything we try to do, including growing our food, obtaining other resources like fresh water, transmitting and processing information, and defending ourselves, becomes harder," writes Homer Dixon in *The Upside of Down.* "And, as the system gets larger and larger and more complex, more and more energy is needed to keep it operating."

Our primary response to this challenge has been to attempt to increase supplies—the energy paradigm of the previous century—despite grand inefficiencies. As evidenced in the tar sands, some of the world's largest energy corporations are adding new oil reserves by, paradoxically, burning up valuable resource inputs—natural gas, water, air, as well as imported machinery, trucks, and workers—to manufacture oil out of dirt. Consequently, a growing portion of the oil that supports our consumer world is getting ever more

expensive, dirtier, and its development, production, and consumption is causing a broad range of unexpected consequences.

Plastic is Power

The world's largest ethylene facility stands tall in the middle of the Canadian
prairies. Ethylene is a hydrocarbon product refined from natural gas, crude
oil, or naphtha that is used to make plastics. If you live in North America
and have recently used a styrofoam cup, a plastic bag, or a plastic outdoor
children's toy, there's a good chance its molecules were formed here. Set
amid farmers' fields in central Alberta, the shining towers and stacks of Nova
Chemical's Joffre plant are built on top of the expansive natural gas reserves
of the Western Canada Sedimentary Basin (WCSB), a rich geological formation of hydrocarbons that also encompasses the tar sands, located a long
half-day's drive to the northeast. The WCSB has served as the anchor for
nearly all of Canada's oil and gas production since 1947, turning Canada into
the world's second largest exporter of natural gas. Nova's sprawling complex
at Joffre is as big as a small town, yet it is mostly empty—much of the work
done here is automated. Three different plants here annually churn out 6 billion pounds of ethylene, and over two billion pounds of polyethylene, a long-
chain polymer that is used to make product containers, plastic films, tubing,
garbage bins, kayaks, and toys. Turning liquid gas into intermediate plastics is
surprisingly straightforward process. Ethane, a colorless, odorless constituent
of natural gas, is heated and then cooled to extreme temperatures, altering
the molecular structure into ethylene, which is a gas at room temperature.
Ethylene is either piped or trucked for intermediate or end-use manufacturing, or processed on-site into polyethylene—polymerizing the gas in long-
chain plastics, resulting in tiny white pellets by the ton. Fifteen percent of
all pellets are bagged and sent to Asia; others are put in boxcars and rolled
out across North America to make plastic packaging, bags, milk containers,
garden sheds, or piping. Coproducts include nylon rope, various kinds of synthetic rubber, and building materials. "Ethane is a primary building block"
says Al Poole, site director, "[of] everything from auto parts, textiles, food
services, and pharmaceuticals."

It was for the rich deposits of natural gas that the Joffre facility was built.
It towers over the verdant plains that first drew settlers in the late 1800s. The
site is 150 acres of orderly, efficient manufacturing capacity. Despite the occasional materials spill—such as an unauthorized 2001 effluent pond release—
the plant hosts a cogeneration plant, increasing efficiency, and carbon capture
for enhanced oil recovery, which sequesters the equivalent of 32,000 cars

annually; most of the visible emissions from the plant stacks are actually water vapor that results from the continuous combustion of natural gas. These operations alone represent 20 percent of Alberta's natural gas consumption, much of which goes into Nova's 416 megawatt cogeneration plant.

Global demand for basic petrochemicals and plastics has increased roughly 4.5 percent annually since the 1980s—with the greatest single-year growth, almost 6 percent, occurring in 2004 when energy prices were double 1999 levels. Americans now consume roughly 100 billion plastic bags annually; producing these bags requires approximately 12 million barrels of crude.

Interest in fuels and plastics all started during the late nineteenth century, when oil, gas, and aromatic hydrocarbons became the focus of experimentation and industrial processing. In 1899, for example, German chemist Hans von Pechmann accidentally discovered polyethylene, which became part of our consumer world during the 1950s. By the early 2000s, an estimated 60 million plastic bags were produced worldwide on an annual basis.

The fruits of the world's industrial carbon chain—polymers, styrene, methane, nitrogen, paraffins—are the lifeblood of the twenty-first century, reflecting an economy increasingly dominated by the likes of Wal-Mart, Exxon, Dow, and Monsanto. All of these global category killers have built themselves upon extracting value from the hydrocarbon chain—and making this value available to consumers in a plethora of low-cost, end-use products. Even chemicals and materials not directly sourced from hydrocarbon feedstocks are usually embodied energy products because they require high-quality energy inputs.

There's a strong historic correlation between the world GDP and petrochemical development. Ethylene, in particular, contributes to prosperity. "Just look at the historic correlation between the world GDP and ethylene demand," argued Dr. Rajesh Ramachandran, then-president of Dow Canada in 2005. "In the history of business as we know it, I'm not sure you can find another such strong long-term correlation in existence."

It's a compelling theory. World ethylene production has almost tripled since 1980. Most consumers don't know that this double-bonded hydrocarbon is the most prolifically produced organic chemical in the world, dating back to 1795, when several Dutch chemists synthesized it as part of efforts to create "Dutch oil" or ethylene dichloride—a handy paint remover and modern-day component of the global environmental hazard (and highly popular petrochemical) polyvinyl chloride, or PVC.

Plastics and chemicals have helped serve as the backbone of rapid industrial growth and consumer plentitude ever since. More recently, efficient and advanced applications of plastics literally stretched valuable hydrocarbon molecules and extended the role of plastic into building materials, transport, and automotives—often ably replacing wood, paper, and steel. The global dispersion of petrochemicals are a map of world power. Since the mid twentieth century, countries with plentiful crude oil but no added-value industries, for example, such as Angola, Nigeria, Iran, Iraq, Russia, are usually oil oligopolies or juntas that funnel resources to richer, more powerful nations through global energy trades. Yet leading OPEC nations, rapidly industrializing Asian nations, and, certainly, Europe and North America in their prime, all shared the trait of having vibrant petrochemical complexes, not democracy, as a common denominator. Finance, influence, and access to resources are increasingly controlled out of Dubai, Shanghai, Beijing, and Singapore. It has something to do with the higher concentration of education and technology required to sustain advanced hydrocarbon industries—nearly 30 percent of chemical industry workers have university degrees, for example—plus the industry's ten times input value multiplier that can, in turn, multiply the nation's own wealth and power.

The odorless pellets of polyethylene produced at Joffre and other plants around the world are a value-added product worth 12 times the cost of the natural gas that is used to manufacture it. Poole estimates that polyethylene demand has grown at about 1.5 times the rate of national GDP in recent decades. And while the land and ocean pollution from waste plastic has also grown considerably—notably the North Pacific "island" of waste plastic reported since the 1990s– packaging itself has become more efficient in recent years, between 250 and 400 percent less mass and volume utilized. Closer to home, phthalates and other plastic additives have become pervasive within our own bodies, leading to an outcry over endocrine disruption and the hazardous use of petrochemicals in daily life. Likewise, it's hard to be energy efficient without plastic: one of the great ironies of modern life is that we have to burn up hydrocarbon in order to save even more hydrocarbon. The Tivek plastic house wrap and closed-cell foam that is commonly seen at residential construction sites requires 35 liters of fuel to create. But once installed, these plastic products save 1,250 liters of heating fuel annually. Polyethylene also now replaces wood in construction applications, and offers a great many options in foam insulation, panelized construction, and high-performance wall construction with insulated concrete forms.

Reducing the amount of plastic used for bags and packaging is partly about cost control—doing more with less hydrocarbon—and partly about advances in organic chemistry. At Nova's nearby research facility, research director Eric

Kelusky shows how long-chain polymers are increasingly customized and engineered to create new kinds of plastic, and to create more product out of the same mass of polyethylene pellets. With plastic bags and other products made out of polyethylene, "the workhorse of plastics," less hydrocarbon can be used to create the same product because longer-chain polymers are now much stronger, while maintaining their supple, rip-resistant qualities. Since the 1970s, the average plastic bag has required 200 to 300 percent less material to manufacture. "Yet the number of things getting packaged has grown even more," says Kelusky. "Thirty years ago, people didn't eat yogurt. And a lot of things that were made of metal, glass or even wood are now made of plastic. It's usually cheaper to use plastic."

Kelusky shows off Nova's laboratory, where the company manufactures short runs of various products with factory equipment. Unlike other plastics that have reactive and noxious additives—such as hormone disruptor Bisphenol A in polycarbonates or chlorine in PVC—basic polyethylene is upgraded mineral oil, so there is little stench or irritant. On one machine is a new variety of film being air-blown into thin sheets, like bubble gum expanding. Polyethylene chips are heated and fed into a large blower—an eight-foot-wide steel doughnut that sends a shimmering circular curtain of thin, molten plastic ten feet into the air, where it is collected, air cooled, and rolled onto spools that are ten feet wide. It is mesmerizing to watch. "It's quite an art to engineer these," he says. "It's all about melting, pumping, and pressure—getting flow of air on each side of the polymer."

Another positive new development was radical reduction in food waste in both the developed and developing world brought out by the advent of packaging films. In India, for example, where refrigeration was minimal, this kind of packaging resulted in less food spoilage, improved product shelf life, and better consumer access to fresh food. Even at home, the ordinary milk bag was invented and improved. "We manipulated the length and the composition of the molecule chains so that milk bags had a special set of properties," says Kelusky. "They now seal better, last longer and do not break easily."

Plastic shipping containers are in the works and would have the advantage of being collapsible, offering radical new efficiencies in the reduction of weight and volume for land and ocean transport—and are "made out of a sheet of plastic the size of this room." says Kelusky. Special extruded foams are also being used to reduce packaging and reduce extra mileage caused by return of damaged goods. "A computer used to have a 2-by-2 foot package, but we reduce this by 40 percent with something that can withstand multiple drops," says Kelusky. "It's about lifecycle analysis: reduce logistics space, shipping costs, returns. There's savings as much as one-half of logistics costs and returns. Saving a small percentage of returns makes a big difference, and allows for more shipping options." This is of particular interest to Wal-Mart, whose money-saving, emissions-saving packaging initiative promised to reduce packaging by 5 percent by 2013.

Nova's Joffre site even ships pellets to China—and some of it is later shipped right back to us as packaging or product. But China soon won't have a need for North American plastic. A new world map of petrochemicals shows that productive capacity is relocating to the East and Middle East. Approximately ten times the polyethylene output of Joffre will be produced in the Middle East by 2013. Although per capita demand for polyethylene is still 800 percent more in developed countries, it will be non-Western nations that will create nearly all new demand for plastics during the twenty-first century. It's the revenge of cheap: For decades, emerging markets provided affordable goods, resources, energy, and labor inputs that raised consumer standards in North America, Europe, and the United Kingdom. Yet the fundamental truth is that these same developed economies are de-industrializing—losing valuable petrochemical capacity, in particular—simply because they can no longer compete on a global basis.

In fact, refinery and petrochemical complexes across North America and Europe have been closing since the first decade of this century. Even within the formerly prosperous petrochemical zone south of the tar sands boom in Alberta, several major sites have closed since 2005, including one of Alberta's original refineries at Devon, which opened in 1950 next to what was once one of the world's largest oil fields, Leduc Number One. Other closures include Edmonton's Celanese plant, and, in August 2006, Dow Chemical announced that it was closing three petrochemical plants in Alberta and Ontario, adding to an estimated 50 manufacturing facilities that Dow Chemical, which is the world's second largest chemical company, has shuttered worldwide since 2003. As one local observed, many large companies just don't see any future here except for bitumen. "It's pretty much dried up around here and they're all going up north. It's in the oil sands now," said Tony McCormick, who started working at the pioneering Devon plant during the 1960s.

The trend is global. In 2008, for example, Dow Chemical announced that it would idle 40 percent of its European styrene capacity (i.e., polystyrene plastic and foam, a common plastic for electronics, containers, packaging), 30 percent of its North American acrylic-acid production (which is essential for other plastics and paints), and shuttered worldwide production of ethylene oxide (an intermediate agent in the production of polyesters). Five thousand jobs and 20 different facilities were eliminated. At the same time, Dow also announced worldwide price increases—as much as 25 percent—in order to offset the rising cost of production, citing everything from the slowdown in American auto sales to the steep rise in global energy prices. "Our feedstock and energy costs are up more than 40 percent compared with the same six months of last year," explained Dow's CEO, Andrew N. Liveris in 2008.

Global price differentials for natural gas and feedstock tell the story: In May 2008, Saudi Arabia's natural gas prices were 700 to 1,000 percent cheaper than those of North America, the United Kingdom, and Europe. New facilities in the Middle East and Asia also carry a price advantage that is resulting in an outflow of high-value jobs and production capacity.

By its own estimates, Dow Chemical's global operations consume the equivalent of a Middle Eastern country's daily gas production. The company claimed that its bill for hydrocarbon feedstocks—natural gas liquids and crude by-products—plus the energy required to manufacture and refine them had increased 400 percent, from $8 billion in 2002 to more than $32 billion in 2007. Dow continued to add new price increases on its petrochemicals into 2009, even as the global economy stalled and the price of crude oil fell to under $40 a barrel. ("Raw material prices are once again on the rise, despite the impact of the global economic downturn," said Mark Bassett, Dow's global business director, in March 2009.)

Some companies are transitioning out of hydrocarbons altogether. The DuPont corporation, which was built on the manufacture of gunpowder and explosives in the nineteenth century, began in the early 2000s to move away from decades of plastic and chemical development and into agribusiness and biotech. Over half the company's 2007 $1.4 billion research and development (R&D) budget was invested in agribusiness, which included biofuels. "We believe we are in a resource-constrained world and it will continue," said Chad Holliday, who was DuPont's chairman in 2007. After selling off 20 percent of its business—its oil interests in Conoco, plus textiles and pharmaceuticals—DuPont is chasing after commercial development of second-generation biofuels, such as cellulosic ethanol, which is, essentially, an automotive fuel derived not from corn kernels, but from corncob waste and wood chips. Critics complained that the company, a still-major producer of plastics and chemicals, might be using ethanol production as a way to market specialized seeds, pesticides, and other agribusiness products. (The promise of cellulosic ethanol as a fuel source from wood chips and corn cobs is to turn alternative fuels from a net energy loss: ethanol produced during the start of 2000 frequently used corn and natural gas to create a product whose value of energy inputs often surpassed actual fuel value—a feat of inefficiency not even managed by the tar sands.)

Because petrochemicals are a twentieth-century business—encompassing manufacturing, well-paid employees, and high-value products—the departure of these industrial giants is a telling sign. "Globally, [North America] is the highest cost location from an energy standpoint," admits Ramachandran. "Add to that, you know, an ethane disadvantage that is even more significant compared to the rest of the world, you've got, you know, almost a perfect storm brewing. I mean it's the worst disadvantage, if you will, for petchem industry. And in the petchem industry about 80 percent of our cost is associated with raw materials and energy."

Nova's Joffre site will soon no longer be the world's largest. With cost advantages all but eliminated in mature Western markets, Dow Chemical is moving investment to the Middle East and Asia, helping to build the world's largest and newest petrochemical complexes using the cheapest natural gas in the world. One week after Dow announced 2008 production declines and price increases for North America and Europe, it announced a $26 billion joint venture with the state-owned Saudi company Aramco to build what may become the world's largest petrochemicals complex. Because natural gas is not globally traded to the degree of crude oil, the locked-in gas reserves of the Middle East are fixed-price bonanzas in the twenty-first century.

In other words, Dow closed its plants not for lack of demand for plastic. Rather, Dow's facilities were closed simply because the energy markets of the West are facing chronic crisis. "It's definitely a very challenging time. We cannot even know the gravity of the challenge that is ahead of us," Ramachandran says. "If we look at it globally, you know, Dow itself has announced the building of the two or three crackers [refining towers that produce petrochemical feedstocks] in the Middle East in the next, you know, three to five years, over 20 crackers being built in the Middle East. Not a single one is being built here."

Running out of affordable hydrocarbons didn't just happen overnight. In hindsight, there has been no small amount of self-sabotage. Jurisdictions like Alberta, for example, have persistently approved large pipeline projects to expedite extraction of its resources internationally and have historically charged cheap royalty rates on hydrocarbons. "It's pipelines and new competition for gas," confirms Nova's Al Poole. "The value that people put on ethane [feedstocks] today is different than 20 years ago."

Valuable petrochemical feedstocks and natural gas are shipped through growing pipeline networks to distant buyers who can pay higher prices. The inefficiencies created by aging plants and a generally wasteful economy within many Western nations haven't helped either. For example, every dollar increase in natural gas prices creates a claimed $3.7 billion annual operating cost increase for American chemical industries—and a similar economic drag on other high-value sectors.

The plain fact is that natural gas is too valuable to be used to burn the oil out of dirt. Within most world markets, natural gas is usually priced much cheaper than crude oil and only reaches price parity with crude on rare occasions. In other words, natural gas offers as much as a 50 percent discount when compared to the energy value embodied by crude oil. (Based on an estimated 6 to 1 thermal equivalence of gas to crude oil, the August 2008 Henry Hub price for natural gas as crude equivalent amounts to $50.94 at a time when crude oil itself was valued at over $120 per barrel.) Exploiting the price differential between lower-cost natural gas inputs and higher-price synthetic crude is currently what makes the tar sands economical. This is a problem, because demand is increasing rapidly and new sources of gas from the Arctic are nowhere in sight. "We currently use a significant portion of Alberta's gas to extract oil [from the tar sands]," says Dow's Ramachandran. "This is akin to using $100 bills to light the candles at the dinner table: Mandating the use of natural gas for [tar sands] power is costly and inefficient."

Consequently, acute competition for affordable hydrocarbons and the rise of dirty energy have become a force of destructive change. For example, tar sands refining on an unprecedented scale is expected to require vast amounts of hydrocarbon distillate, and extracting oil from dirt requires vast quantities of conventional natural gas, possibly enough to completely drain the first Arctic gas to come online via the Mackenzie Valley pipeline project. And like bitumen manufacturing at the tar sands, chemicals and plastic require significant energy resources (sometimes comprising over 75 percent of the cost of production) in order to transform raw hydrocarbons into appliances, plastic packaging, and syringes.

Those who live near a longstanding petrochemical complex—such as polluted communities in Sarnia and Niagara in Ontario, Lake Charles, Los Angeles, and Houston—may rightfully applaud a downturn in petrochemicals. But what has become clear is that plastic is still an indicator of wealth and influence, not unlike the sailing fleets of former imperial nations or gold reserves during the twentieth century. Those who have it tend to prevail, for the simple reason that nearly everything we touch on a daily basis has some sort of petrochemical component.

The erosion of plastic and chemical industries would be far less worrisome, and might even be considered an environmental triumph, if not for two very relevant realities. First, we are years, if not decades, away from transitioning away from plastics and petrochemicals; volatile erosion of an industry responsible for so many products threatens to profoundly destabilize—leading to

food shortages, compromised health—all but the most self-sufficient economies. It's not just about plastic bags. Second, petrochemical manufacture
will play an important role in the production of sustainable solutions, such as
in producing the high-purity silicon wafers that are required for solar power
and computers. High-performance chemicals and materials will continue to
be necessary in a green economy. The unmanaged erosion of this capital-
intensive, skills-intensive technological capacity within major world economies—and the gradual but persistent movement of this capacity to the Middle
East, in particular—is a substantial concern. Second-generation, affordable,
thin-film solar cells; conductive polymers, (the discovery of which resulted in
Nobel Prizes for Alan J. Heeger, Alan G. McDiamid, and Hideki Shirakawa
in 2000), which have been formed into organic LED lighting and organic
solar cells; and infrared solar cells printed on plastic sheets all hold promise for mass-produced renewable power in the future. Chemicals, advanced
materials, and manufacturing will likely be part of a strategic resource that
could radically improve the impact of greenhouse gases.

With the production of solar cells increasing rapidly, who will control
the essential manufacturing inputs and raw materials? Probably not those
nations who staked their future on rapid consumer-driven growth, whose
bloated service economies ignored the perils of de-industrialization and
neglected energy policy, green technology, and energy conservation. The
fate of developed-world debtor nations is becoming more clear: in March
2009, it was announced that Nova Chemicals and its prized Joffre ethane
complex was being sold to Middle Eastern giant International Petroleum
Investment Corporation at a bargain price—$2.3 billion. Nova had simply
leveraged itself too far prior to the great global collapse of 2008, and its stock
plunged 66 percent almost overnight. When the former government-owned
company was taken public in 1998, its stock price was $30; by February 2009,
it was $1.28. Many heralded the sale of the homegrown asset to Abu Dhabi as
a colossal failure of an undergoverned, deregulated industry that had passed
its prime.

It was evidence of synchronous market failure on an astounding number
of levels. But what happened was also quite simple. While Alberta mined
its natural resources, others came to mine Alberta. "There were no rules,"
explains Don MacNeil, an Alberta union president and longtime energy
observer. "We get left with the debt, the greenhouse gases, and the tailings." It is probable that Alberta's cheap natural gas will run out long before
the last bitumen is mined. It's possible that major new pipelines and liquid natural gas terminals for offshore deliveries can't or won't be built fast
enough. And with Arctic gas so distant and industrial demand continuing

to increase, MacNeil wonders, "What are we going to heat our homes with in 2014?"

Eric Kelusky has a suggestion: Burn plastic for its energy value. Most finished plastics actually have a richer energy density—stored energy by mass—than crude oil. In fact, polyethylene and polypropylene plastic has more energy value than biodiesel, jet fuel, and crude oil but less than natural gas and refined gasoline. Plastic is one of the most difficult areas of materials recycling. "I looked at recycling for much of my career," says Kelusky. "The tough thing is the potential mix of materials. Pesticides can get mixed into food grade plastics." Halogenated plastics like PVC contain chlorine or fluorine, for example. In fact one of the ongoing controversies about plastic recycling is that, despite best intentions, consumer plastics can often only be down-cycled into secondary plastics that usually can't be recycled, such as park benches or plastic lumber. Our daily plastics have been engineered for specific applications: microwavability, vapor permeability, flexibility, and rigidity. Some plastic films are engineered to heat and cool at different rates, which is why some prepared-food containers don't burn skin when heated. Even the plastic membrane across most single-use yogurt containers is specially created to be cheap and strong, yet flexible enough to resist pressure. When first introduced on the market, these membranes were made using a lighter plastic, and then grocers worldwide reported mass spoilage because many kids and certain adults couldn't help but puncture the drum-like tops. The plastic bottles used for soft drinks, juices, and water make good polar fleece jackets. But, to date, plastic recycling has done little to stem the use of new, "virgin" hydrocarbons in consumer products.

It is precisely because there are so many different kinds of plastics—with different molecular compositions and physical characteristics—that a household bag of assorted plastic recycling can't so easily be turned into a cheap source of recycled food-grade or manufacturing-grade plastic. The best option is to simply use less plastic. So, in 2008, when Wal-Mart announced a major plastic conservation program, in partnership with Environmental Defense Fund, it was seen as both an environmental and cost-saving advance, expected to eliminate 135 million pounds of plastic waste globally. Customers would still be able to recycle shopping bags. But it didn't quite address the mountains of polyester, nylon, polyethylene, and polystyrene that Wal-Mart and other retailers sell on a daily basis. That's a lot of oil and gas—and carbon emissions.

"Polyethylene seemed a great boon, not least to the food industry, when it was first invented," said Professor Tim Lang of England's Sustainable Development Commission on the anniversary of the plastic's discovery in

2008. "But it is now increasingly being seen as a mixed blessing. It has helped improve food hygiene at the cost of environmental degradation. It is a classic example of a short-term fix now unraveling."

But nations who are short on household savings and energy alternatives can't be too choosy in the twenty-first century. Kelusky advocates that we think practically about our situation. Collectively, Western consumers have a Saudi-sized pool of oil-equivalent plastic in their basements, garages, and backyards—especially after the crash of 2008, when recycling prices fell 50 percent and some Chinese recyclers began to refuse shipments. "The larger opportunity is to turn it back into fuel," says Kelusky, noting that northern Europe leads in research and development on power generation. "The plastic is a rental." It's hard to imagine, but the molecules don't lie: Polyethylene is 15 percent more energy rich than crude oil per liter. "There would be no landfill, and we're short on power. It would be intrinsically better than coal," he says. "If you wanted, you could take your blue box to the power station."

Alternately, to make plastic recycling truly work, we would need to pay more: PVC and poisonous additives like Bisphenol A were what made many plastics cheaper. "A class of polymer that is a step better and doesn't require as much additive: simpler, but better," says Kelusky. "Better for recycling or fuel value because it is almost all hydrocarbon. But not everyone will pay for this. No one wants to pay extra. Over time, this will be a problem."

Across the Desert

On the south side of the Taklamakan Desert, in China's Xinjiang region stands a Central Asian oasis, the edge of a dusty city that was once the center of a great Buddhist kingdom. As early as the second century A.D., Yarkand (*Suoju*, *Sache*, or *Suoche* in Chinese) was responsible for ideas and texts that changed the Chinese empire. Today Yarkand is a marketplace for low-income Uyghurs, Islamic farmers and herders that have lived here for more than five thousand years, and a strategic base for China's domestic security forces. With some of the lowest annual incomes in China, these ethnic-minority farmers and herders scratch out a living from the trickle of moisture that flows from the Kunlun mountain range to the near south. Yarkand is literally wedged in between the outer edge of the Himalayas and a vast desert filled with hidden energy treasure. Along with nearby Kashgar, it borders Pakistan, Afghanistan, and former Russian republics to the west.

Riding a public bus along the desert towards Yarkand, locals jump on and off in towns that are built with bricks and mud, many carrying goods that they will sell at market. There are goats, chickens, and bundles of bread. The bus swerves past slow-moving tractors. On one side of the road is sand and scrub, with the larger desert dunes beyond obscured by haze; on the other side sheep and a few yak graze in dried-up pastures. Minicyclones blow in from the desert and kick up dust storms that obscure the road. The bus suddenly stops in the middle of a long, deserted stretch; more cyclones pass by and a teenage boy wearing a *doppa* (Uyghur traditional hat) steps up into the bus. He has appeared from nowhere and finds a seat while the other riders ignore him. In his palm he cradles a single white egg.

The bus pulls back onto the road and speeds east towards Yarkand. Outside, the scenery changes from yellow desert to scrubby trees and farms. Despite dust storms, freezing nights, and persistent drought, the oases of the southern edge of Central Asia's great desert are surprisingly lush. Watered by centuries-old irrigation channels and tunnels filled by mountain run-off, locals grow cotton, apricots, pomegranates, corn, and walnuts. Climate change has brought drought to this region. According to one government report, temperatures in Xinjiang have increased 1.6 degrees Celsius since the 1980s, well above most averages, and the glaciers that have supplied the oases with water and sustained agriculture have begun to recede. Between dwindling water supply and China's government-led expansion into towns and cities all along the great desert, Uyghur society itself is threatened.

The center of Yarkand has been largely paved over by Chinese developers. Government offices, a modern bus station, and a police detachment line a broad main street lined with concrete planters and benches. It's a template of China's colonial urban form: white tile, blue glass, and concrete that can be found on the edges of its empire from here to Tibet to Inner Mongolia. There is blaring karaoke from the Yarkant Hotel, an older Soviet-era establishment, which was once the local headquarters for the Communist Party. Inside, the archetypical padded armchairs with white doilies stand in a semi-circle, awaiting the arrival of old-school functionaries dressed in Mao suits who will lounge around, smoking cigarettes and drinking tea while issuing edicts. In the hotel's restaurant, Chinese entrepreneurs serve up delicacies in air-conditioned splendor, while Uyghur vendors peddle kebabs and Nan flatbread out on the street in wheel carts. The café, which serves up noodles and lamb, is the liveliest spot in town besides the Sunday market, and on its outer wall is a rough double-sized mural of John Rambo, of the classic 1980s action film *Rambo*. But this roughly painted Rambo, clothed in camouflage gear and fiercely firing off an AK47, looks not like Sylvester Stallone, but like an ethnic Uyghur in fatigues.

It's just another indication that all is not well between the Chinese newcomers and Xinjiang's former Islamic majority. The police here carry

automatic weapons. Locals don't want to be interviewed, politely point-
ing at police and shaking their heads. Nearby, a mostly deserted bowling
alley stands next to a local café. Several blocks away is the Altun Mosque of
Yarkand, which dates back to the tenth century; its prayer hall is still open
but empty. At the bus station travelers have to juggle schedules organized in
Central Asian and Beijing time, since much of the region can hardly agree
on a time zone, let alone mend fences in a struggle that's been simmering
since the first century AD.

All along the edge of the Taklamakan desert, within a few day's drive of the
Pakistani and Afghani borders, the other desert towns—Kashga and Hotan—
show signs of both rapid development and feudal rivalry. In Kashgar, photos
of bloodshed, captured guns, and murdered police are posted to buildings in
an attempt to persuade Uyghurs that Chinese crackdowns against mosques
and outspoken locals are legitimate. Everywhere, large banners put up by
the government urge Uyghurs to follow China's strict one child per family
policy. Islamic resistance to this idea has provoked the assassination of several Chinese enforcement officers. Partially used pharmaceuticals can be
purchased in local bazaars—a reminder that annual income in the Uyghur
heartland remains even lower than in the rest of rural China.

Xinjiang is the site of one of Asia's longest-running intranational conflicts,
a 2,000-year battle between those to whom this is still East Turkestan and
those who see it now as belonging to the Middle Kingdom. Invaded by China
in 1937 and consolidated by Mao Zedong in 1950, Xinjiang rarely captures
international headlines, but open warfare, summary executions, and assassinations are commonplace. It was in Kashgar, the most distant of all of China's
cities, and nearby towns where several fatal incidents took place during the
2008 Beijing Olympics: 20 Chinese police officers and, reportedly, 33 civil-
ians were killed in clashes and attacks during the month of August 2008.
The region remains an area of major concern to international human rights
groups like Amnesty International, who decry "gross and systematic" abuses
that take place there.

For now, the Chinese appear to have largely won this war, largely because
of the long-term scarcity of cheap, accessible, fossil power around the world.
This Central Asian frontier has become crucial to China's economic survival
plans, especially its recent efforts to transition from a low-cost-manufacturing
economy to a higher-value, independent economy. In order to stabilize its
heartland, China needs high-quality energy, lots of it. Xinjiang has an estimated 10 trillion cubic meters of recoverable natural gas, buried deep beneath
the sands of the Taklamakan desert. The largest single source of crude oil
in China, roughly one-third of the country's reserves, is also located here.

Uyghur nationalism stands in the way of the planet's fastest-growing consumers of power in the twenty-first century.

Here, the brute, methodical consolidation of a new fossil-fuel empire is underway. For years, China relied upon imports. A net exporter during the 1980s, China is now the world's third-largest net importer of oil, accounting for nearly 40 percent of new oil demand during the mid 2000s. While China also lead world investment in renewable energy in 2006, "China has poured billions of dollars of investment in building power plants—at a rate of one large power plant (1000 MW) per week," wrote Jiang Lin in *Energy Policy*. "China in 2004 added the entire generating capacity of California or Spain in a single year."

Energy is the single biggest factor behind China's continued ability to sustain growth without imploding. China needs energy to sustain its high output of domestic and export manufacture, especially of high-value, high-margin items like iPhones, laptops, and IT infrastructure. "More than 80 percent of crude oil in China is used in oil processing, chemical fiber manufacturing, and chemical raw material production [for plastics and textiles]," notes the *China Chemical Reporter*. "Sufficient oil supply is the basis for the sustained development of these sectors."

The Chinese government is spending a staggering amount of money to lock up foreign oil. In the early 2000s, China launched an ambitious campaign of energy acquisitions, partially funded by rich dollar reserves created through its bargain trade with Western nations. China now imports more oil from troubled petro state Angola than it does from any other nation, including Saudi Arabia, and has aggressively pursued supplies in Sudan, where China is the country's largest foreign investor. China is spending billions on unconditional loans and grants across Sub-Saharan Africa, essentially purchasing access to resources, including in U.S.-dominated Nigeria, where Americans thought they had a lock on offshore reserves until China signed a $2.27 billion oil deal with the Nigerian government in 2007. Likewise, China announced a $3 billion oil deal with Iraq in 2008, the first major foreign oil deal the country has made since 2003. By 2008, China had extended development and infrastructure loans to Angola for as much as $11 billion, even though NGOs (nongovernmental organizations) estimate that $4 billion in oil revenues have gone missing from Angola's treasury between 1997 and 2002. It is possible that your trendy iPhone or Dell laptop is made of blood oil petrochemicals.

While America and its "coalition of the willing" launched energy-tinged wars in the Middle East, China has been diligently poaching access to many of the world's last great conventional oil reserves. "Oil-related Chinese diplomacy has led to the bizarre accusation by Washington that Beijing is trying to 'secure oil at the sources'," reported the *Asia Times* in 2007. "[Which is] something Washington foreign policy has itself been preoccupied with for at least a century."

There is something very Cold War about China's more recent efforts to secure direct supplies at elevated prices, making what is known as "off take," or bilateral, deals, where the energy is directly purchased and then taken completely off the market. "They didn't care about the price. All they cared about was locking up the supply," one oil executive told Canada's *Globe and Mail* in 2008 on the condition of anonymity. "China's goal is to get direct control of the barrels." This is how China, through multibillion dollar deals with African countries, is literally reserving oil by owning it before it can be offered on the open market. Bidding wars and competition for other resources may not be far behind. "Other commodities, including liquefied natural gas, rice, wheat, fertilizer, and water, may be the next lock-up targets," writes the *Globe's* Eric Reguly. "Sovereign wealth funds from China and the Arab world may wade into the game. Inevitably, more and more commodities will be taken off the global markets. At some point, the Americans and the Europeans will realize that paying market prices alone is not enough to secure supplies."

Energy is shaping up to be the arms race of the twenty-first century—and the global sense of fear of terminal scarcity is precisely what pushed the $218 billion investment in Canada's Athabasca basin. Unprecedented energy competition between trading nations is a singular factor in what will make the IEA's predictions of the $200 barrel of oil eventually hold true.

Yet the quest for cheap continues. As world oil prices rose during the 2000s, China also turned its sights towards affordable domestic frontiers. The Tarim Basin, a geological formation that encompasses much of the Taklamakan desert, holds significant amounts of heavy crude, natural gas, and petrochemical feedstocks. In 2004, China completed a $6 billion pipeline to that will be used to export Xinjiang's hydrocarbon riches. The massive West-East Gas Pipeline runs 4,000 kilometers from the Central Asian capital Urumqi to Shanghai, supplying natural gas to the polluted epicenter of the Yangtze economic boom. Construction on an even larger 6,500-kilometer pipeline began in 2008. Costing $10 billion, it will run from Xinjiang to Guangzhou in the south. When they reach full operational status, both pipelines will carry as much as 50 billion cubic meters of natural gas a year. Only the Three Gorges Dam project, which cost China's government about $25 billion, is larger in economic scale.

Tightly controlled by the Chinese government, Xinjiang is often off-limits to foreign journalists (I'm here on a tourist visa) but not to major multinational oil companies like BP and Shell, who fly their flags up and down Beijing Avenue in Urumqi. And, while tremendous wealth is being taken from the ground beneath these old Silk Road outposts in the Taklamakan desert—a region formerly valued for its cotton and strategic proximity to Russia—little of it has reached the Islamic population: Most Uyghurs, Kazakhs, and other indigenous Central Asians still subsist on less than $200 annually.

China has pledged to modernize Xinjiang for its own good, developing a multibillion dollar plan that involves importing vast quantities of bureaucrats, soldiers, gas pipelines, and workers. "It's a top down approach to development, where the state decides what are the important projects like building railroads, roads, developing the oil exploitation of Xinjiang," Nicholas Becquelin of Human Rights in China told the BBC in 2003. "These are all major infrastructural programs that directly benefit the urban Chinese segment of the population. And there is nothing done seriously on poverty alleviation, rural development or minority empowerment in this program."

Local Chinese were, predictably, the first to enjoy Xinjiang's boom, which has only fueled the longstanding feud. "The Chinese get all the favors and preferential treatment," complains my Urumqi guide, Rebiya. "There are few jobs for we Uyghur." For emphasis, she points her finger like a gun and fires at a Chinese couple strolling by.

I've arrived in Urumqi only a few months after the last major clash between police and Uyghur rebels. As we stroll along, Urumqi presents itself as two cities: a hastily built Chinese city of concrete, glass, and brick—and a Uyghur stronghold, full of ancient mosques and markets. We walk towards the Sanxihangzi Market in the center of town, passing the famous White Mosque—a 200-year-old institution that, she says, is a frequent haunt of secret police. Although Sanxihangzi is the oldest market in Urumqi, Chinese developers gained permission to tear down its northern corner for a gleaming, 14-storey high rise. Its footprint pushed aside fruit vendors and bread peddlers, much to the indignation of locals who consider the market a treasure of Uyghur culture. It was here that some of Xinjiang's worst riots occurred in 2009, when nearly 200 died.

On a typical day, the market is chaos: Pakistani traders wave bolts of imported silk or push cartloads of naan bread—salted and savory—through the crowd. As we walk through the narrow maze of stalls, Rebiya picks out the choicest dried apricots as a gift, along with some sweet melons fresh from the countryside, piled high on a cart. This is a place that still considers firewood a cutting-edge fuel. The earthen ovens that cook bread don't really work with anything else.

In the midst of an energy boom, the Uyghur have become a minority in their own land. The flood of Han settlers, businesses, industrial development, and police into Urumqi has, in turn, fuelled an anti-Chinese campaign that has given Beijing serious cause for concern with political bombings, assassinations, and weapons smuggling. Xinjiang often exceeds Tibet in executions, a fact that China's affluent trading partners have chosen to ignore: China was taken off the United Nations censure list in 2002 because member nations—and trading partners—elected not to question ongoing human rights violations.

Xinjiang's economic divide and sustained political crackdown has pushed the traditionally moderate local population towards fundamentalism, a political development actively exploited by radicals in Pakistan, Afghanistan, and the former Soviet republics of Central Asia. Between 30 and 300 Uyghur Taliban fighters were reported captured by American forces during the United States' War in Afghanistan. Xinjiang's porous border has seen continued trafficking in radical ideas, as well as guns and ammunition.

But a large part of the energy war is diplomacy and propaganda. The September 11 attacks gave Beijing a tremendous political opportunity to clamp down and push ahead in its pipeline plans. Or as one government report was titled: "East Turkestan, An Integral Part of Bin Laden's Terrorist Forces." China has frequently accused protestors and cultural advocates of belonging to the real East Turkestan Islamic Movement (ETIM), a group that terrorism experts estimate has 40 core members, based mostly in Pakistan. Beijing alleges that the ETIM is a "major component of the terrorist network headed by Osama bin Laden." Others speculate part of the violence isn't political but comes from revenge or crime.

Official sources claimed Xinjiang separatists committed more than 200 acts of terrorism in China between 1990 and 2003, killing 162 people and injuring more than 440; Xinjiang police claim there were 800 "separatist incidents" in the first eight months of 2001 alone. Later in 2002, China's Foreign Ministry reported that then–U.S. president Bush and Chinese president Jiang Zemin had agreed that "Chechnya terrorist forces and East Turkestan terrorist forces are part of the international terrorist forces, which must be firmly stopped and rebuffed."

Nevertheless, the real threat of terrorism in Xinjiang remains indeterminate. Expatriate political networks have been subdued, transborder traffic in dissidents has been slowed, clerics are forced into political re-education, birth control is heavily enforced, and even the Uyghur language, a distant relative of Turkish, has been banned from universities and schools for communist cadres. In short, today's Xinjiang bears a harsh resemblance to Mao Zedong's

China during the cultural revolution. It is a zone of enforced progress and cultural oppression.

Because of this, China's quest for cheap energy is surely manufacturing new instability. Some observers predict that anger against China will increasingly become redirected at the United States and its allies. "There's real disillusionment and growing anger, not so much against China, but against the United States. Mosques are now raising warriors to go and fight," said Dru C. Gladney, a Xinjiang expert at the University of Hawaii. Speaking to a Beijing audience in 2003, Gladney reported that American policy in the Middle East is radicalizing the political underground in Xinjiang, which in turn may disable China's long-term ability to export cheap consumer items to the West. "There is no love or sympathy for Saddam Hussein [in Xinjiang] but there's certainly a lot more awareness of international politics and they're certainly in touch with Muslims around the world."

While China's government helps manufacture and amplify Central Asian terrorism, Western corporations have moved in. Despite its competition with China for Nigerian oil, Shell Oil is one of the largest foreign investors in China, with investments totaling $1.6 billion, and had increased its investment to $4 billion by 2006. This includes a share in the $ 4.2 billion Nanhai petrochemicals plant in Guangdong, China's largest single refinery. As one Shell executive explained in 2005, China will likely become the second-largest chemical market in the world by 2020, and the fact that China's per capita consumption of plastics was only 22 kilos annually, compared to Japan's 87 kilos per capita and 100 kilos of America, was a measure of vast sales growth potential. By 2010, Shell intends to have over a third of its petrochemical production in Asia and the Middle East.

Beijing has dubbed Xinjiang its "sea of hope" because of the region's rich energy deposits—but for many foreign multinationals, it is simply a foothold within the fastest-growing energy market in the world. As analysts have noted, Shell's aggressive entry into China is at least partially about cultivating relationships with the Chinese government, in addition to gaining a strategic position at the confluence of Russia, China, and Central Asia. During the early 2000s, Shell was a full partner in the first Xinjiang pipeline project. "The West-East pipeline is a pathfinder for future pipelines and gas from farther afield," explained Shell Exploration (China) managing director Martin Bradshaw in 2002. "[The pipeline] will be in line with international standards and . . . will benefit all ethnic groups." The beginning of a huge trans-Asian pipeline network, one as complete as those seen in Europe and North America, begins in Xinjiang. Yet not long after, China's national oil company dumped its foreign partners and built the pipeline by itself.

With the formula for Central Asian strife now solidly in place, China has begun to express the kind of explicit energy nationalism long predicted for the twenty-first century. "On the street and in the boardroom, there is a growing sense in China that we are now strong enough to do it all alone which I think is wrong," said European Union trade commissioner Peter Mandelson in 2008, regarding ongoing trade obstacles and "an unspoken economic nationalism that implies that foreign investment is no longer wanted or needed."

The inevitable consequence of building a modern-day manufacturing empire is a deep hunger for resources. And in the case of Xinjiang, the old geopolitics of Maoism—the manifest destiny of an ideological state—has been replaced with a one-party state deeply in need of large quantities of secure power. Because if China cannot feed its factories, refineries, and booming cities, then its growth stalls and the delicate political balance of China's post-communist system is potentially outpaced by rural poverty, regional upheaval, and the debilitating cost of imported crude and natural gas. In the West, importing crude oil is still accepted as a necessary evil, even if it indirectly funds terrorism. In China, the prospect of escalating energy costs and excessive oil imports are seen as the end of China's miracle boom—and the onset of chaos and collapse.

The one thing everyone can agree upon is that the world still needs natural gas right now, lots of gas. What this means is that major pipelines (and the people who control them) are on par with the railroads in the nineteenth century. Energy suppliers hold the key to our economy, and those who control transport and product will prosper. A world that starves for lack of natural gas cannot, practically speaking, effectively combat climate change or air pollution.

This is, perhaps, the ultimate measure of our deep and problematic connection to global networks of resource exploration and consumption. On one hand, China's often violent rule over Xinjiang and Tibet might be cause for trade sanctions with any other country that is not so vitally connected with the global supply chain; on the other hand, the more natural gas China burns, the less coal it needs to burn to make the same power. The environmental benefit of the natural gas pipeline is likely reduced demand for other fossil fuels—and even a small offset in China will amount to a massive reduction in greenhouse gas emissions.

But even as China amasses greater wealth and clout, and even begins to green its darkest corners, the nation continues to be challenged by its prerevolutionary past: deep poverty that enables disease, radical Islam, and conflict. Down the road from Yarkand, for example, is the equally ancient city of Hotan, where a mere 14 percent of the area's 1.4 million residents are Chinese. Outside the Chinese core of the city, near a large market is a women's health center and microfinance project, one of many foreign-funded development projects that partners with local and regional government, attempting to raise local incomes above the $1.25-a-day global poverty line. Wages remain low despite billions in loans and grant support from the World Bank—$1.5 billion in 2008 alone—and other agencies for development in China's west. The women's clinic is clean, has medicine, and has windows. "Eighty-five percent of women in the program require some kind of immediate medical attention," says the co-coordinator. "We have 21-year-olds with cervical cancer, mysterious ailments, and diseases long ago eliminated elsewhere, such as typhoid, meningitis, and cholera. Many are prematurely aged, visibly disabled, fighting long-term infections." Yet some of the women in the microlending program are also successful entrepreneurs—selling naan bread, produce, textiles, becoming the bread-winners in their families. It's testament to how selective development can be. Billions of dollars are spent on energy projects in the effort to create affordable fossil power and sustain China's growth miracle (and the West's shopping dependency), yet so many of these benefits have bypassed the people who, literally, live on top of the resource.

It's also testament to the longstanding, moderate version of Islam that has been practiced here that women can earn the family income and speak as freely as men. But progress for all Uyghurs is being eroded by violence and oppression, as well as the incursion of terrorist operatives from abroad who seek to exploit Xinjiang's untapped strife. It is not the Taliban and other covert radicals that locals fear here: it is reprisals from police that keep everyone looking over their shoulder, checking appearances, conversations, and friendships for signs of potentially incriminating antipatriotic behavior.

Hospitality and strength are on full display back in Rebiya's Urumqi home, as she serves up a traditional welcoming feast of rice polo, tomato and cucumber salad, mint tea, and savory noodles. We sit around the low table in the living room to enjoy the feast, trading words for apricot, plum, peach, and melon. Rebiya's cousin pulls out her dutar, a long two-stringed guitar. After an old Turkic folk song, she plays a Ricky Martin tune, the one that blazed across China during the country's first fully televised soccer World Cup in 1999.

Over the drone of the dutar, they sing—*allez, allez, allez*. For all we know, Ricky Martin and the dutar might be the only things holding this place together.

The River Runs North

The Athabasca River runs north through the middle of one of the world's largest continuous bands of boreal forest, to join other rivers and exit into the Arctic Ocean. That this river runs north, and not south, is an important geopolitical fact, says Athabasca Chipewyan chief Alan Adam. If North America's population to the south had to live along this 1,200-kilometer river, he argues, one of the world's largest energy developments would have been shut down long ago. The chief talks of the rare cancers that are showing up in local residents of the small downriver hamlet of Fort Chipewyan, of the toxins found in the area's plants and animals, and, of course, pollution that migrates north from the tar sands sites near Fort McMurray.

The quest for cheap energy inevitably leads us past our cities and malls, down our largest rivers and biggest ecosystems, and into places that are marked by countless shades of green and blue. Places that are not only a global biomass asset, but a growing repository for fugitive effluent and toxins that escape not only tar sands developments, but also millions of consumers and businesses from the south.

It's all outlined on a map on the wall: bitumen leases have been sold halfway along the Athabasca from Fort McMurray. There are industrial projects within a nearly 140-kilometer radius around Fort McMurray. Not only that, potentially rich oil and uranium deposits encircle the community directly, the mineral rights have also already been sold off.

"There's uranium, gold—everything—we are leased out right around the border of our boundaries of our Reserves—everything, all of it," says Adam, circling his hand around the satellite topographic map of the region. "Everybody's attention is on oil sands. The bigger picture is that if these plans were to let go and to keep on going the way they are going, there is no certainty for our people in the future. Nothing at all. And that's why if people were to just stop and think that it has nothing to do with oil sands, it has a bigger picture. This is the whole area that we have to take a look at. And they are drilling here on the lake, not the land—they are drilling in the lakes all along here."

It is no small thing to encircle a northern community like Fort Chip with mining developments and industrial sites: while the hamlet is only 280 kilometers north of Fort McMurray, there is no permanent road access, the muskeg is difficult for prospecting and mining, and air transport is often the only reliable connection. Nevertheless, "there's huge development plans for this area," says Adam. "In 50 years, we would be forced to leave this community. We would be refugees in our own home land. They think I do not know that. I am fully aware. I am fully engaged of all talks from all over the place. I take my position very seriously; that is why I am very serious about what I am doing. People think I was playing a game. I am not playing no game. This is a serious, serious matter."

Fort Chip has been in turmoil since 2006, when the community's former physician, Dr. John O'Connor, went public with his concerns about unusually high incidence of rare cancers in the community of 1,200 predominantly aboriginal people. Not just colon, prostate, and lung cancers, but also six cases of cholangiocarcinoma, a rare bile duct cancer that O'Connor, in an interview with the Canadian Broadcasting Corporation, said should only be seen in the same frequency in a much larger city.

"Our people are dying like flies," says elder Alec Bruno over lunch at the nearby guest lodge. "I thought about maybe, we should move the whole family away from here, away from this lake and the river but then I thought 'why should we move?' Our roots are here; our beliefs, our culture comes from here. This is our home. Why should we move? If anybody is to move, why cannot they move? It is just the way of our people."

Water and animal contamination is a serious issue since many people here still hunt and fish—and, to various degrees, still depend on the land for food. Many couldn't afford to buy all their food from the local store. "We live in isolation here," explains elder Alec Bruno. "We have no roof and our way of life was a simple life until the grabbing of our land. We [still] depend on the land for our life."

At a 2006 regulatory hearing Suncor released a study predicting that, at current rates of development, arsenic levels in local moose meat could increase by 453 times over acceptable levels. Nobody in the community knew about it until months later, when a small item was published in a newspaper story. "When they came up with these preliminary high levels of arsenic, they don't even have the courtesy to inform anyone in the community," said O'Connor at the time.

One of the biggest concerns is seepage from the enormous tailings ponds adjacent to the mines and to the south. All water that moves past the tar sands winds up in the Athabasca Delta to the north, where Fort Chip is located. The largest and oldest of these ponds are either near or directly alongside the Athabasca River. Fish do not live four days in these waters. And there is collectively enough new sludge produced every day to fill 720 Olympic pools. Total waste solids and liquids contain persistent aromatic hydrocarbons (PAHs) equal to what would have been contained in about 3,000 *Exxon Valdez* tankers.

"The ponds leak so routinely, in fact, that they are surrounded by medieval-looking moats equipped with pumping stations to return the seepage to the ponds," writes Andrew Nikiforuk in 2008's *Tar Sands*, the first exhaustive account of bitumen mining in Canada. The first major tailings pond was supposed to be temporary. "Engineers not only miscalculated how long they would need the pond (the initial projection was a few years) but underestimated the fluidity and instability of the tailings. A dam originally designed to be 40 feet high now towers over the river at 325 feet and stretches for two miles."

On a site tour of Suncor, Mark Shaw, the company's director of sustainable development, reports that the company's Pond One is due to be reclaimed by 2010. Parts are "mud mixed with water,"—a total of 255 acres—and are listed, like other ponds, as a company liability in regulatory filings. Shaw is responsible for turning several tailings ponds into "viable landscapes," which would make Suncor the first company to reclaim a tailings pond in the history of the industry.

Shaw and his coworkers would much rather talk about technological innovation, such as the development of "dry tailings"—effluent processed with less water—as well as other environment-related engineering feats that cannot yet be shown because they do not yet commercially exist. It's a little like the greenhouse-gas question: Sure, the oil is dirty, but solutions are immanent. (Don't expect miracles laundering dirty oil though: "Only a small percentage of emitted CO_2 is 'capturable' since most emissions aren't pure enough," said one Alberta government briefing note leaked in 2008. "Only limited near-term opportunities exist in the oil sands and they largely relate to the upgrader facilities.")

There's a strong engineering culture at work here, which is not unexpected given that the development of these pits, ponds, and cities has been the collective brainchild of some of the world's leading technicians and scientists. Yet visitors, taxpayers, and the rest of the world are being asked to trust engineers with managing the consequences of runaway growth. It's a version of the quaint techno-utopianism of the 1950s, except instead of flying cars and space homes, we're asked to believe that industry-led innovation, with some publicly funded subsidies and research, can turn dirty oil clean again. The reality is that the extraction technology at the core of the these massive plants is the same energy- and water-intensive process first invented in the 1920s, and refined to become commercially viable in the 1970s. Among industries like forestry, agriculture, and pharmaceuticals, Canada's energy sector is among the lowest-spending on research and development as a percentage of revenue.

From Central Asia to northern Alberta, the problem with dirty energy is still the same: Those who control the resource often deny responsibility for the environmental, economic, and human rights impacts of resource development. It can be nearly impossible to obtain reliable information on the tar sands, even if you are standing right on the edge of a tailings pond. "There is no leakage from this pond," insists Shaw. "This dyke is largely sand, [filled] with process-affected waters. What we know for sure is that the pond has no leakage."

Shaw argues that the fine clay sediment and bitumen in the tailings settle out and help form an impermeable barrier to keep contaminated water out of what is understood to be a fairly dynamic hydrological environment of muskeg, river, and underground streams. But Suncor obviously has a well-strategized position on the matter, developed to counter investigations by done by several government agencies and the threat of legal action by the First Nations of Fort Chip. "There's really no leakage from the pond," Shaw repeats. "The process-affected water that was part of the dike, rainfall will flush down some [traces]. But no fluid gets from the pond to the river."

It was a cordial but firm denial. Welcome to the Kingdom: The bitumen projects of the Athabasca have become their own semiautonomous jurisdiction, not subject to the same regulatory, environmental, and political accountability as the rest of the continent. The army of trucks, massive tailings ponds, and nonstop capital expansion of the tar sands is the result of companies gaining government-scale powers to self-regulate, self-monitor, as well as influence energy and climate policy. If Suncor says there is no leakage from its tailings ponds, despite substantive evidence that suggests otherwise, the real government has either been slow to challenge the company's assertions or simply echoes them outright. In May 2008, for example, Alberta's environment minister, Rob Renner, claimed that with any leakage "the amount of water that would be outside of the pond itself would be diluted by a factor of about 40 million to one."

There is an authoritarian, antidemocratic reality to this modern energy frontier. Canada sells to and shares heavy-oil technology with China, for example. China's interest in purchasing Canada's bitumen deposits is widely known, and, in 2007, Sinopec, a major Chinese petroleum company, bought 40 percent of the Northern Lights project, the oil sands project in Northern Alberta, which is expected to deliver 1.3 billion barrels of synthetic crude over its lifetime. Both nations share a distaste for the Kyoto climate-change protocol, and growing opposition to dirty oil in 2008 from American environmentalists created a movement in the tar sands industry to move closer to Asian markets in 2009, where most governments do not yet enforce climate controls, carbon taxes, or raise other environmental objections. The exporting of dirty oil's climate change liabilities into the developing world—via multiple pipelines to the Pacific Ocean—has become an real possibility for Canada's tar sands producers, whose responsibility to shareholders is to "get the highest net price to market," as one Husky Energy spokesperson said in 2009.

As the First Nations along the Athabasca River will attest, there is little way of escaping the reach of industry: those who dissent are sometimes blacklisted, which exerts considerable pressure in a region dominated by a single industry. "We have no choice but to seek work [in the tar sands] because our way of life has been destroyed," says Mikisew band official Steve Courtoreille. "Because we've been very outspoken in our belief in trying to protect the environment, we're not treated fairly," he said regarding his band's regional business interests in aviation, construction, and energy services that contributes important income to the community. "We do get threats in terms of losing our contracts. We're not going to get intimidated by anybody who comes and threatens our contracts."

The question still stands: in the pursuit of cheap energy, is the Athabasca becoming an environmental sacrifice zone? "Whenever we raise issues, they are swept under the carpet," says Mikisew representative George Poitras at a panel debate with government and company officials. "Our doctor raised issues about the disproportionate number of health conditions that are showing up in Fort Chipewyan. But what happens? Your government and the federal government launched complaints, as opposed to heeding his advice and [addressing] health conditions and early death from cancers. . . . Do you think the people of Fort Chipewyan are delusional? Do you think we raise trouble just for the sake of it?"

The conflict here is not energy wars between two competing countries, nor is it an outright scramble for resources like a Klondike gold rush or an early California oil field. This contest is about creating new supply as cheaply as possible, and the most efficient way to do this is to minimize regulation and policy that might inhibit growth. Suncor and other companies cannot control the price of steel, the supply of natural gas, nor even labor supply. The tailings ponds were built next to the Athabasca, for example, not because industry had malicious intent, but because it was the cheapest, most convenient spot for their operations; they needed vast water supplies, and being next to the river was an efficient solution.

The tar sands is a manufacturing-logistics operation that happens to produce oil. As James Hoopes wrote in the 2006 anthology *Wal-Mart*, the incredible success of the modern vertically integrated corporation forces us to reconsider what D. H. Robertson once described as "islands of conscious power," which arise in an "ocean of unconscious co-operation like lumps of butter." This was the old notion of the firm and of how essentially undemocratic but managerially powerful competitive companies can successfully coexist with free markets and elected governments. The size of the firm was optimized and often curtailed by its own limits and inefficiencies. (A vision of this also informs more recent arguments that defend globalization as a great global equalizer, creating a "flat world" of many players.) But waves of innovations since the Industrial Revolution have shown that "technological change clearly favoured managerial power over the free market," writes Hoopes. "[T]he economic advantage of the new technology went to large management-intensive firms."

As with finance, energy wealth has often been created through various conflicts of interest. It is estimated that total government revenue from the tar sands will total $123 billion between 2000–2020; for Alberta, it is hoped that this will replace the one-third of its revenue it once collected from conventional oil and gas. Governments responsible for public health and environment are banking on these royalties. Moreover, these same governments are charged with various treaty and legal duties to First Nations even though they directly benefit from the growth and success of companies operating in traditional territories. It goes a long way to explain why there are no stated limits for development, nor is tar sands development itself yet governed by international agreements to reduce greenhouse gases.

In fact, the only relationship that isn't potentially compromised is the one between energy companies and their shareholders. Operations like Suncor and Syncrude are legally bound to create returns for shareholders. This fiduciary duty does not necessarily extend to "external" market concerns such as aboriginal rights, climate change, environment and health impacts. In fact, companies that offer too much and voluntarily adjust operations to respect environmental limits and climate concerns could be served suit for neglecting their duty to produce reasonable returns. This is one of many reasons why tacit self-regulation has largely been a failure within not only tar sands developments, but globally as well, given failed attempts to voluntarily reduce emissions. In the case of the tar sands, it is a well-documented failure, replete with mountains of reports, meetings, consultations, and applications—millions have been spent to document the piecemeal process by which overdevelopment has taken place.

It is green washing by bureaucratic means, and if you untangle the web of responsibility, ownership, and rights, the thread that might actually lead to who is ultimately responsible and accountable for what is happening disappears—it leads nowhere out of this cloud of competing and conflicted interests, as it is a regulatory and legal tangle that few can either comprehend or afford to challenge.

What if, by chance, it wasn't just that oil companies were operating more like leading manufacturers and retailers? What if by moving into late-stage fossil fuels like unconventional crude, the energy company is evolving into something potentially more influential than Wal-Mart itself? The world's most profitable company in 2008 was not Wal-Mart, but ExxonMobil, which owns a controlling interest in the $8 billion Kearl Oil tar sands project launching in 2010 as well as major shares in Syncrude. Ten years hence, when plastic is so valuable people might want to burn it rather than buy more of it, when shipping costs could cull down our avalanche of bargains to a meager flow of semiessential goods, and when consumers themselves discover that liquidity and credit spending cannot support an economy, who will hold more power: a discounter that once sold more diapers than anyone else, or the integrated energy company that can, for a price, alchemize dirt into crude oil?

This sense of historic transition and power transfer hasn't been missed at Fort Chipewyan, where some recount predictions of long-dead elders, who were born before the time of the treaties and before government consolidated influence in the area. "When I was younger, an elder told me that things are going to be different," says Alec Bruno. "In the future, he said that there will be problems with animals and fish. 'You will see some deformities. And when you see deformities, it tells you that there's a problem with the land. And these deformities will tie into your children's future.' To me he was more like a prophet—38 years ago he died."

In its advertising campaigns, ExxonMobil promises "more energy, fewer emissions [and] with technology, we can do both." But that's not what is happening on the ground. By 2009, Alberta's government had admitted that cancer rates in the community were, in fact, elevated. ("The overall findings show no cause for alarm," argued a provincial health official. "But they do, however, point to the need for some more investigation.")

This wasn't the win-win future that some had been promised.

Alec Bruno worked at Suncor when the dike for Pond One was being built, and knew, as likely did the government, that the ponds were leaking. He understands the burden of this knowledge. "They don't want to know," he says, looking out over the lake, "yet they are concerned."

CHAPTER 6

WE, THE RESOURCE

JOURNEYS TO THE END OF CHEAP

Borderlands

It's 4 P.M. and another load has arrived. People file off what looks like a large tour bus and march forward in a rough line. Some are dressed in golf shirts and khakis, others in tee shirts and jeans. Most carry knapsacks, like the ones that college kids haul around. Some people aren't carrying anything.

They walk along a tall chain-link fence toward a bright yellow gate. The scene resembles a shift change at a factory or tourists returning from a packaged day tour. At the gate, someone is selling snacks, and a uniformed guard is stationed there to ensure that everyone passes through without incident. They are illegal immigrants who have been caught by the U.S. Border Patrol in the Arizona desert, and they are being unceremoniously returned to Mexico at the Mariposa border crossing at Nogales, the state's largest international border town. On average, 1,500 undocumented travelers are returned through this gate every day.

Most of the migrants visit the aid station, a large white tent that stands a few hundred feet from the gate, where they receive food, water, discounted bus tickets home, medical assistance, and, for those who may be immediately planning a return trip, warnings about the perils of the Sonoran desert. Inside, migrants arrive and linger, some just to gather themselves before the next stage of their journey—others sit here because they have nowhere else to go. Some have been injured during crossing or capture and are attended to by medics. These are the lucky ones. Since America's Immigration and Customs Enforcement (ICE) ended its "catch and release" policy in 2006, many non-Mexican migrants are detained in the United States without trial. Chasing undocumented workers in America is now a government-sponsored business worth $1 billion annually. Most of America's 580 miles of border wall has been installed along the California-Mexico border, and the security build-up there has pushed migrants east into Arizona. The buses unloading the returned migrants are run by the Wackenhut Corporation, a U.S.-based, multinational security firm that is under contract from the American government.

Off in the distance, U.S. border guards patrol the American side with rifles and dogs. There were an estimated 18,000 U.S. border agents in 2009, twice the number from just a decade ago, plus a large floating pool of military, ICE agents, and others deployed by the Department of Homeland Security. On the Mexico side, there is a single uniformed, unarmed guard at the gate who looks like he would be comfortable working shopping-mall duty; other guards are holed up in buildings and watchtowers nearby. All the while, refrigerator trucks and semitrailers hauling containers of finished products head north, while empties return south.

We're in the geographic center of what has become the world's busiest border crossing. The number of undocumented migrants grew during the 1990s and peaked during the mid 2000s at over 300,000 people apprehended in Arizona annually. "We were walking for three days and were caught," says one farmer from the Mexican state of Michoacan, who is traveling with several cousins. "Migration caught us and deported us.... We're really not sure where we were when they caught us. Maybe we were half way there." Each had paid as much as $3,000 to smugglers so that they might cross, disappear into Arizona, and resurface in California, Georgia, or even Canada with steady employment—in construction, cleaning, landscaping. Workers can make as much as five times the wages they might make at home—$60 weekly back in Michoacan versus $400 to $500 in the United States.

Yet to subsidize the American economy with cheap, undocumented labour, the dangers migrants face are considerable. "There are people with guns that wander around in the middle of the desert," one of the migrants tells me, talking about the bandits who attacked his party. "They are just out there. Plus the route is pretty dangerous, pretty difficult." He's still undecided about his next move, as are many of the others who've just gotten off the Wackenhut bus. It's a long trip back to Michoacan, yet whatever he has seen in the desert has him thinking hard about another attempt.

It's a deadly dilemma that U.S. authorities actually helped to create. The U.S. government under former president George W. Bush authorized millions of federal dollars to be spent on infrastructure, technology, and personnel, including a controversial plan to build additional border fencing at a cost of up to $7 million per mile. The militarization of the border peaked between 2006 and 2008 during Operation Jump Start, when 6,000 armed National

Guard troops were stationed along the border to reduce drug traffic and deter immigration. "The goal was to drive migrant traffic away from cities like San Diego and El Paso and into the remote desert on the assumption it would act as a deterrent," explained journalist Randal Archibold in 2007. "But while there is no way of knowing its overall effect, the strategy is serving at least in part as a funnel for untold numbers of migrants. [And they] cross with little or no knowledge of the desert, whose heat, insects, wildlife, and rugged terrain make it some of the most inhospitable terrain on the planet."

Nearby, at the Nogales headquarters of Grupo Beta, the Mexican state agency responsible for migrants, Jose Mon Martinez shows me just how bad it can get. In a back room, there are file photos of rescued and deceased migrants. One man lost a leg falling off a train and getting caught beneath the tracks. A woman from Chiapas attempted to cross with seven children, not once but five times. Another man jumped from a border wall and fractured both ankles. Others sliced their necks open on barbed wire or mangled their feet wandering five or six days, lost in the desert. Some migrants become delirious with heat and try to bury themselves in the dirt or take off all their clothes under the midday sun. Their bodies are often found shriveled up, partially baked and decomposed. Those who are badly dehydrated might just go to sleep and never wake up. There are even Europeans and Japanese who try to make the crossing for their own mysterious reasons.

Drugs are part of the violent mix, since the relative lawlessness of the Sonoran desert attracts narcotics traffic. Whole pack trains of mules and horses carrying millions of dollars of drugs are sometimes apprehended. Migrants who cross paths with professional criminals in the desert are sometimes executed says Martinez, adding a few more bodies to the more than 5,000 drug-related killings that plagued Mexico in 2008.

Martinez informs migrants of all these risks; some listen and decide to return to their villages and towns, but many don't. "Even if they increase the number of Border Patrol agents, the migration is never going to finish," he says. "It is not going to be stopped."

While the number of workers in Mexico's borderland *maquiladora* factories—factories along the border that operate in duty-free zones—peaked in 2001, due mostly to Asian outsourcing, the migration of people across the Mexican-American border has continued. Mexico's dominant export is people—not just Mexicans, but large numbers of poor farmers from across Central America as well. As Sheldon Zhang reported in his 2007 book *Smuggling and Trafficking*, as many as 3,500 people have died crossing Arizona's southwestern frontier since 1995. When over 500 died in the Sonoran desert during 2005 alone, the Arizona border town of Pima actually had to rent a refrigerated truck to store all the bodies that awaited identification and the county coroner's determination of the cause of death.

Back in Tucson, which is a short drive north of the border, there's constant debate over the immigrant situation. Some locals spend their weekends driving water trucks into the desert and leaving behind maps for incoming migrants. Others want the border locked up tight. "Half of the North American migration occurs in Arizona," says Reverend Robin Hoover, activist pastor and president of Humane Borders, an award-winning humanitarian group that maintains a prominent network of blue water barrels on the American side of the desert. "We have more apprehensions, we have more deaths, we have more agents, we have more boys, more toys, more this, more that. Nobody is happy with this migration. Landowners aren't happy; law enforcement is not happy; healthcare folks aren't happy. I cannot name anybody that is happy. The human rights folks are not happy and the faith communities aren't happy. Civil society is pissed off."

So why does it keep happening? In short, we have come to depend on cheap imports and on the affordability of Latin American labor on both sides of the border. "What we have here is a human artifice called the border that enables us to love Mexican tomatoes more than we love Mexicans," says Hoover. "That's the problem; half of the tomatoes that are consumed in the United States are produced just south of here."

But it is an impermanent kind of cheap, created partially by a discriminatory immigration policy. Many migrants plan to leave the United States and return home within a year or two, but most end up staying longer. In 2000, only about one in ten migrants returned within a year, according to the Public Policy Institute of California. Those who come north from Mexico and Central America stay in the United States because it has become too difficult to re-cross the border. "In its effort to lock people out," writes Maggie Jones, "the U.S. government has instead locked them in."

By 2009, it was clear to nearly everyone that this strategy had failed. Mexican drug violence was at an all-time high, migrants continued to die in the desert, and America's immigration system had created a two-tier model of citizenship. The result was a massive pool of cheap labor stranded within the United States, which had begun to mirror China's pool of displaced farmers. Many were still underemployed and, with limited rights, were vulnerable to labor abuses, homelessness, and substandard health care.

Transnational migration has created a nation within a nation. According to one 2009 Pew Center report, a record 12.7 million Mexican immigrants were living in the United States in 2008—the largest single immigrant population in the world. And an estimated 55 percent of these people are undocumented and subject to summary arrest and incarceration. Amazingly, 11 percent of all people born in Mexico currently reside in the United States, representing a massive human subsidy to a service economy addicted to cheap labor.

Globalization has succeeded mainly through the existence and management of imbalances, the opportunities presented by price differentials in wages, resources, technological, and managerial efficiencies. And so it came to pass that there was an 800 percent wage gain for undocumented workers willing to cross a desert for a booming service economy, or an opportunity to engineer the world's largest company out of stranded labor, hungry consumers, high-volume shipping, and cheap energy. Consequently, borders and borderlands became integral to the production of cheap products. In the first place, borders create pools of stranded labor by limiting mobility of people and facilitating movement of products. More broadly, borderlands and frontiers have always been integral to major economic transformations. Many of the great economic zones of our time are also highly militarized and managed: Singapore, the Mexican-American border, and south China, all of which became wealth and savings multipliers that helped raise standards of living around the world.

Yet trade itself creates displacement. Partly due to inequitable trade agreements that eliminated Mexican agricultural subsidies—leading to $2.5 billion in American corn exports to Mexico in 2006—deep poverty has continued to fill the developed world with people traveling across borders and oceans looking for work. Between 2000 and 2005, for example, Mexico lost an estimated 1.6 million jobs in its rural and urban sectors. The dollars that migrants sent home actually managed to raise average Mexican wages by 8 percent between 1970 and 2000, according to the World Bank.

But, even as trade flourished, Bush-era America "lavished scarce resources solely on hunting down and punishing illegal immigrants," said the *New York Times* in a 2008 editorial. "Its campaign of raids, detentions and border fencing was a moral failure. Among other things, it terrorized and broke apart families and led to some gruesome deaths in shoddy prisons.... But it also was a strategic failure because it did little or nothing to stem the illegal tide while creating the very conditions under which the off-the-books economy can thrive. And without a path to legalization and under the threat of a relentless enforcement-only regime, they cannot assert their rights."

Around the world, an estimated 200 million legal and illegal migrants live outside their countries of origin, according to the World Bank. This major population reallocation is also helping to redefine society and politics in the United Kingdom, Europe, Canada, and Southeast Asia. It represents a major subsidy to most economies, a deep dependence on vast quantities of second-class citizens on hand for landscaping, butchering, and day laboring. These are Filipino nannies in Canada, Pakistani ditch diggers in Dubai, Thai construction workers in Singapore, and Dominican cab drivers in New York.

While internal migrants in India and China still outnumber transnational migrants, the economic value of displaced foreign workers is significant. One 2007 study by the accounting firm Ernst & Young found that curtailment of migration in Britain would decrease the country's economic growth; conversely, continued immigration would boost Britain's growth by as much as 20 percent. And even though many of these European immigrants were as skilled as their U.K. counterparts, they only earned 60 percent of the average U.K. wage. When the EU added eight Eastern European countries into its membership in 2004, it was estimated that 50,000 immigrants would arrive by 2008; instead, over one million legal Eastern Europeans freely entered Britain, infusing its economy with cheap, skilled workers.

The money that migrants send home props up poor households and local economies where conventional forms of globalized trade have failed. This redistribution of global wealth, worker by worker, has helped forestall deeper poverty within many developing world countries. Egypt, for example, receives more in remittances than it collects from the Suez Canal; incoming payments represent 54 percent of Tajikistan's entire economy. The World Bank's Dilip Ratha estimates that 200 million immigrants made $305 billion in remittance payments in 2008, a conservative number that does not include informal and unrecorded payments. These payments to family and community increased globally by 73 percent between 2001 and 2005, and were distributed across an estimated tenth of the world's population. The scale of the remittance economy has surprised many observers, and it underlines the risk of greater poverty and possible crisis should this aspect of globalization fail.

Remittance is also an indirect measure of the savings created by foreign workers within their host economies. Foreign workers and migrants are, on average, making half of what a regular worker would earn. This means, roughly speaking, that they saved their host countries at least $305 billion, which represents a significant labor subsidy. (Not to mention the economic activity of migrants in their host countries). Coincidentally, this amount is nearly identical to Wal-Mart's record-setting sales revenue for 2008, and nearly three times the world expenditure of foreign aid in 2003.

Migrant workers are essential to booming developing economies like China, and help underwrite the rich standard of living enjoyed by most Western nations. Like affordable crude oil, migrants anchored our world of cheap for several decades. Yet many migrants have become tired of taking risks that subsidize developed world households. More are staying on their farms and in their ghettoes; many are returning home. In 2008, the World Bank noted that, for the first time in nearly a decade, remittance payments to Latin America and the Caribbean did not increase, and that overall remittances would decrease as much as 5 percent in 2009. This, even though experts predicted that low-wage migrant labor would remain a relatively secure resource in America, because many resident Americans, even unemployed ones, are slow to take these "low-caste" jobs.

On a bench outside of the Grupo Beta building, several migrants wait for a truck ride out of Nogales, away from the border. They've had enough. "I had this idea of going to the United States to look for work in a restaurant because supposedly you can earn more there," says Jolanda, who most recently cooked in a kitchen in Mexico City. She had been traveling with her brother and some other relatives in the company of a smuggler. "But the experience that I had in the desert was, well, very sad. It is a really sad reality because you come with this kind of vision or illusion of being able to help your family and all that changes when you enter into the desert."

This is one face of deglobalization in the twenty-first century. Jolanda no longer has any expectation of a better life in America, and she is certainly not willing to gamble everything so that Americans can live cheaper. "You really have to fight for your life [out there]. I am going to return to my children and never leave them again."

"The truth is that I actually handed myself in," says Jolanda, as more deported migrants arrive at the Grupo Beta headquarters. "You really come to value what it is that you've left behind in your hometown. You value your family and you value everything that you left behind and just in a few words, you say that 'I am not returning.'"

The Great Consumer Collapse

There's another good reason for migrants like Jolanda to stay close to home. Even though the global income gap between rich and poor increased over the last 20 years—the rich got richer in three-quarters of all OECD nations—migrant, immigrant, and resident communities now have a surprising amount in common. After the great crash of 2008, the kind of insecurity, underemployment, and economic worry that migrant workers have experienced for decades became acutely familiar to working households across the developed world.

Certainly, there have been shared benefits, such as the emergence of transnational communities and greater diversification. Discounting has played a role in this, creating shared consumer cultures. In a 2003 article about Walmex, Wal-Mart's operation in Mexico, the *Los Angles Times* noted that Mexicans had "developed a taste for bagels." By 2009, Wal-Mart had opened its first Hispanic supermarkets in Arizona and Texas, even as Minutemen continued to "arm themselves, come to the border, and defend the country."

But all-access consumerism is likely finished—and with it the augmented buying power and affordability enjoyed by all households around the world is gone. "Suddenly consumers are focused on buying what they have to have as opposed to buying what they want to have," Howard Davidowitz, financial consultant, told the *Wall Street Journal* in June 2008. "This is a permanent change for Americans, who will face a declining standard of living over the next 20 years."

It wasn't supposed to end up this way. For many, the global consumer revolution was about owning a bigger house, a nicer television, and laptops for the whole family. And for others, it meant the promise of affordable household supplies, school supplies, and children's clothing purchased at the local discounter or dollar store. Those who were poor were able to purchase more of what they needed, and those who were already somewhat comfortable acquired better clothes, video games, and furniture. Few households failed to enjoy the consumer credit and product bonanza that began during the 1990s.

But just as global migrant workers became economically integrated with Western nations, consumers themselves became a primary resource. Consumer debt, equity, and spending not only filled our postwar, postindustrial economies with growth and purpose, but also filled the likes of Wal-Mart, Carrefour, Home Depot, and Target with money. And, like any other resource, consumer debt was prospected, exploited, and bought and sold, resulting in the risky practice of massive, unregulated trade in debt derivatives.

In the nice middle-class suburb where I live, there are no abandoned homes or mass foreclosures. It's an older suburban neighborhood, much like any other that can be found in North America. Lawns are mowed, cars are washed, and kids play on the sidewalk. The houses are mostly postwar bungalows, next to which are newly built mini-mansions. There's relatively little crime, the air is clean, and the local public school is great.

But, looking closer, you can see signs of slippage. My neighbors across the alleyway, longtime renters, have been picking up the bottles and cans that we usually leave for homeless bottle collectors. And the homeless guys that are losing out on garbage picking occasionally sleep in our local playground, even though we are miles away from the nearest emergency shelter. In my city, average housing costs consume nearly 45 percent of average income—so you can bet that I'll be at Home Depot whenever I need to fix a toilet or a fencepost, trying to save a few dollars.

Yet if averages are true, most of the families in my neighborhood carry zero cash savings or, just as likely, have significant debt. America's personal savings rate has plunged to nearly zero since the late 1990s, according to the Federal Reserve, and the numbers are similar in Canada. These houses are not merely homes, but singular assets that backstop mortgages, credit cards, and retirement plans. Just one string of bad luck or a few bad decisions, and any one of these homes can be the very thing that drags down an unwitting family into insolvency.

"The bottom line is that there has been basically no wealth creation at all since the turn of the millennium. The net worth of the average American household, adjusted for inflation, is lower now than it was in 2001," wrote Nobel laureate economist Paul Krugman in 2009. "The surge in asset values had been an illusion—but the surge in debt had been all too real. So now we're in trouble—deeper trouble, I think, than most people realize even now."

Our rich consumer universe, even though it cuts prices on an ongoing basis, is failing us. And as we complete the first decade of the millennium, many goods remain affordable, yet our most essential requirements—food, housing, energy, health care, and education—have become considerably more expensive relative to average household income. This paradox of affordability lies at the root of today's consumer crisis.

Besides borrowing against their equity, more people are taking out payday loans and using credit cards to charge basic expenses like groceries. By 2003, the average Canadian household already held more debt than annual income. And by 2008, U.S. household debt had grown to 100 percent of GDP. Britain's Uswitch finance service diagnosed a "spendemic" in the country in 2008, with one in ten adults spending more than they earn on a monthly basis, doubling the number of credit cards over the course of a decade.

There are similarly high ratios in other OECD countries. "The sharp increase in the debt to income ratio in developed countries has raised concerns about a parallel rise in household financial fragility that would affect macroeconomic and financial stability," predicted Europe's Rinaldi and Sanchis-Arellano in 2006. "[Yet] in the short-run the role of financial wealth and housing wealth tends to confirm the idea that wealth is used as a buffer in case of unexpected shocks."

Income insecurity has everything to do with the fast rise of involuntary part-time labor has accounted for most part-time employment growth since 1969 in the United States and follows a similar pattern in OECD nations like Canada and Great Britain. Overall, the employment growth rate actually peaked back in the 1970s, reports the U.S. Department of Labor. "The growth rate of the labor force has been decreasing with the passage of each decade and is expected to continue to do so in the future."

Of course, many middle- and lower-income households had already been suffering for years. This is one major reason why discounters, large and small, moved from the margins of economic life to the very center; people needed savings in the face of insecure income and persistent, increased costs of essential good and services. While luxury products, natural resources, and high-value industries are still important—ExxonMobil or Dow Chemical are unlikely to disappear from the Fortune 500 anytime soon—the realities of today's world heavily favor those who can deliver bargains.

But likely even the world's largest company can no longer protect shoppers. In 2005, Wal-Mart's former CEO Lee Scott famously claimed that the retailer saves consumers up to $100 billion annually through the "negotiating power" of millions of Wal-Mart shoppers. "We touch so many lives," said Scott. "There is almost [nothing] that does not have an interest in what we as a company are doing."

It is true that Wal-Mart and other bargaineers improved many household bottom lines. In one Wal-Mart commissioned study, economists claimed that Wal-Mart's incredible growth between 1985 and 2006 resulted in a cumulative 3 percent decrease in American consumer prices—equaling $957 per person or $2,500 per household. But the world's leading bargainer and its competitors also exert a deflationary pull in economies where they dominate. For example, furniture prices fell 4.1 percent between 2000 and 2004, according to a 2004 study by Washington's Institute for International Economics, largely because production had shifted from North Carolina, the former center of U.S. furniture production, to China. Even as manufacturing jobs disappeared within most service economies, global trade in bargains cushioned the impact of job losses and decline of local economies with lower prices. Even in the United States, the world's nexus of discounting, the average cost of housing, food, and transportation increased 25 percent between 1998 and 2008—despite persistent price drops in everything from female apparel to furniture. And in the homeland of Tesco, the world's fourth-largest retailer, Britain saw grocery prices increase 6.6 percent over the same period, followed by a 4.8 percent increase in Europe.

Even during the height of the crash, consumer prices continued to rise 0.4 percent in February 2009, with the bulk of the increase due to rising food and fuel prices; other commodity prices rose 0.4 percent, the biggest increase since 1999. Amazingly, in the midst of a 20 percent decline in trade with

China, American clothing prices jumped 1.3 percent in the same month, the biggest monthly increase in nearly 19 years (Prices of wholesale imported goods from China decreased generally by 0.5 percent, suggesting that not all savings were passed along to consumers).

In 2007, the International Monetary Fund reported in *World Economic Outlook* that, among 18 developed nations from 1982 to 2002, lower prices and higher productivity resulting from globalization of trade only boosted average real pay by 0.24 percent annually—or $115 for the average American household. That's a significant shortfall from Wal-Mart's claimed 2007 benefit of $1,122 of increased purchasing power per household.

We enjoyed the fruits of a synchronous world, a globe woven tightly through commerce and accelerated by information technology, logistics, porous national economies, and a seemingly infinite thirst for products. Yet what we now have is a consumer economy that is surprisingly hollowed out, spent, and mined.

On paper, many of us are the same. To someone, somewhere, we are all assets or liabilities. This, of course, was the premise of those who devised complicated derivatives for home-based debt, and it was all bundled together by the thousands, regardless of circumstance or debt rating, and sold as generic (if not highly advanced and poorly accounted) financial product. They were bonds backed by mortgage payments, sold quickly and indiscriminately as derivatives, like knockoff fashion; they themselves were complicated wagers on arcane aspects of the original debt.

We are also abstract assets in a broader, more profound way as well. When economies depend on consumer spending, consumers themselves are essential fuel for continued growth. As long as we spend and don't save, our nations remain solvent, more or less.

The combination of bargaineer ingenuity and the virtual wealth of credit-rich populations turned grocers and discounters into some of the world's largest multinationals. Nearly everyone played this convergence like an oil discovery, reaping tremendous early gains, extracting consumer surplus as hard and fast as possible.

Of course it wasn't a resource play, but a reconfiguration. At the very same time that energy companies were bearing down on unconventional crude, our leading service sector companies were busily drilling down for pure "consumer value" with the gusto of a Signal Hill oilman. Energy has become more managerial; it's process and supply-chain driven. Finance and retail, having already mastered these modern arts, focused on the gushers of cash created through derivatives and the steady flow of sales in goods siphoned through big-box power centers.

For years, many communities that hosted major big-box developments have reported essentially the same thing: part of their economy gets extracted, sucked away, and their main streets wind up looking like a ghost town. As the Institute for Local Self-Reliance (ILSR) has documented at length, local losses aren't merely consumer dollars, but lost public and civic resources as well. Full-cost accounting suggests that through new infrastructure and lost tax revenue, plus whatever incentives have been negotiated, "retail development can end up being a net drain on city finances," notes the ILSR. Some case studies suggest, "not only did Main Street retail produce lower service costs, it also generated more property tax revenue per square foot, because those retailers occupied higher-value, often historic, buildings."

Consumerism is failing consumers. If the loss of local, and, presumably, more sustainable local economic assets are the casualties of global retailing, then what happens when low-value, high-volume, carbon-intensive consumer systems begin to fail? The growing landscape of destitute regional malls, decommissioned big-box stores, and gaps in strip mall frontage is not reassuring. In July 2008, before the worst, Home Depot had already closed 15 stores in the United States. "We are seeing significant pressure on the cost side as the price of basic commodities goes up," said CEO Frank Blake. "There isn't a well-worn path guiding us on what all these pressures will do to our business... but there is more risk than opportunities."

The productivity and profit created within modern service economies—the technology, finance, and retail pillars especially—have come with costs and risks that are asymmetrically distributed. In some ways, perhaps the outcomes say it all. There has been a transfer of wealth away from middle and lower classes and a consolidation of wealth in upper classes, both within major consumer nations, and globally as well.

The golden age of global consumerism was surprisingly brief. Spanning the mid-1990s (with breaks for stock market bubbles such as 2001's dot-com crash) through the first decade of 2000, it was, arguably, just over a decade long. During this time, there were tremendous advances in everything from consumer technologies to culinary sophistication to affordable luxury goods. There were also tremendous "advances" in overconsumption and materialism-as-entertainment, the kind of no-limits indulgence that would have floored puritanical Victorians. (In 1877's *Thrift*, Scottish reformer Samuel Smiles wrote, "It is the wastefulness of individuals that occasions the impoverishment of states. So it is that every thrifty person may be regarded as a public benefactor, and every thriftless person as a public enemy.")

While consumers were enjoying the peak of globalization, and others made millions trading on nothingness, the floods gathered: housing asset inflation, underemployment and predatory credit practices, which, in turn, helped fuel homelessness, foreclosures, as well as longer-term instability. By now it is clear that much of this prosperity was leveraged not only on credit and finance, but also on the working assumption that opportune conditions for commerce, production, and consumption would persist indefinitely. This too was a gambit.

Hitting Bottom

Whiz, as he calls himself, drags a Home Depot shopping cart out of the bush near the commuter-train station where he lives in Surrey, a suburb of Vancouver, Canada. It is dusk and we leave his makeshift camp site, a torn pup tent amid scattered clothing and garbage, and set out across an abandoned lot, passing a small wooden cross that remembers a murdered prostitute named Dottie. We are looking for food.

Whiz has been on and off the streets for the last decade. What strikes him now is the growing number of people in the playgrounds and parks of these residential neighborhoods, sleeping rough. "It's busier, for sure," he says. "You look in the trees and bush, you'll find them. Out here, you got to be careful not to trip on someone."

Whiz, net worth zero, is pushing an orange Home Depot cart, trying to find a way to better his situation. He is not so different than countless foreclosed-upon Americans who, at the same moment, may be inside a Home Depot store, pushing their own orange cart in quiet desperation. On paper, we are all the same—broke.

Homelessness is what was a housing crisis looks like without bankers. Whiz and I roll past pawnshops and convenience stores, toward the nearest homeless shelter—one of the few that serve this metropolitan area with a population of 2.1 million. As we approach the building, others with backpacks and shopping carts emerge from the darkness in time to line up for the evening meal, which is prepared and served by a local church. To the amazement of many, the annual number of people living outdoors or in shelters in Surrey nearly doubled during the early 2000s. There are addicts and former university students, young families and washed-up street hustlers. Plenty of people used to live in decent homes. Nearby cities and towns have the same problem, and local governments have taken to bussing the homeless around the Vancouver region in an attempt to find them shelter, medical care, and social assistance.

These are the new migrants of the twenty-first century, a growing population of homeless can be found within nearly all developed nations. And its affecting a broader swath of society. As American, Canadian, and European studies have indicated, a growing percentage of homeless are employed with various low-income jobs. Homelessness is now strongly associated with poverty, increased living costs, the rise of part-time labor, as well as the government policies that often neglected these trends. In America, for example, the average household is earning less than it did in 1999, marking the first time since recordkeeping began that an economic expansion did not result in an aggregate advance in household income. (As of January 2009, reports Steven A. Camarota, "twenty-four million adult, native-born Americans who have no education beyond high school who are either unemployed or not in the labor force, which means they are not even looking for work." That's two-thirds of the entire Canadian population.)

The outcome of the housing boom wasn't just growing homelessness due to inflated housing prices. Disbelief in scarcity itself occurred, as millions appeared to become rich with little or no effort. On paper, they gained worth as markets boomed. Owning property in the right market virtually guaranteed double-digit returns. Not only did this create a housing bubble, it also accelerated the income gap between rich and poor. Many countries, from the EU nations to Canada to Hong Kong, allowed the runaway asset inflation that was creating the new wealth—namely, housing price bubbles—to leave behind the middle- and low-income people who couldn't afford the price of admission. In the United States, subprime mortgages and other high-risk house financing schemes exploited lower-income, minority, and immigrant communities who, understandably, wanted to create their own assets that might one day provide retirement security or a university education for their children. As housing scholar Duncan Maclennan argues, "global conditions had created both greater opportunity and greater inequality, mediated by national finance and policy systems."

For a while, it looked like the new millennium might be lucky for everyone. During the boom, analysts and pundits decided that what we had, in fact, was a "New Economy," one that had attained a state of near-permanent, stable growth on the basis of an unprecedented mix of productivity (through new technology and communications), low unemployment (new service sector jobs), low inflation (partially driven by a mass influx of bargains), and new wealth (stock market booms, increased profits). "Just as the eighteenth and nineteenth centuries marked a change from an agricultural to an industrial economy, and the first three quarters of the twentieth century marked a movement from a manufacturing to a service economy, the end of the twentieth century marked a movement to the weightless economy, the knowledge economy," writes economist Joseph Stiglitz in *The Roaring Nineties*. "[Yet] for all the talk of the New Economy ending the business cycle, the changes of the Roaring Nineties actually may have increased our economic vulnerability, by making the economy more sensitive, more responsive to shocks...We not only exposed the economy to more risk, we also undermined our ability to manage that risk."

But even as Wal-Mart came to the fore as the world's largest company, the dream of the New Economy had begun to sour. Our first decade of cheap stuff was also the decade of Enron. The new millennium presents a more advanced, and possibly more dangerous, set of circumstances. This is Las Vegas, globalized. Or as Nobel laureate Stiglitz argues, modern economies are about "making risk a way of life."

Behind this are deep changes that affect everyone. Debates have raged since the 1990s about how much domestic unemployment and poverty can be directly blamed on the offshoring of manufacture and services. In 2004, for example, *The Economist* claimed that job losses due to offshoring made up less than 1 percent of the total, arguing "the jobs lost are mainly a cyclical affair, not a structural one." Conversely, industry lobby National Association of Manufacturers estimated in 2006 that roughly half of all manufacturing job losses were actually due to productivity gains, not outsourcing. By 2007, Washington's Economic Policy Institute determined that America's trade deficit with China was itself a major cause of job loss, with a significant contribution from bargaineers large and small. "Between 2001 and 2006, [the] growing deficit eliminated 1.8 million U.S. jobs," argued the institute's Robert Scott. "Wal-Mart's trade deficit with China alone eliminated nearly 200,000 U.S. jobs in this period."

As economist Susan Houseman determined in 2007, the degree to which offshoring is integral to Western economies is underestimated because "cost savings from outsourcing and offshoring are often counted as productivity gains, outsourcing and offshoring simultaneously place downward pressure on manufacturing workers' wages." That so much high-tech manufacture moved to China, Mexico, and Southeast Asia in the 1990s has at least as much to do with the astounding labor productivity increases of "961 percent in semiconductors and by an astounding 1,495 percent in computers" as they do with technological advance.

Productivity is key to the trend of "jobless growth" that has afflicted all nations dominated by service economies. Among other things, increased productivity means the profit effect of lost jobs is truly amazing. Between 2000 and 2006, for example, a 3.6 percent increase in the Fortune 500 workforce managed to generate 80 percent more profit. "Companies, burned by the tech meltdown and 2001 recession, "kept payrolls amazingly lean," explained *Fortune* magazine's Shawn Tully in 2007. "Of course, it was easier to do so with large pools of skilled workers available and union power at a nadir. By 2006 companies were barely paying any more for a unit of production than they did in 2000."

The homeless are not outliers; they are the other side of a hollowed-out economy, since many of today's homeless lack income. The continuum of underhousing is profound and speaks to the shortage in real, broadly distributed savings and wealth within many Western economies. As many as 700,000 people are homeless in Los Angeles alone, for example, representing a deep core of dispossession characterized by addiction, violence, and disease. It's profound market failure: housing markets have not provided secure or affordable housing in sufficient quantity. On a broader scale, the United Nations estimates up to 100 million people are homeless worldwide, many of them women and children. Underhousing is more widespread, with an estimated 600 million living in shelter that is unfit, dangerous, or unhealthy.

It is oddly fitting that even on the issue of homelessness, which is a social universe away from the world of derivatives, the emergent solutions are based upon taking risks. America's "homeless czar," Philip Mangano, the much-lauded executive director of the United States Interagency Council on Homelessness, is betting that he can engineer double-digit reductions in the number of street people.

Appointed by President George Bush in March 2002, Mangano has worked with over 220 municipalities and 320 local jurisdictions across the United States to develop and implement 10-year plans to end chronic homelessness. Depending on whom you ask, he's either the last great hope for solving homelessness in North America or the harbinger of collapse. "We found that long-term homelessness was often complicated with things like disability, addictions, mental health, or HIV," says Mangano "[Consequently,] long-term chronic homeless people comprise 20 percent of the homeless population but use 50 percent of the resources. This is expensive. That's why we did cost-benefit analysis."

Mangano stirred controversy as a major proponent of a strategy that focuses upon the minority of chronic, long-term homeless people. Why focus on so-called "chronic cases?" They're the most expensive and use up the greatest portion of resources. It is business logic, as Mangano readily admits, that is concerned mainly with reducing the suffering, lost potential, and expenditure for the vast majority of people whose experience with homelessness is unnecessary.

Conceived in 1988 by the Los Angeles-based agency Beyond Shelter as part of an effort to rapidly house increasing numbers of homeless families, the strategy of "Housing First" represents a major change in national strategy in

North America after governments first began funding and building homeless shelters and emergency response systems.

It's about saving money and saving people at the same time, a model of efficiency and logistics not normally seen in the social services. There are obvious cost savings in rescuing people out of perpetual crisis. Mangano often cites the story of Million-Dollar Murray, made famous in Malcolm Gladwell's February 2006 *New Yorker* article. As the story goes, two frustrated police officers tracked the costs associated with three chronically homeless individuals living in Reno, Nevada. Two racked up $120,000 and $200,000 in hospital expenses in a year. The annual expenses for the third— Million-Dollar Murray—were staggering, more than $1 million for hospitalization, incarceration, detox treatments, and ambulance rides. As Reno officer Patrick O'Bryan quipped, "We spent $1 million not to do anything about him."

Mangano's gamble is that homelessness can be successfully addressed by investing resources into housing those who are hardest to house, the most visible, and long-term homeless that people see on the streets every day. The thing is, most homelessness is not actually street homelessness, neither visible nor chronic. Moreover, "hidden homelessness" is growing fast in previously unlikely places such as suburbs, small towns, and even settlements in the Arctic. Broad swaths of the population now have housing-security problems and are at risk for homelessness. Furthermore, some accuse him of attempting to download homelessness onto local authorities, while political bosses decrease social investments. "While Mangano has been piling up frequent flier points visiting every part of the U.S. to convince state and local governments that they need to take up the responsibility for a 'housing first' policy for the homeless, his political boss—President Bush—has been gutting the U.S. federal government's funding for housing," writes Wellesley Institute's Michael Shapcott.

Canada has accumulated a large homeless population in spite of sustained economic growth. In 2006, the United Nations Committee on Economic, Social and Cultural Rights (UNCESCR) actually delivered a firm but harsh rebuke of Canada for its record on poverty and homelessness. The committee urged Canadian governments to "address homelessness and inadequate housing as a national emergency," and made particular note of the long waiting lists for subsidized housing, inadequate minimum wage levels, social-assistance programs that raised income to only 50 percent of poverty levels, high levels of homelessness and hunger, and unfair treatment of the unemployed. The UN committee was surprised by the paradox of Canada's strong economic performance as a top G7 nation in overall economic performance in 2005 and 2006 and its substantial underclass. "Despite Canada's economic prosperity, . . . 11.2 percent of its population still lived in poverty in 2004," it noted. "[And] poverty rates remain very high among disadvantaged and marginalized individuals and groups."

Nevertheless, putting a price on homelessness has achieved results in battling street homelessness. When the Bush administration finally tallied up its numbers in 2008, the number of chronically homeless people living in America's streets and shelters had dropped 30 percent from 175,914 in 2005 to 123,83 in 2008. While the United States has not yet achieved the kind of success reported by England, which began concerted efforts to reduce deep poverty and homeless as early as 1997, 30 jurisdictions had already reported declines in their homeless populations in 2006, including the 28 percent drop recorded in San Francisco a year ago and a 4 percent dip reported in Denver.

The U.S. National Coalition for the Homeless is skeptical that homelessness overall is actually declining. "The 10-year plans are an excellent step forward, but at the same time we need to remember the existing needs of everyone, to not cannibalize other funding while we do this thing for the chronics," said Zach Krochina, economic justice policy coordinator, in 2006.

Yet the "chronics," as they are sometimes called, are still in the minority, roughly 18 percent of the total homeless population in the United States. Indeed, of the 744,000 estimated homeless people in the United States in 2005, the National Alliance to End Homelessness found that a quarter were chronically homeless and about 41 percent were also in families. "Focusing on the more hard-core people is neglecting the plight of [working] homeless families," reported the *San Francisco Chronicle* in 2006. "In some communities, families constitute at least half of the homeless population. In San Francisco, they constitute up to 20 percent."

While the elimination of 50,000 street homeless in a few years is a significant, if not phenomenal, achievement, urban centers still have growing homeless populations. New York City, for example, reduced the number of chronically homeless people by more than 2,200 in 2008, yet the overall number of people counted as homeless—including families living in motels, as well as those sleeping in cars and other improvised shelters—actually increased by 2218 people between 2005 and 2007, from 48,154 to 50,372. And those who have survived homelessness would go on to face Medicare cutbacks by the same government that got them off the streets. The good news is that a great many working households can be stabilized with income and health care supports. Through homelessness, we are learning that economic security is a grand new policy frontier in the twenty-first century.

Dangerous Goods

Russ Howard has taken a hostage. Surrounded by FBI agents, military contractors, and private security consultants of all kinds, the retired brigadier general stands behind a spectator, points a finger at his head, and says, "You've got 30 seconds to decide before you lose advantage to the shooter—what do you do?"

Given that most people in the room already know how clean, maintain, and fire automatic weapons, the silence that follows his question is surprising. Howard intimidates them. As founding director of the Combating Terrorism Center at West Point, and a former commander of Special Warfare Training Group at Fort Bragg, Howard knows something about risk and conflict in the twenty-first century. "Well, what is it?" he asks again. "You're almost done."

Someone in the back proffers up a "negotiate?" Another asks "stay calm?"

"All wrong—you fight!" says Howard emphatically releasing his hostage to applause. There was a time, he explains, when terrorists would negotiate as part of some kind of a broader political process. Back in the 1970s and 1980s, "we taught people not to resist a hostage event because people survived."

"But now, there's no more taking hostages," says Howard. "Now, they [the terrorists] want a lot of people watching and a lot of people dying."

It's a fine spring day with no security threats or crises on the horizon, at least nothing that would bring extra business to the attendees of this logistics-security workshop. Memories of September 11, 2001, are still fresh on the minds of the people in this room, however. History doesn't work in predictable ways, reminds Howard. Like never before, our technologies can be used against us. If drugs, refugees, bad products, and diseases are often shipped by container, then why not a dirty nuclear bomb?

Just as they multiplied savings our supply chains also amplify threats, both long-term threats from carbon-intensive globalization and of direct, horrific attacks because our global logistics infrastructure can be hijacked with less planning and effort than it took to fly planes into New York's World Trade Center. The quest for cheap has not only failed to make the average household better off, but it also exposes us to new dangers. We've become vulnerable in ways that few would have predicted decades earlier.

"Picture this: a nuclear device goes off at Port of Long Beach," Russell continues. "Al-Qaeda takes responsibility. Who would we nuke? . . . This notion of a transnational as opposed to state actors is different. You can't take the same measures." In addition to the fact that terrorists today are better financed and better trained, they also have greater access to our supply chain. There are approximately 24,000 deep-water cargo ships operating worldwide. This means that somewhere in the world, a container ship makes a port call every ten minutes. For a terrorist, says Howard, that is an incredible opportunity. All anyone needs is explosives, some radioactive material, a detonating technology, and a legitimate-seeming reason to load and ship a container.

But a sophisticated nuclear bomb isn't what worries experts most; they're more worried about dirty bombs, which could target any major link in our supply chain—rail cars, warehouses, transport converge points—causing enormous damage with a very small detonating package—containing any nine commonly used radiological isotopes that are lost, stolen, or misplaced in many countries on a daily basis. And you don't need to travel to a former Soviet republic to easily obtain one. Radioactive material can be sourced from hospitals, construction sites, and research labs. The International Atomic Energy Agency estimates that no less than 110 countries lack adequate controls over radioactive materials that could be used in a dirty bomb. "I'm very surprised that a radiological device hasn't gone off," says Matthew Bunn of Harvard's Belfer Center for Science and International Affairs. "There is a bigger puzzle—why no Al Qaeda attacks since September 11 in the U.S.?"

A dirty nuclear bomb isn't a weapon of mass destruction, but of mass disruption. One computer simulation by the Federation of American Scientists, for example, determined that a detonating a device with 1.75 ounces of cesium could broadcast radioactive fallout over 60 square blocks. "Immediate casualties would be limited to people hurt by the blast," reported the *Los Angeles Times* in 2004, "but the simulation suggested that there would be cases of radiation sickness and that relocation and cleanup costs would reach tens of billions of dollars."

It is hard to detect, even with the portable nuclear "sniffers" that are often stationed around major ports. "You are always going to have difficulty detecting nuclear material," says Howard, "whether it is a device or enriched uranium. . . . This sophistication of the detection equipment—you've got to be so close—it is not something that you can monitor from the air."

What complicates the threat further is that the number of possible targets is immense. Major international ports do have security and monitoring programs, so there are easier and more effective targets. "If I were a terrorist, I would not hit the ports," says Howard. In America, there are a handful of major bridges essential to goods movement, such as the crumbling Gerald Desmond Bridge that connects the port facilities on Terminal Island with downtown Long Beach. "If you really want to cripple economically, you take those out. Pretty easy. It does not have to be a nuclear device, it could be just traditional explosives and sort of lace it with biological [contaminant]. It is the effect of the port, but not in the port."

Less threatening but far more pervasive is the spread of toxic, dangerous, and faulty products. Many discounters—and retailers in general—often have no idea who actually produced their products or what they might contain. The subcontractors who produce goods and parts offshore use such a fluid system of negotiations and bidding, creating a complex supply chain that even some of the world's largest corporations cannot untangle. And if a 2007 survey that found potentially hazardous levels of lead in 35 percent of a 1,200-count toy sample is even remotely accurate, the dangers are very real indeed.

That bin of shiny costume jewelry, that Diego backpack, those sunglasses, countless painted wooden toys—everything is suspect. In recent years, rings and trinkets have been routinely discovered containing more than 50 percent lead (the legal limit in most countries is well under one percent). Children are especially susceptible to lead poisoning, which can permanently impair physical and mental development. The effects of low-level lead exposure can be subtle and hard to trace, but enough concentrated lead finds its way to children to result in several reports of death or critical poisoning each year. Lead can leech out into food, and materials can chip and create ingestible dust. Tragically, even small mistakes with a lead-tainted product can result in critical illness. A gumball-sized piece of toy jewelry ingested by a child in 2004 resulted in bodily lead concentrations 12 times the acceptable limit. A four-year-old in Minneapolis swallowed a single charm bracelet manufactured for Reebok in 2006; the preschooler died within days, and investigators later discovered that the item was nearly 100 percent lead.

Products contaminated by heavy metals first made headlines in the late 1980s, just as international trade in consumer goods began to accelerate. In 1990, the American government launched lawsuits against several toy companies that sold toxic or dangerously designed toys, charging them with 70 violations of Federal safety standards since 1986—consequently, spot testing was introduced. By 2004, a record-setting 150 million pieces of toy jewelry were recalled, setting off repeated waves of consumer anxiety, despite government and businesses reassurances.

In any given year, the product-recall list reads like a product list for the Las Vegas bargain show: holiday ornaments, pillow slipcovers, paint brushes, children's sunglasses, fashion bracelets, Halloween pails, race cars, key chains, and mood rings. The world's three largest dollar store chains accounted for over 1.5 million lead-contaminated products of the total 17 million recalled from American retail in 2007—including Dollar General, which recalled over one million items.

While governments scramble to add safety inspectors and new regulations, it remains nearly impossible to regulate the largest flow of product in the history of trade. As for self-regulation, the extra time and expense doesn't exactly gibe with the reality of discount business. Handheld spectrometers that can accurately detect lead in plastics, paints, and textiles are worth about $29,000 each—equivalent to the monthly living expenses of about 600 Chinese factory workers.

"There will be further product recalls," confirms industry expert Sam Bundy, "[And] there will be a falling out period with some stress on wholesale prices, but given the huge dependency on Chinese manufacturing, especially for small- to midsized retailers, I expect that this is a short term problem. And in the long run it will force Asian manufacturers to raise quality standards." For shoppers, there are no guarantees yet, save for one small consolation; many different labels, from detergent to pet food, are manufactured by the same factory or corporation. Therefore, a dollar store product that is dangerous may be equally so at Wal-Mart or at the local grocery store, whether it's a brand-name or not.

Despite all the bad press, the dangers of toxic toys and household goods have had surprisingly little negative impact on retail sales. Dollar General, for example, increased its 2007 net sales by $325 million; Family Dollar Stores, which recalled 342,000 lead-tainted products in 2007 increased its revenue that year by $440 million.

And sometimes, toxic products fly under the radar of weak government inspection and monitoring systems. When toothpaste tainted with a poisonous antifreeze additive was found in Panama, for example, authorities initially assumed it was a small problem. It wasn't—and 34 countries later, tainted toothpaste was found in Vietnam, Kenya, Tonga, Australia, and Dubai. In 2006 and 2007, more than 900,000 Chinese-made tubes were distributed across the United States and Canada, not only in dollar stores, but in prisons, hospitals, and hotels. Twenty-million tubes turned up in Japan alone.

When the toothpaste scandal first broke in 2006, the Chinese government initially defended "legitimate" companies who used the toxic ingredient, diethylene glycol, as a cheap alternative to glycerin, even after Canada found that levels of the toxin were twice those previously discovered in a cough syrup that killed nearly 138 people in Panama in 2006. "It was inconceivable to me that a known toxic substance that killed all these people could be openly on sale and that people would go on about their business calmly, selling and buying this stuff," said Eduardo Arias, the Panama City resident who, unlike all the importers, governments, and retailers involved, actually read the ingredients label on the toothpaste. When he discovered the diethylene glycol, he complained to authorities.

Nothing prevented China's baby-formula crisis in 2008, when a melamine-contaminated formula sickened 53,000 infants, hospitalized 13,000, and killed four. Melamine is an industrial chemical that is legally used in plastics and fertilizers but illegally used to boost protein content and causes kidney failure or kidney stones. It was also found in candy in several Connecticut stores, pretzels in Toronto, and instant coffee in British Columbia—the coffee showed melamine levels three times that of China's contaminated infant formula. Testing also showed that 36 different Chinese dairy companies tested positive for melamine, which turned up in yogurt and other dairy products. It later was discovered that some Chinese officials knew about the contamination in 2007 and that a public health advisory was delayed in order to avoid embarrassment at Beijing's 2008 Summer Olympics. Several brands of baby formula from south China had been exported elsewhere in Asia and in Africa, prompting more searches for contaminated product.

As Chinese dairy farmers in Hebei explained to the *New York Times*, the dairy company Sanlu, which is 43 percent owned by New Zealand interests, allegedly took advantage of regulatory loopholes, bribery, and corruption and that the melamine was added at company-owned milk stations. Not surprisingly, there was a cost issue behind the crisis; Sanlu and other major dairy companies were trying to operate within the Chinese government's price controls, which were an attempt to check the already troubling inflation on essential goods. The controlled-price milk created intense internal pressures to artificially boost protein content in a country where the price of soy meal feed had increased 60 percent in 2007 and 2008, said the farmers. The virtual monopoly that the major milk companies have on the $18 billion Chinese dairy market has meant many farmers have been forced out of business through low price–fixing and simultaneously blamed for the contamination. ("I was one of the drafters of the China Dairy Products Quality Inspection report," said professor Zhang Guonong of Jiangsu. "I found adulteration is extremely widespread. Urea, soap powder, starch are very popular additives.") Several suspects blamed for the dairy scandal would later be charged and, in 2009, dairy businessmen Zhang Yujun and Geng Jinpin were sentenced to death; three others received life sentences in prison, yet government officials responsible for safety and regulation remained unscathed.

The recall of millions of toys throughout the 2000s had already shaken consumer confidence. Roughly half originated from unsafe materials utilized in Chinese manufacture, and half stemmed from company-side faulty design and execution. One 2007 recall for Aqua Dots after 14 children became sick after ingestion lead back to JSSY, the Hong Kong company that manufactured millions of poisonous toy beads. An inexpensive glue additive, it turned out, mimicked the potent chemical depressant GHB, partially banned for its use as a date rape drug. JSSY had copied the beads after an identical Japanese product, but had used GHB-like glue. What became clear was the lack of regulation and monitoring both in China and import countries, even after previous waves of recalls and promises of reform. The *Beijing News* reported in May 2007 that China's General Administration of Quality Supervision's own results showed that 20 percent of toys and baby clothes failed safety tests. Plush toys were stuffed with low-quality fill and even garbage; other toys easily came apart or broke. The report also mentioned milk powder for babies that contained unspecified chemicals that could pose health risks.

Only a few months later, both Wal-Mart and Carrefour claimed that 99 percent of all Chinese-made toys were safe. "We have been purchasing from China for nearly 26 years," said Wal-Mart China's spokesperson in 2007, "Chinese products are economic in price and guaranteed in quality." While some advances have been made in the realm of ethical sourcing—such as Wal-Mart's 2008 withdrawal from the central Asian republic Uzbekistan in protest of the use of child labor—a great many things get lost within the opaque realm of the supply chain. It's impossible to separate dangerous products from geopolitics, and the need for major retailers to maintain good relations with Chinese authorities.

Mattel's struggles with toy safety are another lesson in the way supply chains multiply risk. When the world's largest toy company announced 7.3 million recalls of its own products in 2007, it was clear that problems weren't limited to knock-offs and bargains. Barbie, Elmo, Big Bird, and Dora toys produced between 2003 and 2006 were recalled. Mattel's CEO Bob Eckert insisted that the company had "rigorous standards" while apologizing for the recalls. He later identified a Chinese subcontractor who had "utilized paint from a non-authorized third-party supplier." There are an estimated 30,000 different toy products on sale at any given moment in the world, yet Mattel's accusation managed to bring world attention to just a few, not to mention anger the world's largest country, despite the fact that it had recalled most of the items because of bad design, not materials.

A month later, Mattel's executive vice president for worldwide operations, Thomas Debrowski, met with Chinese officials to apologize. "Mattel takes full responsibility for these recalls and apologizes personally to you, the Chinese people, and all of our customers who received the toys," he said in a meeting with China's top safety official in Beijing. The "vast majority of those products that were recalled were the result of a design flaw in Mattel's design, not through a manufacturing flaw in China's manufacturers." China, of course, produces 65 percent of Mattel's toys and an estimated 80 percent of the world's toys in total.

By 2009, the Obama administration had increased its consumer safety expenditure by 71 percent from 2007 levels. In hindsight, Mattel was probably wise to lose face and mend relations with the world's largest country. It is still the world's supply chain superpower, even during an economic crisis. And as Mattel learned, you can't just insult China and expect the toys to keep flowing.

No Returns, No Deals

On a long detour through Nogales, Mexico, back to Tucson, I stop by the desert compound of Arizona's Minuteman Civil Defense Corps. Located north of the Sasabe border crossing in the Altar Valley, it is in one of the more desolate and challenging stretches of the Sonoran desert. Here, the self-proclaimed civilian defenders have held a floating guard line against migrants on a part-time basis since 2006. The Minutemen are actually camping on the grounds of the historic King's Anvil Ranch, an hour's drive north of the border, whose owners invited the group to set up operations and scare off trespassers.

Gene Caferolla, Minuteman's state director in Arizona, sits down underneath a large camouflage tent and welcomes me to "Operation Stand Your Ground." Caferolla and two other Minutemen chat about life on the border; they are keen to make it clear that they aren't anti-Mexican. They treat the migrants well, giving out water and food while they are waiting for ICE or Border Patrol to arrive. Like other strident nationalists, they just want to roll back the clock to a time before free trade, back when nation-states were nation-states, and people and product weren't as mobile as the weather.

The Minutemen believe that tighter border controls and stricter immigration rules protect freedom. They seem to cherish an idealized past, when America was a paradise of intact pioneer cultures and national economies, even if that place never truly existed. "My forefathers, they blazed the wilderness trail, fought wars to further this idea and it has just been taken away from us. And that is why we are here," says Caferolla. "This is the end of America as we know it." This call to repel invaders, whether economic or military, reflects deep currents in American culture regarding race and free trade.

A true border that kept everyone in their respective countries would keep Latinos employed in *maquiladoras*, which would be better than having them die out here in the desert. "It needs to be fair trade, not free trade, but fair trade, and it is not," he says. "That's the biggest problem right there. If you want to put just one thing; fair trade, not free trade and until we have that, we are all just going to have a lot of problems in the country."

There are businessmen south of border who would like to turn back the clock as well, to before 2001, when Mexican *maquiladora* factory complexes were still growing. As economies contract globally, and energy prices undermine globalization, many wondered why production hasn't yet returned to Mexico or America.

The seemingly random dangers of the modern supply chain—poison toothpaste, toxic toys—are one reason to promote deglobalization. And certainly, in the face of global recession, there is new pressure to regionalize trade. The modern supply chain is vulnerable to cost and environmental constraints. And it is hard to imagine lowering global greenhouse gas emissions with so much global GDP dependent on moving product around the planet. Transport costs from Mexico are exponentially cheaper, just as Eastern European manufacture continues to service the European Union. Cutting down the traffic on our oceans could be a win-win for the environment and economy. In 2004, the cost of shipping from China was $2,500 per container, and the containerized transport expense for a $12 industrial item was $1.10, but it would cost only $.30 to deliver the same product from Mexico.

Yet there is no restore button that returns resources and jobs back to their original locations. Globalization pursued cheap labor, yet some of the resulting productive capacity appears to be stranded. Whole supply chains are literally stuck in place. This suggests that many of our goods could stay fairly globalized even as globalization itself begins to wane. It's not unlike the reality of bottomed-out consumer spending that threatens the health of service economies: Globalization without cheap inputs, cheap energy, and large-scale efficiencies will not deliver the same degree of affordability and plentitude. Nor will this complex system of production simply move itself closer to consumers when transport becomes chronically expensive. And if globalization cannot scale itself, not only will consumers suffer in a world of disappearing bargains, but transitions to more localized, sustainable trade networks may become more difficult as well.

It's an effect of market inefficiency and existing capital investment. Many of the foundries, factories, and skilled workers in the developed world that lost out to China, for example, are no longer operational or simply no longer exist. For example, while giants like Mattel do have factories in Indonesia and Thailand, where costs are even lower, the toy giant and many other businesses remain surprisingly "captive" within China. It's what toy industry expert Eric Johnson of Dartmouth University described as concentrated manufacturing, a reflection of the fact that globalization was built around clusters and pipelines, not open networks and wealth clouds, in order to achieve maximum cheap. "There are some very large companies in the back end of the supply chain that supply everybody," Johnson explained to *Foreign Policy* in 2007. "China is like the Silicon Valley of toys. There are literally thousands of very good toy suppliers there. There are manufacturers who just focus on plush toys and then there are people who just focus on injection-molded plastic and people who die cast, like Hot Wheels and Matchbox cars. So, for companies that don't do any of their own production, they really don't have anywhere to go but China. Thailand has a toy industry with some big players like Mattel, but it's nothing like China. And it's difficult to shift those capabilities."

China stands alone in certain categories: telecommunications, electronic machinery, and office machines. It has also shown a decided transition away from lower-value exports like apparel, textiles, and footwear. While China still held nearly 15 percent of global apparel exports in 2005, it was less than half of its 1992 share. And the country enjoys a certain undefined amount of semicaptive production, especially in the capital-intensive, technologically advanced factories of Shenzhen, where laptops and iPhones are produced. And China's surprisingly activist labor laws have sent a clear signal to non-state corporations operating within China and to countries that depend on its exports. Get ready to pay more for less.

"The bulk of goods made in China—clothing, toys, small appliances, and the like—probably won't be coming back, because they require abundant cheap labor," predicted *Business Week*'s Pete Engardio in 2008. "If anything, their manufacture will go to other low-wage nations in Asia or Latin America."

Some factory owners and large corporations in China have been scheming to move out of the country, to chase the frontiers of cheap labor as far as logistics networks will allow. Yet no clear "elsewhere" exists because the required size of the labor pool and infrastructure found in China cannot easily be matched. Nowhere else offers the same massive labor pool or the same orchestrated political-logistics-economic convergence that is only feasible in a populous one-party state. China's bargain-industrial complex is particularly irreplaceable in the realm of high tech, capital-intensive consumer products that Shenzhen excels at and Changsha aspires to. Losing a few labor jobs to Southeast Asia will not change China's dominance, especially for capital-intensive exports like iPhones and laptops, which accounted for 64 percent of China's export growth for much of 2007. Indeed, high-tech merchandise accounted for 29 percent of China's total exports in 2007, up from 15 percent in 2000.

While Vietnam is surely an Asian tiger in terms of rapid growth, its overall population, 84 million, is still less than that of Guangdong Province and is only slightly less than 6 percent of China's 1.3 billion population. As a 2008 research report by the Royal Bank of Scotland (RBS) argued, Vietnam "lacks the same scale advantages. Its impact on global trade and inflation will also be marginal." The same is true of more remote locales within China, such as Gansu, Xinjiang, and even Tibet, which lack accessibility and sheer scale of population. High-value manufacturer Japan reported inflation that reached a 27-year record in 2008, which hinged on increased commodity prices for wheat, copper, oil, and coal, reflecting similar trends in Korea and Taiwan. As Japan, the world's second-largest economy, prepared for recession, wholesale inflation attacked the profitability of its exports, which remain the country's main engine of growth. The list of available manufacturing countries that can serve as global alternates to China in the event of political strife, increased costs, or the propensity of the CPC to squeeze foreign corporations, is actually quite small.

Mexico's population, for example, is equivalent to only 8 percent of China's total population, and persistent concerns about its inadequate transportation networks, infrastructure, corruption, and social instability indicate that Mexico is not a ready replacement for the Middle Kingdom. As North America's largest auto-producing nation, Mexico's trade impact is significant, but replicating China's 1990s mix of authoritarian efficiency, deep labor resources, and openness to global capitalism is perhaps impossible. Deglobalization is surely bringing more trade to both Mexico and other nations, but it will not result in the highly bargaineered, optimized supply chains that gave us $25 DVD players and nearly a decade of other price rollbacks.

If China's heartland can't engineer bargains, it's likely that nobody can. "Relocating labor-intensive production to Vietnam from China will have little impact on global consumer goods inflation," reports RBS in "Vietnam: Not Another China." "Hong Kong, Japan, Korea, Taiwan, and the United States accounted for the large share of foreign investment in China during the past decade [because] the labor-cost saving of moving to China was large.... The labor-cost saving of moving to Vietnam from China is far smaller."

A May 2008 McKinsey survey of 1,500 global executives around the world found that "they still see low-cost production as the primary competitive advantage of Chinese companies and expect little change on that front in the next three years." Moreover, "four out of five of the executives also say that they expect to see rising competition from Chinese companies in the next three years."

Hong Kong's business community, an innovative group that almost single-handedly devised the global supply chain decades earlier, would have few qualms about moving their factories to Siberia if there were a clear advantage to doing so. Yet a majority of Hong Kong factory owners surveyed in 2008 still see their future inside China; 14 percent were considering a move to Vietnam, while 29 percent planned to move inland where land and labor costs were still cheaper.

As Hong Kong's business leadership also knows another reason for staying put is China's emerging middle classes, who are an attractive new market for at-home production of goods. Compared to the average debt-ridden Western consumer with credit problems, China's new shoppers come from households with high savings rates and growing incomes. The case for remaining in China is no longer about simply saving money; it's about simultaneously attempting to sell to the world's fastest-growing consumer class.

This is the beginning of a strange and likely riskier new chapter in globalization, where production centers like China become less functional for many bargaineers, yet too few alternatives exist. The consequence of a bargaineered world is that much of our productive capacity disappeared offshore and has failed to return. Collapse is what happens when consumers in a service economy fail to show up and spend their allotted 70 percent share of GDP. Spending backed by cheap credit is the fast-depleting domestic resource of service economies; just as value created through spending and outsourcing became the cash crop for global retailers like Wal-Mart, which allowed them to profit on par with global energy companies like Exxon. Globalization was built upon the extractive economic foundations of the nineteenth and twentieth centuries and created unprecedented savings and prosperity. In the process, the world's largest and most powerful companies became energy barons, bankers, or retailers.

The modern supply chain has reached its own mature phase, and the potential consequences are hardly insignificant if it does indeed lead to a sudden decrease in affordability and accessibility of common products. This kind of modal shift could be a damaging and unmanaged transition—not to a sustainable future, but to increasingly desperate efforts to reinstate globalization back to its year-2000 glory. When things get tough, economics often turns retro, eschewing alternatives too risky or expensive.

We can't assume that market forces will adjust—but we've seen the return of some furniture manufacturing to North America, including IKEA's first major North American factory, in Danville, Virginia, in 2008. The factory added 300 new jobs paying average regional wages of $29,000, and the region has gained a total of 6,000 new jobs since 2004. Previously, 30,000 jobs had been lost to the first wave of offshoring, plus it conceded about $7 million in incentives to IKEA—about $23,000 per job—so return of manufacturing is tempered by the fact that new factories are highly automated and job-efficient.

Yet, re-localized production, the so-called "neighborhood effect," has not happened to the degree or speed that many predicted. Danville represents a mere 2.5 percent of the world's largest furniture manufacturer's overall workforce. "I don't see a surge of employment coming back to the manufacturing sector in the United States," predicted economist Jeffrey Sachs in 2008, on the opening of the $85 million IKEA factory. "That's what some people may be looking for when they hear that globalization will be impeded by rising energy prices. I would say don't hold your breath for that."

A few months later, IKEA announced another major furniture factory partnership in Thailand, worth about $441 million. This call to repel invaders, economic and military, reflects some deep currents in American culture regarding race and economic change over five years. The progressive but highly secretive Swedish multinational plans to open 20 more stores across Asia, as part of its pursuit of the world's strongest growth market in fiberboard furniture, a popular segment that has grown 10 percent annually worldwide. "As part of the company's survival during the global economic slowdown, our expansion in Asia will help offset the plummeting sales in the U.S.," said John Carlsson, IKEA's Asia business manager. "We are only slightly affected by the global economic recession although customers have less purchasing power. We have seen a bigger market share from our competitors who shy away from expensive furniture products."

There's one last reason for not returning production to Western consumers: we've run out of cheap resources. IKEA, for example, is one of the largest single consumers of lumber after Home Depot, and because of this it leans heavily on Russian forests and Chinese factories. Keeping its center of production closer to strategic inputs and emerging markets makes business sense, even at the neglect of its Western outlets. "IKEA now buys more products from suppliers in China than any other country and according to industry analysts this percentage will increase as IKEA relentlessly lowers costs," noted Forest Monitor in a 2006 report (It added that despite the company's claim to sustainable forestry, a Chinese factory representative "had no idea where exactly in Russia the timber was harvested," let alone if it was done sustainably).

Deglobalization will happen and is happening. But former consumer superpowers in the West are hardly protected. It's possible that G8 nations could sometimes just get cut out of tomorrow's supply chain, not unlike unlucky emerging nations who found themselves cut out of shipping networks during the 1980s onward. "There is a lot of discussion about pulling manufacturing back to Europe from China and India because container costs and fuel costs are favoring local production," said Roy Lenders, logistics consultant for Paris-based Capgemini, in 2008. "That trend is evident with a number of companies who are now setting up factories in Eastern Europe to move at least part of their manufacturing back [to China]. Wal-Mart buys most of its plastic products from China. Those products are made with oil, and manufacturers are experiencing huge increases in material costs.... Eighty percent of the raw material costs are related to oil, so production might even go to the Middle East to be close to oil production."

Indeed, supply chains may well attach themselves to nations still able to sustain lavish twentieth-century consumer spending patterns, such as a small minority of energy rich nations who are expected to benefit from persistent, global demand for crude oil. The Middle East is the next frontier. "All of the logistics service providers I know of are operating in Dubai," noted Lenders in an interview with *Site Selection*. "It's a two part strategy to reach companies in the Middle East and to mitigate the rising cost of oil. You can operate an intercontinental hub for both Asia and Europe."

For anxious Americans and their politicians, it is true that major re-localization does happen. Just not always in America.

SECTION III

COST OPPORTUNITY

New kinds of change: building-sized blocks of ice collapse into Neko Bay in Antarctica
Credit: Tiffany Vogel

CHAPTER 7

SHOCK THERAPY

CAN HIGH PRICES SAVE US?

Last Discounts, Final Offer

There is no doubt that most everyone loves a bargain. Bargains represent the core work of the Western civilization for the last 200 years: more, cheaper, better. Accelerated by information technology, enriched by cheap offshore labor, and sustained by the biggest consumer binge in human history, retail discounters elevated the lowly bargain into something ubiquitous and profound. Led by some of the world's largest and most powerful companies, the planet has become economically interlinked in the service of bargains, from the Saudi oil that furnishes South China refineries and factories with petrochemical to the sprawling network of transport and technology that brings plastic to the West. And by the middle of the first decade of 2000, globalization had reached its pinnacle—an avalanche of plasma televisions, iPhones, and discount fashion amid a global asset and securities bubble.

It was the apex of consumerism. Despite low levels of household savings, Western shoppers used cheap credit to buy products of unprecedented affordability and selection. Prices in many sales categories actually decreased—arguably lowering real-time inflation by several points—while countless product innovations delivered more for less.

While a minority of households accumulated great wealth during the 1990s and 2000s boom in financial markets, deals on everything from luxury electronics to household goods became the reward for everyone else. If that meant that our dividend came in the form of flat-screen televisions and not household savings or job security, surprisingly few people seemed to complain. All together, it was a surreal accomplishment: twenty-first century technologies—advanced IT, warehousing, GPS, management—operating full-bore on the economic and environmental assumptions of the 1950s.

Consequently, our continued dependence on shopping and shipping represents a series of gambles on a local, national, and international scale, not the least our dependence on non-renewable energy. Even as oil prices plummeted more than 50 percent late in 2008, the International Energy Agency predicted that oil prices of $100/barrel would return, and then double by 2030. "It is becoming increasingly apparent that the era of cheap oil is over," proclaimed the IEA in November 2008, noting that the development and acquisition cost of hydrocarbon resources—especially resource-intensive unconventional sources like the tar sands of Canada and deep water drilling—as well as new carbon taxes and developing world demand will ensure that affordable crude oil will be a distant memory.

It is possible that we have reached the peak oil equivalent of consumerism well before the proven arrival of peak oil itself. While total credit card debt increased by 50 percent in America between 2000 and 2008, consumer spending as a share of GDP began to drop in 2008. Our consumer universe has contracted with surprising speed: by mid-2009, reported the *Globe and Mail*, many retailers were suffering, with the consumer discretionary sector (non-essentials including automobiles) dropping profits by as much as 97 percent, with the only strong business growth coming from dollar store chains, Wal-Mart, online retailers, and other discounters.

Amazingly, an estimated 38.8 million square feet of retail space went empty in 2009, driven by bankruptcies and closures from Circuit City, Linens 'n Things, and others. That's equivalent to more than 100 Colma-sized power centers standing empty. Vacancies in big-box locations have led to interesting reuses, from gymnastics clubs, churches, charter schools, museums and libraries. But it could be difficult to fill the urban, social, and economic hole left by the slow implosion of retail and wholesale trade within major Western economies. By 2009, America's second-largest mall operator, General Properties, had declared bankruptcy, buried in $25 billion of unmanageable debt. With commercial real estate worth $6.5 trillion, half financed by debt, Foresight Analytics estimated in 2009 that a continued slump could create $250 billion in commercial real estate losses and drag down more than 700 banks. Even before the collapse of 2008, the over-saturation of malls and retail in general had already begun to create decline, not the least Wal-Mart's own dismal performance between 2000 and 2007, when Wal-Mart's stock value dropped 38 per cent.

The decline of the modern shopping mall is one version of consumerism's troubled future, illustrative of the way in which Western consumers are being stripped of their VIP status. Until recently, globalization found new opportunity in borderlands: grey zones of untapped consumer equity, unregulated finance, unconventional crude oil, and complex trade agreements that privileged growth over development. In particular, imbalances of income, environment, trade, and spending are something that all major trading powers continue to manage and address as a requirement of continued growth—with decreasing success. From the Mexican border to transcontinental pollution, the illusion was that there could be deep economic integration but that we could still control outcomes. The assumption was that imbalances would hold and the fences would work, and that growth would continue, even if it was founded on things like depleting resources, asset bubbles, and unsustainable household debt.

The good news is that deglobalization will return balance after years of inequitable growth; the bad news is that it won't be fair. As our universe of cheap contracts, low-income households around the world will suffer from the lack of economic activity and the erosion of affordability. The remittance payments that have stabilized countless poor villages will falter if consumers fail to consume. As everything from copper to oil to water gradually increases in price due to a combination of scarcity and increased demand, it will become increasingly uneconomic to operate the global supply chains that once offered consumers great value.

As the resilience of various other energy, economic, government and social systems degrades in the face of change, there's inevitable insecurity. It's the second law of thermodynamics, which governs the degradation of mature energy systems. "As a system's energy degrades, physicists say its 'entropy'— often described as its disorder or randomness—increases," writes Thomas Homer-Dixon in *The Upside of Down*. "Cities, ecosystems, and human bodies must have a constant input of high quality energy to maintain their complexity and order—their position far from thermodynamic equilibrium—in the face of nature's relentless tendency toward degradation and disorder...And, as the system gets larger and larger and more complex, more and more energy is needed to keep it operating."

In this view, the first stage of globalization created value and wealth multipliers, disruptive change, and innovation—as well as deep imbalances and deeper dependence on non-renewable resources. The second stage, which arguably began the arrival of Wal-Mart as the world's largest company early in the new millennium, is a stage of managed imbalance and resource depletion that threatens not merely deglobalization—the contraction of integrated trade—but also the foundations of security and prosperity that were constructed during the twentieth century.

Unlike previous crashes and bubbles, today's challenges aren't merely the result of market speculation, cyclical inflation, or political manipulation. This time, long-term trends figure prominently: depletion of consumer economies, erosion of Western trade dominance, population growth, energy nationalism, food scarcity, and climate change. After enjoying decades of fierce price competition, shoppers are no longer fully insulated from the threats and pitfalls of a world hooked on bargains. In tomorrow's world, the customer is likely no longer king, rollbacks are rare indeed, and scarcity is a new engine for troubling geopolitics and growing poverty.

The paradox is that a great many countries remain dependant on low-cost consumerism at the very moment that consumerism is faltering. Indeed, spending has been the lifeblood of modern-day globalization. And the truth is that many countries can't afford a slowdown in consumption-based growth. An ongoing global recession could eliminate as much as 20 percent of the world's wealth, according to Nicholas Stern, former World Bank chief economist—a crash that would disproportionately affect lower-income shoppers, minority communities, and developing nations around the world. (Other observers claimed that as much as 45 percent of wealth had been vaporized by 2009, mostly through collapsed financial holdings—yet these losses were mostly limited to the rich 2 percent of the world's population who own an estimated 50 percent of all global wealth.)

Before the crash, some argued that the boom in trade and consumerism posed a win-win set of outcomes for the middle class, the developing world, and titans like Wal-Mart. Shaped by insourcing, outsourcing, and offshoring, the "flat world" has sometimes been heralded as the completion stage of globalization. And our world has certainly seemed flat, at least on the basis of growth in international trade. World merchandise increased in volume 27 times since 1950, as compared to an eightfold increase in world GDP. Industrial tariffs in developed countries decreased from 40 percent in 1950 to less than 4 percent in 2008.

Despite post–2008 efforts to address everything from unemployment to climate change, much of our prosperity is still dangerously dependant upon unsustainable supplies of cheap labor, transport, and energy, and on trade imbalances and consumer debt. As we test the material limits of our world, one deal at a time, our quest for cheap has become a source of crisis in the twenty-first century. From Asia's factory borderlands to rural Mexico, from Las Vegas to the Arctic Circle, we are still attempting to reckon the promise and consequence of everyday low prices. And a single question emerges. Can we survive the bargain?

Meet the New Boss

It's another anniversary of the Tiananmen Square massacre. But nobody dares to mark the occasion: soldiers and plainclothes police prowl the streets of Beijing. Even scraps of paper are inspected and no detail is left unexamined; they're after leaflets, posters, and banners—anything that might remind locals of the tragic crackdown that, according to the government, never really happened. The main part of the square is walled off by a huge barricade that shelters the reconstruction of the world's largest public square, which is running conveniently behind schedule. As soldiers march in formation outside the temporary wall, workers are busily removing the tank treads from Tiananmen marble.

What happened here decades earlier is largely unknown to young Chinese entering the workforce today. As Gereme Barmé describes it, China after Tiananmen is the story of "how comrades have become consumers without necessarily also developing into citizens."

The night before, a lone protester walked in front of Mao's portrait here at Tiananmen Gate of Heavenly Peace and managed to pass off a few antigovernment leaflets before he was stopped by police and hustled into a waiting van, "Long live Chairman Mao! Long live socialism!" proclaimed his manifesto. Protest and nationalism are very nearly synonymous. Rife corruption and high taxes have inspired more Chinese to argue that the country suffers from too little revolution, not too much. But for the most part, Beijing stays silent, not because older people don't remember those pivotal events, but because, today, challenging the status quo is simply not worth spending ten years in jail.

The following morning, a fleet of sports utility vehicles is parked in various places around Tiananmen. Behind the cars' tinted windows, public security officers watch for signs of trouble. Around Tiananmen and beyond are the new opera house and the new bird's nest stadium, which was built for the 2008 Olympics, testaments to the aspirations of the Middle Kingdom to be a superpower, not just in population and production, but also in culture, politics, and global influence, as well.

Anyone here who is looking for a sign of the vibrant democracy movement of 1989 will have to settle for the glorious shopping malls of Beijing. While the People's Liberation Army tromps around the square, networks of gleaming, multitiered malls proffer radical consumerism as China's postdemocratic alternative. Prada, Gucci, and Nike all feature prominently, at prices that sometimes exceed those in New York. Back home, the mall is denigrated, but here in Beijing, it offers genuine escape and relief in the midst of an aggressive police state.

This is how developing nations like China will dominate the future: efficient dedication to growth, dedication to ensuring efficient use of resources required for growth, and more new consumers that anyone has ever seen before. Unfortunately, democracy may have little or nothing to do with it. China and other rapidly industrializing countries have come late to the party, and new efforts forge a new version of the developed world's consumer dreams—appliances, cars, big screen TVs—will have consequences.

As malls decline within Western markets, the newest and grandest mega-malls are now being built by the world's emerging nations. When the West Edmonton Mall in Canada lost its "world's largest" mall designation in 2004, for example, it was Beijing's Golden Resources Mall or "Great Mall of China" that claimed the prize. Nearly 50 percent larger than any mall found in Europe or North America, China's mall was not built for Western tourists—indeed, it is obscurely located past Beijing's Third Ring Road—but designed by China's leadership to connect the nation's emerging middle class with made-in-China products.

It's part of what appears to be a historic transfer of global economic and political power. As pioneering consumer economies in North America and Europe struggle with insolvency, emerging nations have little debt, consumer savings and access to rich productive capacity. After launching South China Mall, the world's largest, in 2005, China moved one step closer to its goal of becoming the world's leading consumer nation during the twenty-first century. Some 500 malls were built across China's mainland between 2005 and 2008. Yet here too, the perils of consumerism are clear. By 2009, the South China Mall was all but deserted, its 1,500 store spaces largely vacant, awaiting millions of middle-class shoppers who don't yet exist.

Very likely the title of the world's largest mall will stay in its current place in Dubai, United Arab Emirates, for quite some time. As financial markets collapsed worldwide, the Dubai Mall opened in November 2008, while the financial markets were in the early throes of collapse. It immediately set new standards for opulence and conspicuous consumption; it boasts gourmet food, haute couture, and the world's largest indoor gold and jewelry market. Within its 6 million square feet, the mall fuses Las Vegas flash, Rodeo Drive–style boutiques, and Mall of America populism and creates a refuge for shopping that could probably withstand a few climate catastrophes. Along with the nearby world's tallest freestanding building, and world's largest indoor ski slope, Dubai's status as a global financial and energy center for the new century means that, as economies face troubling times, the voracious consumerism of the late twentieth century probably has a better chance of survival out on the edge of the Persian Gulf than anywhere else. As long as its oil reserves hold up, OPEC nations may be nearly unique in their continued ability to sustain the kind of giddy shopping binge and consumer bling that the rest of us once dreamed of.

Even if the developing world embraces a fraction of the high-impact consumerism of the West, it will be a world-changing event. From 1.6 billion people in 1900 to 6.8 billion in 2009, world population will reach 9 billion people by 2050, according to the United Nations. That's another two million people who will want cellphones, Barbies, and computers.

Wal-Mart, Carrefour, and other major retailers are already out on the retail's frontiers. In 2009, for example, Mattel announced its intention to "aggressively" pursue expansion in China and abroad after a crushing 46 percent profit decrease during the disastrous 2008 holiday quarter. "We are betting on China's future," said Richard Dickson, Mattel's senior vice president, on the launching of a bright pink, six-storey Barbie store in Shanghai. "We are betting our brand will resonate in China and we are investing heavily."

In 2009, Procter & Gamble launched what it called "the most ambitious expansion plan in company history" to double annual sales—from $80 billion to $175 billion—within 15 years through sales in the developing world. The company announced plans for 20 new manufacturing plants in Asia, Africa, and Eastern Europe. "P&G's center of gravity will shift toward developing markets," said Chief Operating Officer Robert McDonald, noting that the bulk of the world's population don't yet buy detergent, shampoo, and razors in the same massive volumes as Western consumers. With 90 percent of the planet's new babies born in countries without disposable diapers, the world's largest consumer goods manufacturer estimated that by pricing its products for lower-income households, it could more than double its sales of disposables to $20 billion by 2020.

From this point of view, affordable consumerism is actually a doomsday machine. Take the consumer out of the picture and Wal-Mart and its kin present as highly efficient mechanisms to accelerate the depletion of our last reserves of household equity and affordable natural resources. The self-greening of Wal-Mart aside, the company's growth model remains expansive. Likewise, China's "plans for building nearly 100 new coal-fired power stations each year until 2012" means that it will likely surpass the United States in greenhouse-gas emissions by 2009. "The expansion of China's power plants alone could nullify the cuts required under the Kyoto Protocol from industrialized countries," writes Juli Kim of the Wilson Center.

A significant portion of the environmental impact of bargaineering has been hidden in the backwaters of rural Asia, distant energy frontiers, and in the unregulated emissions of shipping fleets in international waters. In 2008, for example, researchers at Carnegie Mellon University determined export production was responsible for 33 percent of all of China's greenhouse gas emissions in 2005, up from 12 percent 1987. Globally, this suggests an economic footprint of considerable size, as the 1.7 billion megatons of CO_2 created by the production of Chinese exports in 2005 actually exceeded all of America's industrial emissions for the same year, and was larger or comparable to levels of national emissions from Japan, Canada, Russian Federation, and the Middle East, respectively.

Yet true to its fate as a leading nation in the twenty-first century, China has already launched large-scale energy efficiency programs and environmental protections—if only because the ruling government well understands that energy insecurity and environmental protest are some of its greatest weaknesses. Asian economies, and China in particular, have often been underestimated in their tenacity and resilience. Ongoing trade and currency deficits that favor China have caused growing anxiety over the future of Western consumer dominance and the fate of globalization.

It's a question that came up during the 2008 U.S. presidential race, expressed over concerns of China's profound ownership of debt and tacit control over the U.S. economy. "The first step that has to be taken is obviously we have to stop mortgaging our economy to China . . . and asking them to finance our debt," campaigned John McCain, in the midst of the 2008 economic collapse. Most analysts at the time disagreed, countering that McCain and others were simply politicking, bashing China when, in reality, most American politicians would be loathe to lead the changes and sacrifices required. "If we really did want to change that, we would need to make fundamental changes on the economy and stop generating a trade deficit. There is no simple solution for that," scolded Ward McCarthy of Stone & McCarthy Research Associates.

There may not be much of a choice, since most leading consumer nations are also debtor nations. One in ten American households, 15 million households, carried zero or negative equity in 2009. By 2010, America's 19 largest banks will face as much as $186 billion in credit card losses, reflecting an unsustainable average of $8,600 in outstanding credit debt per household. In response, major card issuers planned to reduce available consumer credit by 57 per cent between 2007 and 2010, a trend that will not only limit consumer spending power, but force a long-term contraction within the service economy itself.

It's not even clear if Keynesian-style spending and investing can recover a society that is so deeply in debt. "In the last eight years, Americans have spent an extraordinary amount of money and borrowed a lot to make that spending possible," wrote Harvard economist Edward L. Glaeser in 2009, noting that America's national debt nearly doubled since 2000, increasing from $5.7 trillion to $10.8 trillion. Despite this, says Glaeser, "many macroeconomists tell us that all that spending is needed to undo the effects of all that spending."

The strategy to kick-start growth with debt spending was simply twentieth-century common sense. But in the twenty-first century, this strategy threatens a wealth and power transfer, since Western debtor nations are actually raising money for stimulus by selling their securitized debt to current and future rivals, such as China, Russia, and the Middle East. In the case of America, its various debt offerings have yielded progressively worse returns over the last several decades, and China has good reason to think about putting its money elsewhere. ("In the last five years, China has spent as much as one-seventh of its entire economic output buying foreign debt, mostly American. In September 2008, it surpassed Japan as the largest overseas holder of Treasuries," reported the *New York Times* in 2009. "China's voracious demand for American bonds has helped keep interest rates low for borrowers, from the federal government to home buyers. Reduced Chinese enthusiasm for buying American bonds will reduce this dampening effect.")

Charles Morris notes that China's "nuclear option" is to sell its American holdings, even though it would destroy the value of its trillion-plus American-dollar reserves. Instead, "the Chinese have already begun the diversification process, but they are doing it quietly, outside of official reserve accounts."

This could be where Western dominance fails in the new millennium. We simply went broke, and nations with less debt and more discipline took over. With the decline of ravenous consumer demand in the West, trade will be regionalized: intra-Asian, EU, and Middle Eastern trade zones will consolidate.

As America sinks deeper in debt and loses its ability to manage its many challenges, and as corporations move further abroad in search of new growth, China is likely to redefine the future of capitalism. "China will replace the U.S. as the motor of the world economy," as billionaire investor George Soros predicted in May 2009. "The American economy is still bigger than the Chinese. However, China will begin to contribute more and more to global economic growth. Therefore, political power will shift from America to China."

The future of democracy itself is up for grabs. Globalization reached its apex in engineering bargains for Western democracies, but it is ending with an authoritarian consumer superpower, and a small collection of hyper-solvent corporations, including Wal-Mart and ExxonMobil. Certainly, if the Western consumer shops less and saves more—as was evident by 2009—it's good news for the planet. Yet even a slightly more deglobalized world will have to reckon this post-democratic trend: from Wal-Mart to OPEC, everything from electronics to energy to ownership of national debt will be subject to the growing influence of countries and companies that sometimes have no accountability to anyone besides shareholders and cadre members within one-party states.

Compared to India, whose democracy and localized commerce showed strength in the wake of the 2008 financial collapse, there are relatively few nations in ascendancy who might counter this autocratic trend within world affairs. With its fierce competition for global resources, lack of reform on human rights, and unrest within its own hinterlands, China's ruling party has an uncertain trajectory; it could democratize suddenly, as Mongolia did in 1990, but most observers would not bet on this prospect. With a shrinking portion of its GDP dependent on exports (currently about 30 percent, which is less than Germany), it is more likely that China will eventually seek to extinguish its American currency reserves and ownership of American government debt in favor of higher-yield investments. In the end, America's diplomatic, military, and cultural supremacy may matter very little.

The prognosis for developed economies is grim if consumption-fuelled economic activity continues to wane. This is a change from traditional notions of progress. In postwar Europe, for example, Germany became the world's leading export nation through cultivating its engineering expertise and high-value manufacture. Its products and brands, from Adidas to Volkswagen, are synonymous with efficiency and quality. It doesn't do bargains, per se, but sells machines, petrochemicals, components, and services to consumer and producer nations alike. German firms designed part of China's Three Gorges Dam, for example, and supplied some of the massive digging machines and turbines required to accomplish what had become the world's single largest public works project. As the third-largest producer of automobiles and the third-largest book market in the world, Germany exemplifies what post-Obama America might aspire towards: a country that makes real things—valuable things—and champions renewable energy. Yet with over 40 percent of its economic output dependent on exports, Germany's major problem is globalization, and that there are far fewer people on the planet at the end of the millennium's first decade keen to pay retail prices for luxury autos. The German model still requires growth and healthy trading partners. In terms of true-cost pricing for carbon and essential resources, high prices can save us, certainly, but this doesn't mean that high-value trading nations are going to come out ahead.

In the West, people have been slow to realize the depth of this change. That's probably because it seems too ridiculous to admit. "The days when foreigners were willing to finance our deficits for free are gone forever," concludes Morris. "The United States, the 'hyperpower,' the global leader in the efficiency of its markets and the productivity of its businesses and workers, [is] hopelessly in hock to some of the world's most unsavory regimes."

Deglobalization

Andre Alexander points toward the sky. Above him looms a cinderblock shopping mall, three stories high. It is possibly the ugliest building in the Tibetan capital, Lhasa. "That was it," he exclaims. "When this went up, we decided that something had to be done."

Alexander says that the shopping mall—a gray glass-and-brick monster that looks like a fortress—was plopped down in 1993 on the Barkhor, one of the city's most sacred pilgrim routes. At the time, the Chinese government was demolishing Lhasa's inner city to make way for commercial hotels and merchants. Thousand-year-old Tibetan mansions were pulled down and replaced with Chinese-style block housing at a rate of 35 buildings per year during the 1990s.

The Barkhor itself is a broad lane that circles through the heart of Lhasa's 1,300-year-old inner city: crooked roads, alleyways, and passages wind outward from the broad cobblestone street. Ancient, crumbing stone buildings loom over the near-constant orbit of pilgrims. While famous temples and landmarks are being rebuilt across Tibet, Lhasa's historic inner city is gradually disappearing.

The mall inspired Alexander to organize the Tibet Heritage Fund (THF), a joint Tibetan-European effort that, between 1996 and 2000, restored heritage structures within Lhasa's inner city, which is one of Tibet's most historic neighborhoods. Andre sees it as simply leveling the playing field—but it's hard not to forget that we're standing in the middle of an economic and cultural struggle that's carried on ever since the first century. Proud Tibetans point toward the ancient Zhol pillar that stands neglected at the edge of the Chinese-built Potala Square. Erected in AD 764, the pillar records how Tibetan armies once occupied the Chinese capital of Xian. Conversely, Chinese visitors point toward the peaked rooftops found on many temples and correctly identify Han architectural influences.

We pass a corner of the Barkhor where over 70 demonstrators, including monks and nuns, were reportedly shot and killed during 1988 riots, an incident echoed again in 2008. Alexander picks up a *bangdian* apron (a traditional striped sash worn by Tibetan women) from a nearby stand. It was made in Chengdu Province, which lies at the eastern foot of the Tibetan plateau. "Most everything here is imported. Tibetans have so little power in their lives." The local economy has taken a beating since China opened Tibet up for business in the 1990s. A peek inside the shopping mall reveals a bevy of low-budget Chinese trinket stands and electronics merchants, plying cheap goods from Sichuan and Guangzhou. "Tibetan people aren't as competitive as the Chinese," he explains, darting through a throng of pilgrims. "Lhasa's culture is cosmopolitan, but isolated. They didn't always have one billion people to compete with."

Indeed, in Lhasa, Tibetans are no longer the majority. It is a city that is actually several cities: the old inner city of pre-1959 Tibet and the large, modern, ugly Chinese metropolis that has sprung up around it. If you count its suburbs, a prostitute encampment, and several large prison camps, it is a sprawling mess that is like nothing that Tibet has ever seen before.

Previous waves of globalization didn't look like this. As historians Findlay and O'Rourke note in *Power & Plenty*, the first significant wave of globalization was the great Mongol kingdom that encompassed Korea, China, Tibet, eastern Russia, and Central Asia between AD 1000 and 1350. Mongol expansion peaked with the proclamation of Genghis Khan as universal ruler in 1206, followed by capture of Beijing in 1215, and of Kiev in 1240. *Pax Mongolia* was a multiethnic horse army dominated by fierce Buddhists; the military empire encouraged East-West trade across multiple civilizations, resulting in a "nonhegemonic or horizontally linked world system" that indirectly connected Britain and Japan. The Uyghur and Tibetans worked within this system, influencing it with administrative expertise and Buddhist teachings, respectively. Lhasa became an esteemed religious center as successive Mongol khans began practicing Tibetan Buddhism. There were early bargains, too. One 1987 study determined that Chinese silk that sold in Italian markets during the Mongol empire were priced at no more three times its original purchase price in China.

Pax Mongolia eventually faltered, not because it ran out of resources—horses and grasslands remained plentiful—but because it could not manage 22 percent of the earth's land area in the face of China's Ming dynasty. While the Ming sacked strategic Mongolian cities and settlements, most communities and cities remained intact, and Mongols claimed global consciousness as their legacy. (As "Europe came to dominate the world," noted one scholar, "it was possibly because Europe first perceived there was a world to dominate.")

Today, globalization is proving much less resilient, and while global consciousness remains strong—there are healthy transnational communities and non-governmental organizations of all kinds—the material-environmental legacy is that of deep, embedded risk. Even after a few decades of intensive bargaineering, our material systems are losing their capacity to absorb costs and impacts—and are becoming risk multipliers. For example: a growing portion of our economy is increasingly vulnerable to small increases in the price of petroleum, plastic, labor, and other resources. Even the most incremental rise in the cost of plastic threatens to derail the plastic-packaged prosperity enjoyed by Western consumers, Indo-Asian manufacturers, and almost everyone else in-between. In the years before the great crash, for example, Chinese production became more costly due to a shortage of workers, food, and resources, as well as new labor laws that have increased wages. China's inflation surged to an 11-year high in 2008, and food prices jumped by over 23 percent—which, in turn, forced an estimated 20 percent increase in factory wages. This matters because developing countries like China supply nearly half of all Western consumer goods. The slightest cost increases impact retail prices, and the average price of goods from China had already begun to increase in 2007, peaking at an annual 9 percent increase by 2008, after uninterrupted savings throughout the 1990s and early 2000s. Global recession had temporarily reversed this inflationary trend by 2009, yet this fierce price spike underlines the scale of inevitable, chronic high prices in the coming decades. ("It is much more difficult to weed inflation out of the economy than it is to revive an economy that's in trouble," said Bernard Baumohl, managing director of research firm Economic Outlook Group in 2007. "All of this tells us that inflation pressures are likely to build in the future.")

As well, globalization has eroded security and increased inequality. Evidenced by the boom-and-bust economy of Los Angeles's ports, a planet conjoined with countless overlapping supply chains offers little economic accountability or stability. The volatility is unprecedented. Until the global economy went bust in 2008, global trade was increasing an average of 20 percent annually; after the crash, the World Bank reported the steepest drop in demand within rich economies in over 80 years. Mexico and China are among the world's most inequitable countries in terms of absolute rich and poor, and both have been heavily bargaineered for decades.

Bargaineering does not ensure affordability or lasting wealth, yet deglobalization could have serious consequences. "I think there's a real danger that globalization could unravel," economist Niall Ferguson told *The Globe and Mail* in 2009. "There will be blood, in the sense that a crisis of this magnitude is bound to increase political as well as economic [conflict]. It is bound to destabilize some countries. It will cause civil wars to break out that have been dormant. It will topple governments that were moderate and bring in governments that are extreme...."

At the very least, protectionism has returned as trade conditions deteriorate. In 2009, for example, Mexico announced tariff increases between

10 and 45 percent, affecting $2.4 billion of American goods entering Mexico. Everything from cabbage, toilet paper, deodorant, pencils, pork rinds, and Christmas trees were affected. ("Clearly, this was designed to bring about some specific pain," said David Gantz, professor of law at the University of Arizona.)

Our bargain-based world is a monoculture. And monocultures never last. Efforts to shore up yesterday's prosperity—such as the 2009 American bailout and stimulus package, fighting a debt crisis with more debt, spending to positive growth—will not work. Clinging to yesterday's economy is risky at best.

Because of deep interdependence, we can't let globalization fail too quickly or without purpose. The case for intensified local production and consumption is compelling. But rapid deglobalization could backfire. Indeed, without the nongovernmental organizations (NGOs) and the cooperative global networks that economist Jeffrey Sachs advocates, former global powers like Mongolia would have likely imploded late in the twentieth century, so deep was the poverty and lack of development that resulted when Russia pulled out after 70-plus years of occupation in 1990. "The paradox of a unified global economy and divided global society poses the single greatest threat to the planet because it makes impossible the cooperation needed to address [our] remaining challenges," writes Sachs in his 2008 book *Common Wealth*. "We've actually been there before. The first great wave of globalization in the nineteenth century ended up in the blood-drenched trenches of Europe in World War One."

For many of us, deglobalization should offer some relief: economies less tied to unsustainable growth, markets less expectant of unrealistic returns, and consumers less governed by objects of their desire. There is liberation in accounting for environmental and climate impacts, practicing economic non-violence, and realizing that as much as we have attempted to prosper with decoupled forms of commerce, we are still ultimately governed by interdependence. It's a lesson in cause and effect taught not only by globalization now in its twilight years, but also as part of teachings for more than a millennia here in Lhasa, even longer in China, and even longer still in India, where the Buddha himself once instructed monks: "From the arising of this comes the arising of that. . . . From the cessation of this comes the cessation of that."

Ultimately, there is no "Wal-Mart" that exists independent of everything else, but an aggregate of causes and conditions that weaves together the livelihoods of millions. There will likely be no Wal-Mart in 100 years, just as there is only just a shell of America's domestic auto industry now remaining. Part of the ingenuity and technology of the modern megafirm is to influence affairs, sway consumers, and channel resources as though there was actually a singular, monolithic power at work. Yet communities that have fought and won against unwanted big-box stores, as well as governments who have refused to subsidize global commerce, have sometimes found that the reality is more porous, change is possible, and that common sense can sway the balance of things. ("The chance that consumers are ever going to go back to their high-spending ways is not very plausible, nor do I think they should," argued President Obama's chief economics forecaster Christina Romer in mid-2009. "We were a country that needed to start saving more.")

The lesson from previous periods of deglobalization, such as the dark years surrounding the Great Depression leading up to World War II, is that the bad politics, fear and strife can become more damaging than economic losses. Nativist movements, anti-immigration rallies, and nationalist fervor are already part of many countries and it would be unwise to rule out destructive and emotional responses to many consumers losing their reach and buying power. In Buddhist practice, loss of identity is something that people can fear just as much as death. And given that many people in the developed world have known little else but two decades of consumer empowerment and reward, there will be inevitable dissent and fear about a future that guarantees less.

Along the outer edge of Lhasa, Tibetan pilgrims follow an ancient circumambulation route, the Lingkor that was here long before modern development covered it up. They swing prayer wheels and chant *Om Mani Padme Hum* as they follow an obscured path along a freshly built four-lane highway. Pilgrims stop to worship in invisible temples and chortens, torn down in the mad swath of Chinese construction that's transforming the city. But the ancient route is outfitted with several of its own video surveillance cameras; as such the Lingkor displays many of the new elements of global economy. The route passes ancient stone carvings, an electronic stock exchange (Tibet's first), a go-cart track behind the Potala Palace, nondescript brothels, and stations of ever-watchful armed soldiers.

Returning from the Lingkor, I spot a gleaming item from a souvenir stand next to Lhasa's central temple. While the statues and religious trinkets sold along the Barkhor are mostly imported from Nepal and India, several vendors actually sell Tibetan heirlooms, many of which have been stolen from temples. It is possible to barter and bargain for things that are priceless. I recognize one artifact immediately, it is the hand of a golden Buddha, sawed-off at the wrist, frozen in the flat-palmed gesture of generosity.

The Thermodynamics of Cheap

While one part of our economy wages a war on scarcity by burning up high-value resources, another part is rediscovering the negawatt. The negawatt is what scientist Amory Lovins once described as the cheapest energy of all: the energy saved from efficiency and demand management.

Energy efficiency is still the final frontier. During the first major energy crisis of the twentieth century—the OPEC embargo that followed the Yom Kippur War of 1973—green energy took root. How-to books on solar power, passive heating, and wind power sold like hotcakes. Tiny start-up companies began building high-efficiency wood stoves and solar panels; books and magazines promoted a back-to-the land ethos that championed smart energy alternatives. But the movement faltered. Governments took to building nuclear power stations, and, as global oil supplies returned, and consumers enjoyed cheap energy prices again, enough to maintain the cars, homes, and appliances of the high energy society built up during the 1950s and 1960s. Nevertheless, a total of over 150 nuclear power plants were built across North America, all of them commissioned before 1974. Finally, Syncrude opened in 1978 with government support, consolidating Canada's tar sands development as an industry, pioneering the effort to create crude oil out of dirt.

But publicly subsidized megaprojects, luckily, aren't everyone's vision. About 700 kilometers north of the tar sands is the small First Nations community of Whatì. With about 485 residents, the Dogrib people here have fished and trapped in the North Slave Lake region as long as anyone can remember. But for decades, the rustic log homes that overlook rugged Lac La Martre were powered by diesel engine generators that were never quiet and required expensive fuel imported in tanker trucks via a 145-kilometer ice-road trip from Yellowknife each winter.

During an energy audit in 2002, the community discovered that it had been collectively spending over a million dollars annually on fuel for heating and transport. At just over $2,000 per resident, it was an annual energy expense double or even quadruple that of most North Americans. Not to mention the health hazard the burning of diesel created. "Anyone living here is affected by the gas emissions. Adults, children, even if the doors are shut," said elder Jonas Nitsiza in 2002. "If they're sick [or] not feeling well, we know that the power plant is the main reason. The diseases originate from the power plant."

Something had to be done. Beginning in 2002, Whatì embarked on an ambitious plan to achieve greater energy efficiency, seek out green sources of power, and somehow reconcile their energy requirements with the social, health, and economic development of their community. To reach the goal of "prosperous self-sufficiency" elders, youth, and adults worked with consultants and government to reduce greenhouse-gas emissions by 50 percent within three years. Progress was made, and by 2008, plans and financing were being arranged for a $16 million micro-hydro installation. Hydroelectricity, using the abundant water resources of the region, could replace or drastically reduce diesel generation and contribute additional space heating. Solar hot water heaters will add additional capacity. By 2009, Whatì was on its way to becoming a genuinely self-sustaining community.

If you live in the cold north, it is hard to let go of high-quality, dependable source energy from hydrocarbons, even if it is slowly killing us or draining our collective savings. To its credit, the community of Whatì sought to change its energy paradigm before too much damage was done. It's a lesson for the rest of us who are still highly dependent on fossil fuels.

History does not favor societies that fail to manage resource crises. "Societies that don't have enough access to high-quality energy are likely to disintegrate," argues Homer-Dixon in *The Upside of Down*. Between the entropy of our material systems and the destabilization of natural systems, the threat of massive Schumpeterian change is real. "This would be destructive—not creative—catastrophe . . . It would affect large regions and even sweep around the globe, in the process deeply damaging the human prospect. Recovery and renewal would be slow, perhaps impossible."

The Bush administration promised to fast-track America into alternative energy by replacing 20 percent of the U.S. gasoline consumption with renewable fuels by 2017. The result was a rediscovery of the first law of thermodynamics, which holds that energy in any isolated system remains constant and cannot be recreated. When American producers allocated one-third of U.S. corn production to ethanol refining in the early years of the 2000s, not only was the net energy gain often negative (after factoring in energy inputs such as farming fuels, fertilizer, transport), it inevitably resulted in international inflation in food prices. Tortilla prices in Mexico, for example, went through the roof. (It is claimed that second-generation ethanol production, cellulosic ethanol, can successfully run off waste streams and could yield roughly 80 to 85 percent more energy than is required to grow and produce.)

Growth becomes self-sabotage. The creation of "new energy" from unconventional sources is subject to similar constraints. Bitumen energy upgrading, hydrogen energy manufacturing, as well as more extreme high-cost frontier extraction such as deep-water drilling, Arctic drilling, and sub-sea hydrates, all of these manifest a much steeper production cost than previously imagined, both to the consumer and to the planet in general. The actual amount of new energy harvested from this growing pool of marginal resources decreases with each passing decade, especially relative to population growth and the often-inefficient energy demands of both emerging and established economies.

Moreover, we have become highly efficient in some ways but not in others, resulting in asymmetrical outcomes. We are optimized for bargains but not for energy usage, for example. Wal-Mart can squeeze pennies out of manufacturers, reduce packaging, push overhead and labor costs down, and then put the product on a container ship burning bunker fuel and distribute it to big-box stores where everyone shows up in a vehicle that likely is nowhere near as efficient as it could be.

The global supply chain was founded on the operating assumptions of open energy systems, of cheap shipping, of big-box stores accessible by automobile, and of the embodied energy materials themselves—plastics, fertilizer—not subject to serious constraints or consequences. Moreover, the amount of energy required to sustain order in globalization's complex systems is immense. And Wal-Mart's commitment to increase its transport efficiency by 50 percent by 2015 is minimized by the fact that it still seeks to champion and grow from a fundamental business model defined by embodied energy.

Record prices fetched for crude oil during the 2000s led business analysts to question the future viability of a bargain-based world, since everything from the cost of manufacturing to mass container transport depends on affordable energy. As *The Financial Times* of London speculated in 2008, "$100-plus [price of oil] sustained for a year or more would do much more damage to the world economy than anything we have seen so far. The break point may well turn out to be pretty close to where we are now."

But as both economies and environments falter, we are moving away from the illusion of open energy systems—boundless horizons of cheap energy, frontiers of plentiful resources with rich gigajoules of power—to the long-term reality of a closed, planet-based system subject to diminishing returns from non-renewable energy, complications resulting from interconnected economies, population growth, and climate change. The closed energy system of the twenty-first century is twofold: the planet itself and a highly globalized economy that, in surpassing its operational limits, has begun to perform like a stressed climatic system.

Investment allocation tells us a story about our future based on current trends: drilling platforms dot forsaken frontiers around the world; a growing network of pipelines weave across continents in an effort to accelerate commerce; and refineries and petrochemical manufacturers are shutting down operations and relocating around the world in an effort to gain location advantage to cheaper fuel supplies and labor. "The next ten years will be crucial for all countries, including China and India, because of the rapid expansion of energy-supply infrastructure," said Nobuo Tanaka of the International Energy Agency (IEA) in 2007. "We need to act now to bring about a radical shift in investment in favor of cleaner, more efficient and more secure energy technologies."

On the positive side the UNEP reported that worldwide investment in sustainable energy broke records in 2007, with $148.4 billion of new money raised, "investment between now and 2030 is expected to reach $450 billion a year by 2012, rising to more than $600 billion a year from 2020." It was a 60 percent increase from the previous year. Very positive news.

But, global spending on exploration and production in 2008 was $418 billion—nearly triple announced renewable investment in 2007—up from $349 billion in 2007. However, this is more a reflection of the rising cost of securing new oil and gas supplies, including unconventional crude sources and deep drilling in extreme locations. As Bloomberg reported in 2008, for nonstate companies like Exxon, Shell, and ConocoPhillips, "costs more than quadrupled since 2000 as explorers targeted more challenging reservoirs and demand rose for labor and material." Conventional oil used to cost $4 per barrel in 2000, yet by 2007 extraction and production costs had increased to $18, reflecting the same triple-digit cost increases found in the tar sands. Overall, exploration spending increased 120 percent between 2004 and 2007, yet the number of wells actually drilled increased only 52 percent.

The gains from energy efficiency are far more impressive than the declining returns of crude oil exploration—and cheaper too. "Global industry will need to invest an additional US$360 billion in energy efficient technology," reported the United Nations Foundation (UNF) in a landmark 2007 report, "Realizing the Potential of Energy Efficiency." "[But] the lifetime resulting savings in energy costs are estimated to be more than US$900 billion."

"World governments should exploit energy efficiency as their energy resource of first choice because it is the least expensive and most readily scalable option to support sustainable economic growth, enhance national security, and reduce further damage to the climate system," argued the UNF. If G8 nations alone—the richest nations of the northern hemisphere—doubled their rate of efficiency between 2012 and 2030, world carbon concentrations could be stabilized at 550 ppm (admittedly the high end for climate stabilization). G8 nations would also avoid spending $3 trillion on new power generation, save consumers $500 billion by 2030, and return the planet to 2004 energy consumption levels.

These epic savings—essentially, energy bargaineering—are not limited to affluent countries. The IEA argued that China alone could realistically cut its fuel use by 15 percent by 2030, and that energy efficiency could account for as much as 60 percent of this gain. By 2009, many countries had included renewable power and energy efficiency in their economic crisis stimulus packages. In 2009, for example, Britain announced it would commit to 24 million U.K. homes to be near-zero carbon by 2030.

To all efficiency and renewable power skeptics, it must be noted that the early decades of oil and gas exploration were also marked by slow returns. Surprisingly few people knew what to do with the stuff, besides burn it in gas lamps or use it to grease the axles of their horse-drawn carriages. In several decades alternatives may look essential and valuable, especially as renewable power becomes more affordable. The cost of solar photovoltaic cells, for example, has already decreased by 95 percent since the 1970s. There are quantum savings to be achieved in the twenty-first century, just not necessarily at the mall. And not with cheap energy.

The True Cost of Things

Early in 2001, just as Wal-Mart was consolidating its status as the world's largest company, I ventured up into Canada's High Arctic on a magazine assignment to write about climate change. Guided by a local hunter from Resolute Bay in Canada's Qikiqtaaluk region, we traveled out onto the pack ice. Here at Canada's second most northerly civilian settlement, local elders were reporting that the pack ice was breaking up weeks and even months early and behaving erratically. The plane ride into Resolute showed a glimpse of a large crack in the ocean ice, even though it was still February, with daytime low temperatures of minus 40 Celsius. Outside, it was too cold to talk— wind chill here runs upwards of minus 70—and all we could do was gaze off into the distance, across the frozen ocean and the islands of the Arctic, toward a horizon lit by winter twilight. It was silent except for the wind, and yet, beneath us, everything was in motion.

We were traveling on top of the legendary Northwest Passage, the world's last great stretch of unconquered ocean and the direct sea route coveted by explorers going back to the time of Queen Elizabeth. But to the local Inuit, this largely ice-bound channel is a thoroughfare for polar bears, seal, walrus, hunters, wayward explorers, and pack ice. Later, after skidding across the ice on the back of a snowmobile, I recall the troubled stories of local hunters describing freak floods, unusual bouts of open water and surges, and disappearing wildlife—phenomena that run counter to generations of Inuit oral history, but are often reflected in the predictions of those who study climate change. Inuit elders and hunters are losing their bearings on the unfamiliar ice floes, and have begun resorting to GPS units for navigation.

In August 2007, the Northwest Passage was open to marine travel for the first time, making it the world's most northerly navigational route. As ice coverage doggedly disappears across the summertime waters of the Arctic, shipping companies and trading nations are jockeying to run some of the world's biggest container ships and tankers on regular routes through the Northwest Passage well before 2040, the estimated date when all summer sea ice in the Arctic will have disappeared. This major new shipping route is worth billions—whereas it once took 29 days to sail between Rotterdam and Yokohama, it would take just 15 across the Northwest Passage and the Arctic Ocean. For Inuit, environmentalists, and many locals, this presents hazards nearly as alarming as the regional effects of climate change, including oil spills, lost shipping containers, oil drilling, and economic development on land—basically, relocating southern industrial development to the edge of some of our most northerly habitable communities.

"Within a generation the Arctic Ocean will be opened-up to general cargo shipping," said Inuit leader Sheila Watt-Cloudier in 2004, who was nominated for the 2007 Nobel Prize. "This means wholesale social, economic, and cultural change in the circumpolar world, and will bring to the fore long-standing questions of national sovereignty and disputed boundaries. I don't think any of us are ready for these very big issues."

While eroding sea ice is the greatest concern to the Innuit hunters, it is the heavy metals and PAHs this will bring that worry many people more. Mercury accumulates in the Arctic; the persistent cold for much of the year literally freezes it out of the water vapor in the air, where it accumulates on the ground. Caribou eat the lichens; polar bears and hunters—and their children—eat the caribou. "We are eager to manufacture metal, to forge steel, and burn coal. Like in the south, all around the Great Lakes," says one Inuk hunter. "For the average farmer in the south, there is quality control. But for caribou meat, all we can hope for is that it is the same as 100 years ago."

Due to the pervasive presence of contaminants and the high cost of gas and equipment, hunters increasingly have to shop for food. Iqaluit's Northmart is one of a handful of high-latitude supermarkets in the world. It may be howling cold outside, with blizzards blowing in off Frobisher Bay, but inside you can push your cart down the isles with your parka off, surrounded by fresh dairy, bread, and produce. In addition to groceries, Northmart also sells housewares, clothing, and equipment, much like a Wal-Mart supercenter, but smaller, more expensive, and with fewer white people as customers.

This is one view of the future: a world without bargains. Tomatoes and green peppers can be had for $4 a pound, milk for $3 to $4 a liter. A liter of apple juice costs $5.89; hot dog buns are $4.99—and that's after $18 million in annual transport subsidies from the government. Junk food and sweetened juices aren't subsidized, so a gallon jug of cranberry cocktail retails for $41.69.

It's hard to hide the true cost of things up here. Transport costs for green peppers and tomatoes are 20 percent of retail price up here, whereas transport cost as a percentage of sales in the south were less than 2 percent in 2004. Gasoline was $5.67 a gallon by mid-2008 even after $230 million in fuel subsidies—the real cost is likely closer to $11.00 a gallon for gasoline. This is a land that is beyond cheap, a place that Wal-Mart has forsaken.

While wrestling with food inflation, climate change, homelessness, unemployment, and other chronic issues, Nunavut's government had to raise an extra $100 million to cover energy price increases in 2008, or let retail gasoline prices jump 50 percent. If consumer gasoline prices doubled, so too would homelessness, given the large number of at-risk residents that live in Iqaluit and depend on gasoline and fuel oils for power. The local homeless shelter runs nearly full already and winters are deadly. A 2006 government report documented that 13-year-old girls were trading sex for shelter, and single mothers with babies were sleeping inside ATM vestibules; several local homeless men wander the Northmart on any given day, in an effort to stay warm.

Iqaluit is on the cutting edge of many of our most important twenty-first century challenges. "I've got to find that $100 million," said Nunavut energy minister Ed Picco. "Do I take it out of education? Do I take it out of health?" The government has certainly done its part to reduce carbon intensity, future-proof, and generally attempt to cope with the multitude of new pressures it faces. But when it comes down to it—when cheap is eliminated—people are often forced to choose between maintaining their material systems and infrastructure and sustaining public assets like education, and environment. This choice, in fact, happens all the time, yet we don't notice it because the consequences are deferred, delayed, or we're simply not paying attention.

What buys Nunavut time is the curious and much larger phenomenon of our societal capacity to absorb and tolerate high economic costs, particularly energy costs, without collapse. This may suggest hidden strength and resilience of some kind. Or, it may also be a lesson about how systems change in nonlinear fashion. For example. if you travel straight out of Iqaluit, across Frobisher Bay, south and east, you'll be in open water within the upper reaches of the Labrador Sea, an extremely deep stretch of ocean bordered by

Greenland and Labrador. This is the site of North Atlantic deep water, one of the great engines of oceanic currents in the northern hemisphere, responsible for anchoring planetary energy balances. Here, water moves in deep channels, mixing with old waters as it moves into the southern hemisphere. Some deep waters travel for 1,600 years before passing Antarctica, turning north into the South Pacific and finally upwelling in the North Pacific.

As Wallace S. Broecker first noted in 1987, and other climatologists have confirmed since, the great ocean conveyor is characterized by massive thermal inertia. Climate change happens as an echo, and today's emissions don't immediately impact the earth's thermal cycles simply because of the planet's oceanic mass. Change is gradual and unlikely to reflect rapid loads and stresses. The true delayed response is the possibility a climactic flip that occurs once a certain threshold of water salinity and temperature is reached. At that point, as has since been debated, discussed, and fearfully speculated on at length, our climate may destabilize and begin to perform in erratic ways, such as cooling in Northern Europe or accelerated sea level increases. NOAA notes a six-year thermal delay after an "instantaneous change."

For people who are also concerned about the price of big-screen televisions, the take-away lesson is simple: As our material world and our economy begins to perform more like a climactic system under late globalization, we are incurring stresses and strains that likely have critical, much-delayed consequences.

Much like the problem of toxic debt within dangerously flawed financial products, costs and dangers within the modern supply chain are not evident, nor are they passed along to consumers as the true price of things. This goes a long way to explain how a crowded global economy managed to squeeze out persistent growth and productivity despite price increases, volatility, and other challenges. That Wal-Mart can still comfortably fill a supercenter during $150 oil price spikes is an accomplishment, to be sure. But three more years of $150 a barrel oil without reprieve would seriously constrain Wal-Mart's survival tools: its ability to hedge and purchase quantities of services, materials, and energy when prices are low; the continued inability of suppliers in the same situation to absorb costs; and the decreasing likelihood that customers themselves would continue to consume at past rates. On the whole, the story of much of the 2000s was how modest overall price increases actually were, given the impressive increases in food, oil, and other commodities. ("One of the surprises," said Patrick Jackman, a senior economist in the consumer price division of the U.S. Bureau of Labor Statistics, "is that the oil price surges of the 1970s passed through fairly quickly into consumer prices, and this time that is not happening.")

The truth is that the world's biggest corporations have been internalizing costs in an effort to stay competitive, essentially creating consumer welfare. During the oil price spike of 2008, for example, Europe's leading discount airline, the Irish Ryanair, reported that 50 percent of all its costs were fuel-related. Likewise, ExxonMobil claimed that it sacrificed its refining margins in effort to reduce retail gas price increases.

Multinationals can't carry us forever, though. In the future, will there be any savings to pass along to consumers after we finish transporting bargains across the planet? Removing subsidies to consumers and business from the global economy would be a lot like removing automobiles from our cities. It is possible, and even desirable on many levels, but it represents the kind of radical change that people rarely undertake voluntarily. And it is very difficult to convince developing nations to give up fuel and food subsidies. The 48 percent increase in global food prices between 2006 and 2008, for example, had its most destructive impact on the developing world. Approximately 100 million people across Africa, Asia, and the Americas are at critical risk as price increases erode previous gains made against poverty.

But someone has to make sacrifices and take new kinds of risk. The crack in the February ice on the Northwest Passage that I witnessed in 2001 wasn't an isolated event. In March 2008, the British Meteorological Office found that the coldest winter days in Canada and Russia had become four degrees milder since the 1950s. In global terms, a four degree overall increase—not just far northern latitudes—would be a profound event, potentially causing water shortages, initial flooding in coastal cities, and profligate spread of tropical disease.

The Big Fix

High prices might well save us. A world that has no price or tax on carbon, for example, is a world that rewards massive investment in unconventional crude and discriminates against sustainable alternatives. "Every serious study of climate change done in Canada and abroad make the same point," reported *The Globe and Mail*'s Jeffrey Simpson in 2009. "Unless governments put a price on carbon, there cannot be a serious attempt to reduce emissions." Moreover, if the carbon price per ton is too low within any emissions trading system, such as it is in Alberta, at $15 a ton, the low cost is inadequate to stimulate alternatives; it is cheaper for companies to simply pay to pollute.

The true cost of things is a critical question in the twenty-first century. The cost of mitigating the worst effects of climate change could be as much as 2 percent of world GDP, according to Britain's influential 2006 Stern Review, while the cost of inaction would be at least 5 percent or even 20 percent of global GDP. To meet the radical reductions in greenhouse gas emissions that would assuredly stabilize the planet, our entire status quo will be challenged. Yet by 2009, Nicholas Stern, estimated that a green plan to save the future— one that addressed both financial and the environment crises—might be as cheap as just 0.8 percent of world GDP, or $400 billion. That's less than a single year's revenue from all the dollar stores, chain discounters, and global bargaineers combined.

Like the unseen effects of ocean currents and pack ice on global climate, there is a hidden world inside our economies and global systems of interdependence that is surprisingly forgiving and open. This is because many of our obstacles are cognitive and cultural, and problems are not always as concrete as one might think. Sometimes stagnation is the result of deep inertia, not because change isn't possible. We are habituated to cycles: grocery shopping, foraging for deals, or aspiring for better gadgets. There is nothing to suggest that we can't change this up in favor of competitive conservation or extreme local commerce. Like energy efficiency, it's hard to imagine why we didn't do it sooner.

Many people are forsaking malls and searching for value within their own communities. New kinds of co-ops, buying clubs, and barter economies are not merely lifestyle choices, as proffered by "simplicity" gurus and glossy magazines, but real-time alternatives to the challenges of twenty-first-century living. Millions are now experimenting with commerce by different means, often without credit cards, money, or retail outlets. Indeed, relief from the global economy is already available at the local level: an economic underground—a constellation of local currencies, co-ops, and community economic development initiatives—which present a series of immediate alternatives, sometimes as a direct challenge to the growing clout of big-box retailers. As America's Institute for Local Self-Reliance has long argued, there are clear payoffs and gains to be achieved through local commerce. (As one 2007 study in San Francisco found, local bookstores create nearly double the economic activity in the area, and that local toy stores create 2.2 jobs per one million in sales, versus 1.3 jobs created by toy chains.)

Specifically, there are several policy fronts that offer new opportunity and require innovation. First, our world is rife with subsidy, not just obvious subsidy such as public investment in logistics and transport infrastructure or tax breaks for unconventional crude development, but broader freebies such as cheap water, carbon, and clean air. The global interest in carbon taxes is one sign of the future—and preferably flat taxes implemented alongside with cap and trading systems because emissions credit systems have been vulnerable to cheats and manipulation. On a smaller scale, charging for things like plastic bags has been enormously successful: in 2009 British retailer Marks & Spencer reported an 80 per cent reduction in plastic bag usage in a single year after implementing a small fee for single-use bags.

Second, government can and should set outcomes. Policy leadership is paramount in the twenty-first century, and there should be no further hesitation in forming policy objectives on everything from financial regulation to energy efficiency. Deregulation and market-set policy have clearly failed within multiple sectors, laxity in regulation on auto fuel efficiency standards has long created needless health, environmental and economic damage. The extravagant stimulus spending of the late 2000s, however, is not a long-term option for western debtor nations like the United States, and governments will have to conserve spending resources. Yet targeted consumer incentives for future essentials like renewable energy—and not dubious alternative fuels like ethanol—are clearly needed on a broader scale.

Third, trade should no longer be decoupled from public safety, human rights, environment, and national policy. For example, market-based engagement on rights in China—the argument that commerce leads to democracy and rule of law—has been disproven. Did western trading nations willfully neglect Tibet, Xinjiang, and other areas of human rights abuses just to keep bargains flowing across the ocean? It's hard to conclude otherwise. By contrast, when American leaders and NGOs promoted low carbon fuel standards—and likely penalization of high-carbon "dirty" oil imports such as from Canada's tar sands—the impact was immediate, and forced new progress on Canada's lagging environmental policy.

Fourth, income security will be a greater challenge in a deglobalized world. With homelessness peaking even before the crash of 2008, and globalized trade failing to enrich many developing nations, there is much to be done on making local economies and households more resilient. The World Bank estimated in 2009 that weaker economic growth could push as many as 46 million people into poverty. For many people, education, health, and housing became more expensive as electronics and furniture became cheaper. We need to somehow reverse this trend. Localized solutions have succeeded in developing countries, such as micro-lending and financial literacy training, and have growing relevance and application in the developed world.

And finally, we may be forced to save globalization from itself. We need continued growth of global civil society—with NGOs, advocacy groups, and diplomatic efforts to work with developing nations and emerging economic powers, as well as continued international cooperation on climate change, reform in trade and currency systems, undocumented migrants, and shipping emissions. America's withering superpower status will provide new opportunities, but will also leave a vacuum in influence and leadership that must not default to opportunistic and antidemocratic interests.

Until we price the true cost of things, we're faced with an economic tautology: Bargaineering creates the need for further bargains. People may decry the local Wal-Mart, and even deny the developing world the chance to enjoy the same pleasures, but they'll still buy cheap stuff. Until then, consumerism will continue to become, one way or another, one massive conflict of interest.

Those who grew up with the "jobless recovery" of the 1990s may one day live to see the growthless economy. Nations built upon spending, shopping and shipping will eventually consume—and potentially destroy—more than they contribute. Our revolution in affordable consumerism created prosperity, but also low wages, urban blight, environmental damage, labor abuses, and a cookie-cutter model of progress. Add climate change, financial collapse, and competition for global resources, and the modern bargain economy embodies many of the greatest challenges of the new millennium. Despite innovations and gains, ours is the generation during which the plentiful will become scarce—and cheap stuff will prove to be truly expensive.

Setting the real price of a bargain is still up to us. With much guilt-tripping and finger-wagging, Americans in particular have attempted to talk themselves out of trade deficits, big box landscapes, and credit insolvency. It hasn't worked. Nagging shoppers and corporations who pursue value to the ends of the earth will not bring back the middle class, reduce America's dependence on Chinese finance, nor stabilize the earth's climate.

Reforming the cousumer isn't the main challenge. Indeed, most shoppers are far more aware and adaptable then many experts allow. What we need is an honest attempt to institute the true cost of things.

ACKNOWLEDGMENTS

More than any other book that I've written, this one was a product of generosity: I could not have managed the book's scope, or even reached completion, if a great many people had not helped along the way.

In Las Vegas, Athene Kovacic and Sam Bundy introduced me to the ASD/ AMD Trade Show; Danny Kole and other exhibitors made time in the midst of a busy event. Jeff Harrison and Kim Brooke at the University of Arizona opened the door to Tucson's annual Global Retailing Conference. Carrie Fox of Borderlinks guided and translated in Nogales, Mexico. Maryada Vallet of No More Deaths shared research. In Los Angeles, Tom Politeo and Elina Green gave engaged ground tours of the port neighbourhoods, and Arley Baker of the Port of Los Angeles provided a deluxe boat ride amid hulking container ships. Dick McKenna and Manny Aschemeyer gave me a bird's eye view of LA's harbour from the control room of the Marine Exchange. Paul Connolly of OOCL shipping got me onto the docks in the middle of a busy day.

In Hong Kong, Wing Ah Fung and Andrew McAuley were gracious hosts. Nury Vittachi gave good advice at the Foreign Correspondents' Club. Labor activist Han Dongfang illuminated parts of China's mainland. Andre Alexander toured me around Lhasa's old city, and allowed an interview despite security cameras and plainclothes police. More than a few locals in China, Tibet, and Xinjiang, all who cannot be named, played important roles. Throughout Asia, my wife Lisa Caton was a lovely travelling companion and co-conspirator.

In Fort McMurray, Bruce Lourie and Tim Gray of the Ivey Foundation hosted a forward-thinking workshop and summit on the future of the tar sands. Suncor somehow engineered its ground tour of its Millennium Mine to make it nearly impossible for to allow visitors to actually view the mine itself. In Fort Chipewyan, Alec Bruno, Mike Mercredi, and Allan Adam all gave interviews on short notice. In Alberta's petrochemical zone, Dr. Ramesh Ramachandran of Dow Chemical, as well as Al Poole and Eric Kelusky of Nova Petrochemicals were all forthright and accommodating.

I owe an ideas debt to writers like Mike Davis, Barbara Ehrenreich, and Nelson Lichtenstein. But the primary inspiration behind this book is the principle of dependent origination, represented by a broad collection of teachings on interdependence and causality common to all schools of Buddhism. While any unskillful application of teachings is my sole responsibility, I would like to acknowledge Dharma teachers that have been generous along the way: Achariya Doug Duncan, Lama Gyurme Dorje, Karma Gyurmey Rinpoche, Neten Rinpoche, Edmund Jones, and the Clear Sky Sangha.

Early segments of this book first appeared in the *Far Eastern Economic Review, Mother Jones, Fuelling the Future* (Andrew Heintzman and Evan Solomon, eds.), the *Georgia Straight*, and *This Magazine*.

I would also like to thank Hilary McMahon, my agent at Westwood Creative Artists, who understood this project from the beginning, and, more importantly, stood behind it when things got rough. Chris Bucci, my first editor at McClelland & Stewart, gave as much time and patience as was necessary. My current editor at M&S, Trena White, was excellent throughout the editorial process, and helped the manuscript reach its potential. Jake Klisivitch at Palgrave Macmillan translated the project into the United States, and brought the book to market despite constraints on time and space. Thanks to all others who typeset, copyedited, sold foreign rights, and couriered proofs.

The author would like to formally acknowledge the financial support of the Canada Council, as well as Dave Greber Freelance Writers Award. A journalism fellowship with the Sheldon Chumir Foundation for Ethics and Leadership contributed valuable research. Public Interest Alberta funded part of my investigation into petrochemicals and pipelines.

May any shortcomings or mistakes within this work not be a source of distress. *Sarva Mangalam*.

"Whatever degenerations there are in the world,
The root of all these is ignorance"

In Praise of Dependent Origination,
Je Tsongkhapa (1357–1419), translated by Thupten Jinpa

SOURCES

As a reporter, one learns that some of the best and most revealing material is usually found through primary interviews—one-on-one investigations and discussions, ideally in the field. Within the constraints of time and budget, I attempted to complete as much reporting as possible to ensure that key interviews from various locations were mostly my own. Over the course of a ten-year period, and mostly since 2005, primary field-work and reporting was completed in Las Vegas, Tucson, Colma, Hong Kong, Shenzhen, Changsha, Beijing, Shanghai, Los Angeles, Calgary, Fort McMurray, Joffre, Xinjiang, Nogales, Vancouver, Lhasa, Inuvik, and Resolute Bay. Thanks to all who took time to meet and share their knowledge.

In a few instances, such as the 2008 Black Friday shopping fatality at Long Island's Green Acres Mall and the early 2000s unionization campaign in Las Vegas, scene reporting was compiled from secondary sources and cross-referenced with select after-the-fact interviews with participants.

Behind the primary interviews and fieldwork is a small mountain of secondary materials. This book builds upon the work of others, from journalists who documented the rise of global discounting during the 1990s, to scholars who have plumbed the mysteries of rural China, Schumpterian theory, petrochemicals, and the post-2008 financial crisis. Listed below are the books, reports, magazine and newspaper stories that provided figures, context, and quotations. Apologies to anyone not duly credited for their work.

Introduction: Black Friday, 2008

Alpert, Lukas I., Carolyn Salazar, and Christina Carrega. "Victim's life a struggle." *New York Post*, November 29, 2008. http://www.nypost.com/seven/11292008/news/regionalnews/victims_life_a_struggle_141388.htm.

Associated Press. "Personal savings drop to a 73-year low." *MSNBC*, February 1, 2007, http://www.msnbc.msn.com/id/16922582/.

Burritt, Chris. "Wal-Mart profit beats estimates as shoppers are lured by discounts." *Washington Post*, February 18, 2009. http://www.washingtonpost.com/wp-dyn/content/article/2009/02/17/AR2009021703165.html.

Crowley, Kieran. "Worker killed in Wal-Mart stampede." *New York Post*, November 28, 2008. http://www.nypost.com/seven/11282008/news/regionalnews/man_killed__woman_miscarries_in_wal_mart_141313.htm.

Dinopoulos, Elias and Fuat Şener. "New Directions in Schumpeterian Growth Theory," forthcoming in *Elgar Companion to Neo-Schumpeterian Economics*, editd by Horstand Hanusch and Pyka Andreas (Cheltenham, UK: Edward Elgar, 2007).

Dokoupil, Tony. "Is the mall dead?" *Newsweek*, November 12, 2008. http://www. newsweek.com/id/168753.

Hayasaki, Erika. "A very dark Black Friday." *Los Angeles Times*, December 6, 2008. http:// articles.latimes.com/2008/dec/06/nation/na-trample6.

Hughes, C. J. "Foreclosures on island outpace most of state." *New York Times*, February 13, 2009. http://www.nytimes.com/2009/02/15/nyregion/long-island/15forecloseli.html.

Kamer, Pearl M. "Moving a moving Long Island economy." *Newsday*, January 4, 2009. http://www.newsday.com/news/opinion/ny-opfocus5985846jan04,0,4503627.story.

Misonzhnik, Elaine. "Store Closings Could Double in 2009." *Retail Traffic*, November 5, 2008. http://retailtrafficmag.com/news/retail_store_closings_2009/.

Organisation for Economic Co-Operation and Development (OECD). "The Service Economy." Science Technology Industry (STI) Business and Industry Policy Forum Series, 2000. http://www.oecd.org/dataoecd/10/33/2090561.pdf.

Palmer, Kimberly. "The end of credit card consumerism." *U.S. News & World Report*, August 8, 2008. http://www.usnews.com/articles/business/economy/2008/08/08/the-end-of-credit-card-consumerism.html.

Rosenbloom, Stephanie. "All eyes on holiday shopping turnout in bleak economy." *New York Times*, November 28, 2008. http://www.nytimes.com/2008/11/29/business/29black. html?_r=1.

Shopping Centers Today staff. "U.S. retailers see encouraging Black Friday numbers." International Council of Shopping Centers, December 2, 2008. http://www.icsc.org/ srch/apps/newsdsp.php?storyid=2469&region=main.

Winzelberg, David. "Foreclosures up on Long Island." *Spaced Out*, February 18, 2009. http://libn.com/spacedout/2009/02/18/foreclosures-up-on-long-island/.

Wölfl, Anita. "The Service Economy in OECD Countries: STI Working Paper, Statistical Analysis of Science, Technology and Industry." Organisation for Economic Co-Operation and Development, February 11, 2005. http://www.olis.oecd.org/ olis/2005doc.nsf/LinkTo/NT00000B62/$FILE/JT00178454.PDF.

World Trade Organization. "WTO: developing, transition economies cushion trade slowdown. Chart 3: Real merchandise trade growth by region, 2007." World Trade Organization, April 17, 2008. http://www.wto.org/english/news_e/pres08_e/pr520_e. htm#chart3.

1. The Bargaineers: *Fear and Housewares in Las Vegas*

ABC News Blog. "Greenspan to Stephanopoulos: This is 'by far' the worst economic crisis he's seen in his career." ABC News Blog, September 14, 2008. http://blogs.abcnews. com/politicalradar/2008/09/greenspan-to-st.html.

Andersen, Kurt. "American roulette." *New York Magazine*, January 1, 2007. http://nymag. com/news/imperialcity/26014/.

Archibold, Randal C. "Las Vegas makes it illegal to feed homeless in parks." *New York Times*, July 28, 2006. http://www.nytimes.com/2006/07/28/us/28homeless. html?partner=rssnyt&emc=rss.

Associated Free Press. "Merrill bonuses made 696 millionaires: probe." *Google News*, February 11, 2009. http://www.google.com/hostednews/afp/article/ALeqM5gsvuGTj GstoLsG9sl2Xl25mGS_0w.

Bai, Matt. "The new boss." *New York Times Magazine*, January 30, 2005. http://www. nytimes.com/2005/01/30/magazine/30STERN.html.

Bell, Daniel. *The Coming of Post-Industrial Society* (New York: Basic Books, 1976).

Beltrame, Julian. "Canadian manufacturers urged to adapt to new strong dollar reality, or risk dying." *Sympatico MSN Finance*, September 17, 2007. http://finance.sympatico. msn.ca/investing/news/businessnews/article.aspx?cp-documentid=5444721.

Bianco, Anthony. *Wal-Mart: Bully of Bentonville* (New York: Doubleday, 2006).

Bianco, Anthony, and Wendy Zellner. "Is Wal-Mart too powerful?" *BusinessWeek*, October 6, 2003. http://www.businessweek.com/magazine/content/03_40/b3852001_ mz001.htm.

Blodget, Henry. "Amazon peak-day unit orders up encouraging 17% year-over-year." *The Business Insider*, December 26, 2008. http://www.businessinsider.com/2008/12/ amazon-peak-day-unit-orders-up-an-encouraging-17-year-over-year-amzn.

Bureau of Labor Statistics. "Employment Situation Summary." United States Department of Labor, Bureau of Labor Statistics, March 6, 2009. http://www.bls.gov/news.release/ empsit.nr0.htm.

Connolly, Ceci. "At Wal-Mart, a health-care turnaround." *Washington Post*, February 13, 2009. http://www.washingtonpost.com/wp-dyn/content/story/2009/02/13/ST2009021300507. html.

Cooper, Marc. *The Last Honest Place in America* (New York: Nation Books, 2004).

Cutler, Jonathan, and Thaddeus Russell. "Workers of the world…disunite!" *The Christian Science Monitor*, July 6, 2005. http://www.csmonitor.com/2005/0706/p09s02-coop. html.

Dicker, John. "Union blues at Wal-Mart." *The Nation*, June 20, 2002. http://www. thenation.com/doc/20020708/dicker.

Dollar Store Newsletter. "The Greatest Business?" Kole Imports (2005). http://www. koleimports.com/Newsletter/DollarStoreNews1.htm.

eBay Inc. "New study reveals 724,000 Americans rely on eBay sales for income." eBay Inc., July 21, 2005. http://investor.ebay.com/releasedetail.cfm?ReleaseID=170073.

Featherstone, Liza. "Andy Stern: Savior or sellout?" *The Nation*, June 27, 2007. http:// www.thenation.com/doc/20070716/featherstone.

Flowers, Lana F. "Consumers turn to private labels in down economy." *The Morning News: Local News for Northwest Arkansas*, February 20, 2009. http://www.nwaonline. net/articles/2009/02/20/business/022209bizwmtprivate.txt.

Friess, Steve. "Las Vegas sags as conventions cancel." *New York Times*, February 14, 2009. http://www.nytimes.com/2009/02/15/us/15vegas.html.

Gogoi, Pallavi. "Wal-Mart's China card." *BusinessWeek*, July 26, 2005. www.businessweek. com/bwdaily/dnflash/jul2005/nf20050726_3613_db016.htm.

Greenhouse, Steven. "Trying to overcome embarrassment, labor opens a drive to organize Wal-Mart." *New York Times*, November 8, 2002. http://www.nytimes.com/2002/11/08/ us/trying-to-overcome-embarrassment-labor-opens-a-drive-to-organize-wal-mart. html?sec=&spon=&pagewanted=all.

Gullo, Karen, and Margaret Cronin Fisk. "Wal-Mart wins request in bias case." *Washington Post*, February 14, 2009. http://www.washingtonpost.com/wp-dyn/content/ article/2009/02/14/AR2009021400071.html.

Hoopes, James. "Growth Through Knowledge," in *Wal-Mart: The Face of 21st Century Capitalism*, edited by Nelson Lichtenstein (New York: The New Press, 2006).

Human Rights in China. "The All-China Federation of Trade Unions (ACFTU)." Human Rights in China, October 25, 2004. http://www.hrichina.org/public/contents/ article?revision%5fid=18142&item%5fid=18141.

Krafft, Manfred, and Murali Mantrala, eds. *Retailing in the 21st Century: Current and Future Trends,* (Berlin: Springer, 2006).

Leamy, Elisabeth, and Vanessa Weber. "Manufacturers shrink products, but not price." *ABC News,* March 24, 2008. http://www.abcnews.go.com/GMA/story?id=4512700&page=1.

Lee, Christina. "Hot Topic: The dollar store's rising value." goWholesale, February 11, 2009. http://www.gowholesale.com/content/2009/02/11/hot-topic-the-dollar-stores-rising-value/.

Levy, Daniel, and Andrew T. Young. "'The Real Thing': Nominal Price Rigidity of the Nickel Coke, 1886–1959." Emory University (2004). http://129.3.20.41/eps/mac/papers/0402/0402013.pdf.

Meyerson, Harold. "Wal-Mart loves unions (in China)." *Washington Post,* December 1, 2004. http://www.washingtonpost.com/wp-dyn/articles/A23725-2004Nov30.html

NOW with Bill Moyers transcript. PBS, December 19, 2003. http://www.pbs.org/now/transcript/transcript247_full.html.

Parloff, Roger. "The war over unconscious bias." *Fortune,* October 1, 2007. http://money.cnn.com/magazines/fortune/fortune_archive/2007/10/15/100537276/index.htm.

Petrovic, Misha, and Gary Hamilton. "Making global markets: Wal-Mart and its suppliers," in *Wal-Mart: The Face of 21st Century Capitalism,* edited by Nelson Lichtenstein (New York: The New Press, 2006).

Pier, Carol. "Freedom of association at Wal-Mart: Anti-union tactics running afoul of US law." *Human Rights Watch,* no. 2 (2007), http://www.hrw.org/reports/2007/us0507/9.htm.

Plunkett-Powell, Karen. *Remembering Woolworth's* (New York: St. Martin's Press, 1999).

Rosenberg, Arthur. "A look into the future of dollar store retailing." Chain Store Guide, August 2007. www.csgis.com.

Shopping Centers Today staff. "U.K. communities need retail development to boost economy, report says." International Council of Shopping Centers, January 16, 2009. http://www.icsc.org/srch/apps/newsdsp.php?storyid=2476&region=main.

Spethmann, Betsy. "Tuning in at the shelf." *Promo Magazine,* April 1, 2005. http://promomagazine.com/retail/marketing_tuning_shelf/.

Vance, Sandra, and Roy Scott. *Wal-Mart: A History of Sam Walton's Retail Phenomenon* (New York: Twayne Publishers, 1997).

Willis, Ellen. "Escape From Freedom: What's The Matter With Tom Frank (And The Lefties Who Love Him)?" http://journalism.nyu.edu/faculty/files/willis-tomfrank.pdf.

Woellert, Lorraine, and Dawn Kopecki. "Moody's, S&P employees doubted ratings, e-mails say." *Bloomberg,* October 22, 2008. http://www.bloomberg.com/apps/news?pid=20601087&sid=a2EMlP5s7iM0&refer=worldwide.

Working Life Blog. "Showdown in Vegas: Is it over?" Working Life Blog, March 1, 2005. http://workinglife.typepad.com/daily_blog/2005/03/showdown_in_veg_2.html.

Yee, Amy. "Las Vegas bets its chips on intimacy." *MSNBC,* May 2, 2005. http://www.msnbc.msn.com/id/7712207/.

Zeitz, Joshua. "Why Woolworth had to die." *American Heritage,* July 17, 2007. http://www.americanheritage.com/events/articles/web/20070717-woolworth-business-retail-five-and-ten-urbanization-suburbanization-walmart.shtml.

2. Quantum Cheap: *Progress is Price Destruction*

Andersen, Michael, and Flemming Poulfelt. *Discount Business Strategy* (Hoboken, NJ: Wiley, 2006).

Associated Press. "Profit at Mattel is reduced by half." *New York Times*, February 3, 2009. http://www.nytimes.com/2009/02/03/business/03toy.html.

Atkeson, Andrew, and Patrick J. Kehoe. "Modeling the Transition to a New Economy: Lessons from Two Technological Revolutions." Federal Reserve Bank of Minneapolis Research Department Staff Report 296, May 2006. http://www.minneapolisfed.org/research/SR/SR296.pdf.

Atlanta Business Chronicle. "Home Depot sales and profit fall in 2007." *Atlanta Business Chronicle*, February 26, 2008. http://www.bizjournals.com/atlanta/stories/2008/02/25/daily8.html?ana=from_rss.

Barbaro, Michael. "Big retailers scaling back expansion plans and shutting stores." *New York Times*, May 2, 2008. http://www.nytimes.com/2008/05/02/business/02shop.html?_r=1&oref=slogin&ref=business&pagewanted=print.

Barbaro, Michael. "Retailing chains caught in a wave of bankruptcies." *New York Times*, April 15, 2008. http://www.nytimes.com/2008/04/15/business/15retail.html?_r=2&ei=5088&en=7937f306da360689&ex=1365998400&oref=slogin&partner=rssnyt&emc=rss&pagewanted=print&oref=slogin.

Bianco, Anthony. *Wal-Mart: Bully of Bentonville* (New York: Doubleday, 2006).

Broda, Christian, and David E. Weinstein. "Product Creation and Destruction: Evidence and Price Implications." University of Chicago (April 2007). http://www.papers.nber.org/papers/w13041.

Chen, Shaohua, and Martin Ravallion. "The developing world is poorer than we thought, but no less successful in the fight against poverty." The World Bank, August 2008. http://www-wds.worldbank.org/servlet/WDSContentServer/WDSP/IB/2008/08/26/000158349_20080826113239/Rendered/PDF/WPS4703.pdf.

Connolly, Ceci. "At Wal-Mart, a health-care turnaround." *Washington Post*, February 13, 2009. http://www.washingtonpost.com/wp-dyn/content/story/2009/02/13/ST2009021300507.html.

de Vries, Lloyd. "Wal-Mart starts holiday toys price war." *CBS News*, October 19, 2006. http://www.cbsnews.com/stories/2006/10/19/business/main2104968.shtml.

D'Innocenzio, Anne, and Mae Anderson. "Store closings may send customers to survivors." *Yahoo! Canada Finance*, March 3, 2003. http://ca.us.biz.yahoo.com/ap/090303/dead_market_share.html?.v=2.

Engardio, Pete. "Can the U.S. bring jobs back from China?" *BusinessWeek*, June 19, 2008. http://www.businessweek.com/print/magazine/content/08_26/b4090038429655.htm.

Fishman, Charles. *The Wal-Mart Effect* (New York: Penguin, 2007).

Flowers, Lana F. "Wal-Mart completes headquarters layoffs." *Morning News: Local News for Northwest Arkansas*, February 20, 2009. http://www.nwaonline.net/articles/2009/02/21/business/022109bizwmtlayoffs.txt.

Gagosian, Robert B. "Abrupt climate change: Should we be worried?" Woods Hole Oceanographic Institution, January 27, 2003. http://www.whoi.edu/page.do?pid=12455&tid=282&cid=9986.

Gogoi, Pallavi. "Wal-Mart's new growth opportunities." *BusinessWeek*, October 9, 2007. http://www.businessweek.com/bwdaily/dnflash/content/oct2007/db2007108_116420.htm.

Goodman, Peter S., and Jack Healy. "Job losses hint at vast remaking of economy." *New York Times*, March 7, 2009. http://www.nytimes.com/2009/03/07/business/economy/07jobs.html?_r=1&partner=rss&emc=rss.

Gunnison, Liz. "Macy's magic act." *Portfolio*, May 14, 2008. http://www.portfolio.com/news-markets/top-5/2008/05/14/Macys-Solid-Results.

Hansen, James, Makiko Sato, Pushker Kharecha, Gary Russell, David W. Lea and Mark Siddall. "Climate change and trace gases." Philosophical Transactions of The Royal Society, May 18, 2007. http://pubs.giss.nasa.gov/docs/2007/2007_Hansen_etal_2.pdf.

Hoopes, James. "Growth Through Knowledge," in *Wal-Mart: The Face of 21st Century Capitalism*, edited by Nelson Lichtenstein (New York: The New Press, 2006).

Hunter, Mark. "Emerging retail trend: Wal-Mart, the blue retailer." Emerging Trends at Retail Blog, December 4, 2006. http://emergingtrendsatretail.blogspot.com/2006/12/emerging-retail-trend-wal-mart-blue.html.

Norman, Al. "Hey, we cut Wal-Mart in half!" *Huffington Post*, October 25, 2007. http://www.huffingtonpost.com/al-norman/hey-we-cut-walmart-in-h_b_69834.html.

RetailWire. "Consumers choosing to tough it out with Wal-Mart." *RetailWire*, February 22, 2008. http://www.retailwire.com/Discussions/Sngl_Discussion.cfm/12773.

Rosenbloom, Stephanie. "Retail sales slide further, except at Wal-Mart." *New York Times*, March 6, 2009. http://www.nytimes.com/2009/03/06/business/economy/06retail.html.

Rosenbloom, Stephanie. "Wal-Mart outpaces a weak economy." *New York Times*, February 18, 2009. http://www.nytimes.com/2009/02/18/business/18shop.html?partner=rss&emc=rss&pagewanted=print.

Schumpeter, Joseph A. *Capitalism, Socialism and Democracy* (New York: Routledge, 1976).

Spector, Robert. *Category Killers: The Retail Revolution and its Impact on Consumer Culture* (Boston: Harvard Business School Press, 2005).

Strasser, Susan. "Woolworth's to Wal-Mart," in *Wal-Mart: The Face of 21st Century Capitalism*, edited by Nelson Lichtenstein (New York: The New Press, 2006).

Stelter, Brian. "Pressed by the economy, Starbucks lowers its forecast." *New York Times*, April 24, 2008. http://www.nytimes.com/2008/04/24/business/24sbux.html?scp=3&sq=starbucks&st=nyt.

Stempel, Jonathan. "One in five U.S. homeowners with mortgages in negative equity." *Yahoo! UK & Ireland Finance*, October 31, 2008. http://uk.biz.yahoo.com/31102008/325/five-u-s-homeowners-mortgages-negative-equity.html.

Stribling, Dees. "Onward and upward: Research reveals surprising stats about the U.S. shopping center industry." *Shopping Centers Today*, October 2007. http://www.icsc.org/srch/sct/sct1007/onward_upward.php.

Tubridy, Michael. "Defining Trends in Shopping Center History." *International Council of Shopping Centers*, May 2006. http://www.icsc.org/srch/about/impactofshoppingcenters/12_DefiningTrends.pdf.

Wall Street Journal. "Heavy discounting hits sears profit, raising doubts about revival effort." *Wall Street Journal*, February 27, 2009. http://online.wsj.com/article/SB123564718748081221.html?mod=todays_us_marketplace.

Watts, Robert, and Jonathan Oliver. "Britain faces crisis as negative equity to reach 2 million." *Sunday Times*, October 19, 2008. http://www.timesonline.co.uk/tol/money/property_and_mortgages/article4969314.ece.

3. *China Crisis:* The End of Cheap Labor

Amnesty International. "People's Republic of China—Internal migrants: Discrimination and abuse—The human cost of an economic 'miracle'." Amnesty International. http://www.amnesty.org/en/library/asset/ASA17/008/2007/en/dom-ASA170082007en.pdf.

Arrington, Michael. "Foxconn building 800,000 iPhones a week." TechCrunch. http://www.techcrunch.com/2008/08/04/foxconn-building-800000-iphones-a-week/.

Associated Free Press, The. "Wal-Mart signs pay deals with official Chinese unions." *Yahoo! Asia News,* July 25, 2008. http://asia.news.yahoo.com/080725/afp/080725133252business.html.

Barboza, David. "Child labor cases uncovered in China." *International Herald Tribune,* April 30, 2008. http://www.iht.com/articles/2008/04/30/asia/01china.php.

Barboza, David. "China says abusive child labor ring is exposed." *New York Times,* May 1, 2008. http://www.nytimes.com/2008/05/01/world/asia/01china.html.

Barboza, David. "China tells businesses to unionize." *New York Times,* September 12, 2008. http://www.nytimes.com/2008/09/12/business/worldbusiness/12yuan.html.

Barboza, David. "Once sizzling, China's economy shows rapid signs of fizzling." *New York Times,* November 7, 2008. http://www.nytimes.com/2008/11/07/business/worldbusiness/07yuan.html.

Bradsher, Keith. "Exports down sharply for 2nd month in China." *New York Times,* March 12, 2009. http://www.nytimes.com/2009/03/12/business/worldbusiness/12yuan.html?_r=1&partner=rss&emc=rss.

Buckley, Chris. "Update 1: Wal-Mart sees China productivity beating inflation." *Reuters,* February 25, 2008. http://www.reuters.com/article/rbssConsumerGoodsAndRetailNews/idUSPEK6745120080225?sp=true.

BusinessWeek. "China rushes upmarket." *BusinessWeek,* September 17, 2007. http://www.businessweek.com/magazine/content/07_38/b4050055.htm?chan=search.

Cao, Belinda, and Judy Chen. "China needs U.S. guarantees for treasuries, Yu says." *Bloomberg,* February 11, 2009. http://www.bloomberg.com/apps/news?pid=20601080&sid=aG_eSDsmh7rw&refer=asia.

Castle, Stephen, and Mark Landler. "After 7 years, talks collapse on world trade." *New York Times,* July 30, 2008. http://www.nytimes.com/2008/07/30/business/worldbusiness/30trade.html.

Castle, Stephen, and Keith Bradsher. "China's shift on food was key to trade impasse." *New York Times,* July 31, 2008. http://www.nytimes.com/2008/07/31/business/worldbusiness/31trade.html.

Chan, John. "Rising costs throw Chinese manufacturing into crisis." World Socialist Web Site. http://www.wsws.org/articles/2008/mar2008/chin-m17.shtml.

Chen, Shaohua, and Martin Ravallion. "The developing world is poorer than we thought, but no less successful in the fight against poverty." World Bank, August 2008. http://www-wds.worldbank.org/servlet/WDSContentServer/WDSP/IB/2008/08/26/000158349_20080826113239/Rendered/PDF/WPS4703.pdf.

ChinaDaily. "China strives to narrow urban-rural income gap." *ChinaDaily,* October 14, 2007. http://www.chinadaily.com.cn/china/2007-10/14/content_6172555.htm.

ChinaDaily. "Guangdong cracks down on child labor in factories." *ChinaDaily,* May 3, 2008. http://www.chinadaily.com.cn/china/2008-05/03/content_6658027.htm.

ChinaDaily. "Half of China's migrant workers unhappy with social status." *ChinaDaily*, January 13, 2008. http://www.chinadaily.com.cn/china/2008-01/13/content_6389912. htm.

China Labor Bulletin. "No Way Out: Worker Activism in China's State-Owned Enterprise Reforms" in *Rights & Democracy*. International Centre for Human Rights and Democratic Development, May 2008. http://www.clb.org.hk/en/files/File/research_ reports/no_way_out.pdf.

China Labor Bulletin. "Official union must back new migrant worker legislators." *China Labor Bulletin*, March 4, 2008. http://www.china-labour.org.hk/en/node/100215.

China Labor Bulletin. "Shenzhen minimum wage reaches 1,000 yuan per month." China Labor Bulletin, June 5, 2008. http://www.clb.org.hk/en/node/100258.

China Labor News Translations. "Trade Unions at Wal-Mart and Foxconn." China Labor News Translations. http://www.clntranslations.org/article/4/wal-mart.

Dean, Jason. "The forbidden city of Terry Gou." *Wall Street Journal*, August 11, 2007. http:// online.wsj.com/article/SB118677584137994489.html?mod=home_we_banner_left.

Economist, The. "Membership required." *The Economist*, July 31, 2008. http://www. economist.com/business/displaystory.cfm?story_id=11848496&fsrc=RSS.

Engardio, Pete. "Can the U.S. bring jobs back from China?" *BusinessWeek*, June 19, 2008. http://www.businessweek.com/print/magazine/content/08_26/b4090038429655. htm.

Fallows, James. "The $1.4 trillion question." *Atlantic Monthly*, January/February 2008. http://www.theatlantic.com/doc/200801/fallows-chinese-dollars.

Fallows, James. "China makes, the world takes." *Atlantic Monthly*, July/August 2007. www.theatlantic.com/doc/200707/shenzhen.

Frontline. "Is Wal-Mart good for America?" *PBS*, November 16, 2004. http://www.pbs. org/wgbh/pages/frontline/shows/walmart/.

Fu He. "Who did Dagongzhe offend?" *Southern Metropolitan Daily*, November 28, 2007. www.clntranslations.org/article/26/shenzhen-labor-activist-attacked

Gan, Lihua. "A tough context: Establishing the first KFC trade union branch." *China Youth Daily*, July 15, 2007.

Gittings, John. "China's city of dreams—and extremes." *Guardian*, May 5, 1999. http:// www.guardian.co.uk/world/1999/may/05/johngittings1.

Gluckman, Ron. "Han Dong Fan: The man who beat Beijing." *Asiaweek*, July 1997. http://www.gluckman.com/HanDongFang.html.

Goddard Space Flight Center. "Satellite measures pollution from east Asia to North America." *PhysOrg*, March 17, 2008. http://www.physorg.com/news124991552. html.

Goldstein, Carl. "Wal-Mart in China." *The Nation*, November 20, 2003. http://www. thenation.com/doc/20031208/goldstein.

Goodman, Peter S., and Philip P. Pan. "Chinese workers pay for Wal-Mart's low prices." *Washington Post*, February 8, 2004. http://www.washingtonpost.com/ac2/wp-dyn/ A22507-2004Feb7?language=printer.

Haddock, Ronald, and Paul Ngai. "China sourcing: Balancing global and local requirements." Booz, Allen, Hamilton. http://www.boozallen.com/media/file/150753.pdf.

Han, Dongfang. "The Prospects for Legal Enforcement of Labor Rights in China Today: A Glass Half Full," in *China Labor Bulletin*, 2008. www.clb.org.hk/en/files/File/ HDF%20testimony%20for%20CECC%20hearing%20June%202008(1).pdf.

Han, Dongfeng. "A turning point for China's trade unions," China Labor Bulletin, 2008. www.clb.org.hk/en/node/100293.

Harney, Alexandra. *The China Price: The True Cost of Chinese Competitive Advantage* (New York: Penguin Press, 2008).

Harney, Alexandra. "Migrants are China's 'factories without smoke'." CNN, February 3, 2008. http://edition.cnn.com/2008/WORLD/asiapcf/02/01/china.migrants/index. html#cnnSTCText.

Hong, Chen. "Employers boost wages in bid to attract workers." *ChinaDaily*, February 19, 2008. http://www.chinadaily.com.cn/china/2008-02/19/content_6464947.htm.

Keidel, Albert. "China regional disparities: The causes and impact of regional inequalities in income and well-being." Carnegie Endowment for International Peace, December 2007. http://www.carnegieendowment.org/publications/index. cfm?fa=view&id=19685&prog=zch.

Keidel, Albert. "The limits of a smaller, poorer China." *Financial Times*, November 14, 2007. http://www.carnegieendowment.org/publications/index.cfm?fa=print&id=19709.

Kim, Juli S. "Transboundary air pollution: Will China choke on its success?" Woodrow Wilson International Center for Scholars. http://www.wilsoncenter.org/index. cfm?topic_id=1421&fuseaction=topics.item&news_id=218780.

KMPG Huazhen. "Changsha Investment Environment Study 2007." KPMG Huazhen, http://www.kpmg.com.cn/en/virtual_library/Financial_advisory_services/Changsha_ investment07.pdf.

Larson, Christina. "China's pollution revolution." *AlterNet*, January 8, 2008. http://www. alternet.org/environment/72995/?page=entire.

Leslie, Jacques. "The last empire: China's pollution problem goes global." *Mother Jones*, December 10, 2007. www.motherjones.com/environment/2007/12/last-empire-chinas-pollution-problem-goes-global.

Li Qiang. "Hantai Shoe Production Ltd." China Labor Watch. www.chinalaborwatch. org/20080715Wal.htm

Li Qiang. "New Labor Law's Effect on Chinese Workers' Rights." Unpublished paper, 2008.

Matus, K. "Health impacts from urban air pollution in China: The burden to the economy and the benefits of policy." S.M. thesis, Massachusetts Institute of Technology, 2005. http://dspace.mit.edu/handle/1721.1/32282.

Memotrek Technologies blog. "Flash price: Chinese factories under pressure." Memotrek Technologies Blog. http://www.memotrek.com/blog/usb-flash-drives/nand-flash-prices-chinese-factories-under-pressure.html.

Mutikani, Lucia. "McCain's China-free debt plan seen unrealistic." *Reuters*, October 3, 2008. http://www.reuters.com/article/vcCandidateFeed2/idUSTRE49281F20081003? sp=true.

Mydans, Seth. "In Vietnam, even ghosts feel inflation's pinch." *International Herald Tribune*, August 19, 2008. http://www.iht.com/articles/2008/08/19/business/dong.php.

Navarro, Peter. "Report of 'The China Price Project'." Peternavarro.com. http://www. peternavarro.com/sitebuildercontent/sitebuilderfiles/chinapricereport.pdf

Nobrega, William. "Why India will beat China." *BusinessWeek*, July 22, 2008. http:// www.businessweek.com/globalbiz/content/jul2008/gb20080722_942925.htm.

People's Daily. "Newly industrialized cities battle pollution." *People's Daily*, January 14, 2006. http://english.peopledaily.com.cn/2006-01/14/eng20060114_235469.html.

People's Daily. "Wal-Mart licensed for global purchasing center in Shenzen." *People's Daily*, December 5, 2001.

Plafker, Ted. "Stable growth an elusive target for China." *International Herald Tribune*, May 4, 2008. http://www.iht.com/articles/2008/05/01/business/rasiachin.php?page=1.

Qingfen, Ding. "Moving inland." *ChinaDaily*, February 25, 2008. http://www.chinadaily.com.cn/bw/2008-02/25/content_6480234.htm.

Saporito, Bill. "Can Wal-Mart get any bigger? (Yes, a lot bigger, and here's how)." *Time*, January 5, 2003.

Schuman, Michael. "The birth and rebirth of Shenzhen." *Time*, August 14, 2006. http://www.time.com/time/nation/article/0,8599,1226199,00.html.

Scott, Robert E. "The Wal-Mart effect: Its Chinese imports have displaced nearly 200,000 U.S. jobs." Economic Policy Institute. http://www.epi.org/issuebriefs/235/ib235.pdf.

Troy, Mike. "In-sourcing the role of the middleman." *DSN Retailing Today*, December 13, 2004. http://findarticles.com/p/articles/mi_m0FNP/is_23_43/ai_n8577533.

Wang, Shunqin, and Jinliang Zhang. "Review: Blood lead levels in children, China." The Woodrow Wilson Center. http://www.wilsoncenter.org/topics/docs/lead_table_1.pdf.

Wines, Michael. "China outlines ambitious plan for stimulus." *New York Times*, March 5, 2009. http://www.nytimes.com/2009/03/05/world/asia/05china.html.

Wines, Michael, Keith Bradsher, and Mark Landler. "China's leader says he is 'worried' over U.S. treasuries." *New York Times*, March 14, 2009. http://www.nytimes.com/2009/03/14/world/asia/14china.html.

World Economic Forum. "The big debate: Setting the business agenda." Paper presented in World Economic Forum Annual Meeting 2006, January 25, 2006. http://www.weforum.org/en/knowledge/KN_SESS_SUMM_15840?url=/en/knowledge/KN_SESS_SUMM_15840.

Xiangde, Dai and Wu Jinyong. "'Labour's' breakthrough at Wal-Mart." *Business Watch Magazine*, September 4, 2006. http://www.clntranslations.org/file_download/3.

Yoon, Eunice. "China's inflation highest in 11 years." *CNN*, February 19, 2008. http://www.cnn.com/2008/BUSINESS/02/19/china.inflation/#cnnSTCText.

Young, Nick. "How much inequality can China stand?" China Development Brief. www.chinadevelopmentbrief.com/node/1001.

Zhen, Wen. "3000 teachers' protest in South China suppressed." Status of Chinese People Blog, December 17, 2008. http://chinaview.wordpress.com/category/china/south-china/hunan/.

Zhiming, Xin. "NBS: Consumer spending a big GDP factor." *ChinaDaily*, December 11, 2007. http://www.chinadaily.com.cn/bizchina/2007-12/11/content_6312714.htm.

4. Supply Chain Nation: *Cargo Cults of the Twenty-First Century*

American Lung Association. "Pittsburgh and Los Angeles the most polluted US cities." *City Mayors*, May 4, 2008. http://www.citymayors.com/environment/polluted_uscities.html.

Bonacich, Edna, and Juan David De Lara. "Economic crisis and the logistics industry: Financial insecurity for warehouse workers in the inland empire." Institute for Research on Labor and Employment. http://repositories.cdlib.org/cgi/viewcontent.cgi?article=101 4&context=uclairle.

Brekke, Erika. "Cleaning the Ports of L.A." On Earth. http://www.onearth.org/article/ cleaning-the-ports-of-la.

Business Wire. "Economic impact study finds trade moving through ports of Los Angeles, Long Beach and the Alameda Corridor significantly impact California's economy." *Business Wire*, March 22, 2007. http://www.businesswire.com/portal/site/ google/?ndmViewId=news_view&newsId=20070322005938&newsLang=en.

Chu, Hanna. "Signal Hill: From oil to million-dollar views." *Press-Telegram*, August 12, 2007. http://www.presstelegram.com/wwl/ci_6606520.

Court, Jamie, and Judy Dugan. "Big oil buys Sacramento." *Los Angeles Times*, May 14, 2007. http://www.latimes.com/news/opinion/la-oe-court14may14,0,991123.story.

Davis, Mike. *City of Quartz: Excavating the Future in Los Angeles* (New York: Verso, 1990).

Dinopoulos, Elias, and Fuat Şener "New Directions in Schumpeterian Growth Theory," in *Elgar Companion to Neo- Schumpeterian Economics*, eds. Horst Hanusch and Andreas Pyka (Cheltenham, UK: Edward Elgar, 2007).

Erie, Steven. *Globalizing L.A.: Trade, Infrastructure and Regional Development* (Palo Alto, CA: Stanford University Press, 2004).

Fitz, Dennis R. "Characterizing The Range Of Children's Pollutant Exposure During School Bus Commutes." California Air Resources Board. http://www.arb.ca.gov/ research/schoolbus/execsum.pdf.

Fortson, Danny. "Shipping surge prompts CO_2 concerns." *BusinessWeek*, December 11, 2007. http://www.businessweek.com/print/globalbiz/content/dec2007/ gb20071211_579202.htm.

Fung, Victor, et al. *Competing in a Flat World* (Upper Saddle River, NJ: Wharton School Publishing, 2008).

Fung, Victor, and Joan Magretta. "Fast, global and entrepreneurial—An interview with Victor Fung." *Harvard Business Review*, September 1, 1998.

Graham, Wade. "Dark Side of the New Economy." *On Earth*, March 1, 2007. http://www. onearth.org/article/dark-side-of-the-new-economy.

Hanson, Kristopher. "Port is an engine for growth." *Press-Telegram*, February 23, 2007. http://www.presstelegram.com/outlook/ci_5290731.

Howard, John. "Job loss, business impacts seen in proposed sales tax hike." *Capitol Weekly*, August 5, 2008. http://capitolweekly.net/article.php?issueId=xas7u1nejid2da& xid=xb9i5bec3g9fea.

Janofsky, Michael, and Samantha Zee. "Oil exploration companies look to Beverly Hills." *Seattle Times*, July 2, 2008. http://seattletimes.nwsource.com/html/ businesstechnology/2008028848_beverlyhillsoil02.html.

Johnson, Keith. "Big (green) box: Retailers get the energy-efficiency gospel." *Wall Street Journal*, Environmental Capital Blog, June 23, 2008. http://blogs.wsj.com/ environmentalcapital/2008/06/23/big-green-box-retailers-get-the-energy-efficiency- gospel/?mod=relevancy.

L.A. Intifada: Interview with Mike Davis, by Cindi Katz, Neil Smith and Mike Davis (Durham, NC: Duke University Press, 2002). http://www.jstor.org/pss/466432.

Levin, Dan. "China's big recycling market is sagging." *New York Times*, March 12, 2009. http://www.nytimes.com/2009/03/12/business/worldbusiness/12recycle.html.

Levinson, Marc. *The Box: How the Shipping Container Made the World Smaller and the World Economy Bigger* (Princeton, NJ: Princeton University Press, 2006).

Lifsher, Marc. "Long Beach aims to boost output from Wilmington oil field." *Los Angeles Times*, September 9, 2008. http://www.latimes.com/business/la-fi-lboil9-2008sep09,1,4418419.story.

Lin Ii, Rong-gong. "County offers 'inland port' plan." *Los Angeles Times*, July 12, 2007. http://articles.latimes.com/2007/jul/12/local/me-inlandport12.

Long Beach Alliance for Children with Asthma. "Reenvisioning the Landscape of Children's Health." Pediatric Asthma. http://www.pediatricasthma.org/community_coalitions/long_beach_ca.

Los Angeles Times. "A shipshape ports bill." *Los Angeles Times*, July 21, 2008. http://www.latimes.com/news/opinion/la-ed-ports21-2008jul21,0,5370497.story.

Lustgarten, Jeff, Theresa Adams Lopez, and Art Wong. "Economic impact study finds trade moving through ports of Los Angeles, Long Beach and the Alameda corridor significantly impact California's economy." Alameda Corridor Transportation Authority (ACTA), The Port of Los Angeles, and The Port of Long Beach, March 22, 2007. http://www.acta.org/newsroom/Releases/018_REL_ACTA-Port_California_Press_Release.pdf.

Lustgarten, Jeff, Theresa Adams Lopez, and Art Wong. "Updated economic impact study shows that ports of Los Angeles, Long Beach and Alameda corridor remain vital to U.S. economy and international trade." Alameda Corridor Transportation Authority (ACTA), The Port of Los Angeles, and The Port of Long Beach, March 22, 2007. http://www.acta.org/newsroom/Releases/019_ACTA-Port_National_Press_Release.pdf.

Morello-Frosch, Rachel, Manuel Pastor Jr., Carlos Porras, and James Sadd. "Environmental justice and regional inequality in Southern California: Implications for future research." Environmental Health Perspectives. http://www.ehponline.org/members/2002/suppl-2/149-154morello-frosch/morello-frosch-full.html.

New York Times. "'Oil!' and the history of Southern California." *New York Times*, February 22, 2008. http://www.nytimes.com/2008/02/22/timestopics/topics_upton sinclair_oil.html.

Ocampo, Jose Antonio. "The instability and inequities of the global reserve system." United Nations. http://www.un.org/esa/desa/papers/2007/wp59_2007.pdf.

Organization for Economic Co-operation and Development. "Moving up the value chain: Staying competitive in the global economy." Organization for Economic Co-operation and Development. http://www.oecd.org/dataoecd/24/35/38558080.pdf.

Organization for Economic Co-operation and Development. "Structure and trends in international trade in services." http://www.oecd.org/documentprint/0,3455,en_2649_34243_2510108_1_1_1_1,00.html.

Pacific L.A. Marine Terminal. "L.A. basin crude oil supply outlook." Pacific L.A. Marine Terminal, 2008. http://www.pacificenergypier400.com/index2.php?id=62.

Palaniappan, Meena, Swati Prakash, and Diane Bailey. "Paying with our health: The real cost of freight transport in California." Pacific Institute. http://www.pacinst.org/reports/freight_transport/PayingWithOurHealth_Web.pdf.

Paleontological Research Institution, The. "The story of oil in California." The Paleontological Research Institution. http://www.priweb.org/ed-/pgws/history/signal_hill/signal_hill2.html.

Port Strategy. "Maersk machine grinds on mercilessly." *Port Strategy*, September 3, 2008. http://www.portstrategy.com/archive101/2008/september/insight__and__opinion/the_strategist.

Raine, George. "Containerization changed shipping industry forever." *San Francisco Chronicle*, February 10, 2006. http://www.seattlepi.com/business/259042_container ships10.html.

Reynolds, Angela, and Greg Holmes. "Correspondence regarding the Environmental Impact Report for the Long Beach sports park project." from the California Department Of Toxic Substances Control, February 14, 2005. http://www.longbeach.gov/civica/filebank/blobdload.asp?BlobID=9087.

Reynolds, Peggy, Julie Von Behren, Robert B. Gunier, Debbie E. Goldberg, Andrew Hertz, and Daniel F. Smith. "Childhood cancer incidence rates and hazardous air pollutants in California: An exploratory analysis." Environmental Health Perspectives. http://www.ehponline.org/docs/2003/5986/abstract.html.

Rodrigues, Alexandre M., Donald J. Bowersox, and Roger J. Calantone. "Estimation of global and national logistics expenditures: 2002 data update." Michigan State University (2005). https://www.msu.edu/~rodri205/CV/Documents/ISL2005%20Article.pdf.

Rohter, Larry. "Shipping costs start to crimp globalization." *New York Times*, August 3, 2008. http://www.nytimes.com/2008/08/03/business/worldbusiness/03global.html.

Russo, Frank D. "PBS show shines light on Los Angeles and Long Beach Port air pollution and its devastating health effects." California Progress Report, October 21, 2006. http://www.californiaprogressreport.com/2006/10/pbs_show_shines.html.

Sahagun, Louis. "Environmental groups threaten to sue Port of Long Beach over air pollution." *Los Angeles Times*, February 7, 2008. http://www.latimes.com/news/local/la-me-port7feb07,0,2821444.story.

Sahagun, Louis. "Long Beach OKs fee on cargo to fund green efforts." *Los Angeles Times*, December 18, 2007. http://www.latimes.com/features/lifestyle/green/la-me-port18dec18,0,2835624.story.

Sahagun, Louis. "Wilmington looks to a greener future." *Los Angeles Times*, March 2, 2009. http://www.latimes.com/news/local/la-me-wilmington3-2009mar03,0,7927648.story?track=rss.

Schulz, John D. "Logisticians 'survive the slump,' but costs hit 10.1 percent of GDP." *Logistics Management*, June 19, 2008. http://www.logisticsmgmt.com/index.asp?layout=articlePrint&articleID=CA6571518&article_prefix=CA&article_id=6571518.

Stiglitz, Joseph. *Making Globalization Work* (New York: WW Norton, 2007).

Thompson, Don. "California unemployment rate jumps to 10.1 percent." *Forbes*, February 27, 2009. http://www.forbes.com/feeds/ap/2009/02/27/ap6108682.html.

United Nations Conference on Trade and Development. "Productivity of the world fleet and supply and demand in world shipping," Review of Maritime Transport, 2006. http://www.unctad.org/en/docs/rmt2006ch3_en.pdf

United States Environmental Protection Agency. "Brownfields Assessment Pilot Fact Sheet." United States Environmental Protection Agency. http://www.epa.gov/brownfields/html-doc/asignalh.htm.

Wall Street Journal. "Ships draw fire for rising role in air pollution." *Wall Street Journal*, November 27, 2007. http://online.wsj.com/article/SB119611182359704284.html.

White, Ronald D. "High-and-dry areas vie for 'inland ports'." *Los Angeles Times*, May 8, 2005. http://articles.latimes.com/2005/may/08/business/fi-cargo8.

White, Ronald D. "2 big haulers sign on to L.A. port's clean-truck plan." *Los Angeles Times*, August 22, 2008. http://www.latimes.com/business/la-fi-ports22-2008aug22,0,7016817. story.

Wienberg, Christian, and Alaric Nightingale. "Maersk profit advances 40% on oil; shipper buys rival." *Bloomberg*, August 27, 2008. http://www.bloomberg.com/apps/ news?pid=20601085&sid=apot_AgiKjSc&refer=europe.

World Trade Organization. "WTO: Developing, transition economies cushion trade slowdown." World Trade Organization. http://www.wto.org/english/news_e/pres08_e/ pr520_e.htm.

World Trade Organization. "WTO: Developing, transition economies cushion trade slowdown. Chart 3: Real merchandise trade growth by region, 2007." World Trade Organization. http://www.wto.org/english/news_e/pres08_e/pr520_e.htm#chart3.

Wright, Robert. "Buoyant Maersk refloats profit." *Financial Times*, August 27, 2008. http:// www.ft.com/cms/s/0/a163eb9a-743f-11dd-bc91-0000779fd18c,dwp_uuid=e8477cc4- c820-11db-b0dc-000b5df10621.html.

Young, Samantha. "New rules cut ship pollution." *Press-Telegram*, July 24, 2008. http:// www.presstelegram.com/ports/ci_9991063.

5. *All Is Plastic: The Small World of Hydrocarbons*

A to Z of Materials and AZojomo, The. "Shell eyes big opportunities in China." *The A to Z of Materials and AZojomo*, September 22, 2005. http://www.azom.com/News. asp?NewsID=4002.

Adams, Gary. "Petrochemicals…positioning Latin America in a changing global market." Paper presented at the 27th Latin American Petrochemical annual meeting, Buenos Aires, Argentina, November 17-20, 2007. http://www.cmaiglobal.com/ Marketing/News/APLA07_Adams_WebPDF.pdf.

Alberta Department of Energy. "Alberta's Oil Sands 2006." Alberta Department Of Energy, December 2007. http://www.energy.gov.ab.ca/OilSands/pdfs/osgenbrf.pdf.

Banholzer, William F. "Changes in the energy market and their impact on the chemical industry." The Dow Chemical Company, May 2008. http://news.dow.com/dow_news/ speeches/20080502_banholzer.pdf.

Blas, Javier, and Carola Hoyos. "IEA predicts oil price to rebound to $100." *Financial Times*, November 5, 2008. http://www.ft.com/cms/s/0/ca2b5254-ab6a-11dd-b9e1- 000077b07658.html?nclick_check=1.

Bloomberg. "China spending on energy output jumps as demand gains." *Shanghai Zoom Intelligence Co., Ltd.*, October 19, 2006. http://www.zoomchina.com.cn/new/content/ view/16387/81.

Boyle, Edward. "Scoring the scorecard." *Paper, Film & Foil Converter*, September 1, 2007. http://pffc-online.com/mag/paper_scoring_scorecard/.

Calgary Herald. "Alberta promises study in wake of toxic oilsands leak." *Canada.com*, May 27, 2008. http://www.canada.com/topics/news/story.html?id=e2a21fcb-453f-49b3- ad10-23e50a2d0160.

CBC News. "'Comprehensive' review of Fort Chipewyan cancer rates announced." *CBC News*, May 22, 2008. http://www.cbc.ca/canada/edmonton/story/2008/05/22/edm- fort-chip.html.

CBC News. "Fort Chip doctor rails against government inaction." *CBC News*, November 16, 2006. http://www.cbc.ca/canada/north/story/2006/11/15/doctor-disgust. html.

CBC News. "Oilsands-area hamlet supports whistleblower MD." *CBC News*, March 5, 2007. http://www.cbc.ca/canada/story/2007/03/05/alberta-doctor-070305.html.

CBC News. "Plant closure marks end of an era in Devon, Alta." *CBC News*, August 1, 2006. http://www.cbc.ca/canada/edmonton/story/2006/08/01/leduc-end.html.

CBC News. "Secret advice to politicians: oilsands emissions hard to scrub." *CBC News*, November 24, 2008. http://www.cbc.ca/canada/story/2008/11/24/sands-trap.html.

ChemEurope. "Dow Acrylates announces global price increase." *ChemEurope*, March 18, 2009. http://www.chemeurope.com/news/e/98477/.

Chin, Josh, and Zachary Slobig. "Xinjiang's melting glaciers." Chinadialogue, March 20, 2008. http://www.chinadialogue.net/article/show/single/en/1820-Xinjiang-s-melting-glaciers.

China Chemical Reporter. "Petrochemical industry faced with challenges." University of Alberta—China Institute, September 16, 2006. http://www.uofaweb.ualberta.ca/chinainstitute/nav03.cfm?nav03=50494&nav02=49950&nav01=43092.

Condon, Bernard. "Wizard of ooze." *Forbes*, March 3, 2003. http://www.forbes.com/forbes/2003/0303/060.html.

De Souza, Mike. "Calgary Herald—Fines rare for oilsands players." ForestEthics. http://www.forestethics.org/article.php?id=2181.

Dyer, Geoff. "EU hits out at China's economic nationalism." *Financial Times*, September 25, 2008. http://www.ft.com/cms/s/0/acf09624-8b2e-11dd-b634-0000779fd18c.html.

Dyer, Simon. "Ducks just tip of toxic tailings iceberg." Oil Sands Watch, February 17, 2009. http://www.oilsandswatch.org/op-ed/1784.

Dyer, Simon. "Oil sands industry blocks new wetland protection rules." The Pembina Institute, September 16, 2008. http://www.pembina.org/media-release/1697.

Edmonton Journal. "Alberta oilsands man killed by giant truck." *Canada.com*, July 9, 2008. http://www.canada.com/topics/news/national/story.html?id=be60742c-b5fe-4ea3-8a7e-e2bf39923895.

Energy Information Administration. "International Energy Outlook 2008." Energy Information Administration, June 2008. http://www.eia.doe.gov/oiaf/ieo/highlights. html.

Engdahl, F. William. "Darfur: Forget genocide, there's oil." *Asia Times*, May 25, 2007. http://www.atimes.com/atimes/China_Business/IE25Cb04.html.

Frigon, Mathieu. "Fertilizers, ethanol and the peaking of natural gas production in Alberta." Library of Parliament, Economics Division, October 10, 2007. http://www. parl.gc.ca/information/library/PRBpubs/prb0749-e.htm#fn9.

Goode, Erica, and Riyadh Mohammed. "Iraq signs oil deal with China worth up to $3 billion." *New York Times*, August 29, 2008. http://www.nytimes.com/2008/08/29/world/middleeast/29iraq.html.

Haggett, Scott. "High cancer rate near oil sands confirmed." *Globe and Mail*, February 6, 2009. http://www.theglobeandmail.com/servlet/story/RTGAM.20090206.wcancer07/BNStory/National/.

Hannon, David. "Energy prices accelerate the move to the Middle East." *Purchasing*, August 14, 2008. http://www.purchasing.com/article/CA6584559.html?q=energy+prices+accelerate+move+to+the+middle%2C.

Henton, Darcy. "Aboriginals declare war on oil sands," *Edmonton Journal*, August 18, 2008.

Homer-Dixon, Thomas. *The Upside of Down* (New York: Random House, 2006).

Houser, Trevor. "The Roots of Chinese Oil Investment Abroad." *Asia Policy*, January 2008. http://www.nbr.org/publications/asia_policy/AP5/AP5_Houser.pdf.

Huntley, Chris. "Dow announces further price increases, freight surcharges and idling of plants." *Reuters*, June 24, 2008. http://www.reuters.com/article/pressRelease/idUS112199+24-Jun-2008+PRN20080624.

International Energy Agency. "World energy outlook 2007: Fact sheet—global energy demand." International Energy Agency, 2007. http://www.iea.org//textbase/papers/2007/fs_global.pdf

International Energy Agency. "World energy outlook 2007: Fact sheet—oil." International Energy Agency, 2007. http://www.iea.org//textbase/papers/2007/fs_oil.pdf

Jackson-Han, Sarah. "China's 'other Tibetans,' the Uyghurs, stage protests." RFA Unplugged Blog, April 2, 2008. http://rfaunplugged.wordpress.com/2008/04/02/chinas-other-tibetans-the-uyghurs-stage-protests/.

Junaid, Adiat, and Albert Koehl. "KAIROS study reveals billions in Canadian tax subsidies to big oil come at the expense of conservation and climate." *Ecojustice*, April 15, 2008. http://www.ecojustice.ca/media-centre/press-releases/kairos-study-reveals-billions-in-canadian-tax-subsidies-to-big-oil-come-at-the-expense-of-conservation-and-climate/.

Leaton, James. "Unconventional Oil: Scraping the bottom of the barrel?" WWF-UK and The Co-operative Group. http://www.wwf.org.uk/filelibrary/pdf/scraping_barrell.pdf.

Lim, Louisa. "China's Uighurs lose out to development." *BBC News*, December 19, 2003. http://news.bbc.co.uk/2/hi/asia-pacific/3330803.stm.

Lin, Jiang. "Energy conservation investments: A comparison between China and the US." *ScienceDirect*, March 23, 2006. http://www.sciencedirect.com/science?_ob=ArticleURL&_udi=B6V2W-4JJ84F9-1&_user=10&_rdoc=1&_fmt=&_orig=search&_sort=d&view=c&_version=1&_urlVersion=0&_userid=10&md5=f2f41e8ae6911da92cb1676dacfd40ef.

Mingxin, Bi. "World Bank's loans to China total $1.5 bln in 2008 fiscal year." *China View*, June 25, 2008. http://news.xinhuanet.com/english/2008-06/25/content_8436378.htm.

Nikiforuk, Andrew. *Tar Sands: Dirty Oil and the Future of a Continent* (Vancouver: Greystone, 2008).

Pett, David. "Failed oilsands projects could bring runaway costs in line." *Financial Post*, September 22, 2008. http://network.nationalpost.com/np/blogs/tradingdesk/archive/2008/09/22/failed-oilsands-projects-could-bring-runaway-costs-in-line.aspx.

Polczer, Shaun. "Oil sands will play crucial role in future: energy giants." *Financial Post*, July 1, 2008. http://www.financialpost.com/reports/oil-watch/story.html?id=625335.

Ramachandran, Dr. Ramesh. "North American Petrochemicals: Walking a tight rope." *Dow Chemical Canada Inc.*, March 7, 2005. http://news.dow.com/speeches/20050307a.htm.

Reguly, Eric. "Supply on demand: Buyers like China are bypassing commodities markets altogether and going right to the source." *Report on Business Magazine*, June 27, 2008. http://business.theglobeandmail.com/servlet/story/RTGAM.20080618.rmreguly0618/BNStory/specialROBmagazine/home.

Severson-Baker, Chris, and Simon Dyer. "Environmental groups pull out of multi-stakeholder oil sands process." The Pembina Institute, August 18, 2008. http://www.pembina.org/media-release/1678.

Sharp, Rob. "Polythene's story: The accidental birth of plastic bags." *The Independent*, March 26, 2008. http://www.independent.co.uk/news/science/polythenes-story-the-accidental-birth-of-plastic-bags-800602.html.

Smith, Grant, and Jim Kennett. "Not enough oil is lament of BP, Exxon on spending." *Bloomberg*, May 19, 2008. www.bloomberg.com/apps/news?pid=20601087&sid=ajkO05voC8xU&refer=home

Stanislaw, Joseph A. "Power play: Resource nationalism, the global scramble for energy, and the need for mutual interdependence." Deloitte Development, 2008. http://www.deloitte.com/dtt/cda/doc/content/us_er%20JAS_PowerPlay_FINAL.pdf.

Star, The. "Two-mouth fish fuels oil-sands fears." *The Star*, August 20, 2008. http://www.thestar.com/News/Canada/article/481840.

Twice. "Wal-Mart to cut bag usage." *Twice*, September 25, 2008. http://www.twice.com/article/CA6599559.html.

Vidal, John. "Canadians ponder cost of rush for dirty oil." *Guardian*, July 11, 2008. http://www.guardian.co.uk/environment/2008/jul/11/fossilfuels.pollution.

Wall Street Journal. "Canada slips on oil's slide." *Wall Street Journal*, February 19, 2009. http://online.wsj.com/article/SB123500580587718267.html?mod=googlenews_wsj.

Weber, Bob. "Piece of oil sands first to be certified as reclaimed." *The Globe and Mail*, March 19, 2008. http://www.theglobeandmail.com/servlet/story/RTGAM.20080319.oilsands20/BNStory/National/?page=rss&id=RTGAM.20080319.oilsands20.

Wong, Edward. "Attack in West China kills 3 security officers." *New York Times*, August 13, 2008. http://www.nytimes.com/2008/08/13/sports/olympics/13china.html.

6. *We, the Resource:* Journeys to the End of Cheap

Amiti, Mary, and Caroline Freund. "China's export boom." *Finance and Development Magazine*, International Monetary Fund, September 2007. http://www.imf.org/external/pubs/ft/fandd/2007/09/amiti.htm.

Archibold, Randal C. "At the U.S. border, the desert takes a rising toll." *New York Times*, September 15, 2007. http://www.nytimes.com/2007/09/15/us/15border.html.

Archibold, Randal C. "U.S. plans border 'surge' against any drug wars." *New York Times*, January 8, 2009. http://www.nytimes.com/2009/01/08/us/08chertoff.html.

Associated Free Press. "Gap between rich, poor growing, OECD finds." Google, October 21, 2008. http://afp.google.com/article/ALeqM5ibqxRYnbFgCrCxgLG_i57Bx4PXqA.

Associated Press, The. "35 percent of toys contain lead, report says." *MSNBC*, December 5, 2007. http://www.msnbc.msn.com/id/22103641/.

Associated Press, The. "Japan: Wholesale inflation at 27-year high." *New York Times*, August 13, 2008. http://www.nytimes.com/2008/08/13/business/worldbusiness/13fobriefs-WHOLESALEINF_BRF.html.

Associated Press, The. "Personal savings drop to a 73-year low." *MSNBC*, February 1, 2007. http://www.msnbc.msn.com/id/16922582.

Bacon, David. "Trading on Migrant Labor." *The American Prospect*, June 11, 2007. http://www.prospect.org/cs/articles?article=trading_on_migrant_labor.

Barboza, David. "China's dairy farmers say they are victims." *New York Times*, October 4, 2008. http://www.nytimes.com/2008/10/04/world/asia/04milk.html.

Barboza, David. "Death sentences given in Chinese milk scandal." *New York Times*, February 2, 2009. http://www.nytimes.com/2009/01/22/world/asia/22iht-milk.3.19601372. html.

Barboza, David, and Louise Story. "Mattel issues new recall of toys made in China." *New York Times*, August 14, 2007. http://www.nytimes.com/2007/08/14/business/15toys-web.html.

BBC News. "Millions 'spend more than income'." *BBC News*, January 22, 2008. http://news.bbc.co.uk/2/hi/business/7202121.stm.

Berg, KK, HF Hull, EW Zabel, and PK Staley. "Death of a child after ingestion of a metallic charm" from *Morbidity and Mortality Weekly Report*, March 23, 2006. http://www.cdc.gov/mmwr/preview/mmwrhtml/mm55d323a1.htm.

Bogdanich, Walt. "The everyman who exposed tainted toothpaste," *New York Times*, Oct 1, 2007. www.nytimes.com/2007/10/01/world/americas/01panama.html?scp=1&sq=The%20Everyman%20Who%20Exposed%20Tainted%20Toothpaste&st=cse.

BusinessWeek. "China rushes upmarket." *BusinessWeek*, September 17, 2007. http://www.businessweek.com/magazine/content/07_38/b4050055.htm?chan=search.

Capps, Randolph, Michael E. Fix, Jeffrey S. Passel, Jason Ost, and Dan Perez-Lopez. "A profile of the low-wage immigrant workforce." Urban Institute, October 27, 2003. http://www.urban.org/publications/310880.html.

CBC News. "20% of Chinese toys, baby clothes fail safety inspections." *CBC News*, May 28, 2007. http://www.cbc.ca/consumer/story/2007/05/28/china-product.html.

CNBC Video. "Nobel laureate solution." CNBC Video, October 1, 2008. http://www.cnbc.com/id/15840232?video=874100965&play=1.

DeParle, Jason. "World banker and his cash return home." *New York Times*, March 17, 2008. http://www.nytimes.com/2008/03/17/world/asia/17remit.html.

Dwyer, Jim. "In a sea of foreclosures, an island of calm." *New York Times*, September 27, 2008. http://www.nytimes.com/2008/09/27/nyregion/27about.html.

Ebner, David. "A nation of debtors." *Report on Business*, September 26, 2008. http://www.reportonbusiness.com/servlet/story/RTGAM.20080926.wrcover27/BNStory/Business/home.

Economist, The. "Misplaced fears about jobs in America." *The Economist*, March 11, 2004. http://www.economist.com/world/unitedstates/displayStory.cfm?story_id=2501977.

Elliott, Larry. "Migrant workers curb wages and keep interest rates low to boost economic growth." *Guardian*, December 18, 2007. http://www.guardian.co.uk/business/2007/dec/18/economics.eu.

Engardio, Pete. "Can the U.S. bring jobs back from China?" *BusinessWeek*, June 19, 2008. http://www.businessweek.com/print/magazine/content/08_26/b4090038429655.htm.

Evans, David, and Richard Schmalensee. *Paying with Plastic* (Cambridge: Ma: MIT Press, 1999).

Evans-Pritchard, Ambrose. "EU refuses bail-out package despite crisis fears." *Telegraph*, September 25, 2008. http://www.telegraph.co.uk/finance/comment/ambroseevans_pritchard/3075180/EU-refuses-bail-out-package-despite-crisis-fears.html?mobile=true.

Fajnzylber, Pablo, and J. Humberto Lopez. "Close to home: The development impact of remittances in Latin America." World Bank, http://siteresources.worldbank.org/INTLACOFFICEOFCE/Resources/ClosetoHome_FINAL.pdf.

Federal Reserve Statistical Release. "Consumer Credit." Federal Reserve Statistical Release G19, March 6, 2009. http://www.federalreserve.gov/releases/g19/current/default.htm.

Financial Times. "U.S. household debt: A frightening picture." *Seeking Alpha*, August 26, 2008. http://seekingalpha.com/article/92682-u-s-household-debt-a-frightening-picture.

Foreign Policy. "Seven questions: China's total toy recall." *Foreign Policy*, August 2007. http://www.foreignpolicy.com/story/cms.php?story_id=3960.

Frantz, Douglas. "Threat of 'dirty bomb' growing, officials say." *Los Angeles Times*, May 9, 2004. http://articles.latimes.com/2004/may/09/world/fg-dirtybomb9.

Friedman, Thomas L. "The inflection is near?" *New York Times*, March 8, 2009. http://www.nytimes.com/2009/03/08/opinion/08friedman.html.

Gogoi, Pallavi. "Gloomy days ahead for retailers." *BusinessWeek*, July 21, 2008. http://www.businessweek.com/bwdaily/dnflash/content/jul2008/db20080718_996200.htm.

Gordon, Jennifer. "Workers without borders." *New York Times*, March 10, 2009. http://www.nytimes.com/2009/03/10/opinion/10gordon.html.

Hammer, Kate. "Melamine-laced pretzels found on store shelves after recall." *Globe and Mail*, April 10, 2008. http://www.theglobeandmail.com/servlet/story/RTGAM.20081004.wxmelamine04/BNStory/National/home.

Holley, Denise. "Security beefed up at aid station." *Nogales International*, March 3, 2009. http://www.nogalesinternational.com/articles/2009/03/03/news/doc49ad4c53a6d13560159111.txt.

Houseman, Susan. "Outsourcing, offshoring, and productivity measurement in U.S. manufacturing." W. E. Upjohn Institute for Employment Research, April 2007. http://www.upjohninst.org/publications/wp/06-130.pdf.

Jones, Maggie. "Migrants no more." *Mother Jones*, November 2004. http://www.motherjones.com/politics/2004/11/migrants-no-more.

Jones, Yvonne D. "International remittances: Different estimation methodologies produce different results." United States Government Accountability Office, March 2006. http://www.gao.gov/new.items/d06210.pdf.

Kantor, Andrew. "IKEA plans to build factory in Danville, furnish city with jobs." *The Roanoke Times*, October 13, 2006. http://www.roanoke.com/news/roanoke/wb/86839.

Kindleberger, Charles. *Manias, Panics and Crashes* (New York: Wiley, 1996).

Kiviat, Barbara. "Misery loves company: negative equity edition." *Time*—The Curious Capitalist Blog, October 31, 2008. http://curiouscapitalist.blogs.time.com/2008/10/31/misery-loves-company-negative-equity-edition/.

Krugman, Paul. "Decade at Bernie's." *New York Times*, February 16, 2009. http://www.nytimes.com/2009/02/16/opinion/16krugman.html.

Labaton, Stephen. "Agency's '04 rule let banks pile up new debt." *New York Times*, October 3, 2008. http://www.nytimes.com/2008/10/03/business/03sec.html.

Leonhardt, David. "Seeing inflation only in the prices that go up." *New York Times*, May 7, 2008. http://www.nytimes.com/2008/05/07/business/07leonhardt.html.

Longman, Phillip. *The Return of Thrift* (New York: The Free Press, 1996).

Maclennan, Duncan. "Trunks, tails and elephants: The economic case for a modern housing policy," Institute for Governance, University of Ottawa, January 2008.

Marcus, Daniel. "Live Richly, and Prosper." Flow TV (May 27, 2005), http://flowtv.org/?p=580.

McCombs, Brady. "Abuse tales hard to dispel: Critics call short-term custody 'a black hole' for immigrants; US denies claims." *Arizona Daily Star*, October 19, 2008.

McKinsey Quarterly, The. "Competition from China: Two McKinsey surveys." *The McKinsey Quarterly*, May 2008. http://www.mckinseyquarterly.com/Strategy/Globalization/Competition_from_China_Two_McKinsey_Surveys_2147.

Meier, Barry. "Consumer's world: To insure toy safety, U.S. shifts its attack." *New York Times*, August 25, 1990. http://www.nytimes.com/1990/08/25/style/consumer-s-world-to-insure-toy-safety-us-shifts-its-attack.html.

Mencimer, Stephanie. "Why Texas still holds 'em." *Mother Jones*, July 2008. http://www.motherjones.com/politics/2008/07/why-texas-still-holds-em.

Minnesota Department of Health. "Child's death from lead poisoning prompts recall and warning about children's jewelry." Minnesota Department of Health, March 23, 2006. http://www.health.state.mn.us/news/pressrel/lead032306.html.

Mitchell, Stacy. *Big Box Swindle: The True Cost of Mega-Retailers and the Fight for America's Independent Business* (Boston: Beacon Press, 2006).

Morris, Charles. *The Trillion Dollar Meltdown: Easy Money, High Rollers, and the Great Credit Crash* (New York: Public Affairs, 2008).

New York Times. "Getting Immigration Right." *New York Times*, December 26, 2008. http://www.nytimes.com/2008/12/26/opinion/26fri1.html.

New York Times. "Inflation slows for 3rd month in China." *New York Times*, August 12, 2008. http://www.nytimes.com/2008/08/12/business/worldbusiness/12iht-yuan.1.15189908.html.

Otsuma, Mayumi. "Japan wholesale inflation eases as oil prices drop." *Bloomberg*, September 9, 2008. http://www.bloomberg.com/apps/news?pid=20601068&sid=aams5x0rUAac&refer=home.

Qiang, Li. "Textile Sweatshops; Adidas, Bali Intimates, Hanesbrands Inc., Piege Co (Felina Lingerie), Quiksilver, Regina Miracle Speedo, Walcoal America Inc., and Wal-Mart made in China." China Labor Watch, November 20, 2007. http://www.chinalaborwatch.org/200711204textile.htm.

Quint, Mitchell, and Dermot Shorten. "China's gold rush: Should you make the journey east?" Booz Allen Hamilton, January 11, 2004. http://www.boozallen.com/media/file/143177.pdf.

Ratha, Dilip. "Remittance flows to developing countries are estimated to exceed $300 billion in 2008." People Move—World Bank Blog, February 18, 2009. http://peoplemove.worldbank.org/en/content/remittance-flows-to-developing-countries.

Ratha, Dilip, and Maurice Schiff. "Migration and Remittances." World Bank, September 2008. http://web.worldbank.org/WBSITE/EXTERNAL/NEWS/0,,contentMDK:20648762~menuPK:34480~pagePK:64257043~piPK:437376~theSitePK:4607,00.html.

Reuters. "Uzbekistan: Wal-Mart bans cotton." *New York Times*, October 1, 2008. http://www.nytimes.com/2008/10/01/business/worldbusiness/01fobriefs-WALMARTBANSC_BRF.html.

Room for Debate Blog Editors. "The competition for low-wage jobs." *New York Times*, Room for Debate Blog, March 18, 2009. http://roomfordebate.blogs.nytimes.com/2009/03/18/the-competition-for-low-wage-jobs/?scp=3&sq=migrant%20benefit%20economy&st=cse.

Schlisserman, Courtney. "U.S. import prices drop 0.2%; down 0.6% excluding Oil." *Bloomberg*, March 13, 2009. http://www.bloomberg.com/apps/news?pid=20601087&sid=addHCIGsLwIw&refer=home.

Scott, Robert E. "The Wal-Mart effect: Its Chinese imports have displaced nearly 200,000 U.S. jobs." Economic Policy Institute, June 26, 2007. http://www.epi.org/issuebriefs/235/ib235.pdf.

Shipler, David. *The Working Poor: Invisible in America* (New York: Knopf, 2004).

Stein, Ben. "In Financial Food Chains, Little Guys Can't Win." *New York Times*, September 28, 2008. http://www.nytimes.com/2008/09/28/business/28every.html.

Stiglitz, Joseph. *The Roaring Nineties* (New York: WW Norton, 2003).

Swarns, Rachel L. "U.S. reports drop in homeless population." *New York Times*, July 30, 2008. http://www.nytimes.com/2008/07/30/us/30homeless.html.

Thottam, Jyoti. "Why Mattel apologized to China." *Time*, September 21, 2007. http://www.time.com/time/business/article/0,8599,1664428,00.html.

Tilly, Chris. "Reasons for the continuing growth of part-time employment." *Monthly Labor Review*, March 1991. http://www.bls.gov/opub/mlr/1991/03/art2full.pdf.

Toossi, Mitra. "A new look at long-term labor force projections to 2050." *Monthly Labor Review*, November 2006. http://www.bls.gov/opub/mlr/2006/11/art3full.pdf.

Tully, Shawn. "A profit gusher of epic proportions." *Fortune*, April 15, 2007. http://money.cnn.com/magazines/fortune/fortune_archive/2007/04/30/8405391/index.htm.

Waters, Jennifer. "Economy forces major shift in spending." *Wall Street Journal*, June 16, 2008. http://online.wsj.com/public/article_print/SB121338190561972555.html.

Weller, Christian E. "Drowning in debt: America's middle class falls deeper in debt as income growth slows and costs climb." Center for American Progress, May 2006. http://www.americanprogress.org/kf/boomburden-web.pdf.

Willis, Bob, and Timothy R. Homan. "U.S. economy: U.S. consumer price gains accelerate." *Bloomberg*, March 18, 2009. http://www.bloomberg.com/apps/news?pid=20601087&sid=a96UYa3hNIh0&refer=home.

Wood, Greg. "High oil price fuels 'Made in America'." *BBC News*, September 12, 2008. http://news.bbc.co.uk/2/hi/business/7611960.stm.

Wozniak, Lara. "Sorry, Vietnam is not the next China." *BusinessWeek*, May 13, 2008. http://www.businessweek.com/print/globalbiz/content/may2008/gb20080513_415737.htm.

Xinhua. "Wal-mart, Carrefour and Metro find 99 pct of Chinese products qualified." *Xinhua*, September 27, 2007. http://news.xinhuanet.com/english/2007-09/27/content_6803552.htm.

Yardley, Jim. "More candy from China, tainted, is in U.S." *New York Times*, October 2, 2008. http://www.nytimes.com/2008/10/02/world/asia/02milk.html.

Yardley, Jim. "Worried parents in China wait for answers on tainted formula." *New York Times*, September 18, 2008. http://www.nytimes.com/2008/09/18/world/asia/18china.html.

Zhang, Sheldon. *Smuggling and Trafficking in Human Beings: All Roads Lead to America* (Westport, CT: Greenwood Publishing Group, 2007).

7. Shock Therapy: *Can High Prices Save Us?*

Birol, Fatih. "World energy outlook 2007: China and India insights." Climate Action Programme, November 23, 2007. http://www.climateactionprogramme.org/features/article/world_energy_outlook_2007_china_and_india_insights/.

Bloomberg. "Barbie sets up shop in Shanghai." *Globe and Mail*, June 3, 2009. http://business. theglobeandmail.com/servlet/story/LAC.20090306.RSECONDARYTICKER06/ TPStory/?query.

Bradsher, Keith. "China losing taste for debt from U.S." *New York Times*, January 8, 2009. http://www.nytimes.com/2009/01/08/business/worldbusiness/08yuan.html.

Brahic, Catherine. "33% of China's carbon footprint blamed on exports." *New Scientist*, July 28, 2008. http://www.newscientist.com/article/dn14412-33-of-chinas-carbon-footprint-blamed-on-exports.html?feedId=online-news_rss20.

Bromley, Bob, Jesse Row, Matthew Salkeld, Pentti Sjoman, Tim Weis, and Paul Cobb. "Wha Ti community energy plan: Options for energy supply and management for Wha Ti, Northwest Territories." Ecology North and the Pembina Institute, June 2004. http:// www.aea.nt.ca/files/COMMUNITY%20ENERGY%20PLANNING/Whati_Plan.pdf.

Carey, John. "The real question: Should oil be cheap?" *BusinessWeek*, July 23, 2008.

CBC News. "Nunavut braces for pinch of gas price hike." *CBC News*, June 30, 2008. http://www.cbc.ca/canada/north/story/2008/06/30/nunavut-fuel.html.

Chung, Andrew. "Recession is ravaging the world's billionaires." *The Star*, March 12, 2009. http://www.thestar.com/article/600886.

Donohue, Michael. "Mall of misfortune." *The National*, June 12, 2008. http://www. thenational.ae/article/20080612/REVIEW/206990272/1042.

Driver, Anna, and Dave Zimmerman. "Worldwide energy E&P spending seen up 20 pct-Lehman." *Reuters*, June 6, 2008. http://www.reuters.com/article/OILPRD/ idUSN0644385420080606.

Energy Information Administration. "Short-term energy outlook." U.S. Department of Energy, March 10, 2009. http://www.eia.doe.gov/steo.

Energy Information Administration. "U.S. carbon dioxide emissions from energy sources: 2007 *Flash* estimate." U.S. Department of Energy, May 2008. http://www.eia.doe.gov/ oiaf/1605/flash/pdf/flash.pdf.

Expert Group on Energy Efficiency. "Realizing the potential of energy efficiency: Targets, policies, and measures for G8 countries." United Nations Foundation, 2007. http:// www.globalproblems-globalsolutions-files.org/unf_website/PDF/realizing_potential_ energy_efficiency.pdf.

Findlay, Ronald, and Kevin O'Rourke. *Power and Plenty: Trade, War, and World Economy in the Second Millennium* (Princeton, NJ: Princeton University Press, 2007).

Fouché, Gwladys. "North-West Passage is now plain sailing." *Guardian*, August 28, 2007. http://www.guardian.co.uk/environment/2007/aug/28/climatechange.internationalne ws?gusrc=rss&feed=networkfront.

Glaeser, Edward L. "If you got money, it's time to spend some." *New York Times*, February 17, 2009. http://economix.blogs.nytimes.com/2009/02/17/if-you-got-money-its-time-to-spend-some/?scp=5&sq=Keynes&st=cse.

Grynbaum, Michael M. "Core inflation remains steady, presenting a puzzle to the Fed." *New York Times*, October 18, 2007. http://www.nytimes.com/2007/10/18/ business/18economy.html.

Gurria, Angel. "Trade agreement needed now." *New York Times*, April 25, 2009. http:// www.nytimes.com/2008/04/25/opinion/25iht-edgurria.1.12346512.html

International Energy Agency. "The next 10 years are critical—the world energy outlook makes the case for stepping up co-operation with China and India to address global

energy challenges." International Energy Agency, November 7, 2007. http://www.iea.
    org/textbase/press/pressdetail.asp?PRESS_REL_ID=239.

Jones, Sandra M. "Empty boxes." *Chicago Tribune*, April 26, 2009. http://archives.
    chicagotribune.com/2009/apr/26/business/chi-sun-big-box-future-apr26.

Jowit, Juliette, and Patrick Wintour. "Cost of tackling global climate change has doubled,
    warns Stern." *Guardian*, June 26, 2008. http://www.guardian.co.uk/environment/2008/
    jun/26/climatechange.scienceofclimatechange.

Kim, Juli S. "A China environmental health project research brief: Transboundary
    air pollution—will China choke on its success?" Woodrow Wilson International
    Center for Scholars, February 2, 2007. http://www.wilsoncenter.org/index.cfm?topic_
    id=1421&fuseaction=topics.item&news_id=218780.

Leonard, Andrew. "Will China's poverty reduction kill the planet?" *Salon*, April 19, 2007.
    http://www.salon.com/tech/htww/2007/04/19/poverty_reduction/.

Macalister, Terry. "Energy agency sees oil price rising to $200 a barrel." *Guardian*,
    November 7, 2008. http://www.guardian.co.uk/business/2008/nov/07/oilandgas
    companies-energy.

Macklin, Gary. "Volatile market forces produce mixed cost indicators for food distribu-
    tors." *Refrigerated Transporter*, December 1, 2004. http://refrigeratedtrans.com/mag/
    transportation_volatile_market_forces/.

Morris, Charles. *The Trillion Dollar Meltdown: Easy Money, High Rollers, and the Great
    Credit Crash* (New York: Public Affairs, 2008).

Mutikani, Lucia. "McCain's China-free debt plan seen unrealistic." *Reuters*, October 3,
    2008. http://www.reuters.com/article/vcCandidateFeed2/idUSTRE49281F20081003?
    sp=true.

Norris, Floyd. "The upside to resisting globalization." *New York Times*, February 6,
    2009.

Pedersen, Brian J. "Mexican tariffs hit Southern Arizona exporters." *Arizona Daily Star*,
    March 19, 2009. http://www.azstarnet.com/news/284973.

Phoenix Business Journal. "Retailers dump 8.6M square feet of U.S. mall space in 1Q."
    Phoenix Business Journal, April 10, 2009. http://www.bizjournals.com/phoenix/
    stories/2009/04/06/daily80.html?surround=lfn.

Ratliff, Evan. "One molecule could cure our addiction to oil." *Wired*, September 24,
    2007. http://www.wired.com/science/planetearth/magazine/15-10/ff_plant.

Rosenbloom, Stephanie. "Malls test experimental waters to fill vacancies." *New
    York Times*, April 4, 2009. http://www.nytimes.com/2009/04/05/business/05mall.
    html?pagewanted=1&_r=1&dbk.

Sachs, Jeffrey. *Common Wealth: Economics for a Crowded Planet* (New York: Penguin,
    2008).

Stiglitz, Joseph. *Making Globalization Work* (New York: WW Norton, 2007).

Scoffield, Heather. "There will be blood." *Globe and Mail*, February 24, 2009. http://
    www.theglobeandmail.com/servlet/story/LAC.20090224.RFERGUSON24/
    TPStory/?query=niall.

Thompson, John. "Life on Iqaluit's mean streets." *Nunatsiaq News*, November 10, 2006.
    http://www.nunatsiaq.com/archives/61110/news/nunavut/61110_02.html.

Uchitelle, Louis. "Oil prices raise cost of making range of goods." *New York Times*, June 8,
    2008. www.nytimes.com/2008/06/08/us/08oil.html.

United Nations Environment Programme. "Global trends in sustainable energy investment 2008." United Nations Environment Programme, 2008. http://sefi.unep.org/fileadmin/media/sefi/docs/publications/Exec_summary.pdf.

Waldie, Paul. "Homeowners left to 'hope and pray' as foreclosure filings soar." *Globe and Mail*, October 1, 2008. http://www.theglobeandmail.com/servlet/story/LAC.20081001.MELTDOWNSUBPRIME01/TPStory/?query=one+in+10+foreclosure.

Watt-Cloutier, Sheila. "Intervention 1: Remarks made to the Arctic Council Ministerial Meeting, Iceland." Inuit Circumpolar Council Canada, November 24, 2004. http://www.inuitcircumpolar.com/index.php?ID=274&Lang=En.

Weber, Bob. "Exploding fuel prices could take $100 million bite out of Nunavut budget." *RedOrbit*, June 15, 2008. http://www.redorbit.com/news/business/1433675/exploding_fuel_prices_could_take_100_million_bite_out_of/index.html.

Westcott, Kathryn. "Plain sailing on the Northwest Passage." *BBC News*, September 19, 2007. http://news.bbc.co.uk/2/hi/americas/6999078.stm.

World Trade Organization. "WTO: Developing, transition economies cushion trade slowdown. Chart 3: Real merchandise trade growth by region, 2007." World Trade Organization, April 17, 2008. http://www.wto.org/english/news_e/pres08_e/pr520_e.htm#chart3.

INDEX